Automated Knowledge Acquisition

Prentice Hall International Series in Computer Systems Science and Engineering
Developed, Edited and Compiled by Knowledge Systems Research Pty Ltd.
Series Editor: Tharam S. Dillon.

Object-oriented Conceptual Modeling Tharam S. Dillon and Poh Lee Tan.
Automated Knowledge Acquisition Sabrina Sestito and Tharam S. Dillon.

Automated Knowledge Acquisition

Sabrina Sestito

Tharam S. Dillon

Developed and Edited by
Knowledge Systems Research Pty Ltd

PRENTICE HALL

New York London Toronto Sydney Tokyo Singapore

Acquisitions Editor: Andrew Binnie
Production Editor: Fiona Marcar
Cover design: The Modern Art Production Group, Prahran, Victoria
Typeset by: Keyboard Wizards, Allambie Heights, NSW

Printed in Australia by Ligare Pty Ltd, Riverwood, NSW

1 2 3 4 5 98 97 96 95 94

ISBN 013 301136 4

**National Library of Australia
Cataloguing-in-Publication Data**

Sestito, Sabrina
    Automated knowledge acquisition.

    Bibliography.
    Includes index.
    ISBN 0 13 301136 4.

    1. Expert systems (Computer science). 2. Knowledge
    acquisition (Expert systems). I. Dillon, Tharam S.
    II. Title. (Series: Prentice Hall international series
    computer systems science and engineering.

006.33

**Library of Congress
Cataloging-in-Publication Data**

are available from the Publisher.

Prentice Hall, Inc., *Englewood Cliffs, New Jersey*
Prentice Hall Canada, Inc., *Toronto*
Prentice Hall Hispanoamericana, SA, *Mexico*
Prentice Hall of India Private Ltd, *New Delhi*
Prentice Hall International, Inc., *London*
Prentice Hall of Japan, Inc., *Tokyo*
Prentice Hall of Southeast Asia Pty Ltd, *Singapore*
Editora Prentice hall do Brasil Ltda, *Rio de Janeiro*

PRENTICE HALL

A division of Simon & Schuster

Contents

4 Sub-symbolic learning methods — artificial neural networks 94

5 Other machine learning paradigms 129

6 Theoretical considerations 166

7   The extraction of rules and concepts using a single Hebbian neural network   201

8   BRAINNE — automated knowledge acquisition using multi-layered neural networks   217

9   Continuously BRAINNE — automated knowledge acquisition using continuous data   261

Preface

Knowledge acquisition has long been recognized as a bottleneck in the process of development of knowledge-based systems. In the early days knowledge acquisition was done manually through a knowledge engineer interacting with a domain expert. This process was long, tedious and unsatisfactory. Domain experts are often not conscious of the bases of their decisions and therefore have difficulty articulating them in an explicit form. These features have given a strong impetus to the development of techniques for automated knowledge acquisition. The variety of techniques developed over the past few years include:

- decision tree methods
- progressive rule generation
- explanation-based learning
- methods that extract knowledge from neural networks
- genetic algorithm approaches.

This great upsurge in research activity has now reached the point where the subject has matured sufficiently for a general book in the area.

This book clearly explains the various automated knowledge acquisition techniques in a tutorial fashion, making it suitable for both advanced undergraduate and graduate teaching. The book is also valuable for the computer professional who wishes to gain an understanding of these techniques.

Chapter 1 of the book gives a broad description of the nature of knowledge acquisition and defines some of the important concepts.

Chapter 2 discusses the different decision tree methods including those emanating from ID3, the CART family, and statistically based methods such as Goodman and Kruskal's Tau and the Chi-square approach.

Chapter 3 presents the progressive rule generation methods initiated by Michalski and his associates.

Chapter 4 contains a brief review of artificial neural networks. These learning methods develop sub-symbolic representations rather than the knowledge structures associated with traditional Artificial Intelligence.

Chapter 5 details other machine learning paradigms including learning methods that use frames (such as EURISKO), genetic algorithm based techniques, Explanation-based Learning (EBL), and connectionist methods.

Chapter 6 discusses the theoretical issues that impact on machine learning from a neuro-physiological aspect.

Chapter 7 describes the use of a single-layered Hebbian neural network for extraction of production rules and concepts.

Chapter 8 introduces BRAINNE — a method for extracting knowledge in the form of both conjunctive and disjunctive rules using supervised neural networks.

Chapter 9 considers an extension of BRAINNE to deal with data containing continuous attributes.

Chapter 10 gives applications of BRAINNE to real-world problems.

Chapter 11 considers a further extension of BRAINNE to extract symbolic knowledge using unsupervised learning.

Chapter 12 briefly describes manual knowledge acquisition techniques and their relationship to automated knowledge acquisition.

Throughout the book all direct quotations from other sources are indented and set in Roman typeface. Some of these quotations have been slightly altered to conform with the format used within the book.

Acknowledgment

The authors would like to acknowledge the careful and painstaking editing and proofing of the manuscript carried out by Mary Witten. They would also like to acknowledge the kind permission of Knowledge Systems Research Pty Ltd for the use of copyright material in Chapter 12 of this book. Sabrina would like to thank parents, family, and friends for supporting her in reaching for the stars.

Experimental Software

Experimental software implementing several, but not all, of the methods described in this book is available on a 3½" diskette from:

AKT Systems Pty Ltd
PO Box 452
Caulfield East VIC 3145
Australia

The programs were developed using Borland C++ and ObjectWindows for C++. The diskette is suitable for an IBM compatible PC under the Windows environment and includes brief documentation.

Please contact AKT Systems directly for further information regarding pricing and availability.

1

General considerations

1.1 What is knowledge acquisition?

The process of knowledge acquisition pre-dates computers. For instance, when novices or students wish to learn how to carry out a particular task or understand a particular concept or theory, they have to be involved in knowledge acquisition in a very general sense. In simple terms, knowledge acquisition is the process of learning knowledge from one or more sources and passing it on in a suitable form to someone else or to some system. This process involves learning, re-formalizing, transferring, and representing the knowledge. For instance, suppose that in an astronomy class Ernie is taught the concept (or definition) of a black hole. After learning the concept, Ernie will re-formalize it in his own terms, in a way clear to him. Suppose then that a colleague asks Ernie, "What is a black hole?" As Ernie answers the question, he is actually transferring knowledge to his colleague. Thus Ernie has learned the concept of a black hole from his lecturer and/or reference material, re-formalized the knowledge in his own mind, and then transferred that learned knowledge to his colleague. A person (Ernie) has therefore transferred the knowledge from the lecturer to a colleague, as illustrated in Figure 1.1. This is a simple instance of transferring knowledge from a source to a recipient.

1

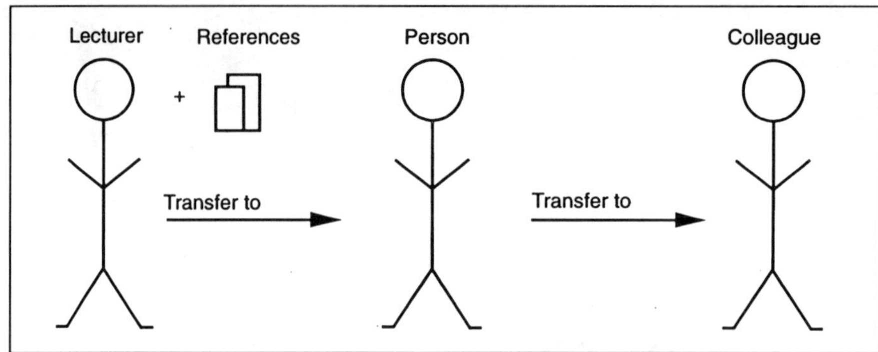

Figure 1.1   Simple example of transferring knowledge from lecturer to colleague

In the computer science field known as Artificial Intelligence (AI), knowledge acquisition can be more formally defined as the transfer of knowledge from one or more sources (e.g., textbooks, manuals, experts) to a computer program, as shown in Figure 1.2. This involves discovering the knowledge and then expressing it in a machine-implementable form.

1.2 Why is knowledge acquisition important?

AI is a well-known field of computer science that has gained increasing acceptance through its various areas of application, such as expert systems (Hayes-Roth et al. 1983), vision, and learning. A significant goal of AI is to understand intelligence itself, in humans as well as in other organisms, and to be able to exploit such understanding to build *intelligent systems;* that is, systems that do intelligent things (DARPA 1988). As a discipline, AI consists of a collection

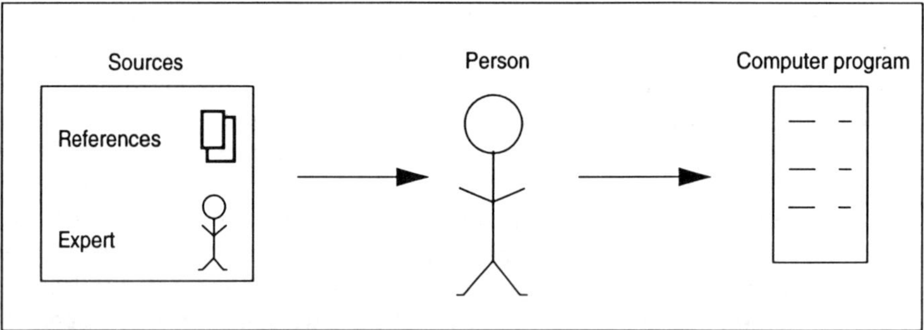

Figure 1.2   Knowledge acquisition as transferring knowledge from some source(s) to a computer program

of techniques, representations, models, algorithms, and programs that have developed since the mid-1950s. Systems developed under this paradigm are referred to as Knowledge-Based Systems (KBS).

Modern knowledge-based systems are different from other computer-based systems in that their basic structure is separated into two major components: the inference engine and the knowledge base, as shown in Figure 1.3. The inference engine contains the reasoning or processing mechanism used by the system; that is, it contains the general problem-solving knowledge. The knowledge base contains the actual knowledge of a problem domain in some suitable format; that is, it contains the domain-specific knowledge. The separation of these components has provided great flexibility in the application of these systems to different problem domains. This structure also makes the system more understandable to the user and easier to modify. Accuracy and completeness of the knowledge in the knowledge base are obviously very important. The basic problem then becomes, "Where does one obtain the knowledge to put into a knowledge base?" This problem is known as knowledge acquisition and it can be defined as (Buchanan et al. 1983):

> *Knowledge Acquisition is the transfer and transformation of problem-solving expertise from some knowledge source to a program.*

The process of knowledge acquisition involves the problem definition, implementation, and refinement. It also involves choosing the knowledge representation to embody the facts and relations acquired from some source. Important sources of knowledge, besides textbooks and other documented knowledge, are human experts and their experiences in the problem domain being considered.

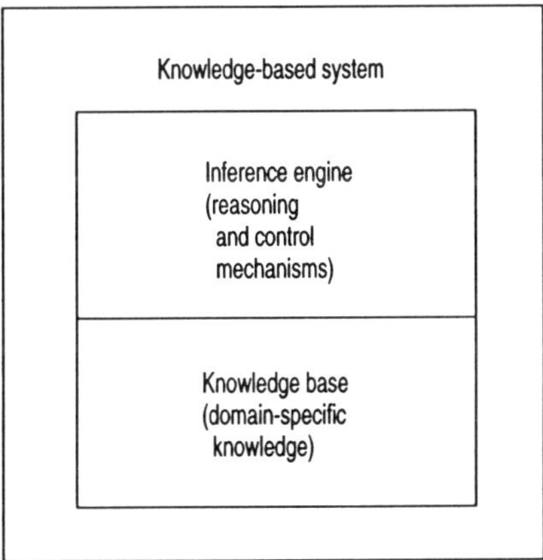

Figure 1.3   A knowledge-based system has an inference engine and a knowledge base

1.3 Using human experts for manual knowledge acquisition

1.3.1 Acquiring knowledge from an expert

The focus in this section is a brief discussion of the methods used to acquire knowledge from human experts. In other words, the source of the knowledge is a human expert, as illustrated in Figure 1.4.

The human experts are specialists, although not necessarily the best, in a narrow domain area. A person, known as a *knowledge engineer*, communicates with the experts to acquire the relevant knowledge, as shown in Figure 1.5. This person also looks at books, manuals, case studies, and other material in order to understand the problem domain. The knowledge engineer frequently has less knowledge about the domain. Hence the restricted nature of the communication between the expert and the knowledge engineer could impede the process of transferring the expertise into a program.

According to Buchanan et al. (1983), several stages of knowledge acquisition have been determined. These stages are *identification, conceptualization, formalization, implementation,* and *testing.* However, this process is not as neat or as well defined as these stages may suggest. The stages are only a simple formulation of the complex activity that takes place during knowledge acquisition.

Chapter 12 elaborates on the manual approach to knowledge acquisition, discussing interviewing techniques, communication with experts, representation of knowledge, and other related issues.

1.3.2 Difficulties with acquiring knowledge from an expert

There are several major difficulties with acquiring knowledge from human experts. One of the most troublesome is the *knowledge mismatch* problem;

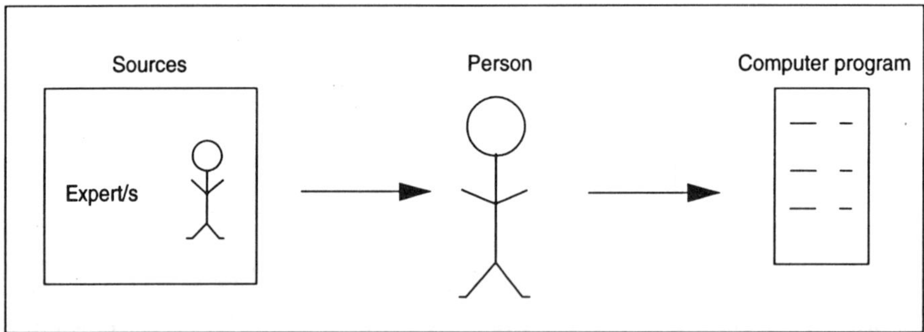

Figure 1.4   Knowledge acquisition using human experts as the source

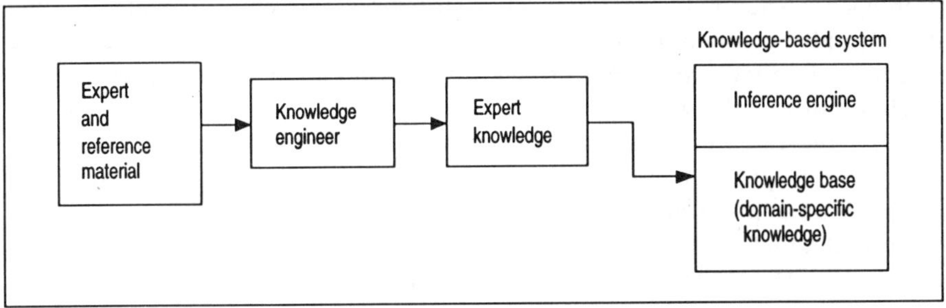

Figure 1.5   Interfacing human experts and knowledge engineers to build knowledge bases

that is, the difference between the way a human expert's own knowledge is structured and the way it is represented in the program. Other difficulties include the inability of humans to express the knowledge they possess, limits of the current technology to represent this knowledge adequately, and the problem of verification and validation of the system.

Attempts to decrease the representation mismatch have involved constructing programs that *learn by being told* and programs that are able to converse in natural language (Buchanan et al. 1983). However, as stated in many articles (Buchanan et al. 1983; Honavar & Uhr 1990; Johnson-Laird 1989; Mozer 1987), the main difficulty in extracting knowledge from experts is that they themselves have trouble expressing or formalizing their knowledge. In other words, experts have difficulty in explicitly quantifying their knowledge and experience in a form understandable to a novice. Johnson (1983) argues that as the level of expertise increases, the ability to articulate the knowledge decreases. Experts also have a problem in describing their knowledge in terms that are precise, complete, and consistent enough for use in a computer program. They sometimes give explanations for their decisions that do not correspond to their actual, perhaps unconscious or compiled, reasons for making the decisions (Johnson 1983). This difficulty stems from the inherent nature of knowledge that constitutes human expertise (Buchanan et al. 1983). Such knowledge is often subconscious and may be approximate, incomplete, and inconsistent. These characteristics of human expertise affect all stages of knowledge acquisition.

The limit of the current technology mainly concerns the representation used to encode the knowledge. The expressive capability of the representation limits the knowledge that can be described and thus is an important consideration (Buchanan et al. 1983; Young 1989). Finally, the knowledge base is being incrementally developed via a cycle of testing and debugging. Isolating a specific bug may require a trace through dozens of inferences involving hundreds of facts. Therefore, the interactions between the stored factual knowledge and the control strategy used must be thoroughly understood. Furthermore, interdependencies between knowledge structures and control strategies that are difficult to comprehend directly could make changes in the knowledge base that cause inconsistencies or deterioration in system performance.

These problems with manual knowledge acquisition have stimulated considerable research effort directed toward the development of automated knowledge acquisition methods. Manual knowledge acquisition requires the expert to be explicit about the reason(s) for making a decision. In contrast, automated knowledge acquisition considers examples of the expert's decisions and tries to extract the knowledge involved automatically.

1.4 Automated knowledge acquisition

As previously stated, the next natural progression of the knowledge acquisition task is to use computers to extract expert knowledge in some way. Thus this field, also known as Machine Learning, seeks to assign parts of the knowledge acquisition task to the computer instead of the knowledge engineer. There are two major benefits from automating knowledge acquisition (Buchanan et al. 1983):

- *Automated methods might be more competent than humans for acquiring or fine-tuning certain kinds of knowledge;*
- *Automated methods might significantly reduce the high cost in human resources involved in constructing expert systems.*

The existing automated knowledge acquisition methods usually involve the examination of a sufficiently large and diverse set of initial conditions and the resulting decisions made by an expert. This set constitutes an example training set used by many computer-based learning methods to determine the underlying facts or decisions used. Note that the factual knowledge captures what is known to be true in a problem domain, while the initial conditions and decisions together capture the strategies of how to solve the problems in the domain.

The computer-based learning methods in this category cover the computer algorithms that proceed from individual cases to general principles, from the particular to the universal. Learning from examples is the most widely used method for automating the process of knowledge acquisition (Kolokouris 1986). Computer-based learning methods that learn from examples include Buchanan and Feigenbaum's META-DENDRAL, Quinlan's ID3, Michalski's STAR algorithms, and Lenat's EURISKO. It is claimed that some of these algorithms (e.g., Michalski's AQ11 algorithm) have constructed better rules than those formulated directly by an expert. These programs are based upon methods for inferring general classification rules from training data. These methods search for common features of the positive training examples that distinguish them

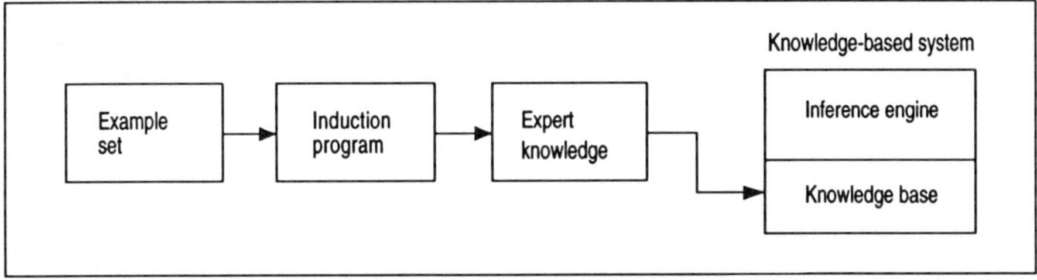

Figure 1.6   Interfacing data and an induction program for automated knowledge acquisition

from the negative examples. This general inductive inference procedure, shown in Figure 1.6, has received considerable attention in AI, philosophy, and psychology (Buchanan et al. 1983).

The acquisition of new declarative knowledge, the organization of new knowledge into general, effective representations, and the discovery of new facts through observations and experiments are all part of the learning process. The study and modeling of this learning process form the subject of machine learning (Carbonell et al. 1983). The central goal of machine learning is to devise mechanisms that transform knowledge from inefficient forms into efficient forms (Wogulis & Langely 1989).

1.5 Concepts and notation used in automated knowledge acquisition

1.5.1 General issues

In this section we discuss various concepts necessary for a better understanding of automated knowledge acquisition methods. Basically, a complete learning system of an automated knowledge acquisition method, as shown in Figure 1.7, comprises:

- a training set
- a learning algorithm
- a symbolic knowledge representation
- an assessment scheme.

1.5.2 Training set

Learning by an automated knowledge acquisition method is accomplished by extracting knowledge from a set of externally supplied examples (Shavlik &

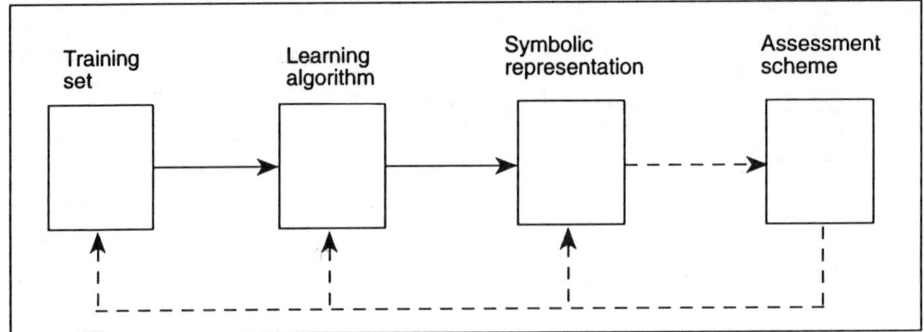

Figure 1.7   A typical learning system

Dietterich 1990a). These examples represent instances of decisions previously made by an expert. They have features or states that describe each instance as well as the decision obtained by the expert. Consider a classification problem such as selecting between poisonous and edible mushrooms. Here, the instances would consist of the features of the mushroom, such as Color and Size, as well as the expert's classification of each instance of a mushroom into POISONOUS or EDIBLE. This set of examples is known as the training set. In many cases, a portion of the examples is used to teach or train the method, while the remaining portion is used to test the knowledge extracted. For instance, the training set found in Figure 1.8 could be used for the classification of animals. Consider the second example in Figure 1.8, which is re-stated below:

$$(\text{Hair, Milk, Pouch, Gray}) \Rightarrow (\text{MAMMAL, MARSUPIAL}).$$

This particular instance states that Hair, Milk, Pouch, and Gray are present, and that the expert has classified the instance as a MAMMAL and a MARSUPIAL. The various parts of the training set will now be discussed.

(Hair, Milk) ⇒ (MAMMAL)

(Hair, Milk, Pouch, Gray) ⇒ (MAMMAL, MARSUPIAL)

(Hair, Milk, Fly, Black) ⇒ (MAMMAL, BAT)

(Feathers, Egglaying) ⇒ (BIRD)

(Feathers, Egglaying, Fly, White) ⇒ (BIRD, PELICAN)

Figure 1.8   A training set for the classification of animals

Features or attributes

The features or attributes in a domain are the characteristics for the various instances encountered in a domain. Generally, when carrying out manual knowledge acquisition, one would seek to retain only the relevant attributes of a domain for a particular application. However, in an automated knowledge acquisition application, one may have difficulty at the outset in determining which attributes are likely to be used by an expert in making a judgment. Therefore, the tendency is to keep a superset of attributes larger than the final set of attributes selected to be important by the learning algorithm.

The values of the input attributes can take various forms. For instance, the presence or absence of a particular feature may be the important issue. In the training set given in Figure 1.8, Hair and Feathers are two such attributes. In the case of these binary attributes, the two values correspond to the presence or absence of the attribute. This could be represented using the notation Hair(T) and Hair(F) to indicate the presence or absence of Hair respectively. Thus the full input vector for the first example in Figure 1.8 would then read:

> (Hair(T), Milk(T), Pouch(Don't Care), Feathers(F),
> Egglaying(Don't Care), Fly(Don't Care), Color(Don't Care)).

This indicates that the attributes Hair and Milk have the value True (T) since they are present, and that the attribute Feathers has the value False (F) since Feathers are absent. Furthermore, the values of the attributes Pouch, Egglaying, and Fly are not important at this point. As this notation is cumbersome, for explanation purposes in this book, only those attributes present are included in the input vector for binary attributes and without the T, which is implicit. Therefore, the assumption can be made that an unlisted True/False attribute is False or not relevant.

Sometimes the specific values of a particular attribute may be important, as in the case of the Color attribute. Color has the value Don't Care in the full input vector previously described, as the attribute is not important at that point. However, in other examples in the training set in Figure 1.8, the values of the Color attribute are relevant. In full notation, the Color attribute and its associated values could be represented as Color(White), Color(Gray), and Color(Black). Again, we avoid cumbersome notation when an attribute has multiple distinct values by including only the actual value of the attribute in the list of inputs. Thus, if Color has the value White, only White is included in the list of inputs. A similarly concise notation is adopted with regard to the outputs, giving the form of the examples in Figure 1.8. This notation is used in explanations throughout the book, but storing an input vector in a database of examples in a machine would require a full representation such as that just discussed.

Now consider the outputs in more detail. The outputs could be simple binary decisions. Examples of binary decisions are whether:

- a mushroom is POISONOUS or EDIBLE
- a plan is ACCEPTABLE or UNACCEPTABLE.

In other cases, particularly for classification problems, the output could belong to one or more categories. Examples of these are:

- an animal could be a MAMMAL, MARSUPIAL, BIRD, REPTILE, etc.
- a plan could be EXCELLENT, GOOD, AVERAGE, POOR, or VERY POOR.

In the general case, one could represent the output as a vector.

In some situations, one needs to represent not just attributes of entities or instances but also relationships between them. The use of a simple attribute vector may not be sufficient. For example, if one wanted to characterize knowledge such as the description of a house, one would need constructs capable of representing relationships, such as Left-Of, In-Between, Right-Of, and Top-Of. Generally one could use a predicate calculus notation for representing such knowledge. Even though these more powerful representations are necessary for describing certain types of knowledge, in this book only an input attribute vector and an output vector will be considered, unless otherwise stated. The concise notation of the instances in Figure 1.8 are typical of the input and output vectors considered. In summary:

$$(\text{Hair, Milk}) \Rightarrow (\text{MAMMAL})$$
$$(\text{Hair, Milk, Pouch, Gray}) \Rightarrow (\text{MAMMAL, MARSUPIAL})$$

are two instances in the training set. In the former, the input attributes Hair and Milk are present, and the output category MAMMAL is True. In the latter, the input attributes Hair, Milk, and Pouch are present, the Color is Gray, and the output categories, MAMMAL and MARSUPIAL, are True.

Type of data

From the previous discussion it is obvious that the type of data being considered is very important. In the preceding training set all of the attributes are discrete. This means that the attributes have a fixed or limited number of values. For instance, the importance of Hair is its presence or absence. This type of attribute is called binary because it only has two possible values. Another type of attribute is multi-valued, such as Color with its possible values of Gray, White, or Black.

Consider now a weather domain. The important features here are the actual numerical values of various parameters such as Temperature and Pressure. These parameters are real-valued and as such have no fixed number of discrete values. They are continuously valued. In many AI methods, the values of such attributes are broken up into two or more classes representing various sub-intervals of the range of possible values.

Noisy and/or incomplete data

Sometimes the training set of examples contains data that has a number of inaccuracies. For instance, in the training set for the animal domain in Figure 1.8, one could have the situation where the third example in the training set:

$$(\text{Hair, Milk, Fly, Black}) \Rightarrow (\text{MAMMAL, BAT})$$

was recorded incorrectly as:

$$(\text{Hair, Egglaying, Fly, Black}) \Rightarrow (\text{MAMMAL, BIRD}).$$

The information could have been erroneously entered or corrupted at some stage. This indicates that the input or output information could be inaccurate. Most real-world data tends to be of this type, because of measurement inaccuracy, entry errors, wrong decisions, or wrongly recorded decisions. Such data is referred to as *noisy data.*

Also, a value for a particular input attribute may not be recorded in an example, because it was not available or because it was inadvertently deleted. For example, a particular medical test may not have been carried out on a patient even though a diagnosis was made. In this case, the example set contains missing data. *Incomplete data* refers to collectively insufficient information, such as a class not being completely determined by given attributes.

One of the challenges facing the various learning algorithms is to be able to learn the knowledge in the presence of such noisy, missing, or incomplete data.

Type of learning — supervised versus unsupervised

A distinction can be made between two types of learning: supervised and unsupervised learning. In supervised learning, each example consists of a set of initial conditions and a set of the resulting actions or decisions. These types of examples are employed by knowledge acquisition methods to learn the underlying knowledge used in the examples. This situation is equivalent to having a teacher who provides the correct set of answers from which the system can learn.

In contrast, each example used by unsupervised learning methods consists of the initial conditions only. That is, there are no appropriate actions or decisions associated with the initial conditions. Here the aim is to understand the underlying statistical structure or patterns in the data. However, unsupervised learning has not been used previously to perform knowledge acquisition of high-level knowledge representations. In supervised learning one thus provides both the input attribute vector and the associated target output vector, while in unsupervised learning one provides only the input attribute vector.

Within the area of automated knowledge acquisition, the primary task studied
has been the acquisition of classification rules from supervised learning methods
(Shavlik & Dietterich 1990b). As such, most of this book is restricted to the
discussion and evaluation of supervised learning methods. However, Chapter
11 presents a method that uses unsupervised learning.

1.5.3 Learning algorithm

General considerations

The learning algorithm learns from a training set of examples and produces
symbolic knowledge. The learning algorithm can be top-down or bottom-up.
A top-down approach learns specific facts from general principles, while a
bottom-up approach learns general principles from specific facts, as illustrated
in Figure 1.9. Many of the existing automated knowledge acquisition methods
use a bottom-up approach. This is because they learn from a set of examples
(i.e., specific facts) and produce general principles (e.g., a set of rules).

It is also useful to distinguish between two types of learning algorithms:

- input space partitioning algorithms
- output space projection algorithms.

To do this, consider an input space and an output space, as shown in Figure
1.10. A point in the input space consists of specific values for the components
of the input attribute vector, while a point in the output space denotes specific
values for the components of the output vector.

An input space partitioning algorithm progressively partitions the input
space, usually by selecting attributes in sequence for partitioning the space.
Typically, one attribute at a time is selected. At some stage it is no longer
necessary to further subdivide the partition. At this stage, one needs to allocate
that particular partition to a given output class, as shown in Figure 1.11.
Therefore, in this approach one needs:

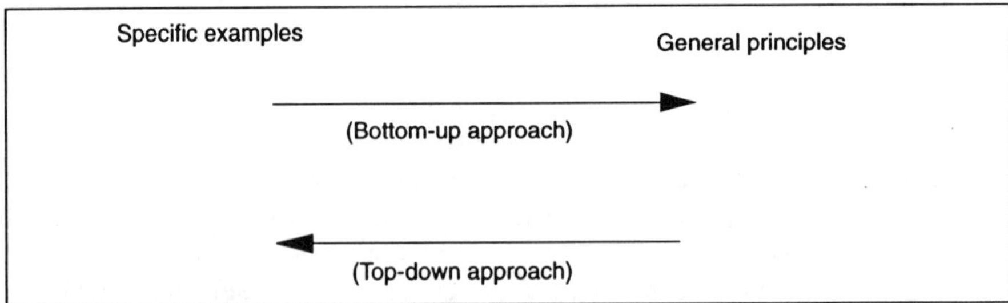

Figure 1.9   Different types of learning algorithm strategies

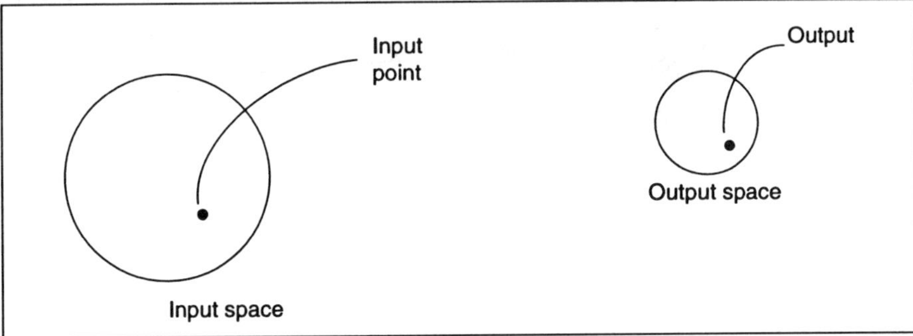

Figure 1.10 An input and output space

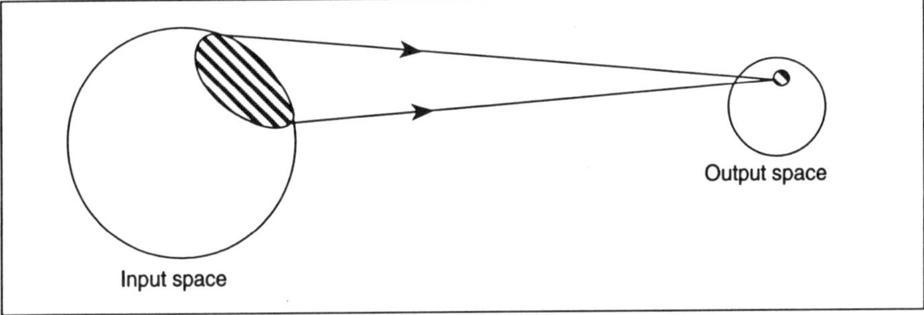

Figure 1.11 An input space partitioning algorithm

- a method for generating the next partition — this typically involves selecting an attribute for subdividing;
- a stopping criterion for halting further subdivisions of a partition;
- a rule for assigning the partition to an output.

Note that more than one partition could be allocated to a given output.

The second approach involves an output space projection algorithm. Here one selects a particular output, which is a point in the output space, and determines the region of the input space that corresponds to it, as shown in Figure 1.12. This is repeated in turn for each of the outputs. Note that since more than one region of the input space could correspond to a particular output, one needs to determine all such regions for each output, as shown in Figure 1.13. In this second approach, one therefore needs:

- a method of relating a given output to points in the input space;
- a criterion for selecting the points that map to that output;
- a criterion for identifying the boundary of the region(s) of interest in the input space.

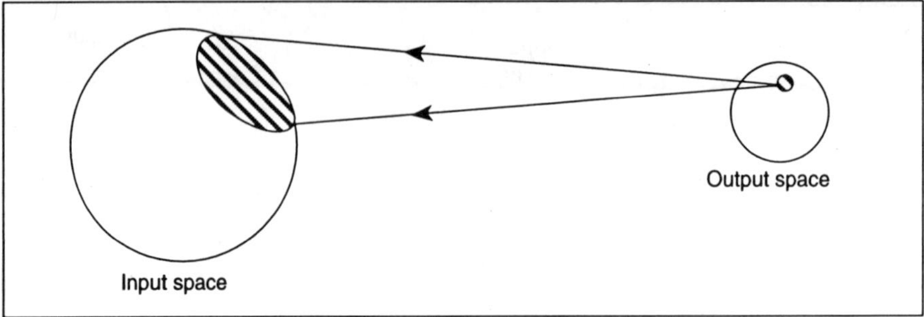

Figure 1.12 An output space projection algorithm

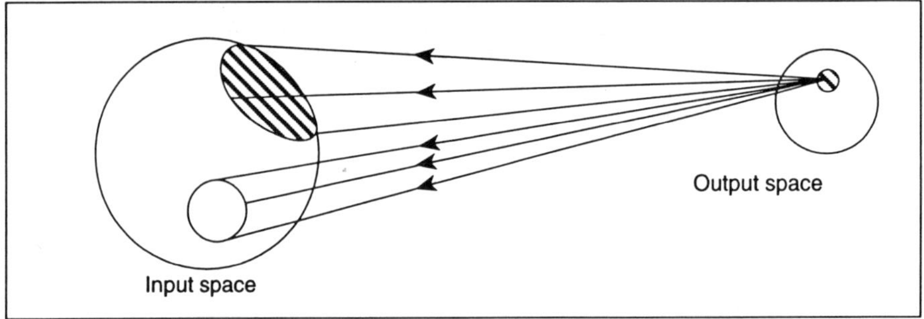

Figure 1.13 Projection to several regions of an input space

The decision tree methods discussed in Chapter 2 and the progressive rule generation STAR methodology discussed in Chapter 3 are examples of the first approach. The neural network based method known as BRAINNE (Sestito 1991), discussed in Chapters 8 and 9, uses the second approach.

The process of inductive learning

Many of the automated learning methods use inductive learning. It is based on the principle of induction that states (Russell 1912):

When a thing of a certain sort A has been found to be associated with a thing of a certain other sort B, and has never been found dissociated from a thing of the sort B, the greater the number of cases in which A and B have been associated, the greater is the probability that they will be associated in a fresh case in which one of them is known to be present.

Induction can be defined as (Honavar & Uhr 1988):

a process by which a system develops an understanding of principles or theories that are useful in dealing with the environment by generalization and specialization from the specific examples or instances presented to it. This includes the process of experimentation and discovery; that is, setting up of hypotheses and then accumulating evidence to confirm or deny their validity.

Induction in machine learning is more restrictive than this general definition. Here the resulting knowledge obtained from the examples is in a format that has more specific applicability, as illustrated in Figure 1.14. For instance, the resulting knowledge may be represented as a set of rules instead of a specific principle defining all the possible rules. This type of knowledge that employs decision trees, production rules, semantic nets, frames, and so on in knowledge-

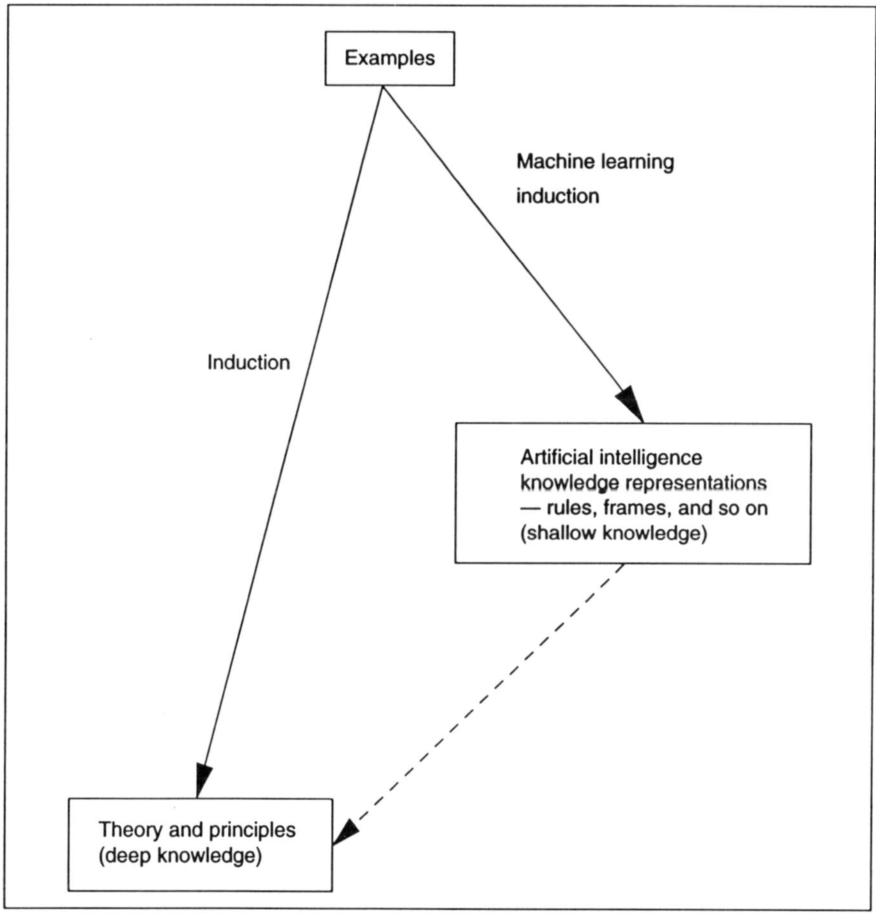

Figure 1.14   Relationship between true induction and machine learning induction

based systems is sometimes referred to as shallow knowledge. In contrast, the deep knowledge produced from induction carried out by humans encompasses a general theory or principle, or a qualitative or quantitative model of the system being considered. Machine-based systems that seek to represent this deep knowledge are referred to as model-based systems.

A number of authors (Charniak & McDermott 1985; Dietterich & Michalski 1981; Forsyth & Rada 1986; Michalski 1983; Mitchell 1979; Winston 1984) view inductive learning in the automated knowledge acquisition area as a heuristic search through a space of symbolic descriptions, generated by an application of certain inference rules to the initial observational statements. The process of generating the goal description (i.e., the most preferred inductive assertion) relies on the complementary operations of specializing and generalizing. Domain background knowledge has also been shown to be a necessary component of inductive learning (Michalski 1983). This background knowledge provides constraints, guidance, and a criterion for selecting the most preferred inductive assertion.

Inductive learning extracts knowledge from examples. Hart (1986) states that the quality of the training set affects the quality of the induced information. The algorithm cannot be used to discover something that is not there. Inductive learning acquires knowledge by drawing inductive inferences. In contrast to deduction, the starting premises of induction are specific examples rather than general axioms.

Knowledge or concept acquisition produces descriptions for classifying objects into classes on the basis of the properties of the objects. Within the machine learning context, an induced hypothesis can be viewed as a concept recognition rule, such that if an object satisfies this rule then it represents the given concept. Descriptive generalizations produce representations specifying properties of objects belonging to a certain class.

The completeness and consistency conditions are the two requirements that must be satisfied for an inductive assertion to be acceptable as a concept recognition rule (Michalski 1983):

- Completeness requires that an inductively derived inference rule for a class should cover every example of that class;
- Consistency requires that no examples of any other classes satisfy the inference rule for the given class as this leads to a contradictory situation.

In other words, the consistency condition assumes that classes are mutually exclusive.

There is also a comprehensibility postulate underlying most of this work. The rationale behind this postulate is to ensure that descriptions generated by inductive inference bear similarity to human knowledge representation and are therefore easy to comprehend (Michalski 1983).

1.5.4 Symbolic knowledge representation

A learning algorithm learns the knowledge and represents it in some symbolic form. In AI, there are several knowledge representation formalisms. Some of these are briefly discussed here.

Production rules

One of the most common knowledge formalisms used in AI is the standard production rule. It consists of a condition-action pair. If the condition part of the rule is met, the rule is fired and the action in the action part of the rule is carried out. The format of a rule is:

IF A THEN B

where A is the condition part and B is the action part. Note that A can consist of a number of premises, A1, A2, ..., An, joined by various connectives. The IF part is also known as the antecedent of the rule, while the THEN part is the consequent of the rule. For example, if a mammal is known to have hair and give milk to its young then the following rule can be constructed to represent this:

IF Hair AND Milk THEN MAMMAL.

Many expert systems use rules to represent their information.

There are two types of rules: conjunctive and disjunctive. A conjunctive rule is defined as a rule containing attributes linked by the AND connective. Therefore, the previous rule is a conjunctive rule. This is the original form of production rules utilized in knowledge-based systems. However, most knowledge-based system building tools today also permit the use of other connectives. A disjunctive rule, in Disjunctive Normal Form, is represented as attributes (which can be in the form of a conjunctive rule) linked together by the OR connective. For instance:

IF (Hair AND Milk AND Egglaying) OR (Hair AND Milk AND Pouch) THEN MAMMAL

is a disjunctive rule. Note that this disjunctive rule is equivalent to the following two conjunctive rules:

IF Hair AND Milk AND Egglaying THEN MAMMAL.
IF Hair AND Milk AND Pouch THEN MAMMAL.

Conjunctive rules correspond to a mapping between the input space and the output space, as shown in Figure 1.15. Disjunctive rules, on the other hand, correspond to mappings such as those in Figure 1.16 for a rule with one OR connective.

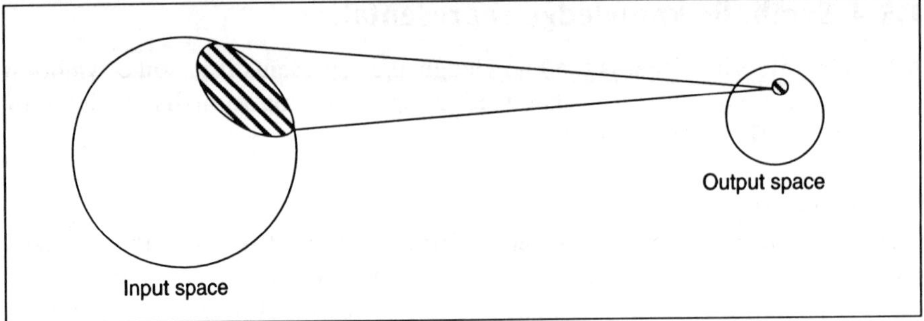

Figure 1.15 Conjunctive rule mapping

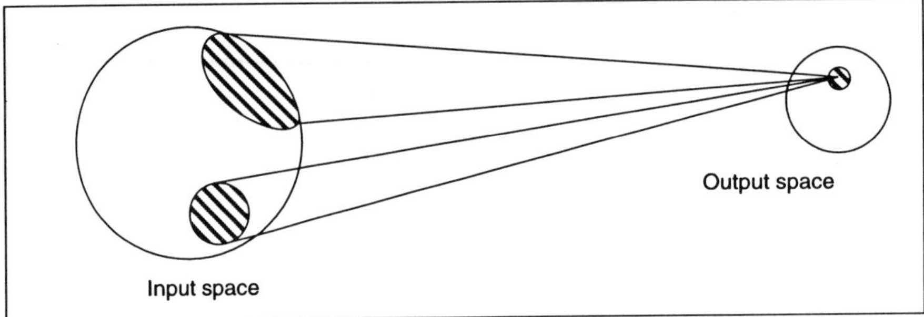

Figure 1.16 Disjunctive rule mapping with one OR connective

Decision trees

A decision tree is a directed graph showing the various possible sequences of questions, answers, and classifications. A decision tree may be a leaf associated with one class. Alternatively, the tree may consist of a test that has a set of mutually exclusive possible outcomes together with a subsidiary decision tree for each such outcome. The process of classifying an object starts at the root of the tree. If this is a leaf, the object is assigned the class associated with that leaf. Alternatively, if the root of the decision tree is a test, the outcome of this test is determined for the given object and the process continues using the subsidiary decision tree of that outcome. An object is thus classified by tracing out a path from the root of the decision tree to one of its leaves. Decision trees are discussed further in Chapter 2.

Frames

Frames are defined as data structures for the representation of stereotypical (normal) situations (Minsky 1975). Frames have names and slot fillers, together with information on how the slots can be filled. These are described in detail in Chapter 5.

Semantic nets

Semantic nets consist of a set of nodes and directed arcs. The nodes represent objects and the arcs depict the relationships between them. For the nodes and directed arcs to be a semantic net, semantics must be associated with the net. The semantics are used to label the nodes and the arcs to describe the objects and the relationships, respectively.

Neural networks

Even though this form of knowledge representation is not symbolic, it is introduced here for completeness. Neural networks were inspired by the architecture of the human brain and various mathematical theories. They comprise a set of nodes connected by weighted links and are trained by example. In Chapter 4 we further describe this representation.

Important considerations

When carrying out automated knowledge acquisition, the developer will choose the symbolic knowledge representation considered to be the most appropriate. This choice will have implications for the type of learning algorithms used.

1.6 A basis for comparing machine learning techniques

In the literature, several methods for comparing the various learning strategies have been presented. Carbonell et al. (1983) are concerned with three basic classifications when comparing techniques. These are classifications on the basis of the underlying learning strategies used, the representation of knowledge or skill acquired by the learner, and the application domain of the performance system for which the knowledge is acquired.

Dietterich and Michalski (1981) have proposed other aspects for consideration when comparing and evaluating various learning techniques. Their criteria include:

- the adequacy of the representation language
- the implemented rules of generalization
- the computational efficiency
- the flexibility and extensibility of the algorithm.

According to Mitchell (1979) and various other researchers (Dietterich & Michalski 1981; Michalski 1983; Winston 1984), concept learning can be viewed as a search problem. Mitchell thus proposed that concept learning techniques can be characterized in terms of the search strategies they have employed. The two broad classes of search strategies that have been employed for concept learning problems are model- and data-driven search strategies.

The knowledge representation employed by the various existing machine learning methods will be used for comparison, as it is an important factor in reflecting the quality and adequacy of the various methods. Besides this, the following factors are also taken into consideration when describing the various methods:

- adequacy and expressiveness of the knowledge representation
- robustness
- completeness and consistency
- bias under certain conditions
- handling of continuous data
- handling of noise
- comprehensibility to human experts and the match with an expert's own reasoning approach.

1.7 Overview of the book

Chapters 2 and 3 discuss methods of automated knowledge acquisition that derive decision trees and rules, respectively. The former chapter discusses ID3 and CART in detail, while the latter describes Michalski's STAR algorithms. These representations are symbolic in nature.

Chapter 4 gives a brief description of neural networks and learning. This computer-based representation was inspired by various mathematical theories and the human brain. These neural networks are distinguishable from other computing devices developed so far, because (DARPA 1988):

- *They are adaptive or trainable — they are not so much programmed, but rather trained with data;*
- *They are naturally massively parallel and thus should be able to make decisions at high speed and be fault tolerant.*

From the point of view of learning from experience, the idea of trainable neural networks is very similar to biological systems (DARPA 1988). While debate continues about the relationship of neural networks to physiological structures, neural networks have been found to be computationally effective in learning patterns from raw data for several different classes of problems (McClelland & Rumelhart 1988; McClelland et al. 1986; Rumelhart et al. 1986). This formalism is reputed to be able to deal efficiently and effectively with noise and conflicting information (Jones & Hoskins 1987; Josin 1987; Kinoshita & Palevsky 1987; Mozer & Bachrach 1990). This learning is considered to be sub-symbolic in nature.

Chapter 5 briefly describes several other symbolic and sub-symbolic learning methodologies. Lenat's frame-based AM and EURISKO programs, genetic-based algorithms, and Explanation-Based Learning (EBL) are all discussed. Other methods, including Gallant's MACIE and Fu's KT algorithms, that use neural networks to extract knowledge are also presented.

The intriguing lure of the way that a human learns is an interesting possibility for machine learning. As such, Chapter 6 discusses various aspects of human learning that could be pertinent to machine learning. In this chapter, various issues in attempting to bridge the gap between the two different paradigms of neural networks and symbolic representations are highlighted.

Chapters 7, 8, 9, and 11 then present a new avenue of automated knowledge acquisition that uses neural networks to learn the knowledge from the training set. These learning methods extract symbolic IF-THEN production rules, concepts, and concept hierarchies from the trained neural network, as shown in Figure 1.17.

Chapter 7 presents the first attempt at extracting knowledge from a neural network. The shortcomings of this method are discussed in that chapter. Chapters 8 and 9 present the BRAINNE method, which does not suffer from the shortcomings of the first attempt. BRAINNE stands for Building Representations for AI using Neural NEtworks. As described in Chapter 8, both conjunctive and disjunctive rules can be extracted. Chapter 9 presents an extension to the BRAINNE method that enables the method to deal efficiently with continuous

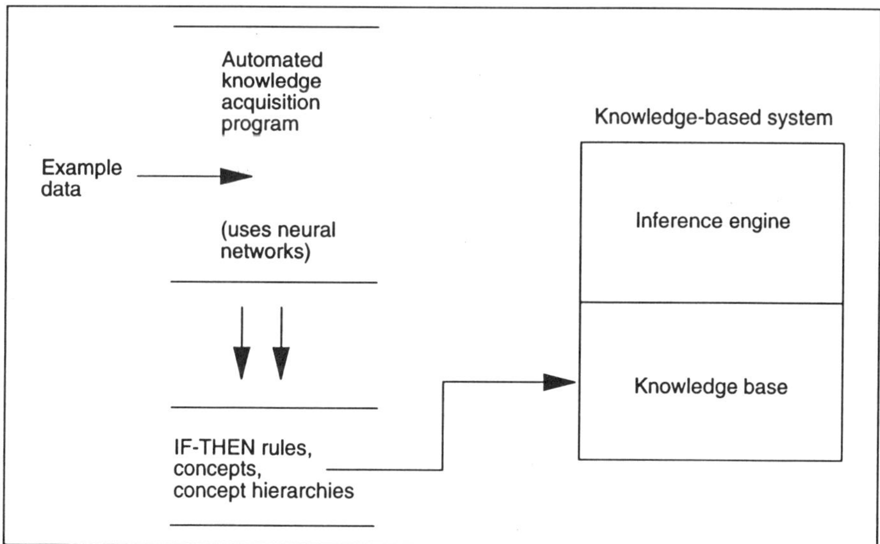

Figure 1.17 The automated knowledge program produces rules that can be put into a knowledge-based system

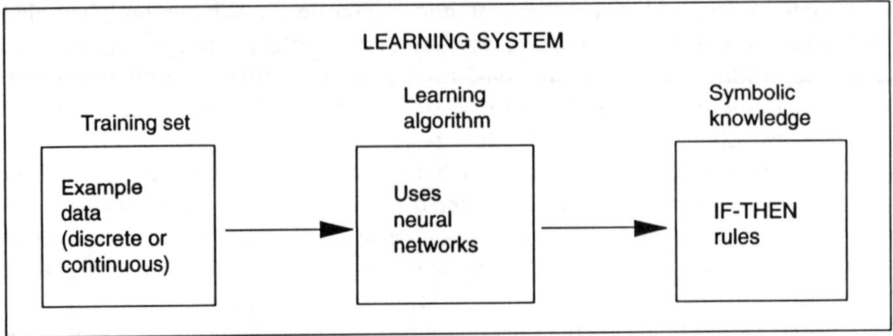

Figure 1.18 The learning system used in BRAINNE

features without prior sub-grouping. In other words, this extension uses the raw (normalized) values as inputs into the learning method and actually produces symbolic rules with the appropriate bounds for the continuous attributes determined. Figure 1.18 illustrates the general framework of BRAINNE. Several case studies of the application of BRAINNE to different problem domains are presented in Chapter 10. They highlight the versatility of BRAINNE and its success in many differing domains.

Chapter 11 presents a method of rule extraction and concept formation that uses an unsupervised Kohonen network. The application of unsupervised neural networks to machine learning is a significant innovation.

Manual approaches to knowledge acquisition are outlined in Chapter 12, the final chapter of the book.

References

Buchanan, B.G., Barstow, D., Bechtal, R., Bennett, J., Clancey, W., Kulikowski, C., Mitchell, T. & Waterman, D.A. 1983, "Constructing an expert system", in *Building Expert Systems,* eds F. Hayes-Roth, D.A. Waterman & D.B. Lenat, Addison-Wesley, Reading, Massachusetts, pp. 127–68

Carbonell, J.G., Michalski, R.S. & Mitchell, T.M. 1983, "An overview of machine learning", in *Machine Learning: An Artificial Intelligence Approach*, eds R.S. Michalski, J.G. Carbonell & T.M. Mitchell, Tioga Publishing, Palo Alto, California, pp. 3–23

Charniak, E. & McDermott, D. 1985, *Introduction to Artificial Intelligence*, Addison-Wesley, Reading, Massachusetts

DARPA (Defense Advanced Research Project Agency) 1988, *Neural Network Study*, AFCEA International Press, Fairfax, Virginia, November

Dietterich, T. & Michalski, R. 1981, "Inductive learning of structural descriptions", *Artificial Intelligence*, vol. 16, pp. 257–94

Forsyth, R. & Rada, R. 1986, *Machine Learning: Applications in Expert Systems and Information Retrieval*, Ellis Horwood, Chichester, UK

Hart, A. 1986, *Knowledge Acquisition for Expert Systems*, Kogan Page, London

Hayes-Roth, F., Waterman, D.A. & Lenat, D.B., eds 1983, *Building Expert Systems,* Addison-Wesley, Reading, Massachusetts

Honavar, V. & Uhr, L. 1988, "A network of neuron-like units that learns to perceive by generation as well as reweighting of its links", in *Proceedings of the 1988 Connectionist Models Summer School*, eds D. Touretzky, G. Hinton & T. Sejnowski, Morgan Kaufmann Publishers, San Francisco, California, pp. 472–84

Honavar, V. & Uhr, L. 1990, *Symbol Processing Systems, Connectionist Networks and Generalized Connectionist Networks*, Technical Report No. 90-23, Department of Computer Science, Iowa State University, Ames, December

Johnson, P.E. 1983, "What kind of expert should a system be?", *J. Med. Phil.*, vol. 8, pp. 77–97

Johnson-Laird, P.N. 1989, "Human experts and expert systems", in *Intelligent Systems in a Human Context: Development, Implications, and Applications*, eds L.A. Murray & J.T.E. Richardson, Oxford University Press, Oxford, pp. 35–46

Jones, W.P. & Hoskins, J. 1987, "Back propagation: A generalized delta learning rule", *Byte*, October, pp. 155–62

Josin, G. 1987, "Neural-network heuristics", *Byte*, October, pp. 183–92

Kinoshita, J. & Palevsky, N.G. 1987, "Computing with neural networks", *High Technology*, May, pp. 24–31

Kolokouris, A.T. 1986, "Machine learning", *Byte*, November, pp. 225–31

McClelland, J.L. & Rumelhart, D.E. 1988, *Explorations in Parallel Distributed Processing: A Handbook of Models, Programs and Exercises*, MIT Press, Cambridge, Massachusetts

McClelland, J.L., Rumelhart, D.E. & the PDP Research Group 1986, *Parallel Distributed Processing, Volume 2: Psychological and Biological Models*, MIT Press, Cambridge, Massachusetts

Michalski, R. 1983, "Theory and methodology of inductive learning", *Artificial Intelligence*, vol. 20, pp. 111–61

Minsky, M. 1975, "A framework for representing knowledge", in *The Psychology of Computer Vision*, ed. P.H. Winston, McGraw-Hill, New York

Mitchell, T. 1979, "An analysis of generalizations as a search problem", *Proceedings of the Sixth International Joint Conference of Artificial Intelligence,* pp. 577–82

Mozer, M.C. 1987, "RAMBOT: A connectionist system that learns by example", in *IEEE First International Conference on Neural Networks*, vol. II, eds M. Caudill & C. Butler, San Diego, California, June, pp. 693–700

Mozer, M.C. & Bachrach, J. 1990, "Discovering the structure of a reactive environment by exploration", in *Neural Information Processing Systems (NIPS) 2*, ed. D.S. Touretzky, Morgan Kaufmann Publishers, San Francisco, California, pp. 439–46

Rumelhart, D.E., McClelland, J.L. & the PDP Research Group 1986, *Parallel Distributed Processing, Volume 1: Foundations*, MIT Press, Cambridge, Massachusetts

Russell, B. 1912, *The Problems of Philosophy*, Oxford University Press, London

Sestito, S. 1991, *Automation of Knowledge Acquisition using Neural Nets*, Ph.D. thesis, La Trobe University, Melbourne, Australia

Shavlik, J. & Dietterich, T. 1990a, "General aspects of machine learning, Introduction", in *Readings in Machine Learning*, eds J. Shavlik & T. Dietterich, Morgan Kaufmann Publishers, San Francisco, California, pp. 1–10

Shavlik, J. & Dietterich, T. 1990b, "Inductive learning from preclassified training examples, Introduction", in *Readings in Machine Learning*, eds J. Shavlik & T. Dietterich, Morgan Kaufmann Publishers, San Francisco, California, pp. 45–56

Winston, P.H. 1984, *Artificial Intelligence*, Addison-Wesley, Reading, Massachusetts

Wogulis, J. & Langely, P. 1989, "Improving efficiency by learning intermediate concepts", *International Joint Conference on Artificial Intelligence (IJCAI-89)*, Detroit, pp. 657–62

Young, R.M. 1989, "Human interface aspects of expert systems", in *Intelligent Systems in a Human Context: Development, Implications, and Applications*, eds L.A. Murray & J.T.E. Richardson, Oxford University Press, Oxford, pp. 20–34

2

Induction algorithms using decision trees

2.1 Introduction

In this chapter, the focus is on machine learning methods that represent their acquired knowledge as decision trees. There are three important families of this type. The first includes CLS (Hunt et al. 1966), ID3 (Quinlan 1986, 1987a), and ACLS systems, while the second involves CART systems (Breiman et al. 1984). The third family uses statistical criteria.

All these systems employ a top-down, divide-and-conquer strategy that partitions the given set of examples into smaller and smaller subsets in step with the growth of the tree. Although they share this common skeleton, systems in this group differ markedly in their selection criteria. These selection criteria form the basis on which the example set is subdivided at each step (Quinlan 1987a).

2.2 Basic information

A decision tree is usually a directed graph consisting of nodes and directed arcs. The nodes frequently correspond to a question or a test. Decision trees have been used in many areas, including pattern recognition, taxonomy, decision table programming, switching theory, databases, machine diagnosis, and analysis of algorithms.

For illustration purposes, consider a decision tree used for classifying a few animals on the basis of whether or not they have Hair or Feathers, and on their Color, as shown in Figure 2.1. Here:

- Hair? Feathers? and Color? are the questions.
- True and False are possible answers to the first two questions, and Black, Gray, and White are possible answers to the third.
- KANGAROO, PELICAN, TUNA, DOLPHIN, and WHALE are the classifications.

As this decision tree shows, the answers to the questions do not have to be binary; that is, an answer does not have to be just two-valued, such as True or False. There can also be a distinct number of values greater than two. Hair? is an example of a question with a binary answer, while Color? is not.

A decision tree has a root node, intermediate nodes, and leaves. The root node is the node from which the decision tree is expanded. Intermediate nodes are nodes that can be further expanded. Leaves are nodes that are not further

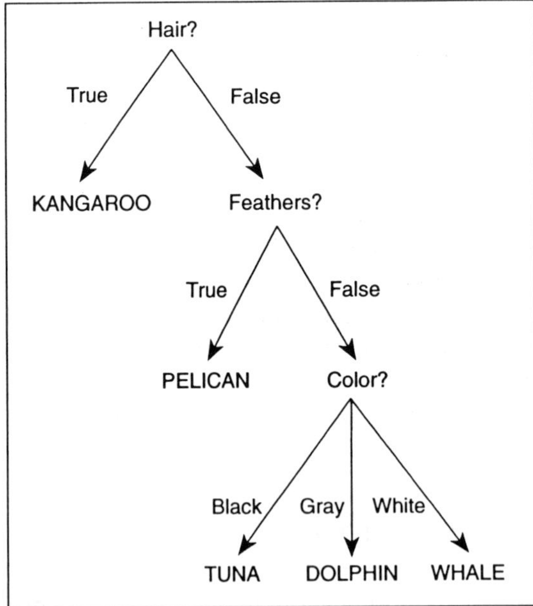

Figure 2.1   A simple decision tree

expanded. Thus in Figure 2.1, Hair? is the root node, Feathers? is an intermediate node, and PELICAN and DOLPHIN are leaves. As leaves are not expanded further, they contain a final decision of the decision tree. In a classification problem, one would assign each leaf to a class. Note that any intermediate node can be considered a root for the subtree starting at that node. This leads to a recursive definition of a decision tree.

At each intermediate or root node, one needs to carry out a test to determine the successor nodes. Thus a decision tree may be considered to be a test that has a set of mutually exclusive possible outcomes together with a subsidiary decision tree for each such outcome. The subsidiary decision tree may be a test or, alternatively, it may be a leaf. Thus in Figure 2.1, Feathers? is a subsidiary decision tree that is a test, while KANGAROO is a subsidiary decision tree that is a leaf.

The root of the tree is the starting point when classifying an example. If it is a leaf, the example is assigned the class associated with that leaf. Alternatively, if the root of the decision tree is a test, the outcome of this test for the given example is determined, and the process continues using the subsidiary decision tree of that outcome. Hence an example is classified by tracing out a path from the root of the decision tree to one of its leaves. For instance, from Figure 2.1, if:

> Hair? = False and Feathers? = False and Color? = Gray
> then classification = DOLPHIN.

2.3 Feature selection criterion

Figure 2.1 illustrates one way of classifying the data found in Table 2.1. An alternative way of classifying the data is given in Figure 2.2.

There are two characteristics distinguishing the decision trees found in Figures 2.1 and 2.2. First, the decision tree in Figure 2.1 is easier to understand than that in Figure 2.2 because the former tree:

- distinguishes between a mammal and other animals after the first partition;
- distinguishes between a bird and other animals after the second partition;
- determines the final categories after the third partition.

example 1	(Hair, Milk, Gray, Medium) $\Rightarrow$ (KANGAROO)
example 2	(Feathers, Egglaying, White, Medium) $\Rightarrow$ (PELICAN)
example 3	(Swims, Medium, Black) $\Rightarrow$ (TUNA)
example 4	(Swims, Large, Gray) $\Rightarrow$ (DOLPHIN)
example 5	(Swims, Large, White) $\Rightarrow$ (WHALE)

Table 2.1 A training set of example data

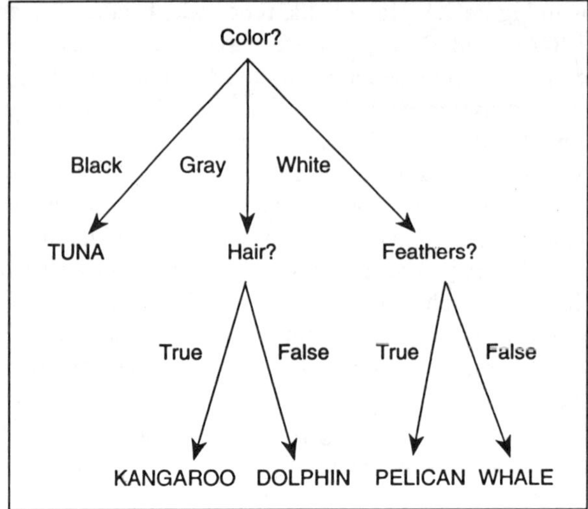

Figure 2.2 An alternative decision tree for classifying the data in Table 2.1

There is no similar conceptual explanation for the decision tree in Figure 2.2. The second distinguishing characteristic involves the positioning of a feature in the decision tree. The aim is to position a feature at some point in the decision tree that generates a tree that is as simple as possible and gives the correct classification. Once again, the decision tree in Figure 2.1 achieves this more efficiently than the tree in Figure 2.2.

Consider now the decision tree shown in Figure 2.3. Here the first partition does not separate out any classes, because there are no leaves. After the first partition, there is a mixture of KANGAROO, PELICAN, and TUNA, and a mixture of WHALE and DOLPHIN. It is only after the second partition of the training set that some of the classes are distinguishable. Also note that when the Color test is used in the decision tree, an empty leaf is generated. An empty leaf is a leaf with no examples. It could be concluded that the tree generated using the Size attribute test as the initial root is not very efficient.

All of these aspects indicate that the ordering of the attributes used in the tests is crucial for the production of an understandable and efficient tree. Thus, when constructing a decision tree, it is necessary to have a means of determining:

- the important attributes needed for the classification
- the ordering of the important attributes.

A feature selection criterion (Carter & Catlett 1987) is used to determine the ranking of the input attributes. Each criterion can be regarded as a test

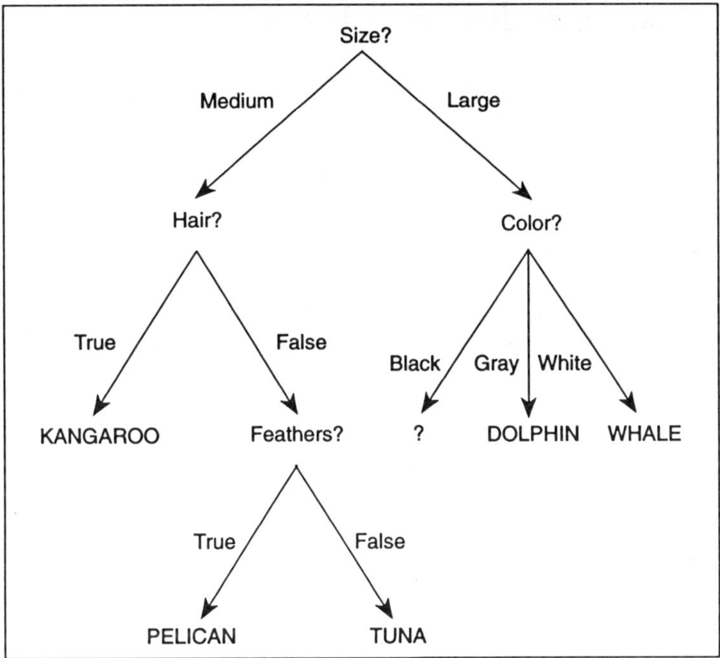

Figure 2.3   A poorer alternative decision tree for describing the data in Table 2.1

commonly restricted to being a function of only one of the attributes. There are several reasons for this:

- It is difficult to define a suitable feature selection criterion for groups of variables taken at a time.
- A combination of variables considered at a node will lead to an increased number of possible children nodes.
- Since decision trees are constructed by examining all possible tests at each stage, increasing the forms to be explored would lead to a significant increase in computational cost (Quinlan 1987a).
- The decision tree may be much more difficult to understand if each test is a complex function (Quinlan 1987a).

Besides being restricted to a function of a single attribute, the exact form of a test is specified by the selection criterion itself. Note here that at each level one has a discrete set of outcomes, no matter what the form of the test. Thus this permits one to define a criterion in a relatively straightforward manner for specifying the structure of a decision tree, given a suitable training set (Quinlan 1987a).

2.4 Learning decision trees

In Chapter 1 we defined an automated learning method as consisting of a training set, a learning algorithm, a symbolic knowledge representation, and an assessment scheme. Figure 2.4 illustrates the type of learning system used in this chapter. It highlights that the symbolic knowledge representation derived by such learning algorithms is a decision tree.

The learning algorithm uses the feature selection criterion to select an attribute on which to divide the training set. This in turn produces a branching or partitioning of the decision tree. The training set is progressively subdivided using attributes determined by the feature selection criterion. A leaf in the tree corresponds to one class only. This class is assigned when all the examples in the particular subdivision have the same class.

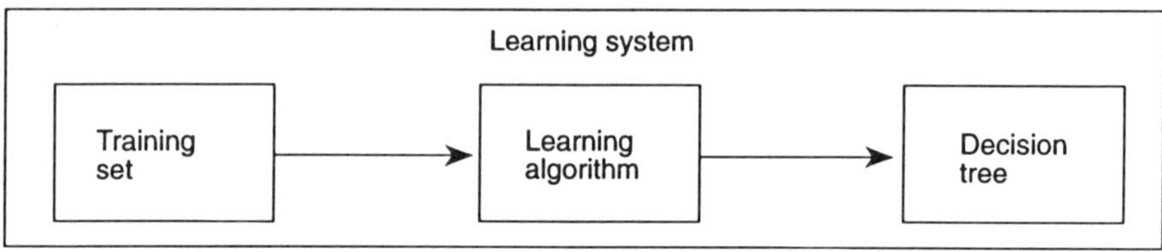

Figure 2.4 A learning system for deriving decision trees

Assuming the existence of some feature selection criterion, consider Figure 2.5, which highlights the procedure of learning decision trees. Let there be 5 examples: E1, E2, E3, E4, and E5 in the training set, each with different classes: C1, C2, C3, C4, and C5. Initially, all of the examples need to be considered. As the examples have different classes, let the initial test for partitioning be T1 and assume it causes E1 to be put into one branch and the remaining examples to be put into another branch. Since E1 is the only example, it would be assigned to the class of that example. Thus a leaf would be produced, labeled as C1. Further partitioning is necessary for the second branch because the examples have more than one class. Let the test for partitioning chosen at this point be T2. This causes example E2 to be put into one branch and the remaining examples into another. The branch with E2 would become a leaf, labeled as C2. Let the next test chosen for partitioning be T3. Assuming that this test has three outcomes, let the 3 remaining examples be uniquely identified, producing 3 leaves labeled with C3, C4, and C5 respectively. At this point, the process is stopped.

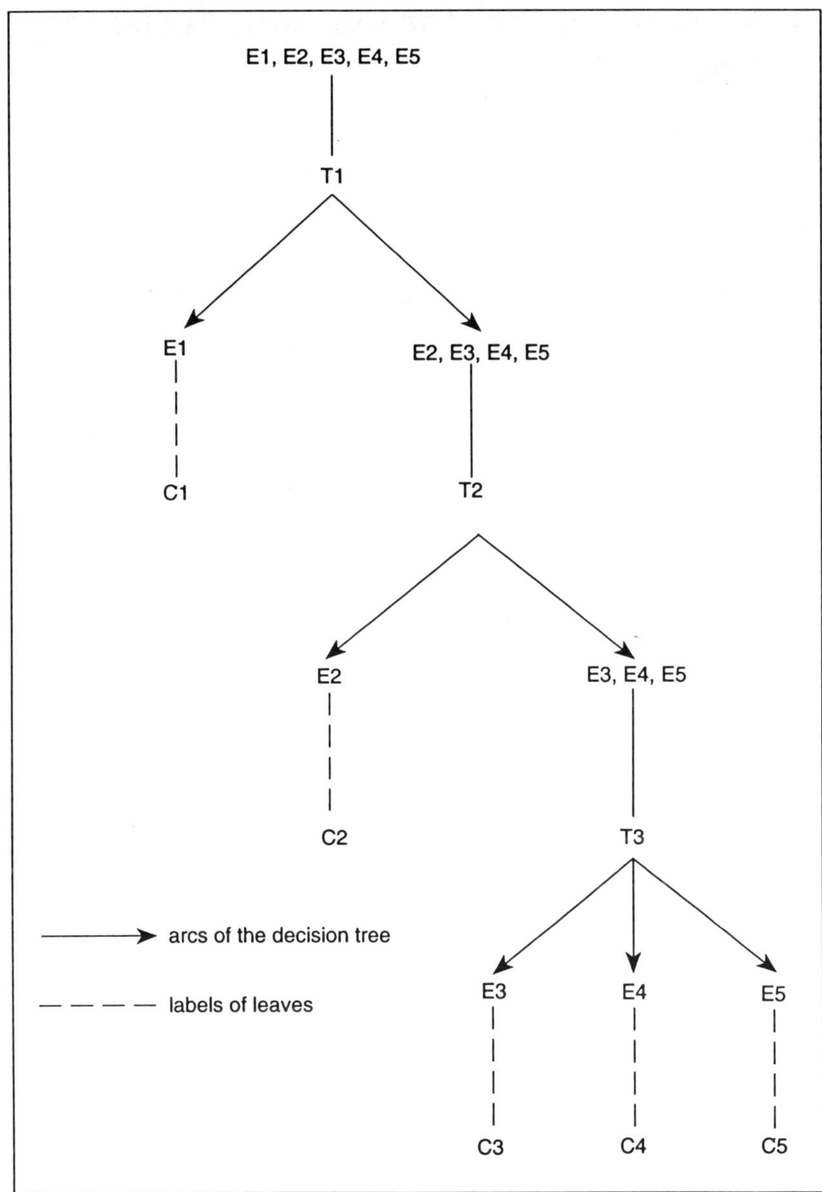

Figure 2.5   An illustration of learning a decision tree

2.5 Basic algorithm for learning decision trees

Hunt's Concept Learning System (CLS) framework (Hunt et al. 1966) is the patriarch of the family of algorithms deriving decision trees. This work first appeared as a proposed model of what people do when given simple concept formation tasks. It was due to Hunt and his associates that this model was used in computer applications. CLS constructs a decision tree that attempts to minimize the cost of classifying an example. This cost has two components:

1. classifying the example correctly
2. classifying the example incorrectly.

CLS uses a look-ahead strategy similar to MINIMAX. MINIMAX is a strategy that explores the space of possible decision trees to a fixed depth, chooses an action to minimize the cost in this limited space, and then moves one level down the tree. In its complete form, the computation required thus increases exponentially with the depth of the look-ahead employed.

To detail the basic algorithm, let a training set S consist of several examples, each belonging to one of the classes C1, C2, C3, ..., Ck. According to Quinlan (1987a), the algorithm for generating a decision tree is given by the following steps:

- *If all examples in set S belong to the same class, say C, the decision tree for set S consists of a leaf labeled with this class;*
- *Otherwise, let T be some test with possible outcomes O1, O2, ..., On. Each example in S has one outcome for T so the test partitions S into subsets S1, S2, ..., Sn, where each example in Si has outcome Oi for T. T becomes the root of the decision tree and, for each outcome Oi, a subsidiary decision tree is built by invoking the same procedure recursively on the set Si.*

Notice that only a subset of attributes may be encountered on a particular path from the root of a decision tree to a leaf. An important question to consider here is whether or not the attributes provide sufficient information for a decision tree to be generated. The attributes are adequate for the induction task unless there are 2 examples in the training set that have the same value for each attribute but belong to different classes. For instance, if the following 2 examples were in the training set, it would be impossible to distinguish between a WHALE and a DOLPHIN:

    example 4   (Swims, Large, Gray) $\Rightarrow$ (DOLPHIN)
    example 5   (Swims, Large, Gray) $\Rightarrow$ (WHALE)

As long as the attributes are adequate, one can always construct a test that produces a non-trivial partition of the training set (Quinlan 1987a).

However, the basic algorithm ignores complexities that arise in real-world induction tasks because the attributes may not be adequate. In this case, it may be necessary to assign a leaf to a set S containing examples from more than one class, either by deciding not to partition such a set or by subsequently replacing the generated decision with a leaf. When S is empty, the choice of which class to associate with the leaf may not matter with the training set examples, but it may be important when the tree is used to classify unseen examples. Further problems arise when there is a need to deal with examples having unknown values for some attributes. An elaboration of these problems and others is given in later sections.

The feature selection criterion plays a central role in the quality of the decision tree as a classifier and its simplicity or complexity. There are basically three groups of algorithms that derive decision trees and use various feature selection criteria. The most well known algorithm of the first group is called ID3 (Interactive Dichotomizer 3), while in the second group the CART (Classification And Regression Trees) algorithm is the most prominent. The third group uses statistically based feature selection criteria. These three groups will now be discussed in detail.

2.6 The ID3 group of algorithms

2.6.1 General aspects

Quinlan's ID3 (1986, 1987a), discussed in detail in the next section, is one of a series of programs developed from CLS. It embeds a tree-building method in an iterative outer shell and replaces the cost-driven, look-ahead of CLS with an information-driven evaluation function. The gain criterion selects the test that maximizes the information gain. Several studies have shown that this gain criterion tends to favor features with more values. One solution to this problem was to use a subset criterion that groups feature values into subsets so all tests have only two outcomes. However, this can lead to decision trees that are unintelligible to human experts and that require a large increase in computation. Quinlan (1986) then proposed a gain ratio criterion to overcome the aforementioned bias. However, there may be a problem with the gain ratio if the denominator approaches zero (Forsyth & Rada 1986).

2.6.2 ID3 in detail

In order to provide a concrete example of this group of methods, Quinlan's ID3 algorithm is discussed in detail in this section. The learning algorithm is presented with a set of examples relevant to a classification task. With this set, the algorithm develops a decision tree from the top down, guided by the frequency information in the examples. The order of presentation of the examples is not important. The learning algorithm requires the examination and re-examination of all the examples at many stages during learning. Therefore, this is a data-driven approach, using a top-down induction method to produce its decision trees (Quinlan 1986, 1987a).

The basic structure of ID3 is iterative. The aim of the method is to produce a tree that correctly classifies all examples in a subset of the training set. All other examples in the training set are then classified using the tree. If the tree gives the correct answer for all of these examples then it is correct for the entire training set, and so the process terminates. If not, a selection of the incorrectly classified examples is added to the initial subset and the process starts again (Quinlan 1986).

A divide-and-conquer strategy is used to construct a decision tree. The choice of the test to partition the training set is crucial if the decision tree is to be simple. Choosing a test reduces to selecting an attribute for the root of the tree and subsequent subtrees. The induction program adopts an information-based method that relies on two assumptions. Let set S represent the training set, and let there be x, y, and z number of examples of classes X, Y, and Z, respectively. The assumptions, according to Quinlan (1987a), are:

- any correct decision tree for S will classify examples in the same proportion as their representation in S. Thus an arbitrary example belongs to class X, Y, or Z with probability:

$$\frac{x}{(x+y+z)}, \quad \frac{y}{(x+y+z)} \quad \text{or} \quad \frac{z}{(x+y+z)} \quad \text{respectively, and}$$

- when a decision tree is used to classify an example, it returns a class. A decision tree can thus be regarded as a source of a message X, Y, or Z, with the expected information needed to generate this message given by:

$$I(X, Y, Z) = -\frac{x}{x+y+z}\log_2\left(\frac{x}{x+y+z}\right) - \frac{y}{x+y+z}\log_2\left(\frac{y}{x+y+z}\right)$$
$$-\frac{z}{x+y+z}\log_2\left(\frac{z}{x+y+z}\right)$$

From these assumptions, the expected information required for the tree with attribute A as its root is given by:

$$E(A) = \sum \frac{x_i+y_i+z_i}{x+y+z} I(x_i, y_i, z_i)$$

where x_i, y_i, and z_i are the number of examples of classes X, Y, and Z respectively with value A_i of the attribute A. The summation gives the total expected information for attribute A. The information gained by branching on A is:

$$GAIN(A) = I(X, Y, Z) - E(A).$$

At each non-leaf node of a decision tree, the gain of each untested attribute must be determined. This gain in turn depends on the value of x_i, y_i, and z_i for each value A_i of the attribute A. Every example must be examined to determine its class and its value of A. Thus, ID3's total computational requirement per iteration is proportional to the product of the size of the training set, the number of attributes, and the number of non-leaf nodes in the decision tree (Quinlan 1987a).

The worth of ID3's attribute-selecting heuristic can be assessed by the simplicity of the resulting decision tree. More importantly, it can be assessed by how well the resulting tree expresses the real relationships that exist in the data between a given class and its attributes. This is demonstrated by the accuracy with which the decision tree classifies examples other than those in the training set. A straightforward method of assessing this predictive accuracy is to use only part of the given set of examples as the training set and to check the resulting decision tree on the remainder.

2.6.3 An illustrative worked example of ID3

The training set used in this section is given in Table 2.2. It contains:

4 inputs:

(Hair, Swims) = (True or False)
(Color) = (White, Brown, or Gray)

(Size) = (Small, Medium, or Large)

3 classes:

(A, B, C) = (KANGAROO, DOLPHIN, WHALE)

Note that the formulae in Section 2.6.2 require computations involving base 2 logarithms. These can be determined from the general relationship:

$$\log_b a = \frac{\log_x a}{\log_x b}$$

example 1	(Hair, Gray, Medium) $\Rightarrow$ (KANGAROO)
example 2	(Hair, Brown, Medium) $\Rightarrow$ (KANGAROO)
example 3	(Swims, Gray, Large) $\Rightarrow$ (DOLPHIN)
example 4	(Swims, White, Medium) $\Rightarrow$ (DOLPHIN)
example 5	(Swims, Brown, Large) $\Rightarrow$ (WHALE)

Table 2.2   The training set for the illustrative example

Hence:

$$\log_2 a = \frac{\log_{10} a}{\log_{10} 2}$$

The first step in the worked example is to determine the root of the decision tree. Therefore, the gain of all of the input attributes needs to be determined.

- There is a total of 5 examples at this point and all input attributes need to be considered:

The total expected information, I, is given by:

$$I(A, B, C) = -2/5\log_2(2/5) - 2/5\log_2(2/5) - 1/5\log_2(1/5) = 1.5219$$

- Consider the input Hair:

The expected information for the various values of Hair is given by:

$$
\begin{aligned}
(\text{Hair} = \text{True}), a_1 &= 2, b_1 = 0, c_1 = 0: \\
I(a_1, b_1, c_1) &= -2/2\log_2(2/2) - 0 - 0 \\
&= 0.0000 \\
(\text{Hair} = \text{False}), a_2 &= 0, b_2 = 2, c_2 = 1: \\
I(a_2, b_2, c_2) &= -0 - 2/3\log_2(2/3) - 1/3\log_2(1/3) \\
&= 0.9183
\end{aligned}
$$

Expected information is given by:

$$
\begin{aligned}
E(\text{Hair}) &= 2/5\ I(a_1, b_1, c_1) + 3/5\ I(a_2, b_2, c_2) \\
&= (2/5 * 0.0000) + (3/5 * 0.9183) \\
&= 0.5509
\end{aligned}
$$

Finally, the gain is given by:

$$
\begin{aligned}
\text{GAIN}(\text{Hair}) &= I(A, B, C) - E(\text{Hair}) \\
&= 1.5219 - 0.5509 \\
&= 0.9710
\end{aligned}
$$

- Similar calculation for the input Swims gives:

$$\text{GAIN}(\text{Swims}) = 0.9710$$

- Consider the input Color, which illustrates the calculation of the gains for the discrete values of Color:

$$
\begin{aligned}
(\text{Color} = \text{White}), a_1 &= 0, b_1 = 1, c_1 = 0: \\
I(a_1, b_1, c_1) &= -0 - 1/1\log_2(1/1) - 0 \\
&= 0.0000 \\
(\text{Color} = \text{Gray}), a_2 &= 1, b_2 = 1, c_2 = 0:
\end{aligned}
$$

$$I(a_2, b_2, c_2) = -1/2\log_2(1/2) - 1/2\log_2(1/2) - 0$$
$$= 1.0000$$

(Color = Brown), $a_3 = 1$, $b_3 = 0$, $c_3 = 1$:
$$I(a_3, b_3, c_3) = -1/2\log_2(1/2) - 0 - 1/2\log_2(1/2)$$
$$= 1.0000$$

Hence:

$$E(\text{Color}) = 1/5\ I(a_1, b_1, c_1) + 2/5\ I(a_2, b_2, c_2) + 2/5\ I(a_3, b_3, c_3)$$
$$= (1/5 * 0.0000) + (2/5 * 1.0000) + (2/5 * 1.0000)$$
$$= 0.8000$$

$$\text{GAIN(Color)} = I(A, B, C) - E(\text{Color})$$
$$= 1.5219 - 0.8000$$
$$= 0.7219$$

- Similar calculation can be carried out for the Size input:

$$\text{GAIN(Size)} = 0.5710$$

From the resulting gains, Hair or Swims could be chosen as the root of the tree at this point since they each have the largest value of the gain. Let the root at this point be Swims. Using this as the first subdivision, examples 1 and 2 are placed into one subtree (Swims = False), while the others are placed into another subtree (Swims = True). The subtree containing examples 1 and 2 becomes a leaf with KANGAROO as the resulting class because this is the class of both examples. The tree at this stage is shown in Figure 2.6(a).

The other subtree contains examples of more than one class. Hence the procedure for calculating the gains must be repeated on this subset.

SUBTREE (Swims = True)

- There is a total of 3 examples at this point and the inputs of Hair, Color, and Size need to be considered:

$$I(A, B, C) = -0 - 2/3\log_2(2/3) - 1/3\log_2(1/3)$$
$$= 0.9183$$

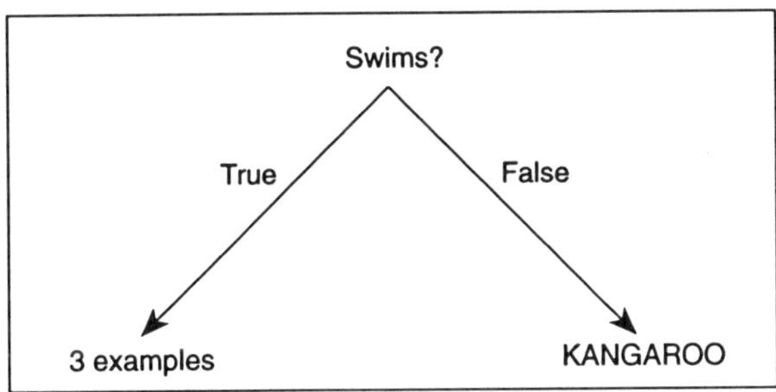

Figure 2.6(a) First subdivision produced for the training set in Table 2.2

- Consider the input Hair:

$$\begin{aligned}
(\text{Hair} = \text{True}),\ a_1 &= 0,\ b_1 = 0,\ c_1 = 0: \\
I(a_1, b_1, c_1) &= -0 - 0 - 0 \\
&= 0.0000
\end{aligned}$$

$$\begin{aligned}
(\text{Hair} = \text{False}),\ a_2 &= 0,\ b_2 = 2,\ c_2 = 1: \\
I(a_2, b_2, c_2) &= -0 - 2/3\log_2(2/3) - 1/3\log_2(1/3) \\
&= 0.9183
\end{aligned}$$

Hence:

$$\begin{aligned}
E(\text{Hair}) &= 0/3\ I(a_1, b_1, c_1) + 3/3\ I(a_2, b_2, c_2) \\
&= (0/3 * 0.0000) + (3/3 * 0.9183) \\
&= 0.9183 \\
\text{GAIN}(\text{Hair}) &= I(A, B, C) - E(\text{Hair}) \\
&= 0.9183 - 0.9183 \\
& 0.0000
\end{aligned}$$

- Similarly, the other gains are:

$$\begin{aligned}
\text{GAIN}(\text{Color}) &= 0.9183 \\
\text{GAIN}(\text{Size}) &= 0.2516
\end{aligned}$$

From these gains, the subtree should be subdivided on Color. Note that the gain obtained from branching on Hair is 0. This is correct because Hair is False for each of the examples in this subtree, even though some of the examples are of different classes. Note also that the gain obtained by branching on Color is equal to the maximum information gain. This also is intuitively correct as each of the examples has different values for Color. The final decision tree is given in Figure 2.6(b).

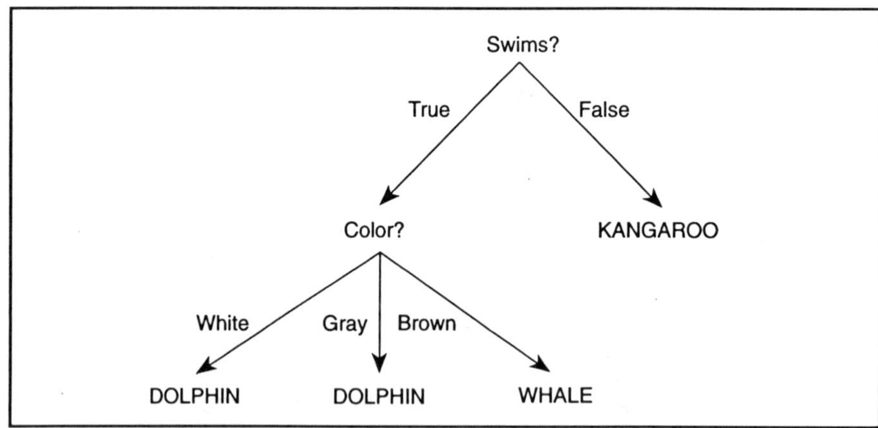

Figure 2.6(b) The decision tree formed for the illustrative training set

2.6.4 LED digit domain example

The example data defining a decimal digit LED display (Breiman et al. 1984) is considered in this section. According to Breiman et al. (1984), each input element of this data was subjected to a 10% random error; that is, a probability of 0.1 that an input element has its correct status inverted. The data consists of 3000 randomly generated examples, each described in terms of 7 binary attributes and 10 equiprobable classes. Figure 2.7 shows a LED decimal digit display.

Using only 500 examples of this noisy data, a very bushy and unintelligible tree was produced, as shown in Figure 2.8. According to Quinlan (1987b), a decision tree comprising an average of 92.2 nodes was produced from the original ID3 algorithm. An average 15.2 production rules were then constructed from the decision tree using various simplification techniques. Quinlan actually used this data for testing improvements to ID3. This example domain illustrates that the original, basic ID3 algorithm has problems dealing with noisy data.

Using a clean subset of the LED example data, the decision tree given in Figure 2.9 was produced. By tracing from the root node to a leaf, IF-THEN type rules can be determined for each leaf. The rules found in Table 2.3 were obtained by collating the various tests and their values for each leaf in the decision tree. For instance, consider the rule defining the leaf labeled with the digit 1 in Table 2.3:

$$((\text{Up-left} = \text{Off}) \text{ AND } (\text{Mid-center} = \text{Off}) \text{ AND } (\text{Up-center} = \text{Off})) \Rightarrow (1).$$

The rule was constructed from the decision tree in Figure 2.9 by taking the right-hand side branch at the root (i.e., Up-left = Off), the right-hand side

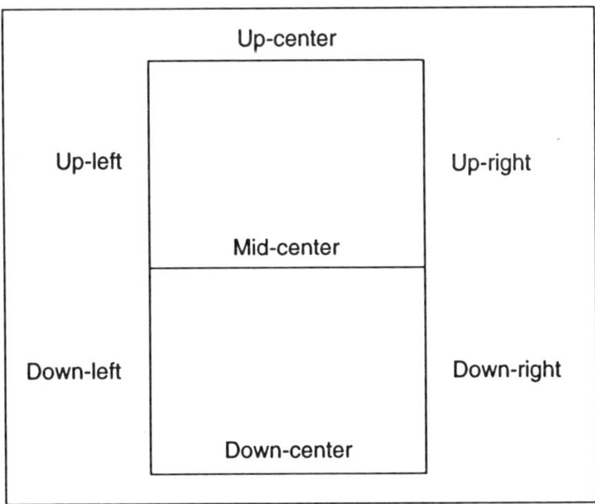

Figure 2.7   A LED decimal digit display

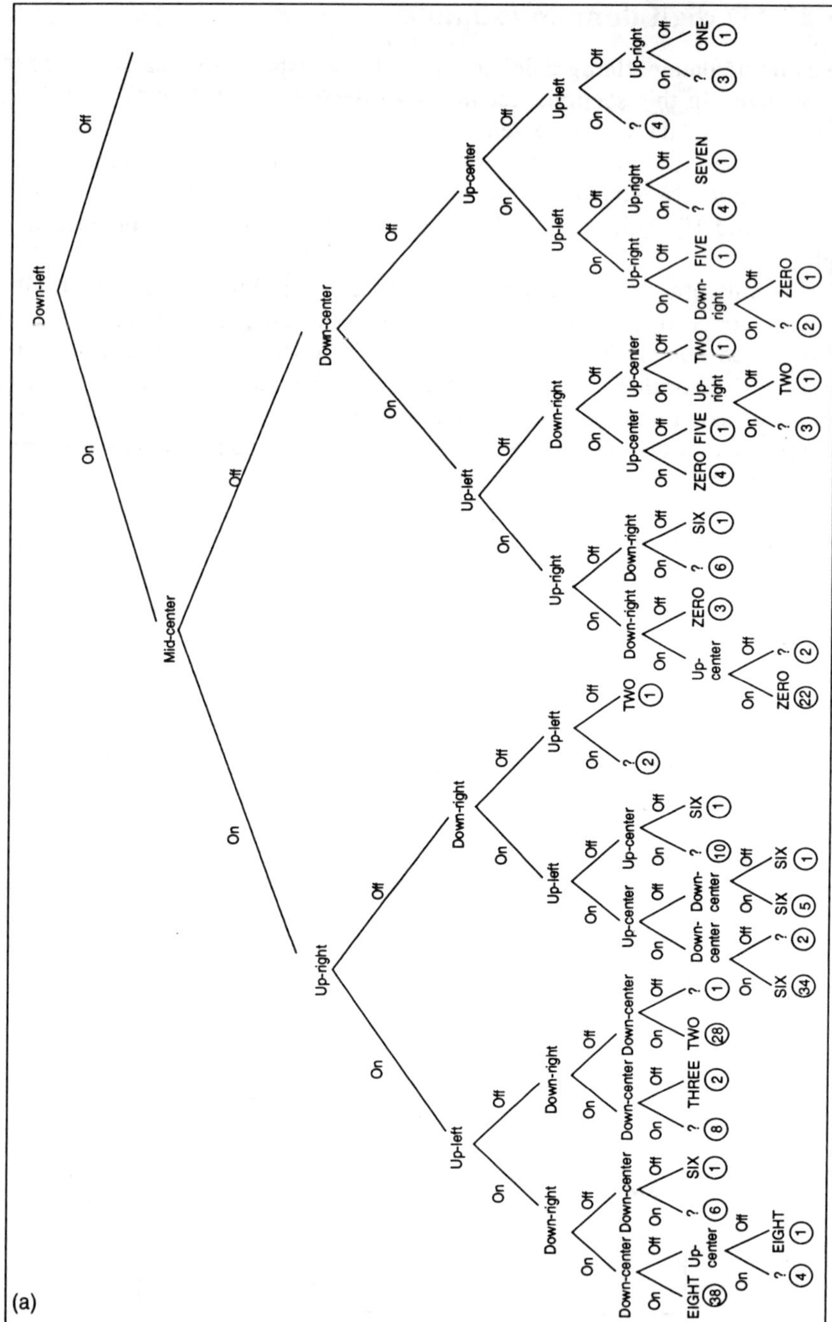

Figure 2.8   Bushy and unintelligible decision tree produced for the noisy LED data

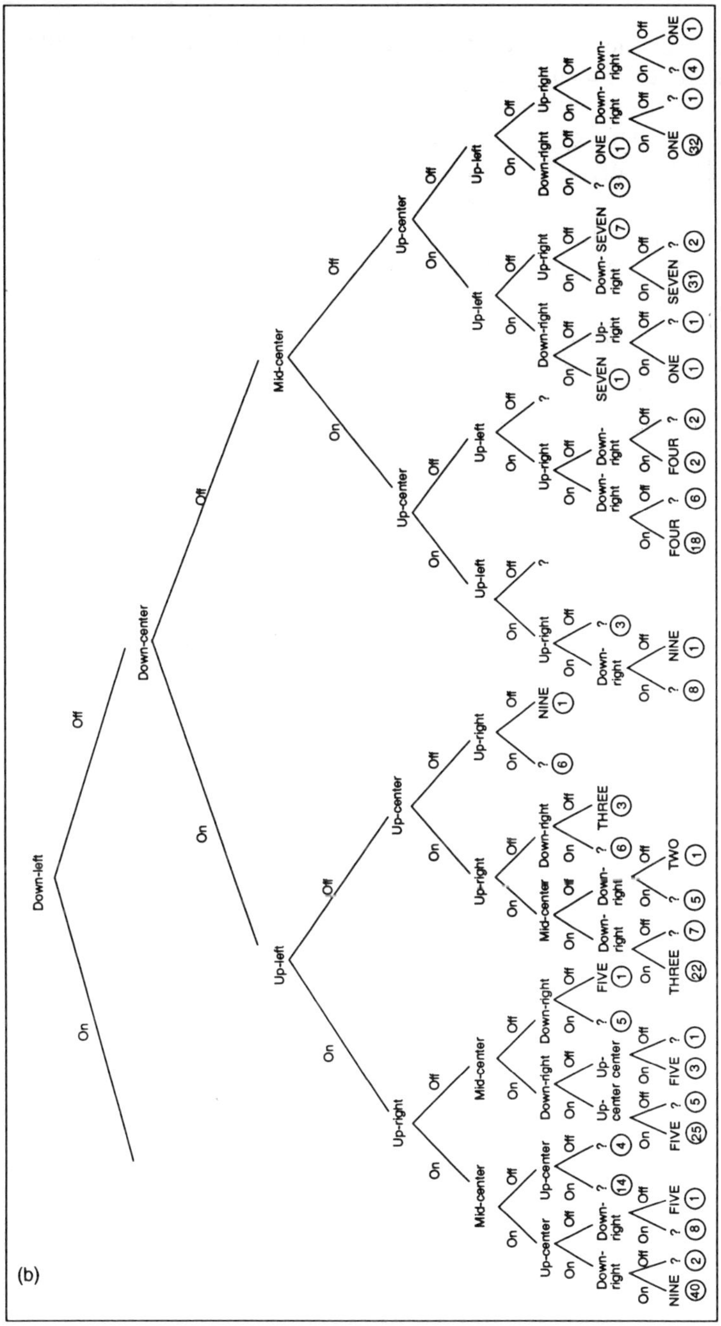

(b)

((Up-left = On) AND (Up-right = On) AND (Down-left = On) AND
   (Mid-center = Off)) $\Rightarrow$ (0)
((Up-left = Off) AND (Mid-center = Off) AND (Up-center = Off)) $\Rightarrow$ (1)
((Up-left = Off) AND (Mid-center = On) AND (Down-left = On)) $\Rightarrow$ (2)
((Up-left = Off) AND (Mid-center = On) AND (Down-left = Off)) $\Rightarrow$ (3)
((Up-left = On) AND (Up-right = On) AND (Down-left = Off) AND
   (Up-center = Off)) $\Rightarrow$ (4)
((Up-left = On) AND (Up-right = Off) AND (Down-left = Off)) $\Rightarrow$ (5)
((Up-left = On) AND (Up-right = Off) AND (Down-left = On)) $\Rightarrow$ (6)
((Up-left = Off) AND (Mid-center = Off) AND (Up-center = On)) $\Rightarrow$ (7)
((Up-left = On) AND (Up-right = On) AND (Down-left = On) AND
   (Mid-center = On)) $\Rightarrow$ (8)
((Up-left = On) AND (Up-right = On) AND (Down-left = Off)
   AND (Up-center = On)) $\Rightarrow$ (9)

Table 2.3   Rules produced by ID3 for a clean subset of LED data

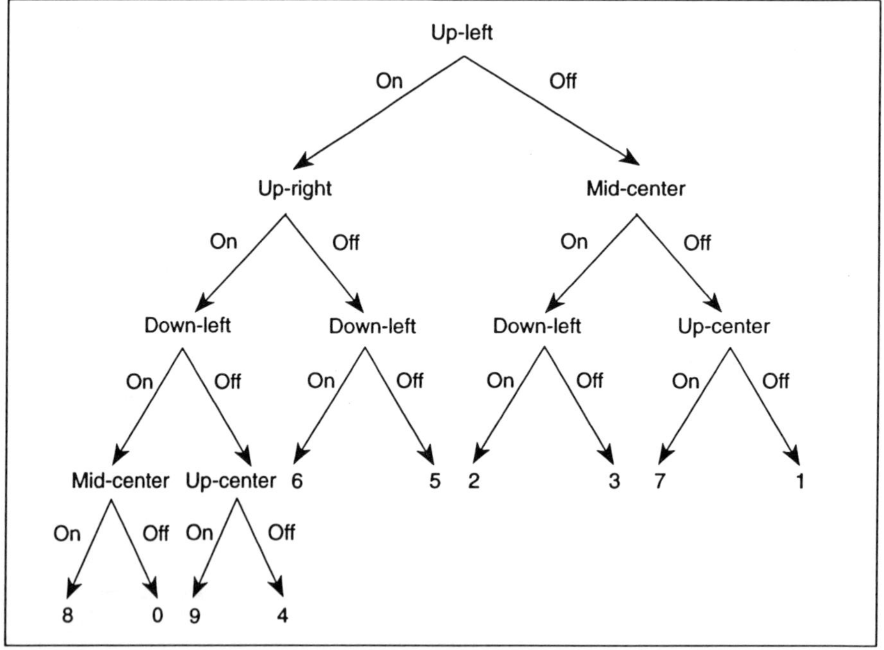

Figure 2.9   The decision tree produced for the clean LED data

branch at the next node (i.e., Mid-center = Off), and the right-hand side branch at the next node (i.e., Up-center = Off). This constitutes the path taken to arrive at the leaf labeled by the 1.

Careful examination of the rules given in Table 2.3 illustrates that the rules are correct in the sense that they do correctly identify the various outputs. However, the rules are not clear to a human observer. They are not the rules that one would expect. For instance, once again consider the rule defining a 1. Figure 2.10(a) shows the LED display with the configuration of this rule:

$$((\text{Up-left} = \text{Off}) \text{ AND } (\text{Mid-center} = \text{Off}) \text{ AND } (\text{Up-center} = \text{Off})) \Rightarrow (1).$$

The rule is essentially saying that if the attributes Up-left, Mid-center, and Up-center are not on, then the example belongs to the output 1. The rule does uniquely define the digit 1 within the context considered. No other output (digits 0, 2–9) has those attributes all Off. However, the actual LED display showing a 1 is that given in Figure 2.10(b). Therefore, one might expect the rule defining a 1 to be:

$$((\text{Up-right} = \text{On}) \text{ AND } (\text{Down-right} = \text{On})) \Rightarrow (1)$$

and nothing more. An important criterion for the applicability or usefulness of a rule is its clarity to a human observer. Note, however, that the above rule

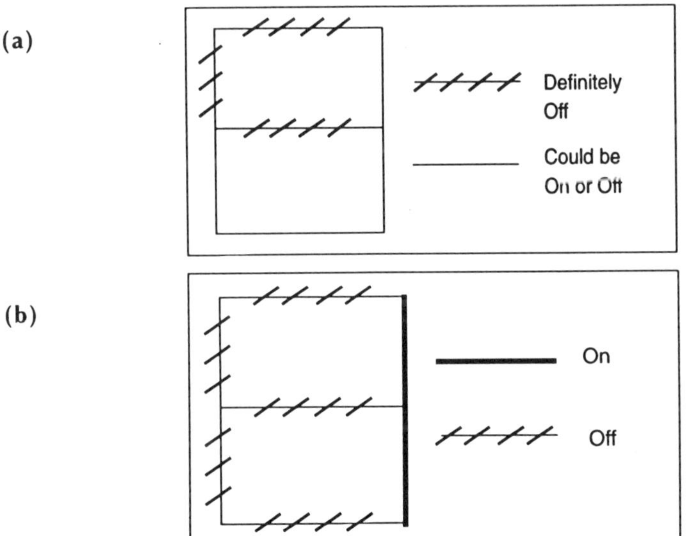

Figure 2.10 (a) The configuration of the LED display for the rule determined by ID3 for the 1 output
(b) The LED display showing a 1

with only two clauses is not unique to a 1. For instance, the 3 output also satisfies it. Including the clauses (Up-center = Off) and (Mid-center = Off) in the rule would make a rule uniquely defining a 1. Thus the following rule uniquely defines a 1 and does not overlap with any other output:

> ((Up-right = On) AND (Down-right = On) AND (Up-center = Off) AND (Mid-center = Off)) $\Rightarrow$ (1).

2.6.5 Problems with these algorithms

As can be seen from the previous examples in this chapter, there are several problems with this type of induction algorithm. Some of these are highlighted below.

Noise

These algorithms have difficulty dealing with noise (Forsyth & Rada 1986; Quinlan 1986). Non-systematic errors in either the values of the attributes or the class information are referred to as noise (Quinlan 1986). The LED domain has illustrated that noise produces large and incomprehensible trees.

Unknown values

These algorithms also have a problem dealing with unknown values. For instance, if the following example were contained in a training set, the basic algorithm has no way of dealing with the unknown value in the Color slot:

> (Swims, Medium, ?) $\Rightarrow$ (DOLPHIN).

A method to overcome this has been proposed by Quinlan (1986). Here, the unknown values of a selected attribute are disregarded when forming the decision trees of the subsets.

Null leaf

A special case arises if the set contains no examples with some particular value of an attribute, giving an empty subset. ID3 labels such a leaf as *null* so that it fails to classify any example arriving at that leaf. This is illustrated in the decision trees in Figures 2.3 and 2.8. A better solution, according to Quinlan (1987a), would be to generalize from the set from which the subset came, and to assign this leaf the most frequent class of the set.

Dead-end leaf

It is also possible to produce a dead-end leaf. This is a leaf that has examples of more than one class, but where no further subdivision is possible. In other words, the leaf contains conflicting examples that cannot be distinguished further. This could indicate erroneous or inconsistent data.

Related to this dead-end leaf problem is the question of whether the chosen attributes provide sufficient information for the production of a complete decision tree. For instance, the following two examples would end up at the same leaf, and yet contain two different outputs:

$$(\text{Swims, Large, Gray}) \Rightarrow (\text{DOLPHIN})$$
$$(\text{Swims, Large, Gray}) \Rightarrow (\text{WHALE}).$$

To deal with these problems, Quinlan (1986) has proposed that two modifications must be made to the basic algorithm. Essentially, the algorithm must be able to work with inadequate attributes and be able to decide that testing further will not improve the predictive accuracy of the decision trees.

Total accuracy required

ID3 subdivides the subset until no single exception remains. Striving for 100% correct rules can cause ID3 to generate very bushy trees with nodes containing very few examples (Quinlan 1986). These nodes are unlikely to be statistically reliable when the tree is later used for classification. Furthermore, large and bushy tree structures are difficult for people to comprehend.

The problem of excessive subdivision could be cured simply by stopping early (Forsyth & Rada 1986). For instance, any subgroup that contained fewer than, say, 5% of the training examples could be deemed too small for further division. When the tree was used to categorize new cases and such a node was reached, the system could give a probabilistic answer. Realistically, such a group is too small to split up any further. There are many domains where certainty is not attainable, and a probabilistic answer based on a reasonable sample is preferred to an exact answer based on a tiny sample (Forsyth & Rada 1986).

A higher order feature selection criterion

As stated previously, in order to be more realistic a function of the attributes could be used for a test. However, there would be a problem with defining a suitable feature selection criterion for groups of variables. Also, as explained earlier, using a function of attributes as a test would increase computational costs and the complexity of the decision tree produced.

Structural relationships

A serious related problem concerns the nature of the description language itself. The decision tree is actually a rather restrictive language. All tests have to be in the form of a comparison between a variable and a constant. Thus this feature-vector notation does not allow one to express structural relationships.

Comprehensibility

Since decision trees are the representation used for learned concepts, the checking of equivalence is not easy. It is difficult for people to understand the learned concept when it is expressed as a large decision tree (Cohen & Feigenbaum 1982). Bushy trees are also difficult for a human to understand. Furthermore, the manner in which the decision is taken may be different from the way a human expert would make it. For instance, the rule determined above by ID3 for the decimal digit 1 on a LED display is not the way a human observer would define a 1.

Continuous data

When dealing with continuous variables, the user has to pre-process the data so that distinct groups are formed. This can be achieved by selecting one or more thresholds on which to subdivide the set. This is somewhat artificial, as it gives no insight into the actual range of the values. For instance, if a threshold of 75° were chosen for a temperature attribute and there were two examples with temperature values of 70° and 10°, then both examples would be put in the same class, even though the values are vastly different. Thus the range of values may not be truly reflected.

2.6.6   Evaluation of these algorithms

There has been a lot of work done to improve ID3 (Cheng et al. 1988; Uthurusamy et al. 1990), including ACLS (Analogue Concept Learning System), which is a generalization of ID3. Both ACLS and ID3 require that each property used to describe examples only has values from a specified set. In addition to properties of this type, ACLS permits properties that have unrestricted integer values. The capacity to deal with such attributes has allowed ACLS to be applied to difficult tasks. ASSISTANT, another direct descendant of ID3, further generalizes the integer-valued attributes of ACLS by permitting attributes with continuous (real) values. Also, rather than insisting that the classes be disjoint, ASSISTANT allows them to form a hierarchy so that one class may be a finer division of another (Quinlan 1986). Further extensions to ID3, found in ID4 and ID5, include the incremental learning of examples (Thrun et al. 1991). Uthurusamy et al. (1990) address the problem of learning useful rules in the presence of inconclusive data and show its application to automobile repair data.

The ID3 family has also adopted pruning. C4, an enhanced version of ID3, has a pruning algorithm called pessimistic pruning (Quinlan 1987b) incorporated in it. In addition, Quinlan (1987b) proposed cost-complexity and reduced error pruning, and an entirely different technique that re-states the decision tree as a set of production rules — a representation medium widely used in expert systems. All of these techniques have been proposed to make decision trees easier to understand.

C4.5, a more recent algorithm (Quinlan 1993):

- deals with continuous input attributes, as CART does (Breiman et al. 1984). The threshold chosen to subdivide a set is the midpoint between two consecutive values of the attribute. However, this can be fairly costly in a large data set as each subdivision is regarded as a separate attribute;
- grows a tree to completion and then prunes it, using an enhanced pessimistic pruning technique;
- allows rules to be obtained by tracing a path from the root to a leaf. However, C4.5 does further pruning on these rules by removing superfluous conditions in the antecedent, using a pessimistic estimate of the accuracy of the rule.

2.7 The CART family

2.7.1 General aspects

The computer algorithm known as CART is the major algorithm of the second group of programs developed from Hunt's CLS. Its name derives from Classification And Regression Trees (Breiman et al. 1984). Like ID3, CART constructs a classification or decision tree by repeatedly splitting the training set into subsets. It aims to find a systematic way of predicting the class to which a particular object belongs. Apart from the goal of producing an accurate classifier, it also attempts to uncover the predictive structure of the problem. A distinctive characteristic of the CART system is its pruning algorithm.

2.7.2 Constructing the tree

The construction of the tree depends on (Breiman et al. 1984):

- the selection of splits
- the decision to continue splitting a node or not
- the assignment of a class to a non-split (non-expanded) node.

A split partitions a training set into two subsets. Thus, in one sense, the splits in CART are similar to the tests used in ID3 for branching. For instance, in Figure 2.1, Hair? would be considered a test in ID3 and a split in CART. However, one important difference is that CART has binary splits only.

When selecting a split, the aim is to optimize the class homogeneity of the resulting subsets (Crawford & Souders 1990). In other words, CART attempts to select a split so that the resulting subsets have examples of only one class.

The goodness of a split can thus be defined as some measure of purity or impurity (Breiman et al. 1984). The splitting of the training set attempts to obtain the best separation of the classes (Atlas & Cole 1990).

A tree is grown in the following manner. Initially, a search is made through all possible candidate splits to find the split giving the largest decrease in some impurity measure. Expansion of a node is stopped when there is no significant decrease in this impurity measure. The class assigned to this non-expanded node is determined by the plurality rules. For instance, consider the hypothetical training set in Table 2.4, containing examples of various types of aquatic vertebrates.

First, all possible splits are determined. For the training set in Table 2.4, this entails the different ways of splitting the input attributes of:

- size with values of (Small, Medium, Large)
- color with values of (White, Silver, Gray, Black)
- length with values of (0.1, 0.5, 1.0, 2.0, 5.0).

Once these splits have been determined, the split generating the cleanest (i.e., most homogeneous) subsets is selected as the best split at that particular point. The impurity measure of the subsets indicates their homogeneity. If this measure is deemed to be adequate for a subset, then any further expansion of that subset is stopped. The class assigned to the subset is that of the majority of the examples in the subset.

example 1	(Small, Silver, 0.1) $\Rightarrow$ (GOLDFISH)
example 2	(Small, Black, 0.5) $\Rightarrow$ (EEL)
example 3	(Medium, Black, 1.0) $\Rightarrow$ (TUNA)
example 4	(Large, Gray, 2.0) $\Rightarrow$ (DOLPHIN)
example 5	(Large, White, 5.0) $\Rightarrow$ (WHALE)

Table 2.4   The training set containing various types of aquatic vertebrates

2.7.3 Standard set of splits or tests

The CART algorithm incorporates a standardized set of splits or tests (Breiman et al. 1984):

- Each split depends on the value of only a single attribute.
- If the attribute C is categorical (i.e., it has a fixed number of possible values $C_1, C_2, ..., C_n$) then the test includes all questions of the form:

  Is C a member of the set S (i.e., is $C \in S$?)?

  where set S ranges over all possible values of the attribute C; that is, $C_1, C_2,$

..., C_n. CART refers to S as a subset of the possible values of the categorical attribute.

- For each continuous or real-valued attribute R, with values R_1, R_2, ..., R_n, the splits (or tests) are of the form:

    Is $R \le V$?

    where V is a real value. The values of V are taken to be midway between consecutive values R_1, R_2, ..., R_n of the attribute R.

To illustrate the technique for constructing the various splits, consider once again the training set in Table 2.4. There are 3 input attributes, two of which, Size and Color, are categorical with values of (Small, Medium, Large) and (White, Silver, Gray, Black), respectively. The Length input attribute is a continuous attribute with possible values of (0.1, 0.5, 1.0, 2.0, 5.0). Applying the above procedure, the resulting splits for this training set would be:

    Is $Color \in \{White\}$?
        $Color \in \{Silver\}$?
        $Color \in \{Gray\}$?
        $Color \in \{Black\}$?
        $Size \in \{Small\}$?
        $Size \in \{Medium\}$?
        $Size \in \{Large\}$?
        $Length \le (0.1+0.5)/2$?
        $Length \le (0.5+1.0)/2$?
        $Length \le (1.0+2.0)/2$?
        $Length \le (2.0+5.0)/2$?

The midway points between consecutive values of the Length attribute are selected as the values used for the continuous input attribute, Length. It is also important to note that all of the splits are binary.

However, the number of splits or tests is not infinite. For categorical attributes, the number of possible splits is obviously limited to the number of possible values of the attribute. For continuous attributes, CART incorporates an interesting, although ad hoc, technique for limiting the number of tests. As stated, the values placed in the tests for the inequalities are halfway between the consecutive distinct values of the continuous attributes.

At each step in the construction of the tree, the algorithm searches through all the attributes and determines the best split by some impurity measure of the resulting subsets. This split is chosen to subdivide the data at that point. The process is continued with each subset until a split, determined to be the best, provides no large or significant decrease in the impurity measure.

2.7.4 Splitting criteria

In the preceding sections, both purity and impurity measures have been mentioned. Here these terms are more precisely defined. CART can incorporate two criteria for defining the goodness of a split. These criteria that determine the optimal split chosen at a particular node in the decision tree are:

- the Gini criterion
- the Twoing criterion.

Gini criterion

The most commonly used impurity function for the CART algorithm is the Gini index (Breiman et al. 1984; Crawford & Souders 1990). It measures the class diversity at a node. The Gini diversity index of node impurity has the form:

$$I(t) = \sum_{j \neq i} p(j|t)p(i|t)$$

where t is the current node being considered, and p(i|t) and p(j|t) are the estimated class probabilities that node t is in class i or j, respectively. These probabilities are sometimes taken to be the proportion of the classes at the node (Breiman et al. 1984). Otherwise, they can be estimated from the training set or supplied by the analyst. The Gini index is simple and quickly computed. Note that in a 2-class problem, the Gini index reduces to (Breiman et al. 1984):

$$I(t) = 2p(1|t)p(2|t).$$

As an illustration of this impurity measure, consider the following:

- Suppose that at some node n1, the subset contains 5 examples of class 1, 10 examples of class 2, and 25 examples of class 3. The Gini diversity index of node n1's impurity, letting p be the proportion of the classes, is:

$$
\begin{aligned}
I(n1) &= \sum_{j \neq i} p(j|n1)p(i|n1) \qquad i, j = \text{classes 1, 2, and 3}\\
&= 2p(1|n1)p(2|n1) + 2p(2|n1)p(3|n1) + 2p(3|n1)p(1|n1)\\
&= 2(5/40*10/40) + 2(10/40*25/40) + 2(25/40*5/40)\\
&= 0.5313
\end{aligned}
$$

- Suppose that at some node n2, the subset contains 2 examples of class 1, 3 examples of class 2, and 35 examples of class 3. The Gini diversity index of node n2's impurity, letting p be the proportion of the classes, is:

$$I(n2) = \sum_{j \neq i} p(j|n2)p(i|n2) \qquad i, j = \text{classes 1, 2, and 3}$$

$$= 2p(1|n2)p(2|n2) + 2p(2|n2)p(3|n2) + 2p(3|n2)p(1|n2)$$
$$= 2(2/40*3/40) + 2(3/40*35/40) + 2(35/40*2/40)$$
$$= 0.2263$$

- The impurity measure for node n2 is smaller than the impurity measure for node n1. This indicates that the subset at node n2 is purer or cleaner than that found at node n1.

One problem with the Gini criterion is that attribute selection is biased in favor of those attributes having more values (Breiman et al. 1984).

Twoing criterion

An alternative approach to measure the impurity of the resulting subsets uses the Twoing criterion. It should be noted that this criterion does not provide an overall measure of impurity, as does the Gini index, but it provides an approach for constructing a tree. The underlying strategy is to reduce the problem to a 2-class problem. The greatest decrease in node impurity can then be determined (Breiman et al. 1984). This is achieved in the following manner. At each node, the classes are separated into two superclasses, denoted by class 1 and class 2 respectively. The problem can then be considered as a 2-class problem. The node with the split that maximizes the change in impurity is then determined. Finally, at that node the superclass that maximizes the change in impurity is selected.

The splits are strategic and the user is informed of the class similarities. Note that at or near the top of the tree, this criterion attempts to group together large numbers of classes similar in some characteristic. Near the bottom, on the other hand, it attempts to isolate single classes (Breiman et al. 1984). One disadvantage of the Twoing criterion is its computational inefficiency.

2.7.5 Pruning

As stated, one of the distinctive characteristics of CART is its pruning algorithm. In fact, Breiman et al. (1984) emphasize the pruning criterion rather than feature selection. They argued that it is more efficient to prune a tree than to stop it growing to completion, because pruning allows one branch from a node to remain and another to disappear, whereas stopping growth removes both branches. Thus CART avoids the pitfalls of stopping rules by first growing a tree of maximum size and then pruning backward in an appropriate manner (Crawford & Souders 1990).

Hence, instead of attempting to stop the splitting at the correct set of terminal nodes, the splitting is continued until all terminal nodes are very small. This results in a very large tree. Next, this large tree is selectively pruned (i.e., recombined) upward, which results in a decreasing sequence of subtrees. Cross-validation or test sample estimates can then be used to determine which subtree has the lowest estimated misclassification rate (Breiman et al. 1984).

The basic idea of pruning is to cut those subtrees producing only marginal benefits in accuracy. It is expected that a simpler pruned tree would achieve better accuracy in predicting unseen cases in the existence of noise.

A minimal cost-complexity pruning approach is used by CART. It involves a process in which a real-valued penalty parameter is steadily increased, with pruning occurring at various threshold values. This yields a nested sequence of minimal subtrees (Crawford & Souders 1990).

The minimal cost-complexity pruning is based on the cost-complexity measure defined as follows:

- Let the complexity of a subtree T be defined by the number of its terminal nodes (i.e., leaves) and be denoted by Tc.
- Let the misclassification cost of the subtree be denoted by R.
- The cost-complexity measure, Rm, is defined as (Breiman et al. 1984):

$$Rm(T) = R(T) + \alpha Tc(T)$$

where the α parameter is the complexity cost per terminal node.

Thus the cost-complexity measure is actually a linear combination of the cost of the tree and its complexity, appropriately weighted; that is, a combination of accuracy and simplicity. For each value of α, the subtree selected is the one with the minimum associated cost-complexity (Breiman et al. 1984). Increasing a leads to an increase in the cost of terminal nodes, thus penalizing a subtree with a larger number of terminal nodes.

Consider the following illustration of minimal cost-complexity pruning:

- Let the complexity cost per terminal node, that is, α, be 0.10.
- Consider the subtree T1, as shown in Figure 2.11(a):

    Let the cost (error rate) of T1, that is, R(T1), be 0.25.
    The complexity of T1 (the number of leaves), that is, Tc(T1), is 3.
    The cost-complexity measure is:

$$
\begin{aligned}
Rm(T1) &= R(T1) + \alpha Tc(T1) \\
&= 0.25 + (0.10*3) \\
&= 0.55
\end{aligned}
$$

- Now, if the right-hand subtree of T1 is replaced with a leaf, the subtree T2, as shown in Figure 2.11(b), results. Note that this pruning would generally cause an increase in errors.

    Let the cost of T2, that is, R(T2), be 0.38.
    The complexity of T2 (the number of leaves), that is, Tc(T2), is 2.

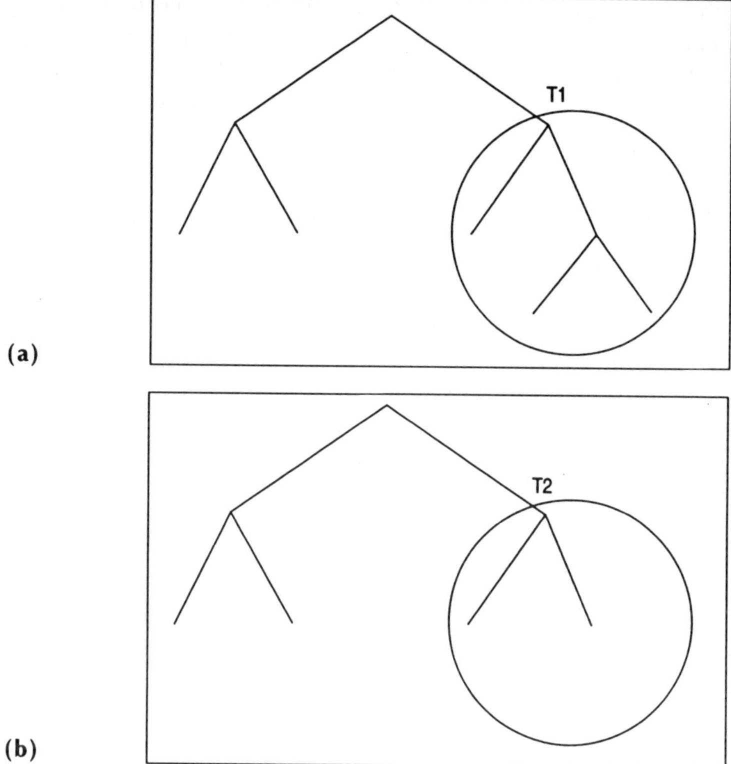

(a)

(b)

Figure 2.11   (a) Subtree T1   (b) Subtree T2

The cost-complexity measure is:

$$Rm(T2) = R(T2) + \alpha Tc(T2)$$
$$= 0.38 + (0.10*2)$$
$$= 0.58$$

- The cost-complexity of T1 is smaller than that of the pruned subtree, T2.
- The pruning relies on the selection of the subtree with the minimal cost-complexity. Therefore, in this case, subtree T1 would not be pruned to T2.

If α is chosen as 0.15 (i.e., weighting the number of nodes more highly than in the example above) then the cost complexity of T1 is 0.70 and that of T2 is 0.68. In this case, a simpler subtree is preferred, and thus T1 would be pruned to T2. This illustrates the problem of choosing an appropriate value of a so that a suitable tree structure is derived.

An obvious problem with this procedure is that of implementation. Clearly, a direct search through all possible subtrees to find the minimal cost-complexity subtree is computationally expensive and not feasible. The simpler approach used initially prunes large subtrees with many terminal nodes. As the tree gets smaller, the procedure tends to cut off fewer subtrees. This results in a decreasing sequence of subtrees (Breiman et al. 1984).

2.7.6 Advantages of CART

CART has several advantages. First, it can be applied to most domains if an appropriate set of tests can be formulated. There is no restriction on the type of attributes, as both continuous and categorical attributes can be processed. The CART algorithm also (Breiman et al. 1984):

- *is extremely robust with respect to misclassified points;*
- *gives an estimation of the misclassification probability of a case;*
- *is invariant under all monotone transformations of individual attributes;*
- *has an automatic stepwise variable selection and complexity reduction.*

2.7.7 Problems with CART

One of the major problems with CART is that it is computationally very expensive. Breiman et al. (1984) suggested using a sub-sampling method to increase efficiency. This works in the following way: if the sample size at a particular node is larger than some value, then a sub-sample from each of the classes present at the node is used to determine the best split. However, the entire example set at the node is sent down the split.

Another difficulty with CART is that the splits or tests are based on only a single variable. Therefore, in situations where class structure depends on combinations of variables, the standard tree algorithm does poorly. If some form of linear structure is suspected, then the set of allowable tests should be extended to include all the linear combinations of the splits. In other cases, certain Boolean combinations of the attributes may be important. However, the number of such combinations increases rapidly with the length of the Boolean expression allowed. In any case, these combinations of tests will increase the complexity and computational efficiency of the tree (Breiman et al. 1984).

As stated, cross-validation gives fairly adequate estimates of the overall misclassification rate. However, the true within-node misclassification rate is not given (Breiman et al. 1984).

The successive nature of node growth is another disadvantage of CART (Atlas & Cole 1990). If the first split made for a problem turns out, given the successive splits, to be sub-optimal, it is very inefficient to change the first split to be more suitable.

Missing values are always difficult to handle. CART uses surrogate splits to deal with these cases. Usually a measure of similarity between any 2 splits for a node is determined. The best split is then used at the node. However, if there are missing values for one or more attributes, the best split of that node with all the other attributes is determined. These secondary (and even tertiary) splits are known as surrogate splits.

2.8 Statistically based approaches

2.8.1 General aspects

In the previous sections, induction algorithms that construct decision trees were discussed. Basically, these algorithms use a divide-and-conquer strategy involving a feature selection criterion to guide the construction of the decision tree. In this section, feature selection criteria based on statistical measures are discussed. These include the Chi-square criterion, Goodman and Kruskal's Asymmetrical Tau, and the Symmetrical Tau.

2.8.2 Motivation

First, a summary of some of the problems with ID3 (Forsyth & Rada 1986; Hart 1984; Zhou & Dillon 1991a, 1991b):

- It needs a complete set of examples.
- The rule cannot be probabilistic.
- Each type of example has equal weighting; hence two identical examples have the same effect as one.
- It cannot deal with contradictory examples.
- The results can be highly sensitive to changes in the example set.
- It has difficulty dealing with noisy, real-world data.
- It has difficulty dealing with continuous features.
- Splitting a node on a feature sometimes forces the use of irrelevant information.
- The decision tree induction approaches are based on the assumption of example set adequacy.
- It fails to extract knowledge for inference under uncertainty.

As stated, the feature selection criterion plays a central role in the quality of the decision tree as a classifier, and its complexity or simplicity. The problem of finding a binary decision tree with a minimum expected number of tests is NP-complete (Zhou & Dillon 1991a, 1991b). Also, it seems that any optimization process over decision trees is computationally infeasible for any reasonably sized data set (Zhou & Dillon 1991a, 1991b). Thus, it is necessary to develop some heuristic that will allow the fast construction of efficient, near-optimal decision trees.

For inductive machine learning in the real world, the following important aspects should be covered by the feature selection criteria (Zhou & Dillon 1991a, 1991b):

- the direct handling of multi-valued features that lead to the construction of multi-branching decision trees;
- the use of a Boolean combination of features;
- the use of a linear combination of features;
- the extension of decision trees as probabilistic classifiers;
- dealing with a mixture of discrete (categorical) and continuous features;
- pre-pruning during tree building.

A very brief introduction to the Chi-square statistic and its use for hypothesis testing is given in the next section. After this, several statistically based feature selection criteria, including Hart's method, are discussed.

2.8.3 The Chi-square statistic and tests of hypotheses

The Chi-square (χ^2) statistic is a measure of the discrepancy between observed and expected frequencies (Hayslett 1976). Smaller χ^2 values mean that the observed and expected frequencies are in close agreement, while larger values of χ^2 mean that the observed and expected frequencies are somewhat apart. The Chi-square statistic is defined in any standard statistical text (Haber & Runyon 1977; Hayslett 1976; Spiegel 1961; Walpole 1982) as:

$$\chi^2 = \sum \frac{(O_i - E_i)^2}{E_i}$$

where E_i is the expected and O_i is the observed frequency. Table 2.5 illustrates the calculation of this statistic.

O_i	E_i	$(O_i - E_i)$	$(O_i - E_i)^2$	$(O_i - E_i)^2/E_i$
95	100	−5	25	0.25
105	100	5	25	0.25
75	100	−25	625	6.25
120	100	20	400	4.00
				$\chi^2 = 10.75$

Table 2.5   The Chi-square statistic (χ^2) obtained by summing the last column

An important use of the Chi-square statistic is for hypothesis testing. When testing statistical hypotheses, one normally constructs a null hypothesis, H_0.

Frequently, the purpose of constructing the null hypothesis is to determine if one can reject it. From this premise, one generally proceeds by determining an alternative hypothesis, H_1, which is accepted if the null hypothesis is rejected. For instance, to prove that one is more likely to draw a ball of one color rather than a ball of another color from a bag containing several balls, one would formulate the following null and alternative hypotheses:

- H_0 : one is equally likely to draw a ball of any color.
- H_1 : one is more likely to draw a ball of one color over another.

Thus in the statistical decision approach, one tests whether the null hypothesis can be rejected. If it is rejected, then the alternative hypothesis can be accepted.

Since the procedure is statistical, there is a finite probability that one may have rejected the hypothesis when it should have been accepted. The level of significance is the maximum probability with which a rejected hypothesis should have been accepted. Levels of significance of 0.05 (5%) or 0.01 (1%) are often used. A level of significance of 0.01 implies that:

- there is a 1% chance that one is rejecting an hypothesis when it should have been accepted;
- there is a 99% level of confidence that the hypothesis was rejected correctly.

One could define a data item falling into a given group of data as an event. If there are k such groups, one has k such events. The observed frequency with which a data item falls into each of these groups is $O_1, O_2, ..., O_k$, and the expected frequency is $E_1, E_2, ..., E_k$. Then the number of degrees of freedom u for the Chi-square statistic is:

$$\upsilon = k - 1.$$

There are standard plots for the Chi-square distribution for different degrees of freedom. From these standard plots, one can obtain a Chi-square value for a given level of significance and degree of freedom. A sample of critical Chi-square values for different levels of significance and degrees of freedom is given in Table 2.6.

		Levels of significance		
		.1	.05	.01
	3	6.25	7.82	11.34
Degrees	4	7.78	9.49	13.28
of	5	9.24	11.07	15.09
freedom	10	15.99	18.31	23.21
	11	17.28	19.68	24.73

Table 2.6   Typical Chi-square distribution values (Hayslett 1976)

As explained earlier, the Chi-square is often used for hypothesis testing. The null hypothesis frequently used is:

- H_0: there is no difference between the observed, O_i, and theoretically expected, E_i, frequencies.

From this point, one can determine the Chi-square value:

$$\chi^2 = \sum \frac{(O_i - E_i)^2}{E_i}$$

and compare it to the critical value at a particular level of significance and degree of freedom. For instance, with 3 degrees of freedom and at a level of significance of 0.05, if the Chi-square value were greater than 7.82 (see Table 2.6), one would reject the null hypothesis and hence conclude that there is a difference between the observed and the expected frequencies.

Consider the following brief illustration of the technique for testing various hypotheses. More detailed discussions can be found in standard statistical texts (Hayslett 1976; Spiegel 1961; Walpole 1982).

- Let the theoretically expected predictions of a population be: 20% level 1 (strongest) swimmers, 40% level 2 swimmers, 30% level 3 swimmers, and 10% level 4 (weakest) swimmers.
- Let 600 people be tested for swimming ability, resulting in: 150 level 1, 290 level 2, 140 level 3, and 20 level 4 swimmers.

The question or hypothesis to be tested is:

Are the samples of the 600 people tested typical according to the theoretical predictions?

- Formulate null and alternative hypotheses:
  H_0 : the predictions for the theoretical population are the same as those obtained for the tested population; that is, level 1 = 0.2, level 2 = 0.4, level 3 = 0.3, and level 4 = 0.1;
  H_1 : at least 2 of the predictions are different from the theoretical values.

- Let the level of significance be 5%, or 0.05.
- Calculate the expected theoretical values for the various predictions, given that there are 600 samples in this case.

$$
\begin{aligned}
E_1 &= 600 * 0.2 = 120 \\
E_2 &= 600 * 0.4 = 240 \\
E_3 &= 600 * 0.3 = 180 \\
E_4 &= 600 * 0.1 = 60
\end{aligned}
$$

- Calculate the Chi-square statistic, as shown in Table 2.7, giving $\chi^2 = 53.48$.
- Determine the degree of freedom and the corresponding Chi-square distribution

O_i	E_i	$(O_i - E_i)$	$(O_i - E_i)^2$	$(O_i - E_i)^2/E_i$
150	120	30	900	7.50
290	240	50	2500	10.42
140	180	−40	1600	8.89
20	60	−40	1600	26.67
				$\chi^2 = 53.48$

Table 2.7   The Chi-square statistic for the illustrative example

value for the 5% level of significance. As there are 4 cases, the degree of freedom is 3. From Table 2.6, the required Chi-square value is 7.82.

- Reject the null hypothesis as 53.48 > 7.82, and hence accept the alternative hypothesis. This means that the 600 samples are not typical of the theoretical predictions of the population.

In statistics, a table known as a contingency table may be used if each member of a sample can be classified according to two criteria (Hayslett 1976). The table thus provides a two-way classification. If one criterion has m values and the other has n, then an m*n contingency table is formed.

For instance, suppose that the samples in a domain can be classified according to the following two criteria:

- Hair Color with values Blond, Brown, and Red
- Eye Color with values Blue, Brown, and Green.

The resulting 3X3 contingency table could have the various values of Hair Color in the rows and Eye Color in the columns. Table 2.8 is an illustrative contingency table for this domain.

In this table, there are 10 samples with Blond Hair Color and Blue Eye Color, 5 samples with Red Hair Color and Green Eye Color, and so on. Note that each sample is entered in the table only once.

The contingency table can now be used to test whether the two criteria, Eye Color and Hair Color, are independent. The technique for calculating the independence of the two criteria is almost the same as that for calculating the Chi-square statistic and comparing it to the typical Chi-square distribution value. However, there are two differences. First, in this case, the expected frequency, E_{ij}, is given by (Hayslett 1976):

$$E_{ij} = \frac{R_i C_j}{N}$$

where R_i and C_j are the total observed frequencies in the ith row and jth column respectively, and N is the total number of samples. Second, the degree of freedom is given by (Hayslett 1976):

		Hair Color		
		Blond	Brown	Red
Eye	Blue	10	15	25
Color	Brown	20	35	10
	Green	15	10	5

Table 2.8   Contingency table for the illustrative domain

$$\text{dof} = (r - 1)(c - 1)$$

where r and c are the total number of rows and columns, respectively.

To illustrate the use of contingency tables and the testing of independence between the two criteria represented in the contingency table, consider the following example based on Table 2.8:

- Formulate the null and alternative hypotheses:

    H_0 : Eye and Hair Color are independent.
    H_1 : the two criteria are not independent.

- Let the level of significance be 0.05. Note that r = 3 and c = 3, and thus the degree of freedom = (3 − 1)(3 − 1) = 4. The total sample size is N = 145. The Chi-square value at a level of significance of 0.05 and 4 degrees of freedom is 9.49 (from Table 2.6).
- Calculate the expected values. The total row and column observed values are:

    $R_1 = 10+15+25 = 50$ $C_1 = 10+20+15 = 45$
    $R_2 = 20+35+10 = 65$ $C_2 = 15+35+10 = 60$
    $R_3 = 15+10+5 = 30$ $C_3 = 25+10+5 = 40$

    and therefore the expected values are:

    $E_{11} = 15.52$ $E_{12} = 20.69$ $E_{13} = 13.79$
    $E_{21} = 20.17$ $E_{22} = 26.90$ $E_{23} = 17.93$
    $E_{31} = 9.31$ $E_{32} = 12.41$ $E_{33} = 8.28$

- Calculate the Chi-square statistic:

$$\chi^2 = \sum \frac{(O_{ij} - E_{ij})^2}{E_{ij}}$$

$$= \frac{(10 - 15.52)^2}{15.52} + \frac{(15 - 20.69)^2}{20.69} + \frac{(25 - 13.79)^2}{13.79} +$$

$$\frac{(20 - 20.17)^2}{20.17} + \frac{(35 - 26.90)^2}{26.90} + \frac{(10 - 17.93)^2}{17.93} +$$

$$\frac{(15 - 9.31)^2}{9.31} + \frac{(10 - 12.41)^2}{12.41} + \frac{(5 - 8.28)^2}{8.28}$$

$$= \quad 23.83$$

- From Table 2.6, the critical value for the Chi-square distribution is 9.49. As 23.83 > 9.49, the null hypothesis is rejected and the alternative hypothesis is accepted. Thus Hair and Eye Color are not independent criteria in this domain.

2.8.4   The Chi-square statistic as a feature selection criterion

Hart (1984) states that the ID3 algorithm would be improved by considering the Chi-square value instead of the information statistic. Pearson's Chi-square statistic provides a test of significance with regard to the independence between variables.

For the Chi-square statistic to be used, a definition of the null hypothesis must be formulated. First, let the problem domain be specified by:

- an attribute A with possible values $A1$, A_2, ..., A_m;
- classes C_1, C_2, ..., C_n;
- the total number of examples, T.

This can be arranged in the form of a m * n contingency table.

One is seeking to determine whether or not the value of attribute A (i.e., A_j) is a good predictor of class C_i. If the values of A are randomly distributed among the classes, then A is not a good predictor of the class (Hart 1984). Hence, one can formulate the null hypothesis to be:

H_0: values of A are randomly distributed over the classes C.

If this null hypothesis is true for each of the A_j then none of the attribute values is a good predictor. This implies that, given a particular value A_j for attribute A, the conditional probability of the example being in C_i is no different from the total probability that the example is in C_i. Thus Hart (1984) formulates the null hypothesis as:

H_0 : *Probability(example is in class C_i | value of attribute is A_j) =
Probability(example is in class C_i) for all i and j.*

If the null hypothesis is rejected, the alternative hypothesis:

H_1 : the value A_j of attribute A is not randomly distributed over C_i

is accepted. This means that some value A_j of attribute A is more likely to be associated with class C_i. Therefore, if a value of A occurs more frequently with class C_i, it can be used as a discriminator for that class.

For calculating the Chi-square statistic, the observed frequency is the number of examples with value A_j of attribute A in class C_i. Hart (1984) defines the expected frequencies as:

$$E_{ij} = \frac{\sum^{k} O_{ik} \sum^{1} O_{lj}}{N} \quad \text{(summation over the current example subset)},$$

where O_{ik} is the observed number of samples in class C_i and O_{lj} is the observed number of samples with attribute A_j. In this case, the number of degrees of freedom is m*n. Using the comparison with the Chi-square distribution value, the null hypothesis would be rejected if the Chi-square value is sufficiently high. This would suggest that the corresponding attribute A is not randomly distributed over C_i and thus did discriminate between the classes. The best discriminating attribute would be the attribute with the highest Chi-square value. This attribute would be the least likely to occur by chance (Hart 1984).

It has been shown that the Chi-square value is equivalent to N times ID3's information statistic (Hart 1984). The use of the Chi-square value has several other features (Hart 1984):

- *The higher number of degrees of freedom means that the Chi-square value has to be correspondingly larger in order to be sufficiently significant;*
- *To make the resulting tree less sensitive to small changes in the training set, it is possible for the algorithm to stop when no Chi-square value is significant at say, the 10% level;*
- *An attribute which has a large number of values may discriminate well by chance.*

The use of the Chi-square statistic as a feature selection criterion has the following difficulties:

- the production of significantly larger trees than the gain criterion (Mingers 1987);
- the extreme sensitivity to small expected frequencies (Mingers 1987) due to instability of the Chi-square statistic for observed frequencies less than 5 (Hayslett 1976);
- the favoring of binary features, leading to very narrow trees with many levels (Mingers 1987);
- the induced decision tree may still be hard to understand because the overall ID3 algorithm has been unchanged (Hart 1984);
- both the gain criterion and the Chi-square statistic still only consider 1 attribute at a time (Hart 1984).

Note finally that even though the Chi-square statistic provides a test of significance with regard to the independence between variables, it does not give a measure of the degree of association between the variables (Hart 1984).

2.8.5   Goodman and Kruskal's asymmetrical measure

Goodman and Kruskal proposed their measure of association, the Asymmetrical Tau, for cross-classification tasks in the statistical area (Zhou & Dillon 1991a, 1991b). In the classification context, a variable could be either a discrete feature with each of its distinct values as a category, or a set of mutually exclusive classes with each class as a category. The Asymmetrical Tau is a measure of the relative usefulness of one variable in improving the ability to predict the classifications of members of the population with respect to a second variable.

The Asymmetrical Tau

Let:

- there be I rows and J columns in a contingency table;
- P(ij) denote the probability that an individual belongs to both row category i and column category j;
- P(i+) and P(+j) be the marginal probability in row category i and column category j, respectively.

From these considerations, the Asymmetrical Tau measure for predicting the category of variable B from the category of variable A is defined by Goodman and Kruskal as (Goodman & Kruskal 1954; Zhou & Dillon 1991a, 1991b):

$$\text{Tau A|B} = \frac{\displaystyle\sum_{j=1}^{J}\sum_{i=1}^{I}\frac{P(ij)^2}{P(+j)} - \sum_{i=1}^{I}P(i+)^2}{1 - \displaystyle\sum_{j=1}^{I}P(i+)^2}$$

By interchanging the roles of A and B, the measure of Tau(B|A) can be determined by:

$$\text{Tau B|A} = \frac{\displaystyle\sum_{i=1}^{I}\sum_{j=1}^{J}\frac{P(ij)^2}{P(i+)} - \sum_{j=1}^{J}P(+j)^2}{1 - \displaystyle\sum_{j=1}^{J}P(+j)^2}$$

Note that unless all non-zero probabilities in the table are in a single row or column, then Tau (A|B) and Tau (B|A) are well defined and not equal to 0 or 1 (Zhou & Dillon 1991a, 1991b).

Goodman and Kruskal developed their asymmetrical measures, Tau(A|B) and Tau(B|A), for cross-classification tasks in the statistical area. These were chosen in some initial studies (Zhou & Dillon 1988) as the basis for designing a new feature selection criterion for constructing decision trees. However, when the Goodman-Kruskal Tau was used directly as a feature selection criterion, it tended to favor features with more values, just like Quinlan's gain criterion and the Gini criterion. A theoretical analysis proved this shortcoming (Zhou & Dillon 1991a, 1991b).

2.8.6 Zhou and Dillon's Symmetrical Tau criterion

Definition

Zhou and Dillon (1988, 1989, 1991a, 1991b) believed that the two asymmetrical measures, Tau(A|B) and Tau(B|A), could still be useful. When the categories of variable A are increased by subdividing existing categories, more is known about variable A and thus the probability of error in predicting the B category according to the A category may decrease. However, the variable A becomes more complex and therefore more difficult to predict. The probability of error in predicting the A category according to the B category may increase with the cost of complexity.

An examination of the various extreme cases inspired Zhou and Dillon to combine a proportional-reduction-in-error (PRE) measure and a cost-complexity heuristic to obtain a balanced statistical-heuristic criterion for building multi-branching decision trees. As a combination of the two asymmetrical measures, Tau(A|B) and Tau(B|A), this new Tau criterion is symmetrical. It is defined as (Zhou & Dillon 1991a, 1991b):

$$\text{Tau} = \frac{\sum_{j=1}^{J}\sum_{i=1}^{I}\frac{P(ij)^2}{P(+j)} + \sum_{i=1}^{I}\sum_{j=1}^{J}\frac{P(ij)^2}{P(i+)} - \sum_{i=1}^{I}P(i+)^2 - \sum_{j=1}^{J}P(+j)^2}{2 - \sum_{i=1}^{I}P(i+)^2 - \sum_{j=1}^{J}P(+j)^2}$$

where, as for Goodman and Kruskal's Asymmetrical Tau:

- the contingency table has I rows and J columns;
- P(ij) = probability that a variable belongs both to row category i and to column category j;
- P(i+) and P(+j) are the marginal probabilities in row category i and column category j, respectively.

According to Zhou and Dillon (1991a, 1991b), Tau has a natural and clear probabilistic interpretation. Suppose that a member of the population is selected at random and the task is to predict this member's A and B category simultaneously. In this case, Tau is interpreted as the reduction in the probability of prediction error. This reduction results from the knowledge of the individual's classification on the second variable, relative to the probability of the error in the absence of that information.

In the context of a feature selection criterion, variable A could be considered as a feature, and variable B could be considered as a class. The associated categories would be the actual values or instantiations of the variables. For instance, the variable A could be Hair Color with associated categories of Blond, Brown, and Red.

Properties of Tau

According to Zhou and Dillon (1991a, 1991b), Tau has a number of interesting properties.

- Tau is well defined in most cases.
- If there exists an i and j such that $P(ij) = 1$ and all other cells contain zero probability then, in this case, feature selection is unnecessary as the categories of both A and B are known with certainty.
- When Tau = 0 (zero association), a feature has no ability to predict the category of another. This occurs if there are no $P(ij) = 1$ and all non-zero probabilities in the table are in a single row or column (i.e., there exists an i or j such that $P(i+) = 1$ or $P(+j) = 1$).
- When Tau = 1 (perfect association), a feature has the perfect ability to predict the category of another variable. This occurs if there is no $P(ij)=1$ and either:
  1. for each j there exists an i such that $P(ij) = P(+j)$, or
  2. for each i there exists a j such that $P(ij) = P(i+)$.
- If no $P(ij) = 1$ and neither perfect nor zero association occurs, then $0 <$ Tau < 1.
- Tau is invariant under permutations of rows or columns.

Merits of the Tau criterion

The Tau criterion (Zhou & Dillon 1988, 1989) has a number of major merits.

- It is a measure of association and has a *built-in* statistical strength to cope with noise.
- Dynamic error estimation conveys potential uncertainties in classification and is crucial for probabilistic decision tree induction.
- Tau processes multi-valued features fairly. There is no bias favoring features with many or few values. This improvement is not at a cost of computational efficiency.
- The Tau criterion is not proportional to the sample size and its proportional-

reduction-in-error (PRE) nature makes it not only a stepwise measure of different features' abilities, but also an overall measure of a particular feature's sequential variation in predictive ability (Zhou & Dillon 1988, 1991a, 1991b). This provides a basis for deleting the features that have become less useful for prediction and helps to prevent splitting when no useful feature remains.

- The criterion has a middle cut tendency that separates a node into two balanced subsets.
- It is able to deal with Boolean combinations of logical features.

Illustrative example

Consider a domain with two input criteria of Height and Eye Color, and one Gender output of Male or Female.

- Let Tables 2.9 and 2.10 represent the contingency tables for Height and Gender, and Eye Color and Gender, respectively.

		Height		
		Tall	Average	Short
Gender	Male	5	4	1
	Female	3	6	1

Table 2.9   Contingency table for Height and Gender for the illustrative domain

		Eye Color		
		Blue	Green	Brown
Gender	Male	3	2	5
	Female	3	1	6

Table 2.10   Contingency table for Eye Color and Gender for the illustrative domain

- Consider Table 2.9 for Height and Gender. The following probabilities can be determined ($I = 2$, $J = 3$):

Probability that an example belongs to both row i and column j:
$P(11) = 5/20$ $P(12) = 4/20$ $P(13) = 1/20$
$P(21) = 3/20$ $P(22) = 6/20$ $P(23) = 1/20$

Marginal probabilities of row i and column j:
rows: $P(1+) = 10/20$ $P(2+) = 10/20$
columns: $P(+1) = 8/20$ $P(+2) = 10/20$ $P(+3) = 2/20$

1. The first term of Tau's numerator:

$$\sum_{j=1}^{J} \sum_{i=1}^{I} \frac{P(ij)^2}{P(+j)} = (25/400)/(8/20) + (9/400)/(8/20) +$$
$$(16/400)/(10/20) + (36/400)/(10/20) +$$
$$(1/400)/(2/20) + (1/400)/(2/20)$$
$$= 0.156 + 0.056 + 0.080 + 0.180 + 0.025 + 0.025$$
$$= 0.522$$

2. The second term of Tau's numerator:

$$\sum_{j=1}^{J} \sum_{i=1}^{I} \frac{P(ij)^2}{P(i+)} = (25/400)/(10/20) + (16/400)/(10/20) +$$
$$(1/400)/(10/20) + (9/400)/(10/20) +$$
$$(36/400)/(10/20) + (1/400)/(10/20)$$
$$= 0.125 + 0.080 + 0.005 + 0.045 + 0.180 + 0.005$$
$$= 0.440$$

3.
$$\sum_{i=1}^{I} P(i+)^2 = (10/20)^2 + (10/20)^2$$
$$= 0.500$$

4.
$$\sum_{j=1}^{I} P(+j)^2 = (8/20)^2 + (10/20)^2 + (2/20)^2$$
$$= 0.420$$

5. Therefore, for Height and Gender:

$$\text{Tau} = \frac{0.522 + 0.440 - 0.500 - 0.420}{2 - 0.500 - 0.420)}$$
$$= \frac{0.042}{1.080}$$
$$= 0.039$$

- Consider Table 2.10 for Eye Color and Gender. The following probabilities can be determined ($I = 2$, $J = 3$):

Probability that an example belongs to both row i and column j:

$P(11) = 3/20$ $P(12) = 2/20$ $P(13) = 5/20$

$P(21) = 3/20$ $P(22) = 1/20$ $P(23) = 6/20$

Marginal probabilities of row i and column j:

    rows: $P(1+) = 10/20$ $P(2+) = 10/20$
    columns: $P(+1) = 6/20$ $P(+2) = 3/20$ $P(+3) = 11/20$

1. The first term of Tau's numerator:

$$\sum_{j=1}^{J} \sum_{i=1}^{I} \frac{P(ij)^2}{P(+j)} = (9/400)/(6/20) + (9/400)/(6/20) +$$
$$(4/400)/(3/20) + (1/400)/(3/20) +$$
$$(25/400)/(11/20) + (36/400)/(11/20)$$
$$= 0.075 + 0.075 + 0.067 + 0.017 + 0.114 + 0.164$$
$$= 0.512$$

2. The second term of Tau's numerator:

$$\sum_{j=1}^{J} \sum_{i=1}^{I} \frac{P(ij)^2}{P(i+)} = (9/400)/(10/20) + (4/400)/(10/20) +$$
$$(25/400)/(10/20) + (9/400)/(10/20) +$$
$$(1/400)/(10/20) + (36/400)/(10/20)$$
$$= 0.045 + 0.020 + 0.125 + 0.045 + 0.005 + 0.180$$
$$= 0.420$$

3.
$$\sum_{i=1}^{I} P(i+)^2 = (10/20)^2 + (10/20)^2$$
$$= 0.500$$

4.
$$\sum_{j=1}^{J} P(+j)^2 = (6/20)^2 + (3/20)^2 + (11/20)^2$$
$$= 0.415$$

5. Therefore, for Eye Color and Gender:

$$\text{Tau} = \frac{0.512 + 0.420 - 0.500 - 0.415}{2 - 0.500 - 0.415)}$$
$$= \frac{0.017}{1.085}$$
$$= 0.016$$

• In summary:

    Tau   =   0.039 for Height and Gender.
    Tau   =   0.016 for Eye Color and Gender.

This implies that Height is a better discriminating criterion than Eye Color in this domain.

2.9 Recapitulation

In this chapter, various machine learning methods for constructing decision trees were presented. Three distinct groups were discussed. ID3 is representative of the first group, CART typifies the second group, while the third group is based on statistical approaches.

The next chapter presents induction algorithms that use a progressive rule generation method known as the STAR methodology.

References

Atlas, L. & Cole, R. 1990, "Performance comparisons between back-propagation networks and classification trees on three real-world applications", in *Neural Information Processing Systems (NIPS) 2*, ed. D.S. Touretzky, Morgan Kaufmann, San Mateo, California, pp. 622–9

Breiman, L., Friedman, J.H., Olshen, R.A. & Stone, C.J. 1984, *Classification and Regression Trees*, Wadsworth International Group, Belmont, California

Carter, C. & Catlett, J. 1987, "Assessing credit card applications using machine learning", *IEEE Expert,* Fall, pp. 71–4

Cheng, J., Fayyad, U.M., Irani, K.B. & Qian, Z. 1988, "Improved decision trees: A generalized version of ID3", *Proceedings of the Fifth International Conference on Machine Learning*, pp. 100–7

Cohen, P.R. & Feigenbaum, E.A., eds 1982, *The Handbook of Artificial Intelligence: Volume 3*, William Kaufmann, Los Altos, California

Crawford, S.L. & Souders, S.K. 1990, "A comparison of two new techniques for conceptual clustering", *International Journal of Pattern Recognition and AI*, vol. 4, no. 3, pp. 409–28

Forsyth, R. & Rada, R. 1986, *Machine Learning: Applications in Expert Systems and Information Retrieval*, Ellis Horwood, Chichester, UK

Goodman, L.A. & Kruskal, W.H. 1954, "Measures of association for cross-classifications", *J. Amer. Statist. Assoc.*, vol. 49, pp. 732–64

Haber, A. & Runyon, R.P. 1977, *General Statistics*, 3rd edition, Addison-Wesley, Reading, Massachusetts

Hart, A. 1984, "Experience in the use of an inductive system in knowledge engineering", in *Research and Development in Expert Systems,* ed. P. Hammersley, Cambridge University Press, Cambridge, pp. 117–26

Hayslett, H.T. 1976, *STATISTICS Made Simple*, W.H. Allen, London

Hunt, E.B., Marin, J. & Stone, P.J. 1966, *Experiments in Induction*, Academic Press, New York

Mingers, J. 1987, "Expert systems — rule induction with statistical data", *Journal of Operational Research Society*, vol. 38, no. 1, pp. 39–47

Quinlan, J.R. 1986, "Induction of decision trees", *Machine Learning*, 1, pp. 81–106

Quinlan, J.R. 1987a, *Learning Decision Trees*, Technical Report 87.5, School of Computing Sciences, NSWIT, Sydney, Australia

Quinlan, J.R. 1987b, "Simplifying decision trees", *International Journal of Man-Machine Studies*, 27, pp. 221–34

Quinlan, J.R. 1993, *C4.5: Programs for Machine Learning*, Morgan Kaufmann Publishers, San Francisco, California

Spiegel, M. R. 1961, *Schaum's Outline of Theory and Problems of Statistics*, Schaum, New York

Thrun, S.B., Bala, J., Bloedorn, E., Bratko, I., Cestnik, B., Cheng, J., De Jong, K., Dzeroski, S., Fahlman, S.E., Fisher, D., Hamann, R., Kaufman, K., Keller, S., Kononenko, I., Kreuziger, J., Michalski, R.S., Mitchell, T., Pachowicz, P., Reich, Y., Vafaie, H., Van de Welde, W., Wenzel, W., Wnek, J. & Zhang, J. 1991, *The MONK's Problems: A Performance Comparison of Different Learning Algorithms*, CMU-CS-91-197, Carnegie Mellon University, December

Uthurusamy, R., Fayyad, U.M. & Spangler, S. 1990, "Learning useful rules from inconclusive data", in *Knowledge Discovery in Databases*, eds G. Piatetsy-Shapiro & W. Frawley, AAAI Press, Menlo Park, California

Walpole, R.E. 1982, *Introduction to Statistics*, 3rd edition, Macmillan, New York

Zhou, X. & Dillon, T.S. 1988, "A heuristic statistical feature selection criteria for inductive machine learning in the real world", *Proceedings of IEEE International Conference on Systems, Man and Cybernetics*, Beijing

Zhou, X. & Dillon, T.S. 1989, "Combining artificial intelligence with statistical methods for machine learning in the real world", *Proceedings of the 2nd International Workshop on AI and Statistics*, Fort Lauderdale, January

Zhou, X. & Dillon, T.S. 1991a, "A statistical-heuristic feature selection criterion for decision tree induction", *IEEE Transactions on Pattern Analysis and Machine Intelligence*, vol. 13, no. 8, August, pp. 834–41

Zhou, X. & Dillon, T.S. 1991b, "Multi-branching decision trees for induction", *Eleventh International Conference on Expert Systems & Their Applications (Avignon '91)*, Avignon, France, pp. 191–203

3

Induction algorithms using progressive rule generation

3.1 Introduction

This methodology comprises algorithms that use logical formulae in disjunctive normal form (Shavlik & Dietterich 1990). The algorithms attempt to produce the simplest expression consistent with the training examples. The initial developers, Michalski and his associates, called it the STAR methodology. Michalski has extended the methodology to incorporate a fairly rich language of features and concepts, and to permit incremental learning. These programs also provide a facility for constructive induction, a method of forming new terms. According to Forsyth & Rada (1986), the description language is more powerful than that in ID3. A distinguishing feature of the algorithms is that they have a facility for providing problem background knowledge to the program that aids in the development of a concept. In this chapter, the STAR, or progressive rule generation, approach is discussed in detail.

3.2 The notion of a Star

In this methodology, a Star is used to denote the possible descriptors of the examples. In order to understand this concept, first consider the training set in Table 3.1. The list of rules in Table 3.2 identifies the outputs of DOLPHIN and EEL according to the training set. In the progressive rule generation or STAR methodology, this list of rules for each output is referred to as a Star. These rules contain the descriptors covering the training set.

example 1	(Swims, Large, Gray) ⟹ (DOLPHIN)
example 2	(Swims, Large, White) ⟹ (DOLPHIN)
example 3	(Swims, Small, Gray) ⟹ (EEL)
example 4	(Swims, Small, Black) ⟹ (EEL)

Table 3.1   An illustrative training set

(Size = Large)   ⟹   (DOLPHIN)
(Color = White)   ⟹   (DOLPHIN)
((Size = Large) AND (Color = Gray))   ⟹   (DOLPHIN)
(Size = Small)   ⟹   (EEL)
(Color = Black)   ⟹   (EEL)
((Size = Small) AND (Color = Gray))   ⟹   (EEL)

Table 3.2   Rules describing the training set in Table 3.1

All the rules in Table 3.2 are not necessary to describe the training set. A smaller set of rules would be adequate to classify the outputs and thus cover the training set. Such a set is given in Table 3.3. The smaller set of rules is sufficient in the sense that the examples in the training set are still correctly covered. In this methodology, this reduced set of descriptors is known as a reduced Star.

(Size = Large)   ⟹   (DOLPHIN)
(Color = Black)   ⟹   (EEL)
((Size = Small) AND (Color = Gray))   ⟹   (EEL)

Table 3.3   Smaller set of rules describing the training set in Table 3.1

As formally described (Michalski 1983):

> *The Star of an event e under constraints F, is the set of all possible alternative non-redundant descriptions of event e that do not violate constraints F. A more restrictive definition is that a Star of event e*

against the event set N (the set of negative examples) is defined as the set of all maximally general expressions that cover (i.e. are satisfied by) event e and that do not cover any of the negative events in N.

In real-world problems, a Star of an event may contain a very large number of descriptions. As such, a theoretical Star is replaced by a reduced Star that contains no more than a fixed number of descriptions. This fixed number of descriptions is selected as the most preferable among all the descriptions according to the preference criterion defined in the problem background knowledge.

Various terms used in conjunction with these algorithms are now defined (Michalski et al. 1986). First, a variable related to a value or a disjunction of values is known as a *selector*. For instance, if the variable is Color and the possible values of Color are Black or White, then a selector representing this would be:

(Color = Black) OR (Color = White).

An alternative notation for this is:

(Color $\in$ {Black, White}).

A *complex* is defined as a conjunction of selectors. Thus the complex

(Color $\in$ {Black, White}) AND (Size = Small)

states that the Color is Black or White and the Size is Small. Finally, the complexes are grouped together into a *cover*. The complexes within a cover can be linked with a conjunction (AND) or a disjunction (OR). These covers represent the IF part of a rule.

3.3 General and simplified versions of the STAR algorithm

Assuming the existence of a technique for generating a reduced Star, the following is a general, greatly simplified version of the STAR algorithm. This version can be viewed as a general schema for implementing various learning methods (Michalski 1983; Thrun et al. 1991). According to Michalski (1983), the steps in the algorithm are:

Step 1.   *Select randomly an event from the set of positive examples (a seed event).*

Step 2.   *Generate a reduced Star (list of complexes with a maximum of m elements) of the seed event against the set of negative examples. In the process of Star generation, apply generalization rules, task-specific rules, and heuristics.*

Step 3.   *In the reduced Star obtained, find the description with the highest preference according to a preference criterion.*

Step 4.   *If the description covers the set of positive examples completely, go to Step 6.*

Step 5.   *If not, reduce the set of positive examples to contain only events not covered by the description and repeat the whole process from Step 1.*

Step 6.   *The disjunction of all the generated descriptions is a complete and consistent concept description. As a final step, apply various re-formulation rules and contracting rules to obtain a possibly simpler expression.*

As an illustration of this algorithm, again consider the training set in Table 3.1. Assuming the existence of a technique for generating a reduced Star, the following highlights the application of the algorithm to the different outputs, DOLPHIN and EEL. Note that the list of complexes in the reduced Star describing each event is limited to a maximum of 3 ($m = 3$).

• DOLPHIN output:

Step 1.   Let the randomly selected positive example of DOLPHIN be the first example:

(Swims, Large, Gray) $\Rightarrow$ (DOLPHIN).

Step 2.   Let the reduced Star (restricted to a maximum of 3 elements), generated in some way to cover the selected positive example and no negative examples, be:

(Size = Large)

(Size = Large) AND (Color = Gray)

(Swims = Yes) AND (Size = Large) AND (Color = Gray).

Step 3.   Let the highest preference according to the preference criterion choose the reduced Star:

(Size = Large).

Step 4.   Does (Size = Large) uniquely identify all the positive examples of DOLPHIN? Yes — go to Step 6.

Step 6.   Final tidying up:

(Size = Large) $\Rightarrow$ (DOLPHIN).

• EEL output:

Step 1.   Let the randomly selected positive example of EEL be the fourth example:

(Swims, Small, Black) $\Rightarrow$ (EEL).

Step 2.   Let the reduced Star (restricted to a maximum of 3 elements), generated in some way to cover the selected positive example and no negative examples, be:

(Color = Black)

(Size = Small)

(Swims = Yes) AND (Color = Black).

Step 3.   Let the highest preference according to the preference criterion choose the reduced Star:

(Color = Black).

Step 4.   Does (Color = Black) uniquely identify all the positive examples of EEL? No — go to Step 5. Note that (Color = Black) is retained on the solution list as the positive example(s) it covers will be removed in Step 5.

Step 5.   Reduce the set of positive examples (to contain only events not covered by the description) by removing example 4. The set of positive examples now only contains example 3:

(Swims, Small, Gray) $\Rightarrow$ (EEL).

Repeat   Steps 1 to 4 for example 3 only.

Step 1.   Let the randomly selected positive example of EEL be the third example:

(Swims, Small, Gray) $\Rightarrow$ (EEL).

Step 2.   Let the reduced Star (restricted to a maximum of 3 elements), generated in some way to cover the selected positive example and no negative examples, be:

(Size = Small) AND (Color = Gray)

(Size = Small)

(Swims = Yes) AND (Size = Small).

Step 3.   Let the highest preference according to the preference criterion choose the reduced Star:

(Size = Small) AND (Color = Gray).

Step 4.   Does (Size = Small) AND (Color = Gray) uniquely identify all the (remaining) positive examples of EEL? Yes — go to Step 6.

Step 6.   Final tidying up:

(Color = Black) $\Rightarrow$ (EEL)

((Size = Small) AND (Color = Gray)) $\Rightarrow$ (EEL).

- Final rules produced for the training set are:

(Size = Large) $\Rightarrow$ (DOLPHIN)

(Color = Black) $\Rightarrow$ (EEL)

((Size = Small) AND (Color = Gray)) $\Rightarrow$ (EEL).

Note that if (Size = Small) had been chosen at Step 2 of the first iteration for EEL instead of (Color = Black), a better reduced Star covering all positive examples of EEL would result.

In the previous illustration, it was assumed that the following were available:

- a technique for generating the reduced Star
- a preference criterion
- generalization and specialization transformations
- the use of background knowledge.

As all of these are crucial for the general algorithm, they are discussed in detail in the next sections.

3.4 Generalization and specialization transformations

Techniques that construct new rules can be used to generate a Star; that is, a series of descriptors covering a training set. Both generalization and specialization transformations can be used for this purpose. A generalization transformation changes a description into a more general description, one that tautologically implies the initial description. A specialization transformation, on the other hand, makes the opposite transformation. Given a description, it generates a logical consequence of it. Note also that generalization rules can be non-constructive (selective) or constructive. Non-constructive rules involve no descriptors other than those in the original rules, whereas constructive rules contain new descriptors.

Generalization consists of using a higher-level description that applies to a

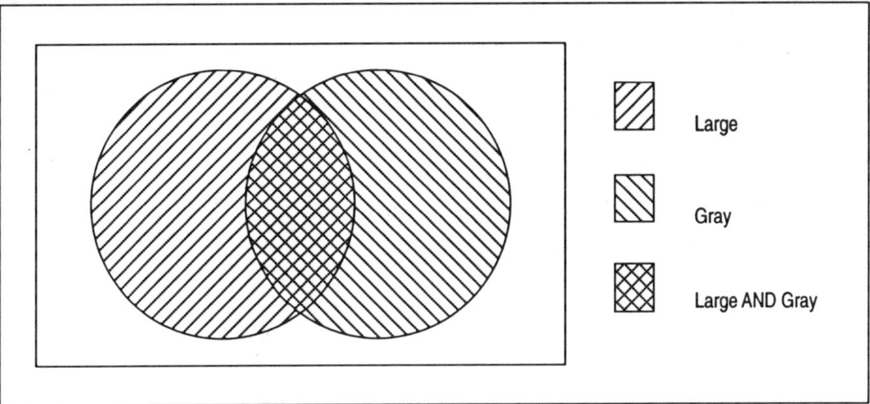

Figure 3.1   A generalization transformation involving dropping a conjunctive term

larger set of objects than the original, more specialized description. Instances of generalization transformations include (Michalski 1983):

- dropping one or more terms from a conjunction of several terms. For instance, as illustrated in Figure 3.1:

  (X is Large) AND (X is Gray)

  can be generalized to:

  (X is Large).

- replacing a constant with a variable in a descriptor. For instance, if Flipper is a constant and X is a variable then, as illustrated in Figure 3.2:

  (Flipper is Large) AND (Flipper is Gray)

  can be generalized to:

  (X is Large) AND (X is Gray).

Specialization results in a more specific description that characterizes a subset of the original set more precisely. Given a description and a negative example, a rule that creates an exception condition and adds it to the initial description is an instance of a specialization transformation (Michalski 1983). The general form of such a rule, as illustrated in Figure 3.3, is:

current description   :   P(X)
negative example   :   P(X) AND Q(X)

then the current description can be specialized to:

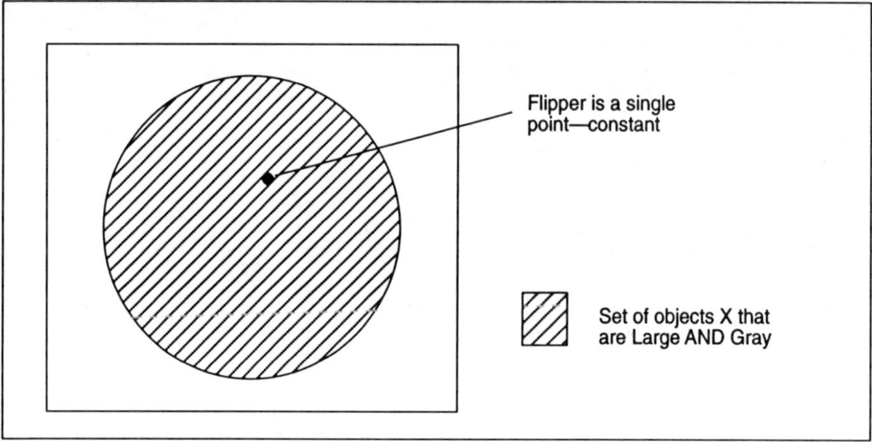

Figure 3.2   A generalization transformation involving replacing a constant with a variable

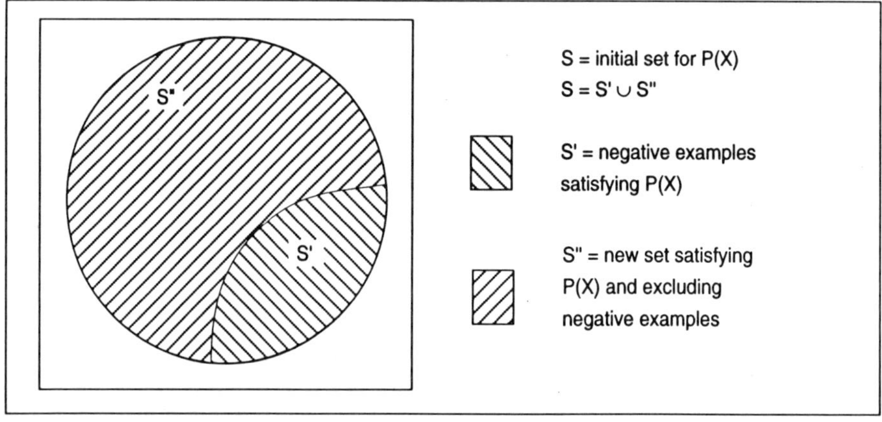

Figure 3.3   A specialization transformation involving adding an exception term

$$P(X) \setminus Q(X)$$

where \ is an exception operator. This exception operator helps define a subset S'' of the original set S (for which P(X) was true) that now contains no negative examples.

To illustrate specialization, consider the following 2 examples from Table 3.1:

example 1:   (Swims, Large, Gray) $\Rightarrow$ (DOLPHIN)

example 3:   (Swims, Small, Gray) $\Rightarrow$ (EEL).

Let the current description for example 1 be:

$$(\text{Swims} = \text{Yes}) \Rightarrow (\text{DOLPHIN}).$$

However, example 3 also satisfies the left-hand side of this description, but it is not an example of a DOLPHIN. Hence it is a negative example. A description for this negative example is:

$$((\text{Swims} = \text{Yes}) \text{ AND } (\text{Size} = \text{Small})) \Rightarrow (\text{EEL})$$

and not DOLPHIN. Thus, the following specialized rule can be obtained:

$$((\text{Swims} = \text{Yes})' \ (\text{Size} = \text{Small})) \Rightarrow (\text{DOLPHIN}).$$

This specialized rule states that if a creature Swims, but is not Small, then the creature is a DOLPHIN.

Each time a generalization or specialization transformation is applied, a new rule is generated. If the various generalization and specialization transformations are freely applied, a large number of rules will be generated covering the training set. This is obviously not efficient because of a possible combinatorial explosion. Some technique is required to search through the constructed rules to determine those that are the best. Problem background knowledge can be used to constrain the number of assertions generated.

3.5 Problem background knowledge

The progressive rule generation, or STAR, algorithms use background knowledge to constrain the space of possible inductive assertions. Problem background knowledge also aids in locating the most desirable assertion(s) and constructing new assertions (Michalski 1983). Background knowledge can be divided into general-purpose and domain-specific knowledge. General-purpose background knowledge consists of constraints and criteria specifying general properties of classifications, while domain-specific background knowledge consists of inference rules for deriving values for new descriptors; that is, for performing constructive induction (Stepp III & Michalski 1986). These inference rules, used for generating internally derived descriptors, are called b-rules, or background rules. Examples of b-rules include expressions of arithmetic and logical relationships, such as the arithmetic relationship:

$$\text{Area}(\text{object}) = \text{Width}(\text{object}) * \text{Height}(\text{object})$$

and the logical relationship:

$$\text{Above}(b1,b2) \text{ AND } \text{Above}(b2,b3) \Rightarrow \text{Above}(b1,b3).$$

Each of these relationships is associated with a condition defining the situation to which it is applicable. These relationships are thus used for constructive induction entailing the derivation of new attributes. Some of the components of the problem background knowledge will now be discussed (Michalski 1983).

An annotation is assigned to each descriptor in the system. Descriptors refer to the predicates, variables, and functions present in the system. The annotation stores the background information of the descriptor tailored to the learning under consideration. For instance, an annotation may include a specification of the domain of a particular descriptor, to restrict the descriptor to a limited set of values. Thus a descriptor representing the age of a human being may have allowable values in the range 0 – 120 years.

The annotation may also detail the structure of the descriptor, including aspects such as whether the values of the descriptor are:

- categorical with a discrete and independent set of possible values;
- linear where the possible values are ordered in some way; or
- structured where the values form a hierarchy or tree structure.

Color with possible values of Red, Black, or White is a categorical descriptor, whereas Age is an example of a linear descriptor. The set CAR, with its subclasses such as SMALL CAR, MEDIUM CAR, and LARGE CAR, forms a taxonomic hierarchy and is an instance of a structured descriptor.

Other aspects that could be included in the annotation assigned to each descriptor are:

- typical examples of a descriptor if the descriptor is a class;
- mean and variance for numerical descriptors;
- a list of the operators that can be applied to the descriptor.

The Lexicographical Evaluation Function (LEF) is another crucial feature of the problem background knowledge. It is used to select from the candidate expressions the one with the most preferred viewpoint of the given goal (Michalski 1983; Stepp III & Michalski 1986). The LEF consists of an ordered sequence of elementary criteria, along with tolerances that control the extent to which different solutions are considered equivalent (Stepp III & Michalski 1986). The LEF is used to define various elementary, easy-to-measure criteria specifying the desirable properties of a classification. Some simple examples of the criteria are (Michalski 1983; Michalski et al. 1986; Stepp III & Michalski 1986):

- the simplicity of the class descriptions;
- the maximization of the number of positive examples covered;
- the minimization of the total cost of the variables used;
- the minimization of the selectors used;
- the number of attributes that discriminate on their own among all the classes;
- the number of attributes necessary to classify the objects into the proposed classes.

As stated, the LEF is defined as an ordered sequence of criterion-tolerance pairs (Michalski 1983):

$$\text{LEF} : (C_1, T_1), (C_2, T_2), \ldots$$

where C_i is the criterion i,

T_i is the tolerance of criterion i, (between 0% and 100%).

These pairs are ordered according to their relevance to a particular domain. According to Michalski (1983), the LEF determines the best assertions from a set of assertions by using the following technique:

- First, all of the assertions are evaluated according to criterion C_1.
- The assertion with the best score from this evaluation is kept, along with all other assertions whose scores fall within the range defined by the tolerance T_1 from the best.
- These retained assertions are evaluated according to criterion 2. The assertion with the best score from this evaluation is kept, along with all other assertions whose scores fall within the range defined by the tolerance T_2 from the best.
- This process is continued until either one assertion is left or the sequence of criterion-tolerance pairs is exhausted. In the latter case, the LEF regards the last set of assertions as equivalent.

Problem background knowledge, which includes the LEF used for selecting the most desirable assertion as well as a lot of other information, is useless if there is no technique available for generating a reduced Star. Some of these techniques are discussed next.

3.6 Generating a reduced Star

3.6.1 General aspects

The various programs based on this methodology use different techniques for generating a reduced Star. However, most of the techniques first separate the training examples into a positive and negative set. The positive set contains the examples of the output being considered, whereas the negative set contains all the remaining examples with other outputs. Next, one example, known as the seed example, is selected from the positive set. A reduced Star is then built covering that seed. The reduced Star is actually the set of all alternative general descriptions that designate the seed example (and possibly other positive examples) and no negative examples (Stepp III & Michalski 1986). Two techniques for generating a Star are described in this section. These techniques are used in the INDUCE and AQ series of programs.

3.6.2 Generating a Star in INDUCE

Discussion

The following steps are used in the technique for generating a reduced Star in the INDUCE program (Michalski 1983):

1. Start with a set of single selectors. These selectors can be extracted from the seed example for which the Star is being generated. Alternatively, they can be inferred from the example by applying constructive generalization rules or inference rules provided by the background knowledge. At this point, some of the negative examples may be covered. The selectors are then ordered according to the LEF.

2. The selectors are specialized by adding other selectors. The selectors chosen for addition are lower in the list sorted by the LEF than the selector being specialized. The new selectors are then inserted in the appropriate position in the ordered list. The number of selectors in a list is restricted to a set size m.

3. Selectors are checked for consistency and completeness. Consistency is reached when the number of negative examples covered is equal to zero. Completeness, on the other hand, is reached when the number of positive examples covered equals the total number of positive examples. Selectors satisfying both criteria are placed on a Solutions list. (If the number of selectors on the Solutions list reaches some set value then the process is stopped.) Incomplete but consistent descriptions are also removed from the current list and placed on a Consistent list. If the number of selectors on the Consistent list is greater than some set parameter, then go to Step 5.

4. Each description left on the current list is specialized by appending a selector to it from the original set of selectors sorted by the LEF. Appended selectors must be of lower preference than the one currently being considered. All or a portion of these lower selectors may be singly appended to each solution. The list is sorted by the LEF and only m expressions are kept. Go to Step 3.

5. Each expression on the Consistent list is generalized. The expressions are once again ranked by the LEF and m expressions are kept. These expressions comprise the reduced STAR.

An important aspect of this technique is that selectors are specialized by appending other selectors with a lower preference than the selectors in the expression. However, the number of descriptions retained is limited by a user-defined parameter, m.

Thus, even though this algorithm involves an extensive enumeration of many combinations of the selectors, it is limited by this parameter. Finally, note that this technique involves the simultaneous consideration of all positive examples at each pass of the algorithm.

Illustrative example

Consider the training set in Table 3.1, which is re-stated as follows:

example 1	(Swims, Large, Gray)	$\Rightarrow$	(DOLPHIN)
example 2	(Swims, Large, White)	$\Rightarrow$	(DOLPHIN)
example 3	(Swims, Small, Gray)	$\Rightarrow$	(EEL)
example 4	(Swims, Small, Black)	$\Rightarrow$	(EEL)

Let the output under consideration be DOLPHIN. Thus the set of positive examples is:

example 1: (Swims, Large, Gray) $\Rightarrow$ (DOLPHIN)

example 2: (Swims, Large, White) $\Rightarrow$ (DOLPHIN)

and the set of negative examples is:

example 3: (Swims, Small, Gray) $\Rightarrow$ (EEL)

example 4: (Swims, Small, Black) $\Rightarrow$ (EEL).

The following is a trace of the application of INDUCE (where the number of selectors on the Solutions or Consistent list must be 2 for the process to terminate, and m is set to 3):

1. The initial ordered selectors are:

(i)   (Swims = Yes)
(ii)   (Color = Gray)
(iii) (Size = Large).

2. The selectors are specialized.

(Swims = Yes) AND (Color = Gray)
(Swims = Yes) AND (Size = Large)
(Color = Gray) AND (Size = Large).

Next, these unordered specializations are ordered according to the LEF. Note that the maximum number of retained descriptors is 3.

(i)   (Swims = Yes) AND (Color = Gray)
(ii)   (Swims = Yes) AND (Size = Large)
(iii) (Color = Gray) AND (Size = Large).

3. The selectors are checked for consistency and completeness.

Selector (i) is both inconsistent and incomplete.
Selector (ii) is consistent and complete and is therefore placed on the Solutions list.
Selector (iii) is consistent, but incomplete, and is therefore placed on the Consistent list.

4. The remaining selector:

(Swims = Yes) AND (Color = Gray)

is specialized by appending a selector of lower preference from the original selector list. Step 3 is then repeated on the result:

(i)   (Swims = Yes) AND (Color = Gray) AND (Size = Large).

3. The selector is checked for consistency and completeness.

Selector (i) is consistent, but incomplete, and is therefore placed on the Consistent list. The number of selectors on the Consistent list is now 2, as required for the process to go to Step 5.

5. The selectors on the Consistent list:

(i)   (Color = Gray) AND (Size = Large)

(ii)   (Swims = Yes) AND (Color = Gray) AND (Size = Large)

can then be generalized. Let the following be the resulting selectors as ordered by the LEF:

(i)   (Size = Large)

(ii)   (Swims = Yes) AND (Size = Large).

These selectors comprise the reduced Star for DOLPHIN. Similar reasoning results in the following selectors for the EEL output:

(i)   (Size = Small)

(ii)   (Swims = Yes) AND (Size = Small).

Final comments

INDUCE was developed to be applied in structural-learning situations; that is, situations in which training instances have some internal structure. It works by considering all the examples at an iteration. This is because each selector is checked for consistency (number of negative examples covered) and completeness (number of positive examples covered). INDUCE seeks to find a few concepts in the rule space, each covering all of the training instances, while remaining as specific as possible. It also applies some model-based heuristics to prune the set drastically so that only a few generalizations are discovered (Forsyth & Rada 1986; Michalski 1983).

3.6.3 Generating a Star in the AQ programs

Discussion

In the AQ series of programs, the generation of a reduced Star has a different emphasis from that of INDUCE. Here, one single positive example or seed is selected at a time (Theron & Cloete 1993). The covering algorithm for generating a reduced Star contains the following steps (Michalski et al. 1986):

While the partial cover does not cover all the positive examples:

1.   Select a seed uncovered by the current partial cover.
2.   Generate a Star covering the seed and no negative examples using the process specified below.
3.   Select the best complex according to some preference criterion.
4.   Generate a new partial cover by appending the best complex to the current cover.

The algorithm can start with an empty initial cover, or the initial cover can be one that was previously learned or one supplied by the user. The steps for generating a Star covering a seed and no negative examples are (Michalski et al. 1986):

While the partial Star covers any negative examples:

2.1. Select a covered negative example.
2.2. Generate a partial Star of the seed against the negative example. This is accomplished by generating all maximally general hypotheses that cover the seed and exclude the negative example.
2.3. Intersect the current partial Star with the partial Star generated against the negative example. This new combination is redefined as the new current partial Star.
2.4. If the number of disjoint complexes exceeds a user-defined threshold, trim the partial Star.

Illustrative example

To illustrate the above technique, consider the training set in Table 3.4.

Let the output under consideration be DOLPHIN. Thus the set of positive examples is:

> example 1:   (Swims, Large, Gray) $\Rightarrow$ (DOLPHIN)
> example 2:   (Swims, Large, White) $\Rightarrow$ (DOLPHIN)
> example 3:   (Swims, Medium, Black) $\Rightarrow$ (DOLPHIN)

example 1	(Swims, Large, Gray) $\Rightarrow$ (DOLPHIN)
example 2	(Swims, Large, White) $\Rightarrow$ (DOLPHIN)
example 3	(Swims, Medium, Black) $\Rightarrow$ (DOLPHIN)
example 4	(Swims, Small, Gray) $\Rightarrow$ (EEL)
example 5	(Swims, Small, Black) $\Rightarrow$ (EEL)
example 6	(Swims, Medium, Gray) $\Rightarrow$ (EEL)

Table 3.4   Illustrative example training set

and the set of negative examples is:

> example 4:   (Swims, Small, Gray) $\Rightarrow$ (EEL)
> example 5:   (Swims, Small, Black) $\Rightarrow$ (EEL)
> example 6:   (Swims, Medium, Gray) $\Rightarrow$ (EEL).

Let the initial partial cover be empty and thus none of the positive examples are covered. A trace of the AQ technique for generating a reduced Star follows:

1. Let the positive seed example be the third example:

    > example 3:   (Swims, Medium, Black) $\Rightarrow$ (DOLPHIN).

2. Generate a partial Star covering the seed and no negative examples. The initial partial Star contains True.

    2.1. Any negative example can be selected, as the initial partial Star covers all negative examples. Let the covered negative example chosen be the fourth example:

    > example 4:   (Swims, Small, Gray) $\Rightarrow$ (EEL).

    2.2. Generate all maximally general hypotheses that cover the seed and exclude the negative example. The seed has different values from example 4 for the attributes Size and Color. The maximally general hypotheses for these attributes that cover the seed and exclude example 4 are:

    > (Size $\in$ {Large, Medium})
    > (Color $\in$ {Black, White}).

    2.3. Intersect each complex in the current partial Star (True at this point) with each complex in the partial Star generated for the seed against the negative example. Thus the new current partial Star is:

    > (Size $\in$ {Large, Medium})
    > (Color $\in$ {Black, White}).

    2.4. The current partial Star does not exceed 4 (assumed to be the number of disjoint complexes allowed).

Within the current partial star (Size ∈ {Large, Medium}) covers negative example 6 and (Color ∈ {Black, White}) covers negative example 5. Therefore, this loop is repeated with the current partial Star as the initial Star.

2.1. Let the covered negative example chosen be the sixth example:

example 6:   (Swims, Medium, Gray) ⇒ (EEL).

2.2. Generate all maximally general hypotheses that cover the seed and exclude the negative example. The seed has a different value from example 6 for the attribute Color only. The maximally general hypothesis for this attribute that covers the seed and excludes example 6 is:

(Color ∈ {Black, White}).

2.3. Intersect each complex in the current partial Star with the complex in the partial Star generated for the seed against the negative example. Thus the new current partial Star is:

(Size ∈ {Large, Medium}) AND (Color ∈ {Black, White})
(Color ∈ {Black, White}) AND (Color ∈ {Black, White})

which simplifies to:

(Size ∈ {Large, Medium}) AND (Color ∈ {Black, White})
(Color ∈ {Black, White}).

2.4. The current partial Star does not exceed 4 (assumed to be the number of disjoint complexes allowed).

Within the current partial star, (Color ∈ {Black, White}) covers negative example 5. Therefore, this loop is repeated with the current partial Star as the initial Star.

2.1. The covered negative example chosen is the fifth example:

example 5:   (Swims, Small, Black) ⇒ (EEL).

2.2. Generate all maximally general hypotheses that cover the seed and exclude the negative example. The seed has a different value from example 5 for the attribute Size only. The maximally general hypothesis for this attribute that covers the seed and excludes example 5 is:

(Size ∈ {Large, Medium}).

2.3. Intersect each complex in the current partial Star with the complex in the partial Star generated for the seed against the negative example. Thus the new current partial Star is:

(Size ∈ {Large, Medium}) AND (Color ∈ {Black, White})
    AND (Size ∈ {Large, Medium})
(Color ∈ {Black, White}) AND (Size ∈ {Large, Medium})

which simplifies to:

$$(Size \in \{Large, Medium\}) \text{ AND } (Color \in \{Black, White\}).$$

2.4. The current partial Star does not exceed 4 (assumed to be the number of disjoint complexes allowed).

3. The best complex is (Size $\in$ {Large, Medium}) AND (Color $\in$ {Black, White}).

4. Append this best complex to the current cover (which is empty) to obtain the new partial cover. The new current partial cover thus becomes:

$$(Size \in \{Large, Medium\}) \text{ AND } (Color \in \{Black, White\}).$$

This current partial Star does not cover all positive examples. Therefore, the previous process needs to be repeated.

1. Let the seed be the only uncovered example:

example 1:   (Swims, Large, Gray) $\Rightarrow$ (DOLPHIN).

2. Generate a partial Star covering the seed and no negative examples. The initial partial Star contains True.

2.1. Any negative example can be selected, as the initial partial Star covers all negative examples. Let the covered negative example chosen be the sixth example:

example 6:   (Swims, Medium, Gray) $\Rightarrow$ (EEL).

2.2. Generate all maximally general hypotheses that cover the seed and exclude the negative example. The seed has a different value from example 6 for the attribute Size only. The maximally general hypothesis for this attribute that covers the seed and excludes example 6 is:

$$(Size \in \{Large, Small\}).$$

2.3. Intersect each complex in the current partial Star (True at this point) with each complex in the partial Star generated for the seed against the negative example. Thus the new current partial Star is:

$$(Size \in \{Large, Small\}).$$

2.4. The current partial Star does not exceed 4 (assumed to be the number of disjoint complexes allowed).

Within the current partial Star, (Size, $\in$ {Large, Small}) covers negative examples 4 and 5. Therefore, this loop is repeated with the current partial Star as the initial Star.

2.1. Let the covered negative example chosen be the fourth example:

example 4:   (Swims, Small, Gray) $\Rightarrow$ (EEL).

2.2. Generate all maximally general hypotheses that cover the seed and exclude the negative example. The seed has a different value from example 4 for the attribute Size only. The maximally general hypothesis for this attribute that covers the seed and excludes example 4 is:

(Size $\in$ {Large, Medium}).

2.3. Intersect the complex in the current partial Star with the complex in the partial Star generated for the seed against the negative example. Thus the new current partial Star is:

(Size $\in$ {Large, Small}) AND (Size $\in$ {Large, Medium})

which simplifies to:

(Size = Large).

2.4. The current partial Star does not exceed 4 (assumed to be the number of disjoint complexes allowed).

3.   The best complex is (Size = Large).

4.   Append this best complex to the current cover (Size = Large) to obtain the new partial cover. The new current partial cover thus becomes:

(Size $\in$ {Large, Medium}) AND (Color $\in$ {Black, White})
(Size = Large).

This does cover all positive examples. Therefore, the preceding process is terminated.

Final comments

This technique focuses on a single positive example at a time. As a result, it seeks the most general description corresponding to a necessary condition for class membership (Cohen & Feigenbaum 1982). The technique works in an incremental fashion with each step appending another conjunctive term (or new selector). The underlying strategy is to introduce new items of evidence one at a time, or a few at a time, and continue to extend the rule to deal with them. Thus, the generated selectors or rules are initially very general but become more and more specific. The technique adds new terms to exclude negative examples, while still covering as many positive examples as possible.

3.7 Programs based on progressive rule generation

AQ11

The AQ11 program was an early attempt at implementing the STAR or progressive rule generation methodology. It found better rules for soya bean disease diagnosis than a human expert (Buchanan et al. 1983; Cohen & Feigenbaum 1982; Forsyth & Rada 1986). The rules obtained discriminated one class from a predetermined set of other classes and therefore performed a classification task (Cohen & Feigenbaum 1982).

AQ15

According to Michalski et al. (1986), AQ15 proved to be a powerful and flexible tool for experimenting with inductive knowledge acquisition. A form of constructive induction (i.e., forming new descriptors) is also implemented in AQ15. The program's background knowledge is expressed in the form of rules that are used to generate new attributes not present in the input data. Michalski et al. (1986) claim that:

- *A major result with AQ15 is a demonstration that knowledge reduction by truncating clauses may lead to a substantial reduction of the rule base without decreasing its performance accuracy;*
- *By varying the degree of generality of rules and applying different evaluation methods, different tradeoffs between the correctness and precision of decision rules are achieved.*

An alternative approach to attribute selection using genetic algorithms is taken in AQ15-GA. The genetic algorithm is used to generate subsets of the attribute set that are assessed using the approach of AQ15. The rules produced are evaluated by measuring the recognition rate (Thrun et al. 1991).

AQ17

In AQ17-DCI, a number of new attributes are generated by a *data-driven constructive induction* approach. Selection of attributes is then based on a special Quality Function (QF) for the attributes exceeding a pre-specified threshold (Thrun et al. 1991).

AQ17-FCLS (Flexible Concept Learning) uses both symbolic and numeric representations as the basis for developing a description of a concept. Two-tiered descriptions are used:

- Basic Concept Representation (BCR) in the form of rules
- Inferential Concept Interpretation (ICI); that is, a weighted evaluation function that sums the contributions of the different conditions in a rule, and compares this with a threshold.

The rules are learned in two steps, the first of which is similar to the STAR algorithm in AQ. The second step specializes the rule and adjusts the threshold accuracy (Thrun et al. 1991).

New attributes are generated on the basis of the analysis of the hypothesis produced in a previous iteration in AQ17-HCI (Hypothesis-driven Constructive Induction) (Thrun et al. 1991).

DLG

DLG (Webb 1991; Webb & Agar 1992) starts with a specific classifier and examines the positive examples, one at a time. The classifier is generalized as required to cover the current example. Each such generalization is accepted only if it improves the classification performance. DLG employs the AQ strategy to develop successive classifiers, each covering different subsets of the positive examples. Thus the clauses of the disjunctive classifier evolve.

3.8 Problems with the STAR algorithms

The various STAR algorithms suffer from (Cohen & Feigenbaum 1982; Forsyth & Rada 1986):

- the absence of a strong model to guide the pruning of descriptions and the termination of the search;
- an exhaustive enumeration of all possible single-step generalizations of the hypothesis involved in the second step in the general STAR algorithm;
- an incomplete method because the STAR algorithm prunes its search.

Note also that these algorithms have no facility for handling continuous data; that is, they deal with discrete-valued descriptors only (Michalski et al. 1986). As with many AI problems, continuous data must be broken up into classes before it can be used.

A major area to be investigated with this methodology is the importance of the generalization/specialization transformations and the background domain knowledge. One question to be answered is whether the incorporation of the background knowledge makes these algorithms more efficient than ID3, for example.

3.9 Recapitulation

This chapter has discussed the various algorithms based on the progressive rule generation or STAR methodology. These algorithms rely on problem background knowledge to guide the search and test the resulting rules. Rule generation relies on a limited enumeration of the clauses that are combined to form the IF part of the rule. This enumeration is a major drawback of the methodology. It may also be difficult to formalize the problem background knowledge.

In the next chapter, sub-symbolic methods of learning are presented. These methods are limited to the discussion of artificial neural networks.

References

Buchanan, B.G., Barstow, D., Bechtal, R., Bennett, J., Clancey, W., Kulikowski, C., Mitchell, T. & Waterman, D.A. 1983, "Constructing an expert system", in *Building Expert Systems,* eds F. Hayes-Roth, D.A. Waterman & D.B. Lenat, Addison-Wesley, Reading, Massachusetts, pp. 127–68

Cohen, P.R. & Feigenbaum, E.A., eds 1982, *The Handbook of Artificial Intelligence: Volume 3*, William Kaufmann, Los Altos, California

Forsyth, R. & Rada, R. 1986, *Machine Learning: Applications in Expert Systems and Information Retrieval*, Ellis Horwood, Chichester, UK

Michalski, R. 1983, "Theory and methodology of inductive learning", *Artificial Intelligence*, vol. 20, pp. 111–61

Michalski, R.S., Mozetic, I., Hong, J. & Lavrac, N. 1986, *The AQ15 Inductive Learning System: An Overview and Experiments*, University of Illinois, Urbana-Champaign

Shavlik, J. & Dietterich, T. 1990, "Inductive learning from preclassified training examples, Introduction", in *Readings in Machine Learning*, eds J. Shavlik & T. Dietterich, Morgan Kaufmann Publishers, San Francisco, California, pp. 45–56

Stepp III, R.E. & Michalski, R.S. 1986, "Conceptual clustering: Inventing goal oriented classification of structured objects", in *Machine Learning: An Artificial Intelligence Approach, Volume II*, eds R.S. Michalski, J.G. Carbonell & T.M. Mitchell, Morgan Kaufmann Publishers, San Francisco, California, pp. 471–98

Theron, H. & Cloete, I. 1993, "An empirical evaluation of beam search and pruning in BEXA", *IEEE Conference on Tools with Artificial Intelligence (TAI '93)*, Boston, Massachusetts, November, pp. 132–9

Thrun, S.B., Bala, J., Bloedorn, E., Bratko, I., Cestnik, B., Cheng, J., De Jong, K., Dzeroski, S., Fahlman, S.E., Fisher, D., Hamann, R., Kaufman, K., Keller, S., Kononenko, I., Kreuziger, J., Michalski, R.S., Mitchell, T., Pachowicz, P., Reich, Y., Vafaie, H., Van de Welde, W., Wenzel, W., Wnek, J. & Zhang, J. 1991, *The MONK's Problems: A Performance Comparison of Different Learning Algorithms,* CMU-CS-91-197, Carnegie Mellon University, December

Webb, G. 1991, "Rule optimisation and theory optimisation: Heuristic search strategies for data driven machine learning", in *Knowledge Acquisition for Knowledge-Based Systems*, eds H. Motada, R. Mizoguchi, J. Boose & B. Gaines, IOS Press, pp. 219–32

Webb, G. & Agar, J. 1992, "Inducing diagnostic rules for glomerular disease with the DLG machine learning algorithm", *Artificial Intelligence in Medicine*, vol. 4, pp. 3–14

4

Sub-symbolic learning methods — artificial neural networks

4.1 Introduction

In Chapters 2 and 3 we presented symbolic machine learning techniques, while this chapter deals with sub-symbolic methods of learning that do not lead to symbolic structures.

The chapter contains a brief overview of artificial neural networks (henceforth referred to simply as neural networks). This discussion only covers those aspects necessary for the development of an automated knowledge acquisition method. Good detailed surveys of this area are provided by Caudill (1987, 1988a–d, 1989a–c), Fahlman and Hinton (1987), Hertz et al. (1991), Hinton (1989), Lippmann (1987), McClelland and Rumelhart (1988), McClelland et al. (1986a), Rumelhart et al. (1986a), and Zurada (1992).

4.2 Background information

An important aspect of connectionist systems is that they learn the knowledge they use by being given, and being trained on, a set of examples. Rather than

94

being programmed, neural networks are trained with examples and therefore, in a sense, acquire knowledge through experience. The advantages of this system are (Aleksander 1989a):

- *The designer does not have to worry about defining formal methods for the representation of the knowledge;*
- *There is no need for exhaustive searches to retrieve the knowledge.*

Thus programmers need not provide neural networks with detailed descriptions of objects being recognized. Instead, a neural network is shown examples of objects and in some cases their identification. The network memorizes these by altering values in its weight matrix to produce the correct response when an object is seen again (Wasserman & Schwartz 1988). A frustrating characteristic of conventional computers is the literal, precise inputs required to produce the desired output. Neural networks, on the other hand, can accommodate variations in their input and still produce the correct output.

Neural networks have two further aspects (Wasserman & Schwartz 1988) that make them invaluable in real-world applications and are similar to the way humans use information.

- Generalization ability — the real world rarely presents information with the precision required. Neural networks accomplish the generalization needed by their structure rather than by elaborate programming. Neural networks therefore provide a far more natural interface to the real world. This is crucial in real-world problems where one cannot train a network in advance for every circumstance it might encounter in the field (Touretzky & Pomerleau 1989). This is an added advantage over traditional symbolic methods (Mozer & Bachrach 1990). Note that generalization performance depends on the size of the training data and the trained network (Rumelhart et al. 1986c).
- Abstraction ability — neural networks can abstract the *ideal* from a non-ideal training set. Through training, neural networks form an internal representation of the salient features of the training set. This feature extraction can produce interesting results (Wasserman & Schwartz 1988).

Parallel Distributed Processing (PDP) models of cognitive processing can be divided into two classes (Smolensky 1986):

- *Local models* — the activity of a single unit represents the degree of participation in the processing of a known conceptual entity (e.g., a word).
- *Distributed models* — the strength of the patterns of activity over many units determines the degree of participation of these conceptual entities.

In other words, where knowledge is represented locally, one unit is used per concept, while in distributed models each concept is represented as a pattern of active units (Wiles 1987). Local representations are often easier for a human observer to understand.

There are several other aspects to consider when dealing with neural networks (Aleksander 1989b). First, neural networks are computationally complete. This means that, given an appropriate neural structure and appropriate training, there is no computational task not available to neural nets. Second, neural networks learn from experience in the form of examples. In contrast, difficulties with conventional rule-based approaches include the fact that the rules are hard to determine and the number of rules in some cases can lead to combinatorial explosions when dealing with complex patterns (Khosla & Dillon 1992, 1993). The performance of neural networks provides a rapid solution to problems such as pattern recognition that, in a conventional computer, could take a long time. Finally, this methodology could provide an insight into the computational characteristics of the human brain.

The connectionist paradigm starts with (Aleksander 1989a):

> *realizing the need to distinguish between the formalized knowledge that may be captured in an expert system and the experience that may need to be stored in a machine to perform a set of less formalized tasks.*

Connectionist systems cut many corners in the process of searching, as does the brain. Hence, once the connectionist implementation techniques have been perfected, the method could provide a means for improving the performance of the more logical processes of knowledge-based systems (Aleksander 1989a).

Working neural networks have major benefits, including the ability to take incomplete data and produce approximate solutions. Massive parallelism gives a neural network a high degree of fault tolerance, associative recall, graceful degradation, and efficiency in dealing with large amounts of data. Neural networks will not replace the conventional methods of computing, especially those dealing with high-speed numeric processing, but will complement them and augment their abilities (Obermeier & Barron 1989; Palmer 1988).

4.3   Basic structure of a neural network

A neural network can be defined as a group of processing elements (neurons) and their interconnections (i.e., synapses or links) (Caudill 1987; Palmer 1988). The early researchers saw these systems as deliberate attempts to model learning in animals (Caudill 1988d).

McCulloch and Pitts laid the basis for the field of neural networks in 1943, by showing that networks of neuron-like elements are general computing devices. This model consisted of binary decision elements (neurons) with suitable interconnections. These were shown to be isomorphic with finite automata and some logical reasoning could thus be attributed to them (Stubbs 1990). The language and techniques were those of standard two-valued logic (Caianiello

1989). The concept of learning was added to this in 1949 when Hebb suggested that synapses are the site of biological learning, and that frequently active synapses should have an increased chance of becoming active again. These premises form a basis of modeling neural networks and also underpin the understanding of how animals learn (Recce & Treleavan 1988).

According to Rumelhart et al. (1986b), there are eight major aspects of a PDP model:

- *a set of processing units (i.e. neurons);*
- *a state of activation;*
- *an output function for each unit;*
- *a pattern of connectivity among units;*
- *a propagation rule for propagating patterns of activities through the network of connectivities;*
- *an activation rule for combining the inputs impinging on a unit with the current state of that unit to produce a new level of activation for the unit;*
- *a learning rule whereby patterns of connectivity are modified by experience;*
- *an environment within which the system must operate.*

In the computer model of a neural network, the simulated neuron illustrated in Figure 4.1 has four important components (Jones & Hoskins 1987):

- *input connections (synapses), through which the unit (i.e. processing element or neuron) receives activation from other units;*
- *a summation function that combines the various input activations into a single activation (this is based on what is known of the function of neurons in the brain (Aleksander 1989a));*
- *a threshold function that converts this summation of input activations into output activations;*
- *output connections by which a unit's output activation arrives as input activation at other units in the system.*

Jorgensen and Matheus (1986) provide a more biological definition of a neuron.

Each neuron in a neural network has many inputs and only one output. Each output can branch to become the input to many other neurons, so that each neuron receives signals from many others. In a typical neural network, most of the inputs to each neuron are from other neurons; the remaining inputs are from the outside. If the sum of the inputs to a given neuron exceeds a set threshold, the neuron is activated and sends a signal to other neurons (Palmer 1988; Stubbs 1990). Thus, some of the nodes of connectionist networks use a sum-of-weighted-inputs function. This is based on the postulated function of the neurons in the brain. Generally, the output *fires* when the total of the inputs to a node each multiplied by the value of a *weight* exceeds some threshold. Adaptation in the node comes from its ability to change the weights in a controlled manner (Aleksander 1989a).

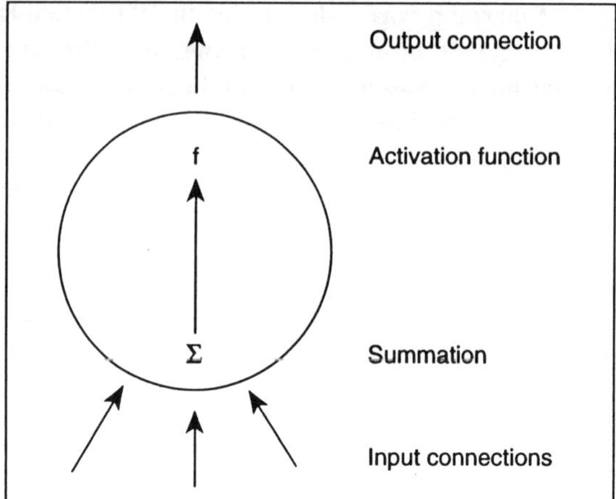

Figure 4.1   Components of a simulated neuron

Each connection between neurons has a weighted value that determines its strength. This connection determines a neuron's contribution to the fire/not-fire decision of the neuron it feeds. In some networks this value can be modified, either from outside the network or by the neurons themselves, and this gives the neural network the ability to learn (Palmer 1988). Therefore, the knowledge of a neural network lies in the inter-unit connections and their weights. Neural networks are basically driven by numerically valued activations that pass from unit to unit. Hence, these activations are said to be at the sub-symbolic level of computation. According to Jones and Hoskins (1987):

> *A network's input, output and internal state can all be characterized by patterns of activation across its nodes.*

Units can be connected to behave like a conjunction (AND) or a disjunction (OR), and it is through the combined effects of a large number of such classifiers and input unit feature detectors that intelligent behavior can emerge from a neural network (Jones & Hoskins 1987; Yang & Dillon 1992). Thus the fundamental premise of connectionism has been that individual neurons do not transmit large amounts of symbolic information.

4.4 Features of a neural network

The neural modeling approach strives to develop general-purpose learning systems that start with little initial knowledge (Carbonell et al. 1983; Michalski

1986). Such a system learns by incrementally modifying the connection strengths between the units, typically by changing the continuous (i.e., not discrete) weights associated with these connections. The system's initial knowledge is provided by the choice of input units representing selected attributes of the objects under consideration, and by the structure and initial strengths of the connections in the network. The connections can have a random structure, one pre-arranged by the designer, or a mixture of the two. Characteristic features of systems built under this paradigm include low levels of a priori built-in knowledge and the use of continuous parameters that are altered in a controlled manner to achieve learning (Michalski 1986). Thus every neural network has what is called a network paradigm or network architecture. This specifies its interconnection structure and the form of the differential equations that determine the behavior of its individual elements (Palmer 1988).

According to Hinton (1989), there are two main reasons for investigating connectionist models: first, because of the claim that these models resemble the brain and, second, because they are massively parallel. A network develops the most plausible interpretation of the input by iteratively updating the states of the units until they reach a stable state. An important choice is whether to represent a continuous physical quantity by the state of a single continuous unit, or by the activities in a set of units each representing the fact that the continuous variable falls within a given range (Dillon et al. 1975). This reflects a decision between a local or distributed model, respectively.

As stated, the actual information in a neural network is not stored in particular locations, as in conventional computers. The information is represented by complex patterns of element stimulations and the adjusted weights associated with each interconnection. This may make neural networks inherently more resistant to damage than traditional computing systems. The loss of a few elements only slightly degrades a neural network's performance, whereas damage to a conventional computer's memory or CPU (Central Processing Unit) usually renders it useless (Palmer 1988). Thus, as the knowledge of a neural network is implicitly represented in weighted links, it is believed that a neural network would be more resistant to noise than traditional AI representations (Jones & Hoskins 1987; Josin 1987; Kinoshita & Palevsky 1987; Mozer & Bachrach 1990).

Attention has recently been focused on a neural network's reputed ability to handle problems involving blurry and unpredictable data. Application areas such as everyday speech cannot be defined by clear-cut rules and data, and so they are difficult to tackle with standard digital computing algorithms. Thus neural network modeling aims to process raw sensory data that is flexible and robust enough to deal with the real, unpredictable world. The prospect of using neural networks as an interface between digital computers and messy, real-world data has stimulated much of the current activity (Josin 1987; Kinoshita & Palevsky 1987).

Attractive features of neural networks include the ability to:

- recall memories (Jorgensen & Matheus 1986) even if some individual processors (neurons) fail (Kinoshita & Palevsky 1987);
- retrieve *nearest-neighbor* data if there is no exact match to the requested information (Jorgensen & Matheus 1986);
- modify stored information in response to new inputs (Kinoshita & Palevsky 1987);
- perform *associative recall* — that is, retrieve original inputs from a degraded version (Kinoshita & Palevsky 1987);
- work with partial and conflicting data (Palmer 1988);
- discover statistically salient features among the stored data (Kinoshita & Palevsky 1987);
- derive solutions to problems that involve a combinatorial explosion in the number of possible answers (Josin 1987);
- deal with noisy and approximate data (Rich 1990);
- learn automatically from training data (Rich 1990);
- learn incrementally, adapting to a changing environment (Rich 1990);
- generalize to situations not encountered before (Rich 1990);
- execute very fast once trained (Rich 1990).

As stated earlier, neural networks are trained on a set of examples. The methods for training neural networks to learn from examples are discussed next.

4.5 How connections are formed — teaching the network

The field of neural networks is very broad. There are many types of neural networks and many different methods used to train them. Typically, in most of them learning involves modification of the weights associated with the links between the various nodes. Some learning schemes are based on correlation between the activation values associated with the connected nodes, while others rely on the error between the desired and the actual network output. Such error estimates may be based on (Honavar & Uhr 1990):

- *extremely specific feedback* — for example, the desired network output provided by a teacher for each input pattern, as used by the Back-propagation method and some of its faster variants;
- *not-so-specific feedback* — for example, the reward/punishment signal used in reinforcement learning;

- *internally derived error* — for example, based on an estimate of the output necessary from a node to produce the overall desired behavior from the network, as used in competitive learning in the Grossberg networks.

Reinforcement learning is a compromise between the other two types of learning, as it requires an input and a graded signal only as an output. This type of learning is less common because of its complexity and lengthy training time, but it has potential for training large modular systems of interconnected neural networks. One fundamental way of distinguishing between various types of neural networks is by the method used to train the network. The learning methods are categorized as supervised or unsupervised learning schemes.

Unsupervised learning comprises those techniques for which the resulting actions or desired outputs for the training sequences are not known. These techniques thus attempt to derive or determine the underlying strategy or features of the data through various methods, such as clustering. Hence, in unsupervised learning, the network is only told the input vectors, and the network itself clusters these inputs into categories (Jabri 1988). Therefore, no target vector exists in unsupervised learning. The input vector is applied to the network and the system *self-organizes* so that a consistent output (possibly unpredictable before training) is produced whenever that input vector is applied. These methods were inspired by the fact that the biological brain contains various topographically ordered *maps*, such that different neural cells respond optimally to different signal qualities (Kohonen 1989). Learning without a teacher implies that the input to a node has certain properties such as inbuilt structure and/or statistical distributions. Unsupervised learning uses competitive learning in that it relies on the notion of a winner among a collection of neurons. Examples of such systems have been highly developed by Kohonen and Grossberg.

Supervised, as opposed to unsupervised, learning techniques require that, given a particular set of initial conditions, the resulting action or desired output be known in the training set. Thus the training set used to train these networks is composed of examples of initial inputs and the resulting conditions or desired outputs. Therefore, in supervised learning, a training pair consists of an input vector and a desired target output vector. The input vector is applied to the network, which then produces an output vector. The difference between the output produced by the network and the target output constitutes the error. This error is used to modify network weights in a manner that reduces the error in subsequent training cycles. Some have argued that supervised learning is not biologically plausible as no teacher resides in a biological system to direct training or to compare responses against desired outcomes (Ackley 1989). Nevertheless, many supervised learning algorithms have produced excellent results in the computer science area and seem to be promising avenues for solutions to practical problems (Wasserman & Schwartz 1988).

In this chapter, only the following supervised learning methods are considered (as they are used in Chapters 7 to 9):

- single-layered neural networks, which have only input and output units;
- multi-layered neural networks, where the first layer is the input to the network, the last layer is the output of the network, and one or more intermediate layers represent inner abstractions used to process information.

Chapter 11 describes a Kohonen network that uses unsupervised learning.

At this point, it is important to define the term *example*. Every example in the training set used to train a supervised neural network is denoted by two n-tuples or vectors, comprising the inputs of the example and the desired target output, respectively. Hence, if a domain comprises m inputs denoted by $(x_1, x_2, ..., x_m)$ and n targets denoted by $(t_1, t_2, ..., t_n)$ then:

- the input attribute vector of example k is denoted by:

$$X_k = (x_1, x_2, ..., x_m)$$

- the target output vector of example k is denoted by:

$$T_k = (t_1, t_2, ..., t_n).$$

Corresponding to this example, the network produces an output vector O_k for the input vector X_k:

$$O_k = g(X_k)$$

where g is not explicitly defined, but implicitly defined in the weights and links of the neural network.

4.6 Activation functions

Before discussing the various learning rules, it is important to note that the activation of a unit in a particular network is dependent upon the activation function or transfer function associated with a particular model. To use these transfer or activation functions, the net input to a unit must first be calculated. The net input to a unit is defined by the sum of the values or activations of the input units times the corresponding weights, plus an optional bias term associated with the unit; that is (McClelland & Rumelhart 1988):

$$net_j = \sum_i W_{ij} X_i + bias_j$$

where net_j is the net input to unit j,

W_{ij} is the weight of the link from unit i to unit j,
X_i is the input value of unit i, and
$bias_j$ is the bias term associated with unit j.

The activation of the output unit is then determined using this net input according to the activation function. The output is given by:

$$O_j = f(net_j).$$

Several variants of the f activation function are possible (McClelland & Rumelhart 1988):

- *linear:* the activation of the output unit j is its net input

$$O_j = net_j$$

- *linear threshold:* the activation of the output unit j is set to 1 if its net input exceeds 0 and is set to 0 otherwise

$$O_j = \begin{cases} 1 \text{ if } net_j > 0 \\ 0 \text{ otherwise} \end{cases}$$

- *stochastic:* the activation is set to 1, with a probability p given by the function

$$p(O_j=1) = \frac{1}{1 + e^{-netj/T}}$$

- *continuous sigmoid:* the activation of the output unit j is related to its input according to the non-linear function

$$O_j = \frac{1}{1 + e^{-netj/T}}$$

This is a continuous function, mapping the net inputs that range between + and – infinity to real numbers between 0 and 1. Here, T is a parameter used to define the slope of the sigmoid function in the non-saturated region. When used in a simulated annealing model, it is interpreted as the temperature.

The various methods for teaching supervised neural networks are outlined next. For single-layered networks, Hebb's Rule and the Delta Rule are described, while for multi-layered networks, Back-propagation is discussed.

4.7 Single-layered neural networks

4.7.1   General aspects

These simple neural networks consist of a set of input units connected to a set

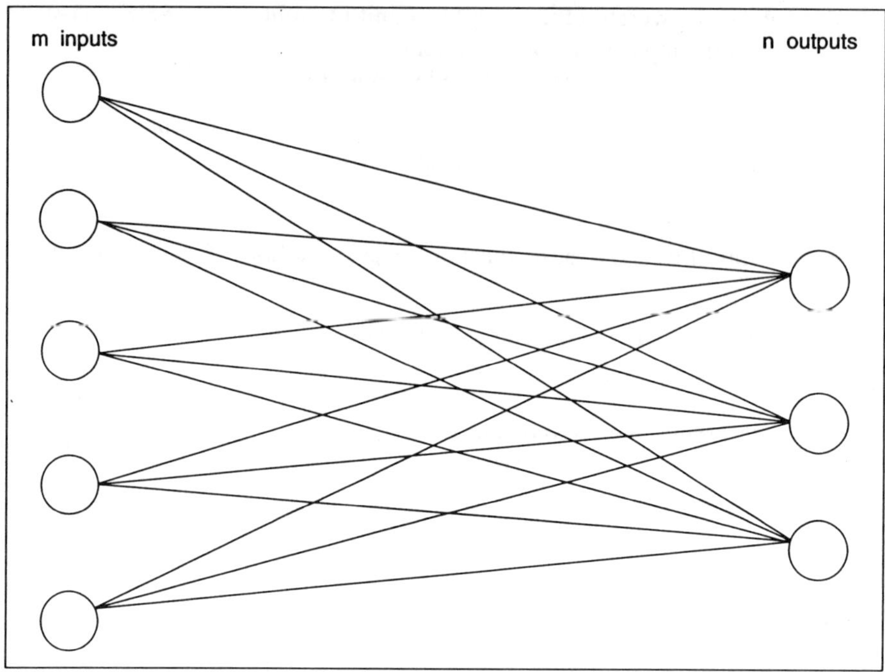

Figure 4.2   Single-layered neural network with m inputs and n outputs

of output units by a single layer of weighted links, as shown in Figure 4.2. Two classical learning rules, namely, Hebb's Rule (McClelland & Rumelhart 1988; McClelland et al. 1986b) and the Delta Rule (Jones & Hoskins 1987; McClelland & Rumelhart 1988), have been widely used for training these networks.

4.7.2 Hebb's Rule

The basic premise behind Hebb's Rule is that when two cells fire at the same time, the strength of the connection between them should be increased. A simple mathematical formulation for this increase in a supervised learning environment is:

$$\Delta W_{ij} = \varepsilon \, X_i \, T_j$$

where W_{ij} is the weight of the link between input i and output j,
X_i is the input value (or activation),
T_j is the output of unit j in the learning sequence, and
ε is the learning rate parameter.

Assuming initial weights are zero and exposing the network to a sequence of learning events indexed by p, the value of any weight at the end of a series of learning events is (McClelland & Rumelhart 1988):

$$W_{ij} = \varepsilon \sum_p X_{pi} T_{pj}.$$

Thus, the W_{ij} calculated will be proportional to the correlation between the inputs and the targets.

This type of network consists of linear units only. Hence the activation of an output produced by the network is equal to the net input; that is, the activation of an output is simply the weighted sum of the total inputs into a unit plus the bias term. Assuming bias = 0, the activation of an output unit is given by:

$$O_j = \sum_i X_i W_{ij}.$$

The correlation property of Hebb's learning rule can be an advantage because these correlations sometimes produce useful associative learning (McClelland & Rumelhart 1988). This means that units correlated together in the past will excite each other. However, this correlation property can also be a disadvantage as simple correlation between units is not sufficient for a network to learn complex associations.

This type of learning is essentially limited to sifting linear statistical associations from background noise. If the input is unpatterned (random sequences of random combinations of features), there is nothing to be learned. To learn useful behavior, some input information must reflect systematic pattern association. The Hebbian model also has a number of stability and saturation problems (McClelland & Rumelhart 1988).

The normalized dot product of two patterns composed of +1's and −1's only provides a measure of the correlation between the patterns. The value of the normalized dot product is (McClelland & Rumelhart 1988):

- *1, if the two patterns are identical*
- *−1, if the two patterns are exactly opposite*
- *0, if the elements of one vector (i.e. pattern) are completely uncorrelated with the elements of the other.*

Thus, the similarity of the patterns is crucial for the performance of the network. Cases where the normalized dot product is zero should be further considered. The patterns with this property are orthogonal or uncorrelated, which is not the same as being opposite or anticorrelated. These patterns cannot be learned with this learning rule as it relies on correlations. This orthogonality limitation is a major problem with Hebb's Rule.

Linear dependence and linear independence should be introduced here. These notions refer to whether a pattern can be written as a linear combination of another pattern.

- If there is at least one pattern that can be written as a linear combination of another pattern in the set, then the entire set is referred to as a linearly dependent set.
- Alternatively, if no patterns (or vectors) can be written as a linear combination of another pattern, then the set is known as a linearly independent set.

To ensure that arbitrary associations of a set of input patterns can be learned, the input patterns must form a linearly independent set (McClelland & Rumelhart 1988). This is another major limitation of Hebb's Rule.

Owing to these limitations, a learning rule is required that finds connection strengths that are not simply proportional to the correlations of the activations of the units. The Delta Rule, discussed in the next section, is one possible solution.

4.7.3 The Delta Rule

The Delta Rule is a simple learning rule used to train a network with only a single layer of connections joining input units to output units. This learning rule has the ability to form and modify its own weights, reflecting the strengths of the connections between the nodes. The Delta Rule is normally used with a sigmoid activation function but it can be used with other activation functions.

This rule uses the difference between the desired or target activation, and the obtained activation to guide the learning. The basic strategy underlying the rule is to adjust the strengths of the connections to reduce this difference or error measure progressively (McClelland & Rumelhart 1988). Before training begins, connections between all input nodes and each of the output nodes are formed, with each connection being given a small, random, initial weight.

Learning is carried out by iteratively cycling through the training pairs. This continues until an acceptably low level of error is achieved. The network is activated with a given pattern p from a training pair and produces an output O_p. The error is obtained by subtracting O_p from the corresponding target pattern T_p of the same training pair. This gives the discrepancy between the actual and the desired behavior of the network. The Delta Rule seeks to minimize the weighted mean square error of these deviations; that is, it minimizes the following error function (McClelland & Rumelhart 1988):

$$E = \sum_p E_p = \tfrac{1}{2} \sum_p \sum_j (T_{pj} - O_{pj})^2$$

where j refers to the outputs and takes values 1 to n. It carries out this minimization by using steepest (i.e., gradient) descent. Mathematically, the change in W_{ij} is given by:

$$\Delta W_{ij} = -\varepsilon \frac{\partial E}{\partial W_{ij}}$$

where ε represents the learning rate. Assuming a linear activation function, it can readily be shown that this gives:

$$\Delta W_{ij} = \varepsilon X_i E_j$$

where

$$E_j = T_j - O_j.$$

Thus, the change in the weight W_{ij} of the connection between input unit i and output unit j is a function of the activation of the input unit X_i and the delta or error $(T_j - O_j)$ associated with the jth output unit (Jones & Hoskins 1987; McClelland & Rumelhart 1988).

In summary, training with the Delta Rule uses the following method. For each pattern, the units are turned on and their effect on each output unit is observed. The resulting activation reflects the current connections in the network. The difference between the obtained output and the training target (i.e., $T_j - O_j$) is then determined. Hence the strengths of the connections can be adjusted according to the equation for ΔW_{ij}. This method is repeated as the procedure cycles through the training inputs several times, with the resulting strengths of the connections calculated after each cycle. The output obtained for a certain output unit is given by summing up the pairwise products of the inputs on the current trial with the weights obtained at the end of the preceding trial.

The correct set of weights is approached if the training procedure is continued for several iterations. Each iteration, or training epoch, results in a set of weights that is closer to the required solution. The measure of closeness to the required solution is given by the value of E, as defined above. The resulting error measure reduces over epochs, as does each change in the strengths of the connections. Thus the value of E indicates the *correctness* of the trained network.

The Delta Rule essentially assigns credit (or blame) to the input units according to their activation levels. The more active an input unit, the more responsible it is for the current distribution of activation among the output units (Jones & Hoskins 1987). This error-correcting learning rule, then, is much more powerful than Hebb's Rule. Also, the Delta Rule overcomes the orthogonality limitation of Hebb's Rule because all patterns have an effect on the training (McClelland & Rumelhart 1988).

The Delta Rule is effective for calculating a set of weights where the relationship between the inputs and outputs is linear. Therefore, this rule will determine a set of weights for a single-layered neural network. However, the version of the Delta Rule applied to a single-layered neural network cannot be used with data where the relationship between the inputs and outputs is either non-linear and continuous, or discontinuous. This has led to the development of more advanced neural networks capable of modeling complex domains effectively. Methods for dealing with these types of multi-layered neural networks are presented in the next section.

4.8 Multi-layered neural networks

4.8.1 General aspects

Multi-layered neural networks consist of an input layer, an output layer, and one or more intermediate layers containing hidden units (units that have no direct contact with the outside world). A multi-layered network with one hidden layer is shown in Figure 4.3.

Hidden units can represent abstractions that cannot be directly encoded from the environment via input nodes; that is, interesting internal representations not part of the input or the output can be modeled through the hidden units (Hinton & McClelland 1988). By only having one set of input units and one set of output units, it is possible to represent what is already in the data and nothing more. So, if the data is discontinuous or non-linear, the innate representation is inconsistent and the mapping required cannot be learned. Adding the third layer to the network allows it to develop its own internal representation of the mapping (Caudill 1988b). It has been shown that a three-layered neural network (i.e., with one hidden layer) can approximate any non-linear continuous transformation (Funahashi 1989; Hornik et al. 1989). The addition of a fourth layer permits the approximation of discontinuous transformations (Sontag 1990). Multi-layered neural networks have other advantages: they make it easier to find the correlations between a large number of variables, and they are efficient for modeling non-linear domains (Atlas et al. 1990).

One of the problems with multi-layered networks is that the architecture chosen for a particular problem is fairly arbitrary. In other words, the number of hidden units and hidden layers chosen is presently ad hoc. There are two extremes when selecting the number of hidden units: one using very few hidden units and the other using a large number of them.

There are several reasons for wanting to use as few hidden units as possible (Kruschke 1988):

- Networks with fewer free parameters are less likely to overfit data and are therefore better able to generalize.

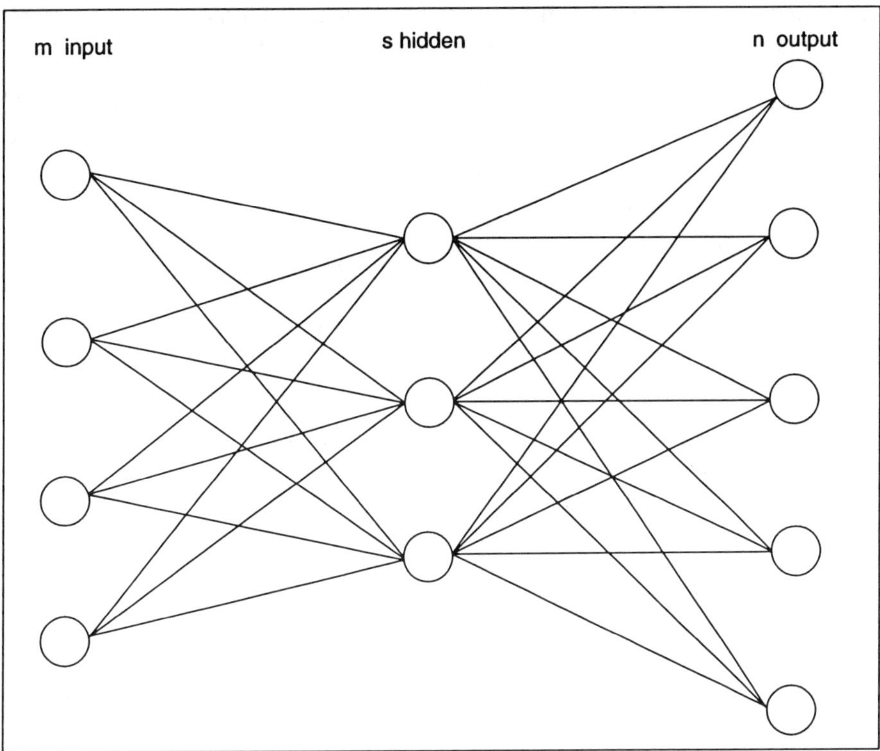

Figure 4.3   A multi-layered neural network consisting of m inputs, n outputs, and s hidden units

- Meaning is more easily assigned with fewer hidden units.

However, there are also reasons for wanting to use a large number of hidden units:

- Local minima are less prevalent with a larger number of hidden units (Rumelhart et al. 1986c).
- Learning time varies inversely with the number of hidden units (Plaut & Hinton 1987).
- Kruschke (1988) reports Smolensky as stating that the use of too few units may allow interpretation of these as atomic representations. It can then be argued that this is not connectionism but symbolic processing.

Further studies might yield enough results to permit some rule of thumb for determining the number of hidden units, dependent on the properties of the domain to be modeled (Morgan & Bourlard 1990; Sietsma & Dow 1988).

In summary, multi-layered networks have difficulty allocating resources;

that is, determining the optimal number of hidden units for a particular problem. If too many units are used, it is not only wasteful, but also could negatively affect the performance of the network. Too many hidden units implies too many free parameters to fit the training data. Their ability to generalize to novel test patterns could be adversely affected. On the other hand, if too few hidden units are allocated, then the network would not even have the power to represent the training set (Sun et al. 1988).

Back-propagation is the most widely used technique to train multi-layered neural networks (Caudill 1988b; McClelland & Rumelhart 1988; Rumelhart et al. 1986c). This method is discussed in the following section. Improvements to the basic Back-propagation method and new learning rules are discussed later.

4.8.2   The Back-propagation Rule

The development of a powerful generalization of the Delta Rule that can arrive at a set of connections between the input, output, and hidden units in a multi-layered system has had a large impact in this field. To some extent it explains the renewed interest in neural networks. This generalized rule is the Back-propagation Rule.

Back-propagation, like the basic Delta Rule, finds the values of all of the weights that minimize the function using a method of gradient descent. After each pattern has been presented, the error on the pattern is computed and each weight is moved down the error gradient toward its minimum value for that pattern (McClelland & Rumelhart 1988). The total error is defined by:

$$E = \sum_{p} E_p = \tfrac{1}{2} \sum_{p} \sum_{j} T_{pj} - O_{pj})^2$$

where T_p is the target vector and O_p is the output vector for the pth pattern, and j refers to the specific outputs.

Gradient descent essentially makes a change in the weight proportional to the negative of the derivative of the error in the current pattern with respect to each weight, as shown in Figure 4.4. Thus, the weight from unit i to unit j is changed by computing the derivative of the error function with respect to W_{ij} and applying the following rule, after presentation of pattern p:

$$\Delta W_{ij} = -\varepsilon \frac{\partial E_p}{\partial W_{ij}}$$

where ε is the constant of proportionality and E is the error function. The constant of proportionality, also referred to as the learning rate, is an important parameter in the application of this method. A small learning rate is frequently

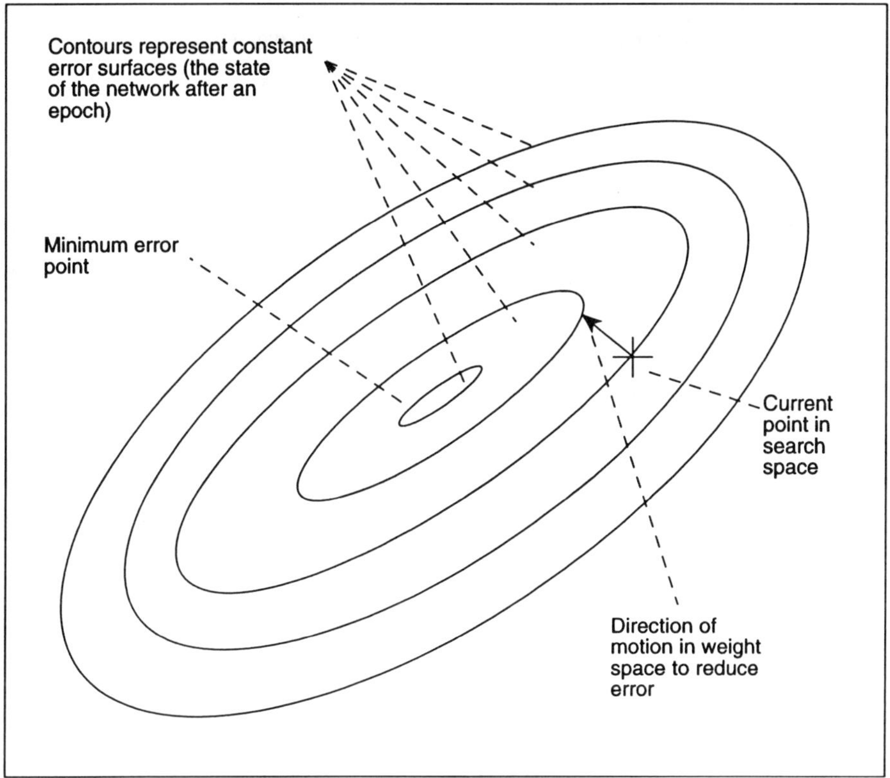

Figure 4.4   Illustration of steepest gradient descent

used in gradient descent procedures. Larger values can give an initial faster convergence, but oscillation about the minimum can result (Rumelhart et al. 1986c).

Since multi-layered neural networks are being discussed in this section, the change in weights ΔW_{ij} must be calculated separately for each layer. Therefore, consider a three-layered network with m inputs, n outputs, and s hidden units, as shown in Figure 4.3. Let the weighted links between the input and hidden layers be represented in the weight matrix U and the weighted links between the hidden and output layers be represented in the weight matrix V, as shown in Figure 4.5. Figure 4.6 shows the basic notation used in the following discussion. It highlights that for each unit in the network, except for the input units, a weighted sum of the inputs into the unit is determined. This value is then used in a transfer or activation function to calculate the activation or output of the unit.

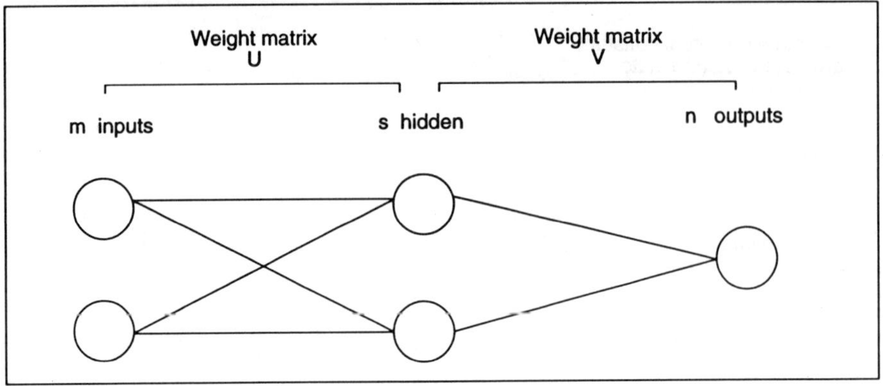

Figure 4.5   Two weight matrices representing the different links in a multi-layered network

Letting i, h, and o represent the input, hidden and output units, respectively, it follows that:

$$\Delta V_{ho} = - \varepsilon \, \frac{\partial E}{\partial V_{ho}}$$

for the hidden to output layer represented in weight matrix V, and

$$\Delta U_{ih} = - \varepsilon \, \frac{\partial E_p}{\partial U_{ih}}$$

for the input to hidden layer represented in weight matrix U. The following Back-propagation rules can be derived for each pattern p:

$$\Delta V_{ho} = \varepsilon \, \delta_{po} \, O_{ph}$$

for hidden to output layer weight changes, and

$$\Delta U_{ih} = \varepsilon \, \delta_{ph} \, X_{pi}$$

for input to hidden layer weight changes. These equations state that the weights for each layer should be changed by an amount proportional to the product of a δ term (available to the unit receiving the input), and the activation (of the unit sending the activation) (McClelland & Rumelhart 1988).

The calculation of the δ terms is a recursive process that starts with the output units. For an output unit, δ is given by:

$$\delta_{po} = (T_{po} - O_{po}) \, f_o'(net_{po})$$

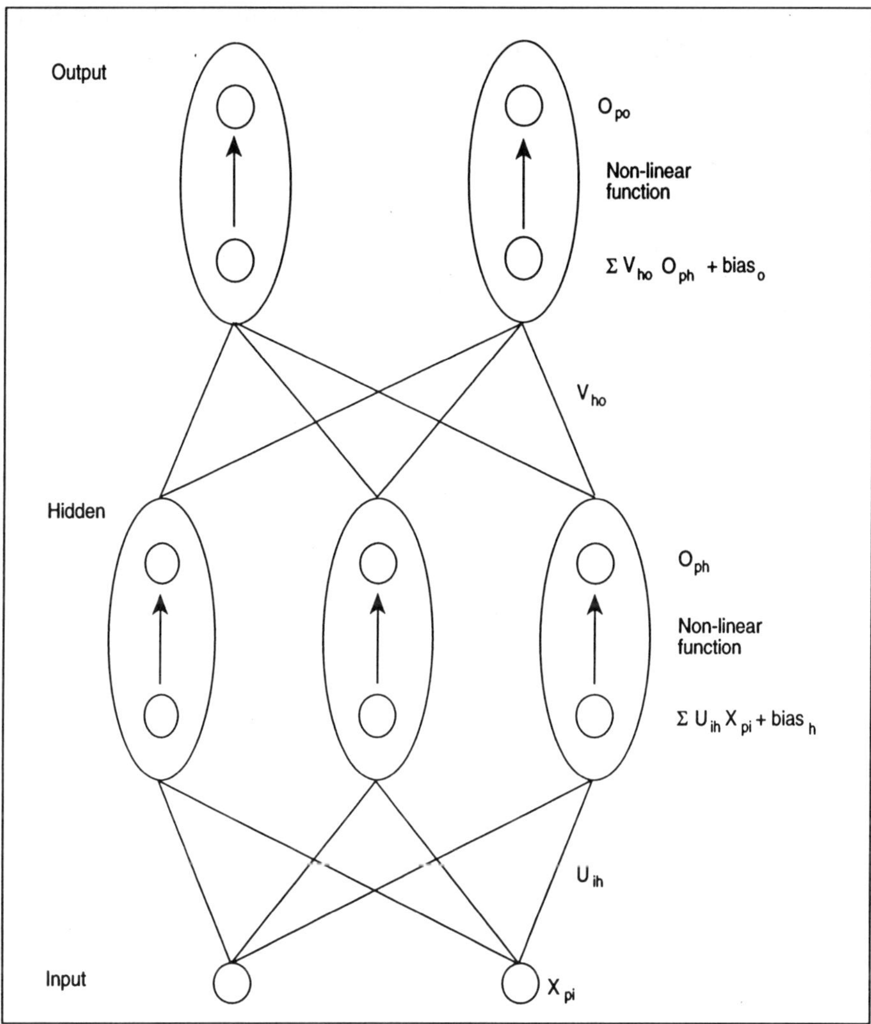

Figure 4.6   Basic terms and flow of information and activation for Back-propagation for pattern p

where T_{po} is the target output,

O_{po} is the output activation of the network,

net_{po} is the net input of unit o, given by:

$$net_{po} = \sum_h V_{ho}\, O_{ph} + bias_o, \text{ and}$$

$f_o{}'(net_{po})$ is the derivative of the activation function with respect to the change in the net input to the unit.

The power of the Back-propagation Rule comes from its assignment of deltas to hidden units. These units receive no direct feedback from training patterns in the outside world. These deltas are then used to carry out alterations to the weights from the input units to the hidden units, in the case of a network with one hidden layer. The delta term for hidden units, for which there is no specified target, is determined recursively as a function of the delta terms of the units to which it directly connects and the weights of those connections (Jones & Hoskins 1987; McClelland & Rumelhart 1988). It is given by:

$$\delta_{ph} = f_h{}'(net_{ph}) \sum_o \delta_{po} V_{ho}$$

The basis of the computation of deltas for the hidden units is to propagate, back through the network, errors that are based on the observed differences between the values of the output units and a target training pattern. This is accomplished by first computing the deltas for the output units. These are then propagated backward to all units in the layer below that point to the output units. These units, in turn, propagate their received deltas backward to units that point to them, and so on, until the input level is reached. Hence the deltas drive the network's weight changes (Jones & Hoskins 1987).

The Back-propagation learning rules require that the derivative of the activation function $f_i{}'(net_i)$ exist. Thus, this activation function should be a continuous non-linear function. The following activation function is most commonly used with Back-propagation (McClelland & Rumelhart 1988):

$$O_{pg} = \frac{1}{1 + e^{-net_{pg}}}$$

for unit g. To apply the learning rule, the derivative of this function with respect to its total input net_{pg} must exist and is given by:

$$\frac{\partial O_{pg}}{\partial net_{pg}} = O_{pg}\,(1 - O_{pg})$$

In summary, for the hidden to output layer, weight matrix V is changed according to:

$$\Delta V_{ho} = \varepsilon\, \delta_{po}\, O_{ph}$$

where

$$\delta_{po} = (T_{po} - O_{po})\, O_{po}\, (1 - O_{po})$$

For the input to hidden layer, weight matrix U is changed according to:

$$\Delta U_{ih} = \varepsilon\, \delta_{ph}\, X_{pi}$$

where

$$\delta_{ph} = O_{ph}\,(1 - O_{ph})\, \sum_{o} \delta_{po}\, V_{ho}$$

The application of the Back-propagation Rule involves two phases, as shown in Figure 4.7. First, the input is presented to the network. This input is propagated forward through the network to compute the output value O_{po} for each output unit. This output is then compared with the target, T_{po}, to calculate the delta terms for each output unit. The second phase involves a backward pass through the network. During this phase, the delta terms, δ_{ph}, are calculated for each hidden unit, using the deltas, δ_{po}, for the output units, as indicated previously. Thus, for each weight, the product of a delta term δ associated with the unit to which it projects, and the activation of the unit from which it projects, can be calculated (McClelland & Rumelhart 1988; Rumelhart et al. 1986c).

An important aspect of gradient descent learning is that it makes larger changes to the parameters with the biggest effect on the measure being minimized. In the case of Back-propagation and the Delta Rule procedures, the changes to the weights are proportional to the effect the weights have on the summed square error, E. With gradient descent, the weight change vector points in the *locally* steepest error drop.

In multi-layer networks there is a possibility of complex surfaces with many local minima, as shown in Figure 4.8. In these cases, a gradient descent method may have difficulty finding the best solution to a particular problem.

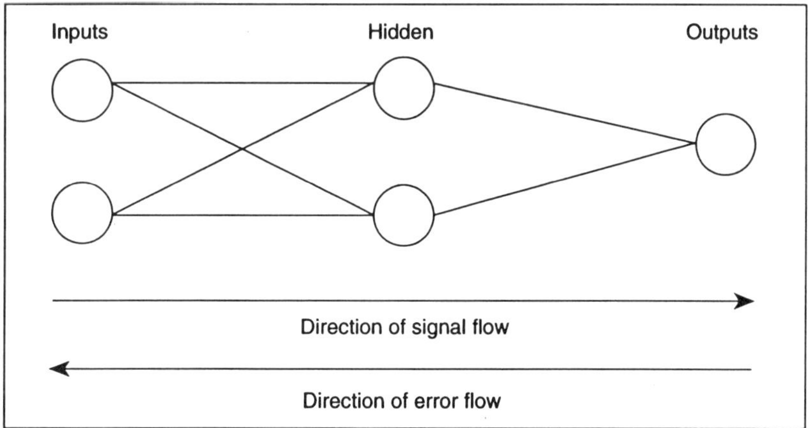

Figure 4.7   Flow of information during Back-propagation

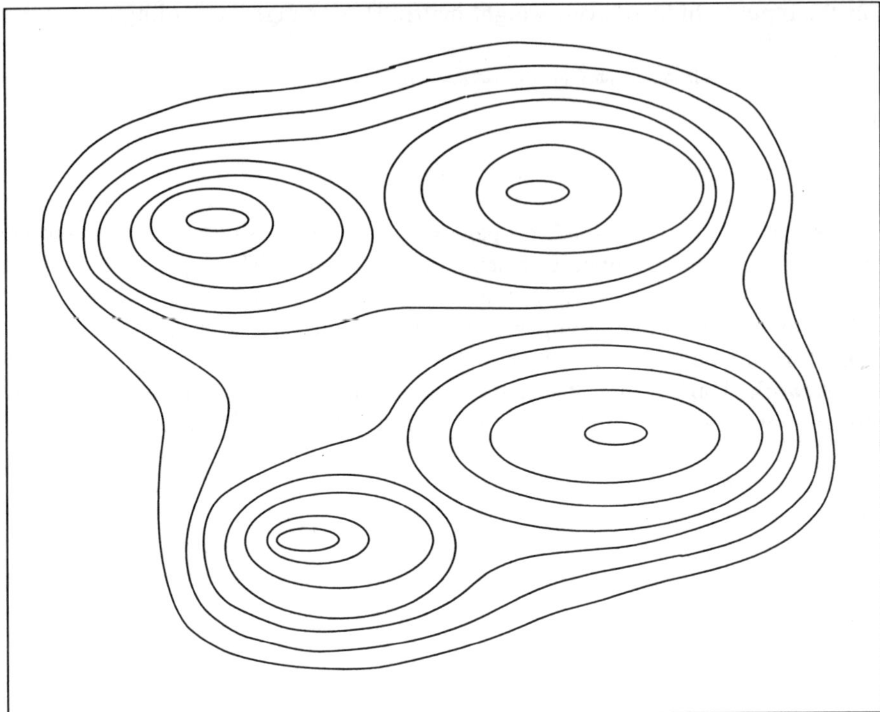

Figure 4.8   A complex surface with several local minima

For such problems, gradient descent can get stuck at local minima that are not globally optimal. Local minima seem less frequent in problems with many hidden units. At the other extreme, local minima can be more common with too few hidden units (McClelland and Rumelhart 1988).

Neural network implementations involving the Back-propagation Rule are demanding on computational resources. One suggestion to overcome the slow convergence problem is to use a completely different machine architecture that supports massively parallel computation (Jones & Hoskins 1987).

Another simple way to increase the convergence rate is to increase the learning rate, but this leads to oscillation around the minimum. An alternative method is to modify the Back-propagation learning rule to include a *momentum term*. This can be accomplished for weight matrix W by the following rule (McClelland & Rumelhart 1988):

$$\Delta W_{ij}(n+1) = \varepsilon\,(\delta_{pj}\,O_{pi}) + \alpha\,\Delta W_{ij}(n)$$

where the n parameter indicates the example number and α is the momentum constant. This α momentum constant determines the proportion of the past weight change that should be used in the calculation of the current direction of movement. The momentum constant is assigned values between 0 and 1. The effect of the addition of a momentum term to the Back-propagation steepest descent rule is illustrated in Figure 4.9. This momentum term has the effect of filtering out high-frequency variations of the local error surface in the weight space (McClelland & Rumelhart 1988). For the first step, no ΔW_{ij} previously exists. Hence, the first step is a pure steepest descent step, as shown in Figure 4.9.

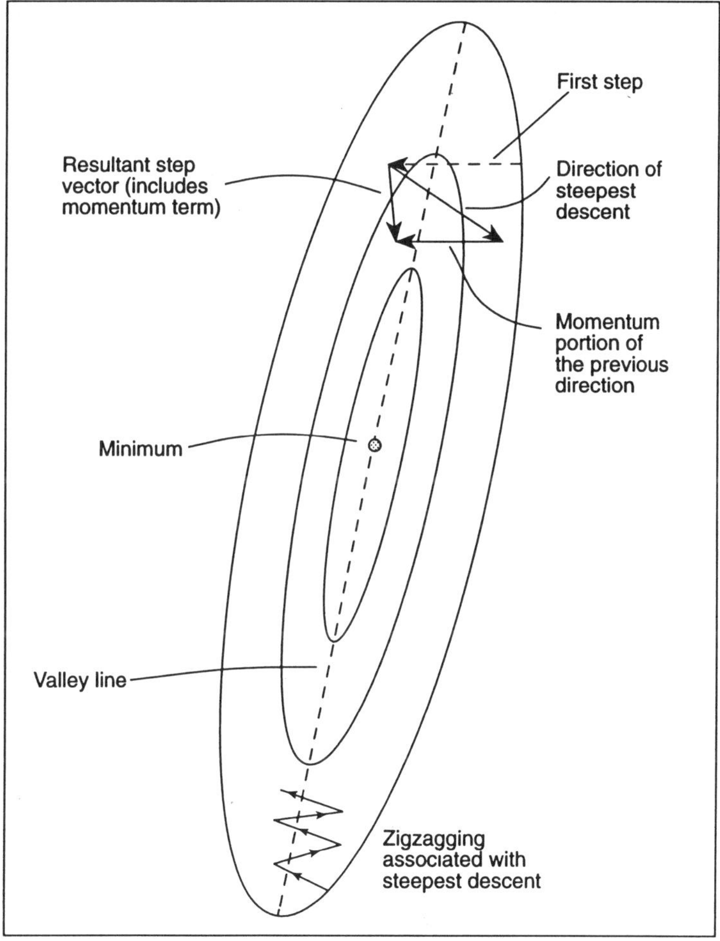

Figure 4.9 The steepest descent path and the effect of an added momentum term on the steepest descent

4.8.3 Problems with Back-propagation

There are several problems with Back-propagation. The algorithm does not scale well to large systems, is slow to converge to a solution, gets stuck in local minima, and is not neurally plausible.

First, consider the scaling problem (Montana & Davis 1989; Roth 1989). Back-propagation works well on simple training problems. However, as the problem complexity increases (owing to increased dimensionality and/or greater complexity of the data), the performance of Back-propagation degrades rapidly. Since the network represents a parallel or co-operative process, each added unit interacts with every other unit. This becomes a serious problem when the size of the network becomes large (Sun et al. 1988), making Back-propagation not feasible for many real-world domains.

The use of the steepest descent procedure is extremely slow in simulations and thus training is extremely slow (Hinton 1989; Wasserman & Schwartz 1988). The path taken by steepest descent to reach a solution can zigzag so much that the path does not move significantly toward the solution, particularly in the presence of valleys in the error surface. This is one of the major drawbacks of Back-propagation but, as can be seen in section 4.9, much work is proceeding to improve the training. One proposed solution uses *conjugate gradient methods* instead of steepest descent. These methods are an improvement over steepest descent because not only is the immediate gradient considered, but also the surrounding curvature.

Back-propagation learning can be viewed as a non-linear optimization problem where the cost function being minimized is an error function. With supervised learning, this function represents the difference between the target and output vectors. Local minima plague a simple gradient descent search in all but the simplest cases. If a local valley is found, the algorithm cannot escape even though there may be a much lower valley just over the next hill. Researchers have used simulated annealing to solve such problems (Wasserman & Schwartz 1988). Thus the performance degradation of Back-propagation appears to stem from the fact that complex spaces have nearly global minima that are sparse among the local minima, and gradient search techniques tend to get trapped at local minima. With a high enough gain (or momentum), Back-propagation can normally escape the local minima (Montana & Davis 1989).

Finally, the Back-propagation method is considered to be neurally implausible (Hinton 1989; Wasserman & Schwartz 1988). Also, it is hard to implement in hardware because it requires the flow of errors to be backward, and the units to use different input-output functions for the forward and backward passes (Hinton & McClelland 1988). However, Back-propagation is a computer-based algorithm that has had some success in modeling some real-world domains (McClelland & Rumelhart 1988; Rumelhart et al. 1986c), and this is the only aspect of importance in this book, since its purpose is not to model biological phenomena.

4.8.4 Comparisons with ID3

Mooney et al. (1989) compare ID3, the Perceptron, or Delta Rule, and Back-propagation and their results show that the Perceptron learning algorithm, with regard to its accuracy and run-time, is comparable to ID3. Although Back-propagation generally takes one to two orders of magnitude more time to train than the other two algorithms, its accuracy on novel examples is always equal or superior to the others. Back-propagation does perform better when dealing with noisy data. This work indicates the need to speed up the training of Back-propagation by exploiting its intrinsic parallelism. There is also a problem of human comprehension: symbolic approaches produce easy to understand rep-resentations, while networks of weights are hard to interpret. Of course, large decision trees, which may be produced by ID3, are also difficult to comprehend. These issues of human comprehension are discussed further in Chapter 6.

Fisher and McKusick (1989) compare ID3 and Back-propagation on the basis of both prediction accuracy and length of training. Back-propagation attains a slightly higher accuracy, but not significantly so. However, Back-propagation requires many more training presentations and so training for it requires up to several orders of magnitude more time. Regardless of the noise level or domain complexity, Back-propagation always achieves a greater accuracy than ID3, but significantly more observations are required. Another difference is the shape of the learning curve. ID3 quickly achieves high levels of accuracy and then gradually converges on its asymptotic value. In contrast, the slope of the learning curve for Back-propagation is more gradual and uniform.

Other related issues are raised by Fisher and McKusick (1989):

- *One weakness of ID3 is that it is monothetic; learning considers the utility of a single attribute at a time. On the other hand, Back-propagation is polythetic; the values of multiple attributes are simultaneously considered in summations.*
- *ID3 assumes that all observations are available for processing at the same time, while Back-propagation processes observations as they become available.*
- *A more overt distinction is the manner in which the two paradigms explore their respective search spaces. AI systems typically reconstruct the space upon demand, as it is only defined implicitly by operators and an initial state. In contrast, most connectionist systems pre-enumerate a subset of the space, which is implicit in the number and interconnections between the nodes. Problems arise if too much space (slow convergence) or too little space (the concepts cannot be learned) is pre-enumerated.*

4.9   Improvements to Back-propagation and modifications to architecture

Several researchers are attempting to improve the efficiency of Back-propagation. Ho (1989) has explored the computational potential and limitations of the multi-layered connectionist model, concluding that increasing width (i.e., the maximum number of neurons in one layer) is better than adding layers.

Sietsma and Dow (1988) provide a method that prunes a neural network to improve efficiency. Here it was found that noise resistance improves when useless or repetitive units are removed, and using distorted or noisy signals in the training set improves the performance of the network considerably. LeCun et al. (1990) also conclude that removing unimportant weights from a network gives better generalization. Improved speed of learning and/or classification can be expected and fewer training examples are required. This resulted from using second derivative information to make a trade-off between the network complexity and training set error.

Becker and LeCun (1988) explored the application of Newton's Method and other optimization methods to improve the convergence of Back-propagation. The use of steepest descent procedure is extremely slow in simulations. Several other techniques, such as the conjugate gradient procedure and second order Newton methods, can overcome this slow convergence. The accuracy of the approximation is controlled by the number of units per layer, and not the number of layers (Lapedes & Farber 1988).

Recurrent Back-propagation has been proposed by Simard et al. (1988) through the addition of feedback connections into the previously considered feed-forward networks. These nets have the following advantages (Simard et al. 1988):

- The network is more neurally plausible.
- There is reduced sensitivity to noise and synchronization problems.
- They may learn faster.
- They have a better ability to restore incomplete or corrupted patterns.

Some problems with these nets include an increased tendency to converge to local minima, and performance deteriorates with complex tasks.

An interesting new connectionist learning mechanism for the generation of a network was proposed by Honavar and Uhr (1988, 1989). The mechanism enables the network to modify its own topology by growing links and recruiting links as required. The network grows new links as needed, under guidance from feedback, aided by network structures enabling it to monitor its own performance over time. Recent anatomical and physiological studies (Honavar & Uhr 1989) suggest that learning may involve alteration of the number and the pattern of synaptic interconnections in the brain, in addition to changes in the synaptic weights. Hence, in multi-layered connectionist networks, a combination of generation (a mechanism involving the growing or recruiting of new links and nodes) and reweighting by Back-propagation of the error, appears to yield more powerful learning than reweighting alone (Honavar & Uhr 1988).

Fahlman (1988) proposed Quickprop, alleged to be considerably faster than the standard Back-propagation method. It is also claimed that the program appears to scale up very well as the problem size increases. Instead of performing simple gradient descent, Quickprop uses successive values of the gradient of the error surface in weight space to estimate the location of a minimum (Lang & Witbrock 1988). It then changes the weights to move directly toward this minimum. The two principal assumptions of the algorithm are that the error surface is concave, and the surface is locally quadratic. Recent results indicate that this algorithm is faster than standard Back-propagation (Lang & Witbrock 1988).

Cascade-Correlation, a more recent algorithm also developed primarily by Fahlman and Lebiere (1990), is claimed to be the fastest learning algorithm for supervised neural networks. Instead of adjusting the weights in a network of fixed topology, Cascade-Correlation begins with a minimum network and then automatically trains and adds new hidden units one by one, creating a multi-layer structure. Once a new hidden unit has been added to the network, its input-side weights are frozen. This unit then becomes a permanent feature detector in the network, available for producing outputs or for creating other more complex feature detectors. Cascade-Correlation has several advantages over other existing algorithms: it learns very quickly, the network determines its own size and topology, it retains the structures it has built even if the training set changes, and it requires no back-propagation of error signals through the connections of the network.

Finally, Jacobs (1988) stated that existing connectionist learning techniques will prove impractical when applied to real-world problems. Hence he proposed to incorporate domain knowledge into the connectionist system. Jacobs concluded that the best method of solving real-world problems is to group together a collection of connectionist systems into a large control system. A hierarchical organization provides the proper framework for co-ordinating the communication between the networks. The advantage of this collective approach is that each individual network is never faced with the task of solving a large problem in its entirety.

4.10 General problems with neural networks

General problems that have arisen with using multi-layered neural network formalism include:

- the modeling, so far, of stationary data only
- the ad hoc choice of the number of training examples
- the opaqueness of initial attributes.

In the work done to date, there has been no attempt to deal with non-stationary data. With this type of data, past trends do not necessarily reflect the current or future trends of the data. Dillon et al. (1975) allude to the problem of predicting power system loads using neural networks. They solved the problem by first removing the trend component by exponential smoothing, and then predicting the residual using a neural network. The total load was then determined by adding the predicted residual to the trend component. However, this approach merely acknowledges the weakness in neural networks for dealing with this problem, and removes it from the task that the neural network is supposed to solve. A more recent solution, proposed by Dillon et al. (1991) and Peng et al. (1990), uses an Adaptive Neural Network to forecast short-term load in a power system. The Adaptive Neural Network approach is also detailed by Park et al. (1991).

Associated with this trend-detecting problem is the choice made for the size of the learning sequence; that is, the number of examples to be used for training. The learning stage of the network is normally only carried out once for any problem or system. Thus, the number of events or examples initially considered can be critical since they determine the initial strengths of the connections, and it is through the changing strengths of these connections that a network learns from experience. If the size of the learning sequence is too small, the complete model of the system would not be developed after training. In this case, the network would waste time and resources in producing a complete model that would have been developed sooner if the learning sequence were larger. On the other hand, if the size of the learning sequence is too large, then the network may contain behavior no longer present in the actual system, in the event that the system is non-stationary. A method to determine the optimal size of the learning sequence is thus needed.

Finally, a major concern with neural networks is their complexity (Niida et al. 1989). They are seen as black boxes where meaningful relationships between the inputs and the outputs cannot be easily obtained (Niida et al. 1989; Towell & Shavlik 1992). Many people cannot accept this *black box* point of view, where all that matters is that the machine works, regardless of why it works (Patarnello & Carnevali 1989). The knowledge that the network acquires is encoded in its numerical weights. As highlighted by many researchers (Carbonell 1989; Fahlman & Hinton 1987; Fozzard et al. 1989; Goodman et al. 1989; Mozer 1987; Saito & Nakano 1990; Touretzky & Pomerleau 1989), it is not easy to decipher the network's solution to a problem when all one has is a set of floating-point numbers. Consequently, connectionist systems have very little power of explanation (Mozer 1987). To gain acceptability of the network as a realistic model, it is necessary to develop some method of extracting this information into a form that humans can easily understand. A user of a system needs to know how the system reached its conclusions in order to have confidence in it. This credibility factor is important for the acceptance of any working system. To provide information about a neural network, a symbolic representation of the knowledge could be used. As this form is more compact and precise, it is more acceptable to humans.

4.11 Recapitulation

The approach in developing PDP models is completely different from the symbolic AI approach. The goal of learning in these models is not the formulation of explicit rules or symbolic knowledge structures. Instead, the basis of these models is the acquisition of the connection strengths that allow a network of simple units to act as though it knew the rules. Learning essentially consists of adjustment of the strengths of connections between the units.

The machine learning techniques discussed in Chapters 2 and 3 are essentially symbolic in nature; that is, the knowledge is represented as symbols. The representations discussed in this chapter are sub-symbolic, as only numerically valued activation passes from unit to unit. The next chapter outlines several other learning methodologies, involving symbolic and sub-symbolic approaches. Later chapters use these neural networks as the basis of learning symbolic representations.

References

Ackley, D. 1989, "Associative learning via inhibitory search", in *Neural Information Processing Systems (NIPS) 1,* ed. D.S. Touretzky, Morgan Kaufmann, San Mateo, California, pp. 20–8

Aleksander, I. 1989a, "Connectionist systems: information technology goes brain-like (again!)", in *Intelligent Systems in a Human Context: Development, Implications, and Applications,* eds L.A. Murray & J.T.E. Richardson, Oxford University Press, Oxford, pp. 47–52

Aleksander, I. 1989b, "Why neural computing? A personal view", in *Neural Computing Architectures: The Design of Brain-Like Machines,* ed. I. Aleksander, North Oxford Academic, London, pp. 1–7

Atlas, L., Cole, R., Connor, J., El-Sharkawi, M., Marks II, R.J., Muthusamy, Y. & Barnard, E. 1990, "Performance comparisons between Back-propagation networks and classification trees on three real-world applications", in *Neural Information Processing Systems (NIPS) 2,* ed. D.S. Touretzky, Morgan Kaufmann, San Mateo, California, pp. 622–9

Becker, S. & LeCun, Y. 1988, "Improving the convergence of Back-propagation learning with second order methods", in *Proceedings of the 1988 Connectionist Models Summer School*, eds D. Touretzky, G. Hinton & T. Sejnowski, Morgan Kaufmann, San Mateo, California, pp. 29–37

Caianiello, E.R. 1989, "A theory of neural networks", in *Neural Computing Architectures: The Design of Brain-Like Machines*, ed. I. Aleksander, North Oxford Academic, London, pp. 8–25

Carbonell, J.G. 1989, "Introduction: Paradigms for machine learning", *Artificial Intelligence*, vol. 40, pp. 1–9

Carbonell, J.G., Michalski, R.S. & Mitchell, T.M. 1983, "An overview of machine learning", in *Machine Learning: An Artificial Intelligence Approach*, eds R.S. Michalski, J.G. Carbonell & T.M. Mitchell, Tioga Publishing, Palo Alto, California, pp. 3–23

Caudill, M. 1987, "Neural networks primer, part I" *AI Expert*, December, pp. 46–52

Caudill, M. 1988a, "Neural networks primer, part II" *AI Expert*, February, pp. 55–61

Caudill, M. 1988b, "Neural networks primer, part III" *AI Expert*, June, pp. 53–9

Caudill, M. 1988c, "Neural networks primer, part IV" *AI Expert*, August, pp. 61–7

Caudill, M. 1988d, "Neural networks primer, part V" *AI Expert*, November, pp. 57–65

Caudill, M. 1989a, "Neural networks primer, part VI" *AI Expert*, February, pp. 61–7

Caudill, M. 1989b, "Neural networks primer, part VII" *AI Expert*, May, pp. 51–9

Caudill, M. 1989c, "Neural networks primer, part VIII" *AI Expert*, August, pp. 61–7

Dillon, T.S., Morsztyn, K. & Phua, K. 1975, "Short term load forecasting using adaptive pattern recognition and self-organizing techniques", *Fifth Power Systems Computation Conference (PSCC)*, Cambridge, London, vol. 1, September, pp. 2.4/3

Dillon, T.S., Sestito, S. & Leung, S. 1991, "An adaptive neural network approach in load forecasting in a power system", *First International Forum on Applications of Neural Networks to Power Systems*, Seattle, Washington, July

Fahlman, S.E. 1988, "Faster-learning variations on Back-propagation: An empirical study", in *Proceedings of the 1988 Connectionist Models Summer School*, eds D. Touretzky, G. Hinton & T. Sejnowski, Morgan Kaufmann, San Mateo, California, pp. 38–51

Fahlman, S.E. & Hinton, G.E. 1987, "Connectionist architectures for artificial intelligence", *IEEE Computer*, January, pp. 100–9

Fahlman, S.E. & Lebiere, C. 1990, "The Cascade-Correlation learning architecture", in *Neural Information Processing Systems (NIPS) 2*, ed. D.S. Touretzky, Morgan Kaufmann, San Mateo, California, pp. 524–32

Fisher, D. & McKusick, K. 1989, "An empirical comparison of ID3 and Back-propagation", *International Joint Conference on Artificial Intelligence (IJCAI-89)*, Detroit, pp. 788–93

Fozzard, R., Bradshaw, G. & Ceci, L. 1989, "A connectionist expert system that actually works", in *Neural Information Processing Systems (NIPS) 1*, ed. D.S. Touretzky, Morgan Kaufmann, San Mateo, California, pp. 248–55

Funahashi, K. 1989, "On the approximate realization of continuous mappings by neural networks", *Neural Networks*, vol. 2, pp. 183–92

Goodman, R., Miller, J. & Smyth, P. 1989, "An information theoretic approach to rule-based connectionist expert systems", in *Neural Information Processing Systems (NIPS) 1*, ed. D.S. Touretzky, Morgan Kaufmann, San Mateo, California, pp. 256–63

Hertz, J., Krogh, A. & Palmer, R.G. 1991, *Introduction to the Theory of Neural Computing*, Addison-Wesley, Reading, Massachusetts

Hinton, G.E. 1989, "Connectionist learning procedures", *Artificial Intelligence*, vol. 40, pp. 185–234

Hinton, G. & McClelland, J. 1988, "Learning representation by recirculation", in *Neural Information Processing Systems*, ed. D.Z. Anderson, American Institute of Physics, New York, pp. 358–66

Ho, C. 1989, "On multi-layered connectionist models: Adding layers vs. increasing width", *International Joint Conference on Artificial Intelligence (IJCAI-89)*, Detroit, pp. 176–9

Honavar, V. & Uhr, L. 1988, "A network of neuron-like units that learns to perceive by generation as well as reweighting of its links", in *Proceedings of the 1988 Connectionist Models Summer School*, eds D. Touretzky, G. Hinton & T. Sejnowski, Morgan Kaufmann, San Mateo, California, pp. 472–84

Honavar, V. & Uhr, L. 1989, "Generation, local receptive fields and global convergence improve perceptual learning in connectionist networks", *International Joint Conference on Artificial Intelligence (IJCAI-89)*, Detroit, pp. 180–5

Honavar, V. & Uhr, L. 1990, *Symbol Processing Systems, Connectionist Networks and Generalized Connectionist Networks*, Technical Report No. 90-23, Department of Computer Science, Iowa State University, Ames, December

Hornik, K., Stinchcombe, M. & White, H. 1989, "Multilayer feedforward networks are universal approximators", *Neural Networks,* vol. 2, pp. 359–66

Jabri, M.A. 1988, "An introduction to electronic neural networks", in *Proceedings of Neural Networks — Their Implementation in VLSI*, ed. M. Jabri, Sydney University Electrical Engineering, Australia, November, pp. 75–96

Jacobs, R.A. 1988, "Initial experiments on constructing domains of expertise and hierarchies in connectionist systems", in *Proceedings of the 1988 Connectionist Models Summer School*, eds D. Touretzky, G. Hinton & T. Sejnowski, Morgan Kaufmann, San Mateo, California, pp. 144–53

Jones, W.P. & Hoskins, J. 1987, "Back-propagation: A generalized delta learning rule", *Byte*, October, pp. 155–62

Jorgensen, C. & Matheus, C. 1986, "Catching knowledge in neural networks", *AI Expert*, December, pp. 30–41

Josin, G. 1987, "Neural-network heuristics", *Byte*, October, pp. 183–92

Khosla, R. & Dillon, T.S. 1992, "An integrated neuro-expert system model for real-time systems", in *International Joint Conference on Neural Networks (IJCNN)*, vol. I, Beijing, China, November, pp. 154–9

Khosla, R. & Dillon, T.S. 1993, "A symbolic-connectionist model for time critical and diagnostic domains", *Proceedings of the Thirteenth International Conference on Artificial Intelligence, Expert Systems and Natural Language*, vol. 1, Avignon, France, May, pp. 233–42

Kinoshita, J. & Palevsky, N.G. 1987, "Computing with neural networks", *High Technology*, May, pp. 24–31

Kohonen, T. 1989, "Speech recognition based on topology-preserving neural maps", in *Neural Computing Architectures: The Design of Brain-Like Machines,* ed. I. Aleksander, North Oxford Academic, London, pp. 26–40

Kruschke, J.K. 1988, "Creating local and distributed bottlenecks in hidden layers of Back-propagation networks", in *Proceedings of the 1988 Connectionist Models Summer School*, eds D. Touretzky, G. Hinton & T. Sejnowski, Morgan Kaufmann, San Mateo, California, pp. 120–6

Lang, K.J. & Witbrock, M.J. 1988, "Learning to tell two spirals apart", in *Proceedings of the 1988 Connectionist Models Summer School*, eds D. Touretzky, G. Hinton & T. Sejnowski, Morgan Kaufmann, San Mateo, California, pp. 52–9

Lapedes, A. & Farber, R. 1988, "How neural networks work", *Neural Information Processing Systems*, ed. D.Z. Anderson, American Institute of Physics, New York, pp. 442–56

LeCun, Y., Denker, J.S. & Solla, S.A. 1990, "Optimal brain damage", in *Neural Information Processing Systems (NIPS) 2*, ed. D.S. Touretzky, Morgan Kaufmann, San Mateo, California, pp. 598–605

Lippmann, R.P. 1987, "An introduction to computing with neural nets", *IEEE Acoustics, Speech and Signal Processing (ASSP) Magazine*, vol. 4, no. 2, April, pp. 4–22

McClelland, J.L. & Rumelhart, D.E. 1988, *Explorations in Parallel Distributed Processing: A Handbook of Models, Programs and Exercises*, MIT Press, Cambridge, Massachusetts, pp. 83–137

McClelland, J.L., Rumelhart, D.E. & the PDP Research Group 1986a, *Parallel Distributed Processing, Volume 2: Psychological and Biological Models*, MIT Press, Cambridge, Massachusetts

McClelland, J.L., Rumelhart, D.E. & Hinton, G.E. 1986b, "Appeal of parallel distributed processing", in *Parallel Distributed Processing, Volume 1: Foundations*, D.E. Rumelhart, J.L. McClelland & the PDP Research Group, MIT Press, Cambridge, Massachusetts, pp. 3–44

Michalski, R.S. 1986, "Understanding the nature of learning", in *Machine Learning: An Artificial Intelligence Approach, Volume II*, eds R.S. Michalski, J.G. Carbonell & T.M. Mitchell, Morgan Kaufmann, San Mateo, California, pp. 12–13

Montana, D. & Davis, L. 1989, "Training feedforward neural networks using genetic algorithms", *International Joint Conference on Artificial Intelligence (IJCAI-89)*, Detroit, pp. 762–7

Mooney, R., Shavlik, J., Towell, G. & Gove, A. 1989, "An experimental comparison of symbolic and connectionist learning algorithms", *International Joint Conference on Artificial Intelligence (IJCAI-89)*, Detroit, pp. 775–80

Morgan, N. & Bourlard, H. 1990, "Generalization and parameter estimation in feedforward nets: Some experiments", in *Neural Information Processing Systems (NIPS) 2*, ed. D.S. Touretzky, Morgan Kaufmann, San Mateo, California, pp. 630–7

Mozer, M.C. 1987, "RAMBOT: A connectionist system that learns by example", in *IEEE First International Conference on Neural Networks*, vol. II, eds M. Caudill & C. Butler, San Diego, California, June, pp. 693–700

Mozer, M.C. & Bachrach, J. 1990, "Discovering the structure of a reactive environment by exploration", in *Neural Information Processing Systems (NIPS) 2*, ed. D.S. Touretzky, Morgan Kaufmann, San Mateo, California, pp. 439–46

Niida, K., Tani, J., Hirobe, T. & Koshijima, I. 1989, "Application of neural networks to rule extraction from operation data", *AIChE Annual Meeting*, Paper No. 6g, San Francisco

Obermeier, K.K. & Barron, J.J. 1989, "Time to get fired up", *Byte*, August, pp. 217–24

Palmer, D.A. 1988, "Neural networks: Computers that never need programming", *I & CS*, vol. 61, no. 4, April, pp. 75–7

Park, D.C., El-Sharkawi, M.A. & Marks II, R.J. 1991, "An Adaptively Trained Neural Network", *IEEE Transactions on Neural Networks*, vol. 2, no. 3, May, pp. 334–45

Patarnello, S. & Carnevali, P. 1989, "Learning capabilities of Boolean networks", in *Neural Computing Architectures: The Design of Brain-Like Machines*, cd. I. Aleksander, North Oxford Academic, London, pp. 117–32

Peng, T.M., Hubele, N.F. & Karady, G.G. 1990, "Conceptual approach to the application of neural networks for short-term forecasting", *IEEE Inter-national Symposium on Circuits and Systems*, New Orleans, May, pp. 2342–5

Plaut, D.C. & Hinton, G.E. 1987, "Learning sets of filters using back-propagation", *Computer Speech and Language*, vol. 2, pp. 35–61

Recce, M. & Treleavan, P. 1988, "Computing from the brain", *New Scientist*, May, pp. 61–4

Rich, E. 1990, "Expert systems and neural networks can work together: Interview of Elaine Rich by Ware Myers", *IEEE Expert*, October, pp. 5–7

Roth, M.W. 1989, "Neural-network technology and its applications", *Heuristics*, vol. 2, no. 1, pp. 46–62

Rumelhart, D.E., McClelland, J.L. & the PDP Research Group 1986a, *Parallel Distributed Processing, Volume 1: Foundations*, MIT Press, Cambridge, Massachusetts

Rumelhart, D.E., Hinton, G.E. & McClelland, J.L. 1986b, "A general framework for parallel distributed processing", in *Parallel Distributed Processing, Volume 1: Foundations*, D.E. Rumelhart, J.L. McClelland & the PDP Research Group, MIT Press, Cambridge, Massachusetts, pp. 45–76

Rumelhart, D.E., Hinton, G.E. & Williams, R.J. 1986c, "Learning internal representation by error propagation", in *Parallel Distributed Processing, Volume 1: Foundations*, D.E. Rumelhart, J.L. McClelland & the PDP Research Group, MIT Press, Cambridge, Massachusetts, pp. 318–362

Saito, K. & Nakano, R. 1990, "Rule extraction from facts and neural networks", *International Conference on Neural Networks (ICNN-90-PARIS)*, Paris, France, July, pp. 379–82

Sietsma, J. & Dow, R. 1988, "Neural net pruning — why and how", *IEEE International Conference on Neural Networks*, vol. 1, pp. 325–33

Simard, P.Y., Ottway, M.B. & Ballard, D.H. 1988, "Analysis of recurrent back propagation", in *Proceedings of the 1988 Connectionist Models Summer School*, eds D. Touretzky, G. Hinton & T. Sejnowski, Morgan Kaufmann, San Mateo, California, pp. 103–12

Smolensky, P. 1986, "Neural and conceptual interpretation of PDP models", in *Parallel Distributed Processing, Volume 2: Psychological and Biological Models*, J.L. McClelland, D.E. Rumelhart & the PDP Research Group, MIT Press, Cambridge, Massachusetts, pp. 390–431

Sontag, E.D. 1990, *Feedback Stabilization using Two Hidden Layer Nets*, Report SYCON-90-11, Rutgers Center for Systems and Control, October

Stubbs, D.F. 1990, *Neurocomputers*, Springer-Verlag

Sun, G.Z., Lee, Y.C. & Chen, H.H. 1988, "A novel net that learns sequential decision process", in *Neural Information Processing Systems*, ed. D.Z. Anderson, American Institute of Physics, New York, pp. 761–6

Touretzky, D.S. & Pomerleau, D.A. 1989, "What's hidden in the hidden layers?", *Byte*, August, pp. 227–33

Towell, G. & Shavlik, J. 1992, *The Extraction of Refined Rules from Knowledge-based Neural Networks*, Machine Learning Research Group Working Paper 91–4, University of Wisconsin, Madison

Wasserman, P.D. & Schwartz, T. 1988, "Neural networks, part 2", *IEEE Expert*, Spring, pp. 10–15

Wiles, J. 1987, *A Comparison of Parallel Distributed Models of Memory*, Technical Report No. 313, Basser Department of Computer Science, University of Sydney, Sydney, Australia, October

Yang, H. & Dillon, T.S. 1992, "Neural network construction of Boolean functions used in process control", in *IEEE International Workshop on Emerging Technologies and Factory Automation*, eds R. Zurawski & T.S. Dillon, CRL Publishing, London, pp. 521–4

Zurada, J.M. 1992, *Introduction to Artificial Neural Systems*, West Publishing Company, St Paul, Minnesota

5

Other machine learning paradigms

5.1 Introduction

The previous chapters dealt with various existing symbolic and sub-symbolic automated knowledge acquisition methodologies. In this chapter, we give brief descriptions of several other paradigms. The symbolic methods include the inductive algorithms, AM (Lenat 1982, 1983a) and EURISKO (Lenat 1983b), that use frames; machine learning programs known as classifier systems that use genetic algorithms; and Explanation-Based Learning (EBL) that uses the explanation of why a particular example is an instance of a concept to construct operational recognition rules (Minton et al. 1990). The sub-symbolic approaches involving the use of neural networks include the methods of Sethi, Gallant, Niida, and Saito and Nakano, McMillan et al.'s CONNECTIONIST SCIENTIST GAME, Fu's KT algorithm, and Towell and Shavlik's SUBSET and NofM algorithms.

5.2 Induction algorithms using frames

5.2.1 Frames

The inductive algorithms, AM and EURISKO, use the knowledge representation formalism known as frames. Some of the features of frames are presented next, while the algorithms are discussed later.

Minsky (1975), who originated the frame concept, described a frame as:

> *a data structure for representing a stereotypical situation, like being in a certain kind of living room, or going to a child's birthday party. Attached to each frame are several kinds of information. Some of this information is about how to use the frame. Some is about what one can expect to happen next. Some is about what to do if these expectations are not confirmed.*

A frame is a structure for holding a collection of interrelated knowledge about a concept, a physical object, or an event. It is a very effective knowledge representation of a stereotypical object. The structure of a frame is characterized by a frame name and a number of slots. Detailed descriptions are given by Charniak and McDermott (1985) and Dillon and Tan (1993).

Consider the frame for Rental Car 1 in Figure 5.1, an adaptation of the RENTAL frame given in Dillon and Tan (1993). Each of the slots provides information related to some aspect of Rental Car 1. The values of the slots can be:

- numeric — for example, 12, 24
- logical — that is, True or False
- symbolic — for example, Melbourne
- procedural — for example, Procedure Price_Calculation.

When constructing a frame, restrictions can be placed on the possible values of some slots. Such restrictions affect:

- the type of the value, and/or
- the range of the value.

A technique for attaching control information to a slot is also required. This control will either:

- control access to the slot, or
- control how information in a particular slot is to be treated.

Facets are used to provide the means of attaching control information to a slot. Classically, there are three types of facets associated with slots:

- *Value facets* — these control the actual values, such as 12 and 24, that are placed in the slot.

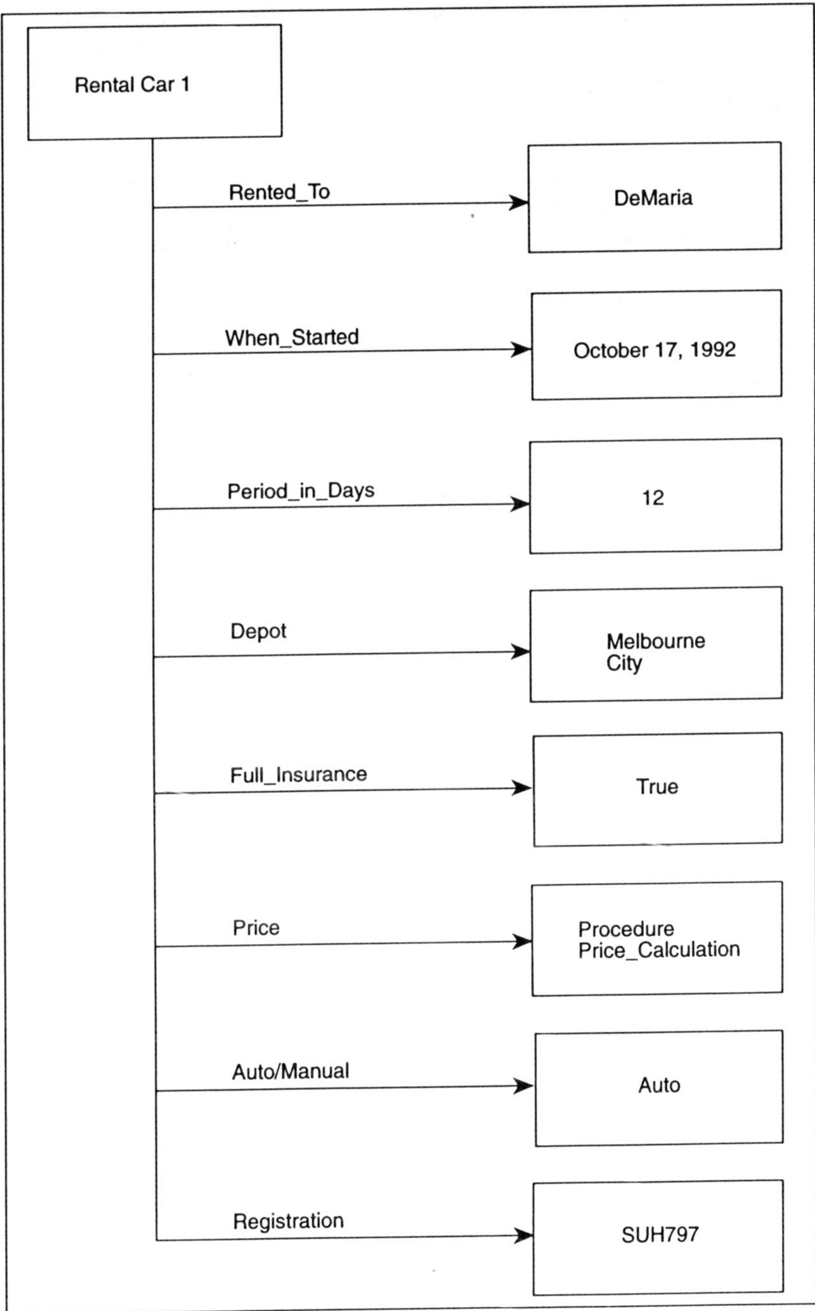

Figure 5.1   A frame representing Rental Car 1

- *If-needed facets* — it may be necessary to activate a function or procedure to return a value for a particular slot. For example, if the price for Rental Car 1 is required from Figure 5.1, then the procedure Price_Calculation is called. A procedure such as this is known as a *daemon;* it is only called when the value of the price is required. Hence, this type of facet is known as an if-needed facet. In addition to associating a function or procedure with an if-needed facet, it is possible to associate a single rule or rule set with a particular slot. The rule set is activated when the value in the slot is required.
- *Default facets* — if a particular slot does not have a definite value or a function associated with it, a default value can be used. This value is assigned by the default facet and, under weak assumptions, it is the most probable value.

The frame in Figure 5.1 refers to a particular rental car, Rental Car 1. The representation of a specific or particular item is an *instance*. A *class*, on the other hand, is a set or collection of objects or concepts. It can also be represented as a frame. Thus the frame representing RENTAL CAR would be a class. Subclasses of a frame represent the specializations of the class. Hence TELSTAR is a specialization of MEDIUM CAR, which is a specialization of RENTAL CAR, while Rental Car 1 is an instance of CELICA, which is a specialization of MEDIUM CAR and RENTAL CAR. This class structure is illustrated in Figure 5.2.

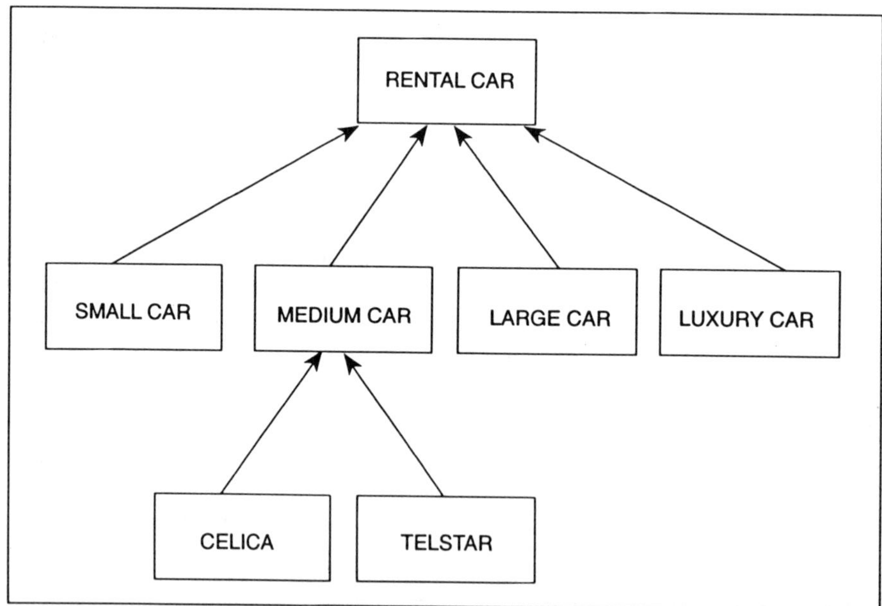

Figure 5.2   The class structure of RENTAL CAR

An important feature of frame-based systems is the inheritance by subclasses of the properties of superclasses. The two types of links commonly used between frames are the instance link and the ISA link. An instance link gives an individual instance of the class of objects currently being considered; that is, it gives one element of a set. The ISA link picks up a subclass of a particular class; that is, it gives a subset of a larger set. The ISA hierarchy thus defines the structure through which inheritance takes place. The slot values, default values, and the procedures or functions associated with the if–needed facets are all inherited by the subclasses. Restrictions associated with slots are also inherited.

It is possible to specialize or over-ride any of these properties at a particular level of the hierarchy. In this case, any subclasses below that level in that branch of the hierarchy would inherit those changed quantities, while any classes at a higher level or in a different branch would not be affected. This leads to a more compact storage of knowledge and a more efficient representation. When every subclass has only one parent superclass immediately above it, the system has single inheritance. When there is more than one parent superclass above a subclass, then there is multiple inheritance from both the parents.

5.2.2 Learning algorithms using frames

The two algorithms that use the frame representation are AM and its successor, EURISKO, both developed by Douglas Lenat (1982, 1983a, 1983b). The algorithms internally use frame-like data structures, called units, to represent almost everything in the system. Each field in the unit is called a slot and describes one feature of the concept. For instance, the ISA slot specifies subclass/superclass relationships. There is also a WORTH slot that specifies the value of a unit, on a scale of 0–1000. As well as describing concepts, a unit can be used to delineate rules and metarules. A metarule is a rule about other rules, such as:

- *if a rule is very rarely true, try to generalize it.*

EURISKO uses the same formalism to represent both rules and metarules. These meta, or discovery, rules modify existing units, leading to more meaningful and possibly new units (Forsyth & Rada 1986). A discussion of the basic mechanisms and the AM algorithm is presented in the next section. This is followed by an explanation of the EURISKO algorithm.

5.2.3 Basic mechanisms and AM

When extracting knowledge from an expert, not only are the facts required, but also the informal judgmental rules or heuristics that guide the expert in rapid decision-making. A collection of special heuristics guides the discovery of new domain facts and conjectures.

This approach is based on the hypothesis that discovery can be adequately guided by a large collection of heuristic rules. To test this hypothesis, Lenat designed a LISP program called AM (Artificial Mathematician). It develops new concepts under the guidance of a large body of heuristics. The domain of the program is elementary finite set theory (Lenat 1982).

Communication between local heuristics is via an agenda mechanism. This mechanism is a global list of tasks for the system to perform and reasons why each task is plausible. AM is able to perform several tasks, including (Lenat 1982):

- defining a new concept
- exploring some feature (property, slot, attribute) of an existing concept
- examining some empirical data for regularities.

The task with the best supporting reasons is selected and executed.

Each concept is represented internally as a data structure with a couple of dozen slots. Initially, most slots of most concepts are blank. There are 115 of these structural modules initially provided, each one corresponding to an elementary set-theoretic concept, such as union or intersection. This provides AM with an immense space to begin exploring (Lenat 1982).

The slots can be (Lenat 1982, 1983c):

- filled at the time the concept is created
- changed with time
- incrementally updated to reflect statistical records
- filled only as a result of AM executing a specific task
- initially defined in terms of other more primitive slots and their values filled in when they are first requested.

During processing, new notions could emerge that may be granted full concept module status. Each new module has dozens of blank slots, resulting in the rapid growth of the space of possible actions (i.e., blank slots to be filled in). The body of heuristics generates new slot fillers and concepts, as well as pruning ones that are no longer considered promising avenues for investigation. Because of the large size of the search space, this second aspect of providing criteria for steering the search is an important function. AM has a collection of some 250 heuristic rules to guide this search (Lenat 1982, 1983a, 1983c).

The general principle used in AM is that if a heuristic is relevant to a concept, then it is also relevant to all its specializations. According to Lenat (1982), three kinds of actions: *Analogize, Satisfice,* and *Remember,* are initiated by the heuristics:

- *Analogize* seeks to extend the scope of an action to apply to other similar situations.

- *Satisfice* seeks to determine actions that are similar to a given action within a given situation.
- *Remember* seeks to determine actions that might apply in a given situation by remembering actions that applied in the past in similar situations.

AM extends its knowledge base, rediscovering hundreds of common concepts and theorems. Some heuristics are used to (Lenat 1983c):

- select which specific feature of what concept to explore next;
- find some appropriate information about the chosen feature;
- prompt AM to notice simple relationships between known concepts;
- define promising new concepts to investigate;
- estimate how interesting each concept is.

AM's activities enlarge upon a given body of mathematical knowledge.

AM was not designed to prove anything, but it conjectured many well-known relationships, including the concept of prime numbers and De Morgan's Laws. Everything that AM does can be viewed as testing its underlying body of heuristic rules. The greatest difference between AM and typical heuristic search procedures is that AM has no well-defined target concepts or target relationship. Rather, its goal criterion or sole aim is to maximize the quality of the activities it performs, as determined by the priority rating of the top tasks on the agenda (Lenat 1983a).

The two relevant conclusions reached from the research on AM are (Lenat 1982):

- *It is possible for a body of heuristics to effectively guide a program in searching for new concepts and conjectures involving them.*
- *As new domains of knowledge emerge, the old corpus of heuristics may not be adequate to serve as a guide in those new domains; rather, new specific heuristics are necessary.*

AM's ultimate failure apparently was because of its inability to discover new, powerful, domain-specific heuristics for the various new fields it uncovered (Lenat 1983a, 1983c).

5.2.4 Overview of EURISKO

EURISKO was developed as the successor system to AM. Its field of expertise is not mathematics or diagnosis, but rather heuretics, the study of heuristics. Lenat (1982) defines heuretics as:

> the study of the informal, judgmental rules of thumb that underlie expert knowledge-based systems.

Thus, EURISKO has a collection of heuristics that gather data about their own performance, synthesize new group members, and modify old ones (Lenat 1982). The program is therefore capable of discovering new heuristics, as well as new concepts. The term *meta-heuristics* is used to denote heuristics that inspect, gather data about, modify, and synthesize other heuristics.

The fundamental assumption of the EURISKO project was that the discovery and modification of useful new heuristics were qualitatively similar to the task that AM had already worked on. In EURISKO, the initial frames also include heuristics attached to slots, permitting heuristic synthesis. AM had primitive operators like coalesce, compose, and intersect, to which EURISKO added new operators for heuristics, capable of generating, evaluating, and modifying these heuristics. As for AM, the EURISKO program uses a collection of heuristics to guide it. These heuristics, which can be thought of as meta-heuristics or metarules, serve to (Lenat 1983a):

- *propose plausible synthesis and modifications to perform;*
- *propose experiments to try;*
- *warn about implausible constructs and actions on which the program is spending time.*

When designing EURISKO, the most important decision was not to distinguish meta-heuristics from heuristics.

As EURISKO matures, it interacts less as a pupil and more as a co-researcher. The program should quickly notice when new concepts are related to existing ones. EURISKO, like AM, creates new concepts by specializing existing ones, generalizing (either from existing ones or from newly gathered data), and analogizing. EURISKO demonstrated that (Lenat 1982):

- *these processes themselves can be guided adequately by a group of heuristics;*
- *there is no need to distinguish such meta-heuristics from object-level heuristics;*
- *analogy has as much potential as generalization or specialization.*

5.2.5   Applications of EURISKO

The aim of any discovery program such as EURISKO is to be able to use the same method to discover concepts, conjectures, and heuristics in several domains. Thus EURISKO has been applied to domains such as naval fleet design for a tournament of wargaming, evolution, games, heuretics, knowledge representations, and VLSI design.

Wargaming and VLSI are claimed by Lenat (1983b) to be its greatest success so far. In the wargaming implementation, the program won the same tournament two years in a row. EURISKO did produce many heuristics. However, Lenat himself weeded out heuristics deemed invalid or undesirable, and rewarded those he understood and liked. Final credit for the wins should thus be given to both Lenat and EURISKO, as neither won alone (Lenat 1983b).

In the area of VLSI, EURISKO produced, through its application of a symmetry heuristic, a very powerful yet simple device that simultaneously computes NANDs and ORs. These devices now form the primitive building blocks of some chip designs.

From these applications, Lenat (1983b) concluded that many heuristics of the following three types should be available:

- heuristics that generate (suggest plausible moves);
- heuristics that evaluate (judge the worth and determine specific problems with the discoveries);
- heuristics that prune (eliminate implausible paths before they are explored too deeply).

Another conclusion made was that the language used to represent the concepts must be a natural one, given the set of objects and operators. In addition, new heuristics discovery, an appropriate knowledge representation, and its maintenance are critical issues (Lenat 1983b).

5.2.6 Problems with these algorithms

One of the problems encountered with EURISKO was that too many heuristics can be created. In the wargaming application, the program came up with all the innovative design and design rules, and recognized the significance of most of them. However, it was Lenat, a human observer, who filtered through all of the generated rules and who occasionally noticed errors or flaws in the synthesized design rules. These flaws would have wasted inordinate amounts of time before being corrected by EURISKO (Lenat 1983b). Lenat, himself has stated that this is a problem with EURISKO. Thus, it seems a method needs to be developed that uses a tougher and more restrictive criterion for constructing rules.

Fundamentally, these algorithms are not totally supervised learning techniques, as they do not rely on the known target outputs of situations to guide the learning. In AM and EURISKO, the goal of learning is not specific. Their goal is to formulate viable observations in specific domains. Also, the algorithms are not totally automated as Lenat, the main creator of the programs, vetted the resulting output.

5.3 Genetic algorithms

5.3.1 Introduction

Genetic algorithms refer to a class of adaptive search procedures based on principles derived from the dynamics of natural population genetics (Grefenstette

1990). These search procedures exploit the mechanics of natural selection and natural genetics. Survival of the fittest is thus combined with mechanisms for generation of new candidates to form search algorithms.

John Holland (1975) first developed genetic algorithms. His aim was to abstract and rigorously explain the adaptive process of natural systems. From this, software systems that capture the evolutionary mechanisms of natural systems have been developed. These genetic algorithms provide robust search procedures for complex spaces.

Some of the general characteristics of genetic algorithms include (Goldberg 1989):

- working with a coding of the parameter set
- searching from a population of points, rather than a single point
- using a pay-off function
- using probabilistic transition rules.

We will now discuss these characteristics. First, the parameter set used in a problem is coded as a finite length string. To explain this, consider the following:

- Problem: determine the best days for making interstate phone calls.
- In this case, the parameters are the seven days of the week. Therefore, to code the parameter set as a finite length string, a string of length 7 with each element representing a different day of the week is chosen.

In general, the parameter set is coded into:

$$A = a_1 a_2 ... a_n,$$

where $a_1 a_2 ... a_n$ represents the individual parameters in the set of size n. The individual parameters are binary, with values of either 1 or 0. This encoding is required by the genetic algorithm for several reasons, including the flexibility to apply the three operators of reproduction, crossover, and mutation on the strings, as discussed below. New strings are created by applying these three string operators. Genetic algorithms actually work by processing and manipulating a group of coded strings. As these coded strings are used in determining the solution, genetic algorithms are regarded as working with a group of points simultaneously. To search effectively through the strings, some form of pay-off value is required for each string. These pay-off values are objective function values used to guide the search through the strings (Goldberg 1989).

The coding of the parameter set is usually over an extended alphabet and not just over 0 and 1. This extended alphabet includes a hash symbol #, representing a *don't care* or *wild card* symbol (Booker et al. 1990; Goldberg 1989). Thus, the # matches either a 0 or 1, as illustrated below:

- Suppose the following strings are in the population being considered:

```
0110011     1111111
0010010     0111010
```

- The string ##1##1#, represented in the extended alphabet, matches each string in the population above. To match this string, a string must have a 1 in both positions 3 and 6; the other elements are not relevant.

The flexibility of this notation is apparent, as large groups of patterns can be stated in a concise form. Thus, the notation greatly simplifies the analysis of genetic algorithms because it explicitly recognizes all the possible similarities in a population of strings.

There are three important operators commonly used in genetic algorithms; reproduction, crossover, and mutation. The first operator, reproduction, is a process in which individual strings are copied according to their objective function values (Goldberg 1989). These objective function values represent a measure of goodness that needs to be maximized. Copying strings with higher fitness values gives those strings a higher probability of contributing one or more of their offspring to the next generation. In the natural world, this is equivalent to natural selection, resulting in the survival of the fittest. Crossover occurs when members of the newly reproduced strings are mated at random. This is the second operator used by genetic algorithms. Goldberg (1989) argues that much of the power of genetic algorithms derives from the combination of reproduction and crossover that provides structured, though randomized, information exchange. Mutation, the third operator, usually plays a less significant role in the operation of genetic algorithms. It allows the random generation of values in the string.

To illustrate these operators, let string 1 be 11011 with an objective function value of 0.25, and string 2 be 11101 with an objective function value of 0.50.

- Applying the reproduction operator to the two strings results in string 2 being reproduced because it has a higher objective function value.
- Applying the crossover operator, assuming the crossover point in the string is the third position, results in the following:

```
original strings:     11011     gives new strings:     11111
                      11101                            11001
```

- Applying the mutation operator to the two strings may result in the following (mutation being the random inverting of a bit in the string):

```
original strings:     11011     gives new strings:     11010
                      11101                            11001
```

Comprehension of a genetic algorithm's manipulation of building blocks is crucial (Booker et al. 1990). Building blocks are high-performance schemata that are combined to form strings with expected higher performance. The schemata or similarity templates are strings over the extended alphabet {0,1,#} (Booker et al. 1990; Goldberg 1989). According to Booker et al. (1990):

> *A genetic algorithm rapidly explores the space of schemas, a very large space, implicitly rating and exploiting the schemas according to the strengths of the rules employing them.*

Two useful schemata properties are (Goldberg 1989):

- order — the number of fixed positions present in each schema
- length — the defining length of each schema; that is, the distance between the first and last specific string positions.

The generating procedure samples the schemata with above average instances more regularly. This results in further confirmation of the useful schemata and degradation of the less useful. The overall average strength is thus increased. This leads to an ever-increasing criterion that a schema must meet to be above average. Also, the generating procedure uses the distribution of instances rather than the most recent, best schemata. This helps the system to be more robust and to overcome local minima that misdirect development. The better than average building blocks are rapidly accumulated by the generating procedure. The strengths are determined by the regularities and interactions in the environment (Booker et al. 1990).

5.3.2   Classifier systems

The most common genetics-based machine learning architecture is known as a classifier system. These have served as the basis for a number of adaptive experimental systems (Grefenstette 1990). A classifier system learns syntactically simple string rules, called classifiers, that guide the performance in an arbitrary environment (Goldberg 1989). Classifier systems have three major parts, as illustrated in Figure 5.3. The *performance system* interacts directly with the environment (Booker et al. 1990). The second part, *credit assignment*, determines

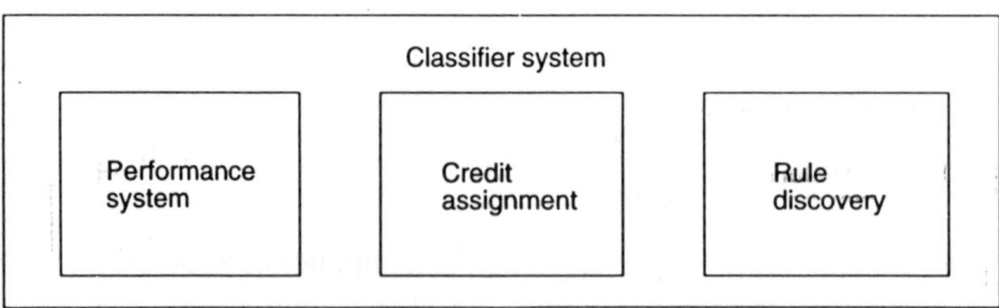

Figure 5.3   The three components of a classifier system

the effectiveness or usefulness of the resulting rules. The remaining part of the system, *rule discovery,* utilizes genetic algorithms. Thus, classifier systems represent quite a different approach to rule learning (Grefenstette 1990). Each of the three parts will now be discussed in detail.

Performance system

This system is a type of rule-based production system. Thus the form of rules in a classifier system is:

IF <condition> THEN <action>.

Unlike typical rule-based systems, however, the conditions and actions in a classifier system are restricted to be fixed-length strings. The benefits of this include (Goldberg 1989):

- *All strings under the permissible alphabet are syntactically meaningful;*
- *Fixed string representation permits string operators of the genetic kind.*

The explicit pattern recognition is provided by using a *don't care* or *wild card* symbol.

In typical rule-based systems, some form of conflict resolution is required to determine which rule to fire, if several match on a given cycle. However, in classifier systems, parallel activation of rules is allowed during a matching cycle, permitting multiple activities to be co-ordinated simultaneously. Note that when classifier systems must choose between mutually exclusive, competing alternatives, they use competitive arbitration strategies (Goldberg 1989).

In general, classifiers send messages that are placed on a message list. This message list provides a centralized form of communication between the various rules, as the messages can activate other classifiers. These messages within a classifier system are simply finite length strings over a finite alphabet, and can be defined as (Goldberg 1989):

<classifier> ::= <condition> : <message>

where

<condition> is a fixed string over the alphabet $\{0,1,\#\}$,
\# is a wild card symbol, and
<message> is a fixed string over $\{0,1\}$.

An example of a classifier is:

01# : 100

where 01# is the <condition>, 100 is the <message>, and : is the delimiter. Once the classifier's condition is matched, the classifier becomes a candidate to post a message on the message list. Whether it does or not is dependent upon the classifier's value or weighting (Goldberg 1989).

Credit assignment system

Each individual rule is assigned a measure or strength. This indicates the utility of the rule to the system's goals or external pay-offs obtained (Grefenstette 1990). Credit assignment in classifier systems is performed by a Bucket Brigade algorithm (Booker et al. 1990; Goldberg 1989). According to Grefenstette (1990), this algorithm:

> *shifts strengths among rules via an economic metaphor, where rules are viewed as both producers and consumers of messages on the message list.*

A competition is held among the classifiers, in the sense that the classifier with the highest *bid* answers the relevant messages (Booker et al. 1990). In many systems, the bids are managed by an internal currency. The exchange and accumulation of the internal currency provide a natural figure of merit. A classifier's bank balance is used as a fitness function, and subsequent payment of bids serves as a source of income to the previously successful message senders (Goldberg 1989). Note that classifiers may be reproduced, crossed, or mutated. The competitive nature of this system ensures that good, profitable rules survive, while the bad, unprofitable rules die off. When a number of rules match on a given cycle, the rules compete to post their messages on the message list by bidding a portion of their strengths (Goldberg 1989; Grefenstette 1990). Bids are also affected by the specificity of the rule's conditions. A more specific rule can make a higher bid. The higher bidders (the relevant, high- strength rules) get to post their messages. Bids are paid to the rules that, on the previous cycle, supplied the messages that determined the winning rules on the current cycle. Ultimately, the environment directly rewards rules that successfully complete the desired task. This scheme encourages the flow of strength back to rules that set the stage for later, ultimately successful, rules. The net result is that each rule's strength indicates its general utility to the overall system (Grefenstette 1990).

Bucket Brigade is a clean procedure for evaluating rules and deciding among competing alternatives (Goldberg 1989). However, a way to inject new, possibly better rules into the system is still needed. For this purpose, genetic algorithms with the operators of reproduction, crossover, and mutation are used.

Rule discovery

New rules are discovered by genetic operators applied to existing rules, selected on the basis of strength. Given an appropriate representation of rules, the theory of genetic search suggests that the new rules will share many of the important building blocks that led to the success of their parents. The newly created rules compete with established rules in the survival process (Grefenstette 1990).

Genetic algorithms select high-strength classifiers as parents and form offspring by recombining components from the parent classifiers (Booker et al. 1990). The weak classifiers are displaced by the offspring in the system entering into competition, and being activated and tested when their conditions are satisfied.

During the application of the genetic algorithm to the classifier system, identifiable patterns or features (i.e., attribute values) spontaneously evolve. These schemata, expressed as strings containing specific values in a number of positions and leaving the rest unspecified, capture combinations of useful features. Thus a schema gradually represents a set of strings containing equivalent values in certain specified positions (Oosthuizen 1989).

From an implementation point of view, several parameters are required for the application of genetic algorithms. First, a proportion parameter specifying the amount of population replaced by the genetic algorithm operators must be defined. The number of time steps between genetic algorithm calls must also be defined (Goldberg 1989):

- deterministically — after X cycles, where X is some value
- probabilistically — after some average period, or
- conditionally — on particular events, such as the lack of a match or poor performance.

Illustrative classifier system

Consider as an example, adapted from Goldberg (1989), a domain with the classifiers listed in Table 5.1. Recall that <classifier> ::= <condition> : <message> and # is a wild card symbol.

Index	Classifier
1	#01:100
2	#10:111
3	1#0:010
4	10#:110

Table 5.1   List of classifiers in the illustrative domain

Using these classifiers only with 001 as the given initial string, a trace of the processing of the strings follows:

- First, there is an attempt to match the given initial string 001 with the conditions of strings 1 to 4, listed in Table 5.1.
- String 001 matches:
    string 1, which posts the message 100. This message is added to the message list.

- Current message list: 100
- String 100 matches:
    string 3, which posts the message 010, and
    string 4, which posts the message 110.
- Current message list: 010
                           110
- String 010 matches:
    string 2, which posts the message 111.
  String 110 matches:
    string 2, which posts the message 111, and
    string 3, which posts the message 010.
- Current message list: 111
                           010
- String 111 matches:
    no classifier, so no new message is posted.
  String 010 matches:
    string 2, which posts the message 111.
- Current message list: 111
- String 111 matches:
    no classifier, so no new message is posted.
- The process is terminated.

This example will now be reworked with the inclusion of a credit assignment system to determine the various rule strengths. Let the initial rule strengths be 1000 and the bids for each rule be 10% of the rule strength. Recall that the bid is subtracted from the strength to give the new rule strength for a matching classifier. Also, the bid is paid to the previously successful message sender. Using 001 as the given initial string, a trace of the processing of the strings follows:

- Initial state of the population:

Index	Classifier	Strength
1	#01:100	1000
2	#10:111	1000
3	1#0:010	1000
4	10#:110	1000

- String 001 matches:
    string 1, which bids 10% of 1000 = 100 and posts the message 100.
  The strength of string 1 is then updated using current strength − bid = 1000 − 100 = 900. Since the external environment supplied the initial message string, it receives payment of the bid.

- Current message list: 100
- Current state of the population:

Index	Classifier	Strength
1	#01:100	900
2	#10:111	1000
3	1#0:010	1000
4	10#:110	1000

- String 100 matches:
    string 3, which bids 100 and posts the message 010, and
    string 4, which bids 100 and posts the message 110.
  String 1 is the previously successful message sender and so it receives payment of the bids from strings 3 and 4.
- Current message list: 010
                          110
- Current state of the population:

Index	Classifier	Strength
1	#01:100	1100
2	#10:111	1000
3	1#0:010	900
4	10#:110	900

- String 010 matches:
    string 2, which bids 100 and posts the message 111.
  String 110 matches:
    string 2, which bids 100 and posts the message 111, and
    string 3, which bids 90 and posts the message 010.
  Strings 3 and 4 are the previously successful message senders and so they receive payment of 100 and 190, respectively. Note that string 3 both receives a payment and pays a bid. Hence its updated strength is given by $900 + 100 - 90 = 910$.
- Current message list: 111
                          010
- Current state of the population:

Index	Classifier	Strength
1	#01:100	1100
2	#10:111	800
3	1#0:010	910
4	10#:110	1090

- String 111 matches:
    no classifier, so no new message is posted.
- String 010 matches:
    string 2, which bids 80 and posts the message 111.
    String 3 is the previously successful message sender and so it receives payment of the bid from string 2.
- Current message list: 111
- Current state of the population:

Index	Classifier	Strength
1	#01:100	1100
2	#10:111	720
3	1#0:010	990
4	10#:110	1090

- String 111 matches:
    no classifier, so no new message is posted.
- The process is terminated after a system reward is paid to the classifier(s) with a message remaining on the message list. In this case, assume a system reward of 200.
- Final state of the population:

Index	Classifier	Strength
1	#01:100	1100
2	#10:111	920
3	1#0:010	990
4	10#:110	1090

After determining the rules with the highest strengths, the genetic algorithm can come into play. The genetic operators of reproduction, crossover, and mutation can be applied to the rules with the highest strengths. As classifiers 1 and 4 have strengths of 1100 and 1090 respectively, let the following operators be applied to them:

        string 1: #01:100   gives new strings: #0#:100
        string 4: 10#:110   101:110

for the crossover operation at the third position

        string 1: #01:100   gives new string: #01:100

for the reproduction operation.
Thus, the new list of classifiers after the first pass is given in Table 5.2. The previous process is repeated until the population of classifiers converges to some number of strong individuals (Michalewicz 1992).

Index	Classifier
1	#01:100
2	#10:111
3	1#0:010
4	10#:110
5	#0#:100
6	101:110
7	10#:110

Table 5.2   New list of classifiers after the initial pass

This simple example serves to illustrate both the path through a domain (with different strings sending messages) and the internal manipulation of bids and currency. In addition to bids made and payments received, some systems include a tax levied at each time step to diminish the effect of non-productive rules. De Groot (1970) also suggested the addition of a random noise term to the bid as a catalyst for activity.

5.4 Explanation-based learning

5.4.1 Introduction

Unlike inductive learning, which learns by abstracting common properties from multiple examples, Explanation-Based Learning (EBL) systems consider why a particular example is an instance of a concept. The explanations are then converted into operational recognition rules. Thus, while inductive learning is data-intensive, EBL is analytical and knowledge-intensive (Minton et al. 1990).

The goal of EBL can be stated as follows:

Given a theory T and examples, find a deductive consequence T' of T such that T':

- performs correctly on the examples
- is more efficient than T.

Some of the key issues for generating the new theory T' are now discussed. In a given domain, a series of operators can be applied in moving from some initial point in the input space to some target point. As shown in Figure 5.4, at any point in the state space, there are several different operators that could be used. Therefore, there are several alternative ways of generating a path to the target set or point from some initial point. One approach for bringing some order to this process is to record all of the past solution paths from the initial

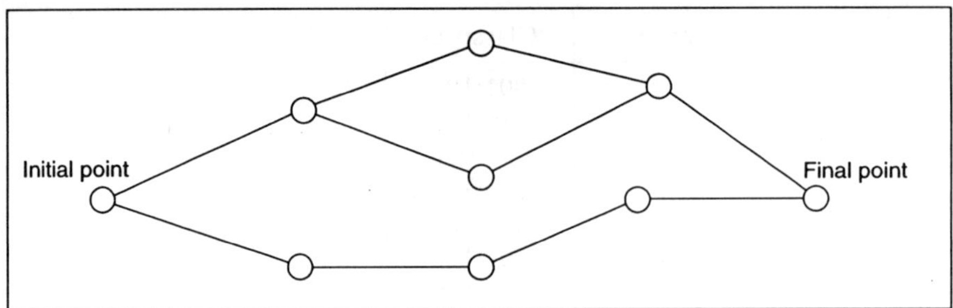

Figure 5.4   The effects of operators on state space

point to the target. These represent the solution description. Thus, when a new problem is encountered, it is checked against the problem description. However, this strategy will only work if an exact match of the solution description has been discovered (Shavlik & Dietterich 1990). In this approach, a new problem is actually being checked against constants in these past solutions, which is definitely not efficient or reliable.

An alternative technique is to generalize the solutions of the path somehow from an initial problem description to a final state so that irrelevant terms are removed and constants are replaced by variables (Mitchell et al. 1990; Shavlik & Dietterich 1990). The new problems encountered are then matched to the generalized problem description to obtain a solution.

The important consideration here is how to generalize the solution path. It is critical in this procedure to determine initially those parts of the problem description that are essential in obtaining the solution. It is also necessary to determine exactly how the final solution depends upon the details of the problem description (Shavlik & Dietterich 1990). As claimed by Shavlik and Dietterich (1990):

> *The key insight of explanation-based learning is that a record of the problem-solving steps taken to get from the initial problem description to the final solution state provides the necessary information for generalizing the solution path. This record is often called an "explanation".*

Thus, EBL systems learn by analyzing explanations of problem-solving behavior (Mitchell et al. 1990).

EBL methods actually generalize from a single example by analyzing why that example is an instance of the concept. This is cast in the form of an explanation. The explanation formed describes the concept in terms of a set of the relevant features. This allows the instances of the concept to be recognized effectively (Minton et al. 1990).

The methods based on the EBL paradigm have a fundamental theme in which there is a general goal or target concept that the system is attempting to learn. The power of the existing EBL algorithms comes from their ability to construct an explanation after observing a single example. This power of EBL stems from its use of a domain theory to drive the analysis process. The explanation attempts to determine why an example is an instance of a target concept. According to Minton et al. (1990):

> *Computing the weakest conditions under which the explanation holds produces sufficient conditions for recognizing the goal concept.*

A common misconception about EBL is that it actually performs no learning since it is provided with the definition of the concept. EBL takes the position that any discovered new knowledge enabling the system to improve its efficiency is better. The definition of the concept that the system receives as input is non-operational; that is, the definition is most probably computationally impractical to use for the recognition of instances of the concept. EBL transforms the given definition into one that can be used as an efficient recognizer of the instances of the concept. In other words, it constructs an operational description (Minton et al. 1990).

Another feature of EBL is the role of the example. In principle, given a complete domain theory, the concept's definition could be transformed into an operational description without the example. However, the example has two functions (Minton et al. 1990):

- It makes the search more tractable by guiding the search for an operational description.
- It leads to recognizers (i.e., sufficient conditions) that are likely to be applicable because it is an instance of the concept.

5.4.2 EBL components

The input and output of EBL can be specified as follows (Mitchell et al. 1990):

Given:

> — *goal concept: A concept definition describing the concept to be learned. (It is assumed that this concept definition fails to satisfy the operationality criterion.)*
> — *training example: An example of the goal concept.*
> — *domain theory: A set of rules and facts to be used in explaining how the training example is an example of the goal concept.*
> — *operationality criterion: A predicate over concept definitions, specifying the form in which the learned concept definition must be expressed.*

Determine:

> — *A generalization of the training example that is a sufficient concept description for the goal concept and that satisfies the operationality criterion.*

Some of these components are elaborated below.

Goal concept

This component of EBL is concerned with determining the goal or target concepts. These target concepts specify the conditions under which one should utilize a given optimization strategy. In some systems, the goal concept is provided by the user. In others, the important goals are pre-programmed into the system. For instance, in the system known as PRODIGY (Minton et al. 1990), there are four types of target concepts (SUCCEEDS, FAILS, SOLE-ALTERNATIVE, and GOAL-INTERFERENCE):

- If the control choice leads to a solution then the chosen alternative SUCCEEDS, and if it leads to a non-solution it FAILS.
- If all but one of the alternatives fail, then the successful alternative is known as the SOLE-ALTERNATIVE.
- If a previously achieved goal is undone, then the alternative chosen is known as GOAL-INTERFERENCE.

Obviously these four possible target concepts do not represent the complete range of potential target concepts. Most implemented systems have used a single strategy, that of learning from success (Minton et al. 1990). In a few cases, the system derives its own goals as sub-goals of a larger plan (Shavlik & Dietterich 1990).

Scope of the theory

The scope of the theory determines the space of explanations that the system can generate for a given target concept (Minton et al. 1990). Recall that EBL methods need to understand why a problem-solving attempt failed or yielded a sub-optimal solution, in order to enhance the understanding of the domain. Thus a theory that describes the relevant aspects of the problem solver is required. Also necessary is a theory that describes the task domain. These two theories enable EBL techniques to construct a better description of the example.

In most cases the domain theory can be automatically constructed by examining the domain and extracting the relevant operators, inference rules, and control rules. However, the problem theory is usually hand-coded. This problem, or architecture theory, describes how the problem solver actually works. In combination, the theories provide a means for showing that a particular optimization strategy is applicable (Minton et al. 1990).

Mapping method

The techniques used to transform the problem solver trace (or example) into an explanation constitute the mapping method. In some cases, such as STRIPS and SOAR, the explanation is directly built from the sequence of operators or productions formed by the problem solver in some past situation (Minton et al 1990; Shavlik & Dietterich 1990). In other cases, the problem solver's actions are gathered first and then analyzed. This analysis tries to determine whether the actions satisfy the target concepts. PRODIGY uses a search tree generated by the problem solver to construct explanations, with the mapping performed by an explanation-based specialization technique (Minton et al. 1990). Current implementations of Explanation-Based Generalization (EBG), a well-known EBL method constructed by Mitchell et al. (1990), seem to rely on a theorem prover to construct explanations (DeJong & Mooney 1990). Observing the problem-solving actions of an external agent is a fourth approach to constructing explanations. Editing and adapting previous explanations provide another technique (Shavlik & Dietterich 1990).

Operationality criterion

This criterion takes into account the usefulness of the constructed explanation and the technique used to determine whether the explanation satisfies the criterion. It considers the computational costs and benefits of the transformations used (Minton et al. 1990). The terms in which the output concept definition is expressed are also included in this criterion (Mitchell et al. 1990).

The operationality criterion has an added use, apart from imposing a requirement that the learned concept definition must be correct. It also requires that the learned concept definition be in a usable form before learning is complete (Mitchell et al. 1990). This forces the learned concept to be in a practical form that can be used and not in theoretical terms only.

The EBG method

The EBL method known as Explanation-Based Generalization (EBG) (Mitchell et al. 1990), as defined in Table 5.3, illustrates the interplay between the various EBL components.

The first step separates the relevant feature values in the example from the irrelevant ones and constructs an explanation from the relevant ones. This explanation is examined in the second step to determine the particular constraints on these feature values. These are analyzed in terms of deciding which feature values are sufficient for the explanation structure to apply in the general case. In order to perform these steps, EBL methods such as EBG assume that the learning environment has the following available: knowledge of the domain, goal concept, and operationality criterion (Mitchell et al. 1990). A detailed

---

The EBG Method

1. Explain: construct an explanation in terms of the domain theory that proves how the training satisfies the goal concept definition.
(This explanation must be constructed so that each branch of the explanation structure terminates in an expression that satisfies the operationality criterion.)
2. Generalize: determine a set of sufficient conditions under which the explanation structure holds, stated in terms that satisfy the operationality criterion.
(This is accomplished by regressing the goal concept through the explanation structure. The conjunction of the resulting regressed expressions constitutes the desired concept definition.)

Table 5.3   Mitchell's EBG method (Mitchell et al. 1990)

analysis of the EBG method and its shortcomings is given by DeJong and Mooney (1990).

5.4.3 Illustrative example

An adaptation of the example in Shavlik and Dietterich (1990) of the EBL algorithm known as Mooney's EGGS follows. In this illustrative example, the simple domain theory can be represented by a collection of rules, as listed below:

- *support-humans(?x) AND planet(?x) fi ClassM(?x)*
  states that if an object is a planet and it can support humans then it is a ClassM planet.
- *emits-no-light(?y) $\Rightarrow$ planet(?y)*
  states that a planet emits no light of its own.
- *oxygen(?z) $\Rightarrow$ support-humans(?z)*
  states that humans live on something that has oxygen.
- *photosynth-plants(?u) $\Rightarrow$ oxygen(?u)*
  states that oxygen is present if there are plants that photosynthesize.

The specific training example:

> photosynth-plants(Earth) AND emits-no-light(Earth)

states that Earth has photosynthetic plants and emits no light of its own. From this, one is asked to show that the Earth is a ClassM planet; that is,

> ClassM(Earth).

It can be shown that Earth is a ClassM planet simply by applying the rules in the domain theory.

- Given that Earth has photosynthetic plants, applying rule:

  photosynth-plants(?u) $\Rightarrow$ oxygen(?u) results in
  photosynth-plants(Earth) $\Rightarrow$ oxygen(Earth).

  Hence, Earth has oxygen.

- Given that Earth has oxygen, applying rule:

  oxygen(?z) $\Rightarrow$ support-humans(?z) results in
  oxygen(Earth) $\Rightarrow$ support-humans(Earth).

  Hence, Earth can support humans.

- Given that Earth emits no light, applying rule:

  emits-no-light(?y) $\Rightarrow$ planet(?y) results in
  emits-no-light(Earth) $\Rightarrow$ planet(Earth).

  Hence, Earth is a planet.

- Given that Earth is a planet and it can support humans, applying rule:

  support-humans(?x) AND planet(?x) $\Rightarrow$ ClassM(?x) results in
  support-humans(Earth) AND planet(Earth) $\Rightarrow$ ClassM(Earth).

  Hence, Earth is a ClassM planet.

The solution path depicted in Figure 5.5 applies to the specific planet, Earth. To be of wider use, this solution must be generalized so that it can be applied to other instances. EGGS uses an explanation structure in which the original general rules replace the instantiated rules in the explanation to achieve this (Shavlik & Dietterich 1990). Such a structure is shown in Figure 5.6,

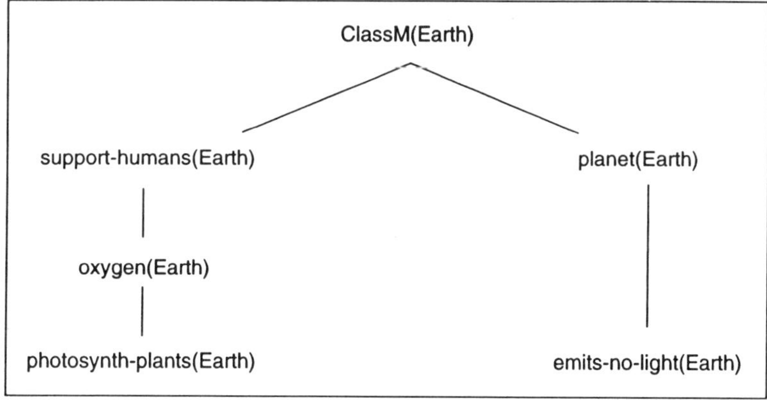

Figure 5.5   Solution path for the illustrative example

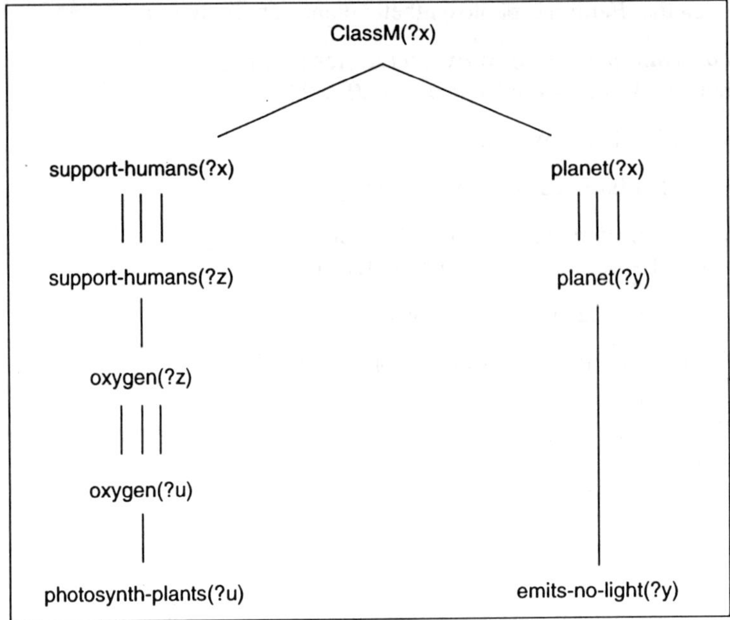

Figure 5.6   A generalized solution to the illustrative example

where triple parallel lines indicate where the consequent of one rule must unify with the antecedent of another (Shavlik & Dietterich 1990).

Finally, EGGS would produce the general rule:

$$\text{photosynth-plants}(?z) \text{ AND } \text{emits-no-light}(?z) \Rightarrow \text{ClassM}(?z).$$

5.5 Connectionist methods

5.5.1 Introduction

The methods discussed so far are symbolic in nature. AM and EURISKO use the knowledge representation formalism known as frames. The machine learning genetic algorithms manipulate a string of bits representing the population. Explanation-based learning employs a non-operational theory and converts it into an operational theory with the use of an example.

The next group of methods described in this section are sub-symbolic in nature. The first method is an approach for converting decision trees to neural nets. Most of the others use neural networks for rule extraction. The method known as BRAINNE, discussed in Chapters 8 and 9, represents a novel approach to rule extraction using neural networks.

5.5.2   Sethi's method

An approach proposed by Sethi (1990, 1991) converts a decision tree into a neural network. The decision tree is initially constructed using some machine learning method, such as ID3 or CART. The neural network is not fully connected as it directly follows the structure of the decision tree. Thus, the number of units in the hidden or intermediate layers is pre-defined. Non-linear activation functions are associated with each neuron (Sethi 1990).

Some of the rules used to construct the neural network from the decision tree are (Sethi 1990, 1991):

- *The number of neurons in the first layer of the layered network equals the number of internal nodes of the decision tree. Each of these neurons implements one of the decision functions of the internal nodes. This layer is called the partitioning layer.*
- *All leaf nodes have a corresponding neuron in the second hidden layer where the ANDing is implemented. This layer is the ANDing layer.*
- *The number of neurons in the output layer equals the number of distinct classes or actions. This layer implements the ORing of those tree paths that lead to the same action.*
- *The connections between the neurons from the partitioning layer and the neurons from the ANDing layer implement the hierarchy of the tree.*

An important feature is evident. The number of neurons needed in each layer is known exactly and there is a way of specifying the desired response for each of these neurons. Except for the neuron representing the root node, the remaining nodes do not have connections with all the neurons in the adjacent layer. This architecture is known as an Entropy Net.

Solving the credit assignment problem for the intermediate layers involves determining the target for each intermediate hidden node. In the Entropy Net, this is automatically achieved during the tree design phase when different paths are assigned different class labels. When an example given to the network is known to be an instance of class C, then only one neuron in the ANDing layer produces an output of 1, while the remaining neurons produce a 0. Therefore, for this layer credit assignment is simple. It enhances the response of the neuron producing the highest output among the group and suppresses the remaining neurons of the group of the ANDing layer (Sethi 1990). This is similar to the winner-take-all competitive nets used by neural network approaches in the self-organizing or unsupervised mode of operation. Once the appropriate neuron has been identified in the ANDing layer for a given example, the desired output from the partitioning layer is also established because of the tree-to-network architecture. The credit assignment problem is thus solved (Sethi 1990).

Using this approach, Sethi (1990) claims that learning time is reduced. The initial network constructed from the decision tree is a reasonably good start for selecting the number of hidden units. As such, incremental learning can be very fast, leading to reduced training time. Training is not achieved by Back-propagation, which takes a long time because of the partial connections in the network. Instead, the presence of the hierarchy is exploited and developed into a suitable training method (Sethi 1991).

To enhance generalization, one needs to associate the sigmoid function or some other soft non-linearity with every neuron. The non-linearity changes a binary signal to an analogue signal. Thus, small changes do not affect the response of the neuron, and the ability to deal with noise and variability is enhanced (Sethi 1990). With the soft non-linearity, the network is allowed to adapt its connection strengths to overcome the rigidity of the decision tree classifiers (Sethi 1991).

5.5.3   Gallant's method

Gallant (1988) examined expert systems with connectionist networks as their knowledge bases. These were called *connectionist expert systems*. As part of this research, Gallant developed MACIE, a stand-alone expert system inference engine that interprets such knowledge bases. Several traditional expert systems employ IF-THEN production rules to represent the knowledge base, while connectionist expert systems use a neural network model for this purpose. The most difficult, time-consuming, and expensive task in building an expert system is constructing and debugging its knowledge base. Gallant believes that the learning power of connectionist models can be harnessed for expert system construction. However, the question of the connectionist model's ability to give reasonable justifications for its conclusions is of prime importance. The work presented here does not attempt to extract a set of rules from the connectionist knowledge base; it attempts to generate an explanation for a particular conclusion. Gallant decided to use IF-THEN rules for the purpose of explanation. Thus, the user can ask the system why it concluded that a particular cell was True or False, and the system answers with an IF-THEN rule. These IF-THEN rules are generated by the inference engine as needed for explanations, and are not represented explicitly in the knowledge base.

In generating these explanations, it is assumed that the system has already inferred that a cell, say $x8$, has a value of True. From this, a minimal subset can be selected of the currently known information that is sufficient to make this inference. The following calculations are performed (Gallant 1988):

- *List all inputs that are known and contributed to the ultimate positivity of the discriminant for x8.*
- *Arrange the list by decreasing absolute value of the weights.*

- *Generate clauses for an IF-THEN rule from this ordered list until*

$$\left\{\sum_{inputs\text{-}used\text{-}for\text{-}clause} \mid W_i \mid\right\} > \left\{\sum_{remaining\text{-}inputs} \mid W_i \mid\right\}$$

is satisfied.

Gallant (1987) describes extensions of MACIE for handling noise and redundancy.

From this premise, it would seem possible to examine a connectionist network and produce every related IF-THEN rule. However, this procedure would only work for a very small connectionist network because the number of implicitly encoded IF-THEN rules can grow exponentially with the cell inputs (Gallant 1988). Saito and Nakano (1990) also highlight that this method suffers from a combinatorial explosion because of the number of implicit rules in the network.

Gallant (1988) reasons that connectionist expert systems are not a psychological model; he states that *connectionist researchers interested in psychological modeling would probably argue that MACIE is an implausible model of human reasoning.* In agreeing with this, he argues that expert systems generally do not reason as humans do. Gallant believes that humans seldom follow logical rules in daily life. However, such rules may be constructed to justify or explain their actions to other humans. Therefore, according to Gallant (1988), requiring a system to be rule-driven and a model of human reasoning is not psychologically plausible. The desire for a practical system led Gallant to favor performance over modeling. This resulted in a system much closer to conventional expert systems than to psychological models.

Gallant (1988) believes that connectionist expert systems present a promising approach to the knowledge acquisition problem for expert systems. These methods are most appropriate for classification problems in environments where humans tend to generate brittle and perhaps contradictory IF-THEN rules.

5.5.4 Niida et al.'s method

If the dominant relationships for a connectionist system are to be extracted, then it is necessary to find an effective way of decreasing the complexity of the neural network into what is called a skeleton network. The method developed by Niida et al. (1989) uses this approach. The skeleton network is created by a multi-level optimization method guided by a human decision-maker. From this skeleton network, redundancy is decreased by removing links and/or hidden units.

The basic steps of this method are summarized below (Niida et al. 1989):

1. Define the problem by specifying output variables and alternative input variables.
2. Collect and check the validity of pattern data by dividing the pattern data into two groups for learning and evaluation.

3. Select the input nodes from the alternative input variables.
4. Create the skeleton networks by two-level optimization; that is,
    (i) orthogonality among the input nodes, and
    (ii) the randomness between the input and output nodes.

5. Evaluate further performance of the skeleton networks by using the evaluation pattern data. Sensitivity analysis to input values is also checked. If not satisfied, go back to step 3.
6. Where good performance is achieved, the dominant relations can be extracted from this network.
7. The relationships obtained should be explained and analyzed by experts, or should be used to obtain further knowledge from experts in explicit forms.

The sixth step of extracting the dominant relationships is the critical part of this method. After creating a skeleton network various links will remain. The weight of each link has a sign and a value. If the absolute value of the weight is high, the link represents a strong relationship between the source and destination nodes. The following two knowledge extraction rules are then used (Niida et al. 1989):

- *If the weight of the lower (i.e. input to hidden) and upper (i.e. hidden to output) link have the same sign, the total effect from an input node to an output node is positive.*
- *If the links have different signs for their weights, the effect is negative.*

The rules produced are totally dependent upon obtaining the correct skeleton network. The construction of this skeleton network is guided by a human and thus is not truly automated. Apart from this, the extraction of the rules is totally dependent upon the correct links remaining as part of the network. This could be difficult for large problems. This solution also seems to be restricted to a three-layered network.

5.5.5 Saito and Nakano's RN method

The RN method, developed by Saito and Nakano (1990), produces rules that are expressed in disjunctive normal form, as it is an intuitive form for humans. Two phases compose the method (Saito & Nakano 1990). The first generates candidates for rules from neural networks and facts. The key idea in this phase is to employ a perturbation approach that makes use of the positive and negative facts. The second phase then selects the useful rules from the candidates. Saito and Nakano (1990) believe that using both a network and facts will prevent the combinatorial explosion that is likely if only a network were used.

The basic algorithm is (Saito & Nakano 1990):

RN1. Generate a candidate for rules:

   RN1-1. Generate a positive rule:

   RN1-2. If the positive rule has covered some negative facts,

      then

            RN1-2-1. Pick a negative fact and generate a negative
            rule.
            RN1-2-2. Modify the positive rule by subtracting the
            negative rule.
            RN1-2-3. Continue until the positive rule does not
            cover any negative fact.
   RN2. Continue until every positive fact has been examined.

To generate the positive/negative rules, the positive and negative output regions are first determined for the output unit of the neural network. Then for a positive/negative fact, each attribute value is changed gradually in predetermined constant steps; that is, first the attribute value is increased until the output level has changed to another region, and then it is decreased to another region. Since the upper and lower limits are thus obtained, an interval corresponding to the attribute is determined. According to these intervals, a positive/negative rule is generated (Saito & Nakano 1990).

5.5.6 McMillan et al.'s CONNECTIONIST SCIENTIST GAME

The intention of the approach proposed by McMillan et al. (1991) is to mimic the scientific method of discovery in order to extract rules from a network.

The method uses an iterative approach that:

- trains a network, analogous to the observation and intuition phase of a scientist;
- extracts rules, analogous to the hypothesis phase of the scientific method;
- injects the rules back into the network, analogous to the testing by experimentation phase of the scientific method.

The solution presented by McMillan et al. (1991) relies upon a special purpose architecture, tailored for an individual domain, that reflects the structure of the rules. For this architecture, a special learning technique trains the network. Correct rules defining the output are then produced from this.

There are several obvious drawbacks to this solution. First, how does one construct a special purpose architecture to reflect the rules, if the rules are not known? Second, and more importantly, this solution totally relies on the special purpose architecture for the specific problem domain. The solution is thus only applicable to that specific problem domain, and a different special purpose architecture must be developed for different problem domains. However, the aim of any learning or discovery program is to develop a generic algorithm that can be utilized for several different problem domains (Lenat 1983b). A generic learning algorithm allows what was learned with one domain to be used with another problem domain, resulting in less effort and time to produce a solution.

5.5.7 Fu's KT algorithm

The KT algorithm developed by Fu (1991) translates a trained neural network into a rule-based system. The algorithm consists of two sequential phases (Fu 1991):

- *A network is trained using Back-propagation;*
- *The KT algorithm is applied to the trained net to obtain a set of rules, each represented as:*

  premise(antecedent) $\Rightarrow$ *conclusion(consequent).*

Some details underlying the algorithm need to be presented. If the activation of a clause in the antecedent falls within various ranges, then certain assumptions are made. For some α and β, where $\beta > \alpha$, these assumptions are:

- range (0 to α) — represents a 0 or no, and
- range (β to 1) — represents a 1 or yes.

These restrictions follow directly from the sigmoid activation function used by Back-propagation. KT recognizes two important kinds of attributes:

- Pos-atts — attributes linked to a particular concept with positive weights;
- Neg-atts — attributes linked to a particular concept with negative weights.

Once again, this is based on the fact that the sigmoid function used by Back-propagation is a monotonically increasing function, restricting the activation values to between 0 and 1.

The KT algorithm works by searching for rules that are able to confirm a given concept (i.e., output) independently (Fu 1991). The antecedent of any such rule should have an activation greater than β, as stated above. The selected rules form a set of all combinations of, at most, k pos-atts. Each rule can confirm the concept if all neg-atts are absent. Each such rule or rule combination is then searched in an attempt to determine those rules that can confirm the concept in the presence of some or all neg-atts. The next phase interchanges the roles of pos-atts and neg-atts; that is, the method searches for rules that produce an activation level less than α.

In multi-layered networks, it is difficult to recognize the pos-atts and neg-atts for a final concept. To deal with multi-layered networks, KT learns rules on a layer-by-layer basis (Fu 1991). Eventually, rules are rewritten in input attribute terms that link directly to a final (target) concept. To construct rules between the hidden layer and the output layer, each hidden unit is treated as an attribute. These hidden attributes are also categorized into pos-atts and neg-atts. Rules in this layer are then rewritten in terms of the rules in the next layer closer to the input of the net. Rewriting therefore starts with the output layer and is repeated until the attributes are associated with the final concept. After rewriting, a rule is deleted if it contains an attribute and its negation, or conflicting attributes.

Even though the number of attributes in the premise part is limited, there is still a need to check every possible combination of attributes. Using the notion of pos-atts and neg-atts avoids the combinatorial explosion of this search (Fu 1991). For example, to learn a confirming rule, one can always assume that pos-atts absent in the premise part are absent, and neg-atts absent in the premise imply that the corresponding attributes are present.

The KT algorithm actually uses an abstraction technique (Fu 1991). Thus KT can be regarded as a process of generalization of the input and output relationships of the network. The performance of KT cannot be better than the performance of the neural network. However, consistency of the resulting rules is obtained, as confirming rules and corresponding negating rules cannot fire simultaneously because there is no overlap between the activation ranges. This has the side effect of no rule being formed for the inputs corresponding to activations between α and β. Finally, limiting the number of attributes to k in the premise part may result in important rules being overlooked.

5.5.8 Towell and Shavlik's SUBSET and NofM algorithms

Towell and Shavlik (1992) state that the units in a Back-propagation neural network normally have an activation equal to:

$$O_j = f\left(\sum_i W_{ij} X_i + bias_j \right)$$

where
O_j = output of unit j,
W_{ij} = weight of unit i to j,
X_i = output of unit i,
$bias_j$ = bias of unit j, and
$f(z)$ = activation function
$= \dfrac{1}{1 + e^{-z}}$

Hence the activation of a unit is a function of the sum of the weighted inputs to a unit plus the bias. In broad terms, if the summed weighted input exceeds the absolute value of the bias, then the activation will be near one. If the opposite is true and the bias is negative, then the activation will be approximately zero. From this premise, rule extraction methods look for ways in which the weighted sum is guaranteed to exceed the absolute value of the bias so that the activation is near to one (Towell & Shavlik 1992).

The basic task of rule extraction reduces to searching each unit for the set of incoming links with summed weights exceeding the absolute value of the bias. The logistic function guarantees that the units have non-negative activations. This allows the rule extraction method to take the sign of a link's weight into consideration and indicate the manner in which an attribute should be used. Positively weighted links therefore give rise to non-negated antecedents, while negatively weighted links can only give rise to negated antecedents. However, the extracted rules make errors using only these considerations due to the combined effect of the links with low weight that have not been included in the rules (Towell & Shavlik 1992).

Towell and Shavlik's SUBSET method attempts to find subsets of incoming weights that exceed the absolute value of the bias on a unit. The major problem with SUBSET is the cost of finding all such subsets. Hence, SUBSET looks for subsets using a branch-and-bound algorithm that is limited in terms of the number of rules it may find. This method is similar to that of Saito and Nakano, who establish an ad hoc ceiling on the number of antecedents in the extracted rules.

The NofM method (Towell & Shavlik 1992), on the other hand, searches for rules in terms of:

IF (N of the following M antecedents are true) THEN ...

In this formalism, if N=M then only conjunctive rules are produced and if N=1, then disjunctive rules are produced. The NofM algorithm is given in Table 5.4.

---

(1) With each hidden and output unit, form groups of similarly weighted links.

(2) Set links weights of all group members to the average of the group.

(3) Eliminate any groups that do not significantly affect whether the unit will be active or inactive.

(4) Holding all links weights constant, optimize biases of all hidden units and output units using the backpropagation algorithm.

(5) Form a single rule for each hidden and output unit. The rule consists of a threshold given by the bias and weighted antecedents specified by remaining limks.

(6) Where possible, simplify rules to eliminate superfluous weights and thresholds.

Table 5.4   The NofM algorithm for rule extraction (Towell & Shavlik 1992)

Using a standard clustering method, the first step groups links into equivalence classes. The equivalence class idea is the key to the NofM algorithm because it allows the algorithm to consider groups of links and not individual links within the group. The next step attempts to identify and eliminate those groups with low link weights and few members, as they are considered to have little effect on the outputs. The biases on the units are then optimized by freezing the weights on the links so that groups stay intact. The network is then retrained using Back-propagation with the activation function slightly modified to reflect the rule-like nature of the network. This modified training only alters the biases of the units. Finally, rules can be formed.

Towell and Shavlik (1992) state that the NofM method is able to extract a good set of rules from trained networks. They claim that the rules are meaningful and, in some cases, superior to the knowledge-based neural network in classifying and testing examples. The reason given for this is that the rule-extraction process reduces overfitting of the training examples. Also, rule extraction is (Towell & Shavlik 1992):

> *an extreme form of pruning in which links and units are pruned and actions are taken on the remaining network to transform the network into a set of rules.*

Some of the limitations of these methods raised by Towell and Shavlik (1992) are:

- *Large shifts in the meaning of the units as a result of training can make the extracted rules difficult to comprehend;*
- *Domain theories may not provide a sufficiently-rich vocabulary to allow a knowledge-based neural network to accurately learn a concept;*
- *The methods have not been tested on a broad set of problems.*

5.6 Recapitulation

This chapter has briefly described various symbolic and sub-symbolic learning methods such as Lenat's EURISKO, Gallant's MACIE, and Fu's KT algorithms. The next chapter discusses various theoretical considerations of human learning. These aspects provide an insight into an alternative approach for automated knowledge acquisition that uses neural networks.

References

Booker, L.B., Goldberg, D.E. & Holland, J.H. 1990, "Classifier systems and genetic algorithms", in *Machine Learning: Paradigms and Methods*, ed. J.G. Carbonell, MIT Press, Cambridge, Massachusetts, pp. 235–82

Charniak, E. & McDermott, D. 1985, *Introduction to Artificial Intelligence*, Addison-Wesley, Reading, Massachusetts

De Groot, M.H. 1970, *Optimal Statistical Decisions,* McGraw-Hill, Sydney, Australia

DeJong, G. & Mooney, R. 1990, "Explanation-based learning: An alternative view", in *Readings in Machine Learning*, eds J. Shavlik & T. Dietterich, Morgan Kaufmann Publishers, San Francisco, California, pp. 452–67

Dillon, T.S. & Tan, P.L. 1993, *Object-Oriented Conceptual Modeling*, Prentice Hall, Sydney, Australia

Forsyth, R. & Rada, R. 1986, *Machine Learning: Applications in Expert Systems and Information Retrieval*, Ellis Horwood, Chichester, UK

Fu, L. 1991, "Rule learning by searching on adapted nets", *Proceedings of the Ninth National Conference on Artificial Intelligence (AAAI-91)*, Anaheim, California, pp. 590–5

Gallant, S. 1987, "Automated generation of connectionist expert systems for problems involving noise and redundancy," *AAAI Workshop on Uncertainty*, Seattle, July

Gallant, S. 1988, "Connectionist expert systems", *Communications of the ACM*, vol. 31, no. 2, February, pp. 152–69

Goldberg, D.E. 1989, *Genetic Algorithms in Search, Optimization, and Machine Learning,* Addison-Wesley, Reading, Massachusetts, pp. 217–307

Grefenstette, J.J. 1990, "Genetic algorithms and their applications", in *The Encyclopedia of Computer Science and Technology, Volume 21,* eds
A. Kent & J.G. William, AIC-90-006, Naval Research Laboratory, Washington DC, pp. 139–52

Holland, J. 1975, *Adaptation in Natural and Artificial Systems*, University of Michigan Press, Ann Arbor

Lenat, D. 1982,"The nature of heuristics", *Artificial Intelligence*, vol. 19, pp. 189–249

Lenat, D. 1983a, "Theory formation by heuristic search. The nature of heuristics II: Background and examples", *Artificial Intelligence*, vol. 21, pp. 31–59

Lenat, D. 1983b, "EURISKO: A program that learns new heuristics and domain concepts. The nature of heuristics III: Program design and examples", *Artificial Intelligence*, vol. 21, pp. 61–98

Lenat, D. 1983c, "The role of heuristics in learning by discovery: Three case studies", in *Machine Learning: An Artificial Intelligence Approach*, eds R.S. Michalski, J.G. Carbonell & T.M. Mitchell, Tioga Publishing, Palo Alto, California, pp. 243–306

McMillan, C., Mozer, M. & Smolensky, P. 1991,"The CONNECTIONIST SCIENTIST GAME: Rule extraction and refinement in a neural network", *Proceedings of the Thirteenth Annual Conference of the Cognitive Science Society*, Erblaum, Hillsdale, New Jersey

Michalewicz, Z. 1992, *Genetic Algorithms + Data Structures = Evolution Programs,* Springer-Verlag, Berlin

Minsky, M. 1975, "A framework for representing knowledge", in *The Psychology of Computer Vision,* ed. P.H. Winston, McGraw-Hill, New York

Minton, S., Carbonell, J.G., Knoblock, C.A., Kuokka, D.R., Etzioni, O. & Gil, Y. 1990, "Explanation-based learning: A problem solving perspective", in *Machine Learning: Paradigms and Methods,* ed. J.G. Carbonell, MIT Press, Cambridge, Massachusetts, pp. 63–118

Mitchell, T., Keller, R. & Kedar-Cabelli, S. 1990, "Explanation-based generalization: A unifying view", in *Readings in Machine Learning,* eds J. Shavlik & T. Dietterich, Morgan Kaufmann Publishers, San Francisco, California, pp. 435–51

Niida, K., Tani, J., Hirobe, T. & Koshijima, I. 1989, "Application of neural networks to rule extraction from operation data", *AIChE Annual Meeting,* Paper No. 6g, San Francisco

Oosthuizen, G.D. 1989, "Machine learning: A mathematical framework for neural networks, symbolic and genetic-based learning", in *Proceedings of the 3rd International Conference on Genetic Algorithms,* ed. J.D. Schaffer, Morgan Kaufmann, San Mateo, California, pp. 385–90

Saito, K. & Nakano, R. 1990, "Rule extraction from facts and neural networks", *International Conference on Neural Networks (ICNN-90-PARIS),* Paris, France, July, pp. 379–82

Sethi, I.K. 1990, "Entropy nets: From decision trees to neural networks", *Proceedings of the IEEE,* vol. 78, no. 10, October, pp. 1605–13

Sethi, I.K. 1991, "Decision tree performance enhancement using an artificial neural network implementation", in *Artificial Neural Networks and Statistical Pattern Recognition: Old and New Connections,* eds I.K. Sethi & A.K. Jain, Elsevier Science Publishers, Amsterdam, pp. 71–86

Shavlik, J. & Dietterich, T. 1990, "Improving the efficiency of a problem solver", in *Readings in Machine Learning,* eds J. Shavlik & T. Dietterich, Morgan Kaufmann Publishers, San Francisco, California, pp. 429–34

Towell, G. & Shavlik, J. 1992, *The Extraction of Refined Rules from Knowledge-based Neural Networks,* Machine Learning Research Group Working Paper 91-4, University of Wisconsin, Madison

6

Theoretical considerations

6.1 Introduction

As seen from the previous chapters, the existing machine learning methods for automating the process of knowledge acquisition have many unresolved problems. As a consequence, these methods are not widely used in real-world applications. However, there seems to be a more basic difficulty with these methods that is more conceptual than technical.

In some respects, people are better than computers at performing certain tasks. They are far better at a wide range of natural cognitive tasks such as recognizing objects in natural scenes, communicating in natural languages, and retrieving contextually appropriate information from memory (McClelland et al. 1986b). In fact, people can be extremely clever at capturing regularities and formulating abstractions concerning some repetitive task or situation (Patarnello & Carnevali 1989). In the view of some researchers, such as McClelland et al. (1986b), humans are better at these skills than a computer because the human brain employs a basic computational architecture that is more suited to dealing with the tasks. These tasks generally require the simultaneous consideration of many pieces of information and constraints. Thus, any model that exploits this architecture would seem to be more closely tied to the physiology of the brain than any other information-processing model.

It is believed that the brain consists of a large number of highly interconnected nodes that apparently send very simple excitatory and inhibitory messages to each other. The properties of the nodes used in many models based on the architecture of the brain were inspired by neural hardware. However, neurophysiological plausibility is not the primary concern of the models. Their computational aspects are of greater importance (McClelland et al. 1986b).

In this chapter we discuss various features of human learning and the human brain from a machine learning perspective. Computer-based models inspired by the architecture of the human brain contain many of the essential human processing facilities, such as insensitivity to noise, graceful degradation, and learning from experience (Norman 1986). Such methods have had some success in modeling (i.e., learning) various complex domains (McClelland & Rumelhart 1988; McClelland et al. 1986a; Rumelhart et al. 1986). However, the actual knowledge learned by these computer-based models is not in a form understandable to a human. To remedy this, the first step of any new learning method should allow the computer-based model to learn from a set of examples (in other words, from experience). A knowledge acquisition method should then be developed to extract the learned knowledge from this computer-based model in a form understandable to a human, as shown in Figure 6.1.

Numerous people in the AI area have commented on the richness of the human brain (Arbib 1989; Boden 1989a; Carbonell 1989; Collins & Smith 1988; Rendell 1987; Tattersall 1989). This richness provides motivation for a computer-based model that seeks to capture some elements of the architecture

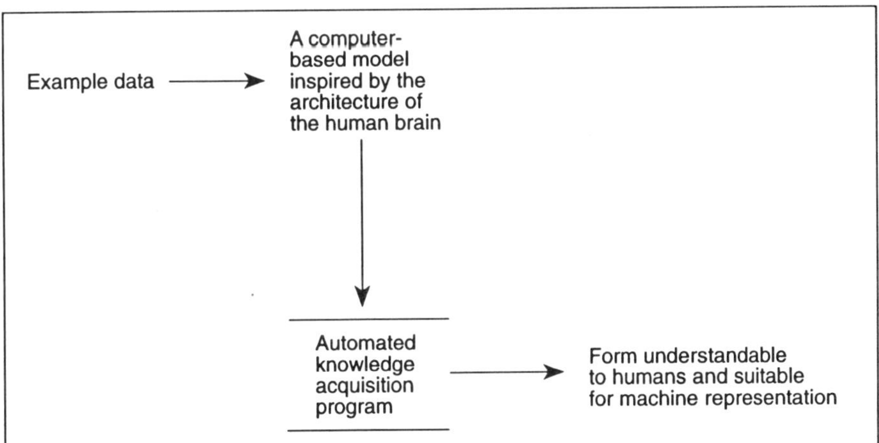

Figure 6.1   Building a knowledge acquisition program using a computer model inspired by the architecture of the brain

of the human brain. More importantly, it also provides some indications and theoretical justifications for the development of a better and more efficient method of acquiring knowledge on a machine.

6.2 Some issues of human learning

This section is not intended as a survey of human learning, but rather as a discussion of some aspects of human learning considered to have implications for machine learning. In addition, the focus is on learning with a view to acquiring knowledge for problem-solving.

All difficult problem-solving tasks require the use of knowledge. This knowledge must be understandable, easily modified, and expressed so that it can be applied in many situations (Rich 1983). But how does a human acquire knowledge? Learning, which is the process of acquiring knowledge, has many definitions in the literature. Wolff (1987) regards learning as:

> *a process of building and refining a knowledge structure towards a form which is optimally efficient for the several functions it must serve.*

The *International Encyclopedia of the Social Sciences* (Sills 1968) defines learning as:

> *a relatively permanent change in a behavioral tendency, which occurs as a result of reinforced practice. Here, learning is considered to consist of the formation of stimulus-response connections.*

A more psychological definition of learning is given by Rich (1983):

> *Learning refers to the change in a subject's behavior to a given situation brought about by its repeated experiences in that situation, provided that the behavior change cannot be explained on the basis of native response tendencies, maturation or temporary states of the subject.*

These definitions are too general to be useful here, as they give no indication of how to integrate new knowledge into existing knowledge. Kochen (1974) defines cognitive learning more specifically as:

> *a process for utilizing experiential inputs to shift representation so that an increasing variety of problems can be recognized, formulated, coped with.*

Thus, the concept of learning covers a wide variety of aspects.

Learning ability is no doubt central to human intelligence (Michalski 1987). This ability permits humans to adapt to the changing environment, to develop a great variety of skills, and to acquire expertise in a large number of specific domains. People are capable of learning from information carried by different sources and expressed in a variety of forms. This information can be encoded with or without errors, at different levels of abstraction, with different degrees of precision, and with varying relevance to the knowledge ultimately acquired. Learning can therefore be seen as the improvement of general cognitive capacities under outside influence (Boden 1987).

Gennari et al. (1989) view human learning as a gradual process of concept formation. In this case, the agent observes a series of objects or events, and hence induces a hierarchy of concepts that summarize and organize the experience. This is similar to conceptual clustering, which helps humans to understand the world better and to make predictions about its future behavior.

Important characteristics of human learning are as follows (Ohlsson 1987):

- *Improvement is gradual and continues after a correct solution has been found;*
- *Practice effects transfer from one problem to another;*
- *Errors are frequent during practice;*
- *Multiple trials are needed before a problem is mastered;*
- *Effects of practice depend upon the order of the practice problems.*

The learning process therefore is:

- slow, because of errors disappearing only gradually;
- repetitive, as a human needs repeated attempts before a solution path is mastered;
- dependent on what other problems have been solved.

Basically, humans continue to improve their performance over long periods of practice. They readily transfer what they have learned to other problems within the same domain. Hence, key factors in human intelligence are the ability to combine information in new ways, and the ability to identify and utilize the knowledge that is relevant to a particular problem (Anderson 1983). It also involves choosing what to process from among a set of alternatives.

The aspect of transferring knowledge is an important issue. A transfer of knowledge is said to occur when a problem solver applies knowledge gained while solving one set of problems to a different set (Ohlsson 1987). For such a transfer to be possible, what is learned during practice must be processed in such a way that it is applicable to the new target. With the experience accumulated during practice, the aim is to develop heuristics that apply to the target problem.

A related issue is when and how a skill is acquired. This is associated with the transition from a declarative base for the performance of a skill to a procedural base for using the skill (Anderson 1983, 1988). At the current stage of research, this transition is unclear and difficult to capture (Bruner et al. 1956). While several proposals have been made, the ACT* theory developed by Anderson is the most widely applied theory of the human acquisition of cognitive skills (Ohlsson 1987). ACT* is a rule-based system in which rules are implemented in a psychologically and neurally plausible manner. Anderson (1983) established that the symbolic processing involved in the theory could be implemented in terms that were plausible, given what is known about the nature of brain computations on neural activation levels.

The basic premise of the ACT* framework follows. The ability of humans to acquire complex skills distinguishes humans from other creatures (Anderson 1983, 1990). There may be a significant innate component to this successful acquisition, but it is totally implausible to suggest that humans have evolved special faculties or organs for mathematics, chess, and so on. People have become expert at activities that could not have been anticipated. According to Anderson (1983, 1988), there must be some basic set of principles that spans a broad range of computational tasks. The human mind is considered to be general-purpose; that is, the same data structures and processes can be used in programs for language and for problem-solving. This requires a single set of principles underlying all of cognition, with no principled differences or separations of faculties. In other words, Anderson claims that all higher-level cognitive functions are achieved by the same underlying structure.

6.3 Concept or category formation

The capacity to categorize enables humans to handle everyday information. According to Bruner et al. (1956), categorization is:

> *to render discriminably different things equivalent, to group the objects and events and people around us into classes, and to respond to them in terms of their class membership, rather than their uniqueness.*

Once categories have been learned, they can be used without further learning. The learning and usage of such categories are elementary forms of cognition by which humans adjust to their environment. Given a set of observations, humans thus acquire concepts that organize these observations and then use them in classifying future experiences (Gennari et al. 1989).

Selective perception is the process whereby an organism chooses from a large number of features available via its environment (Rendell 1987). The best discriminating feature is most likely to be selected. Hence categorization should yield the most information for the least cognitive load (Rendell 1987).

Without concepts, each new instance would have to be freshly responded to (Pollio 1974); that is, concepts provide the informational basis for classifying newly encountered objects or events. Encountering and identifying new instances is the essence of why a concept is such a powerful tool (Klausmeier et al. 1974). A concept is a mental activity that brings together two or more situations, experiences, or objects into a relationship. Via concepts, past experience can be used in a given situation (Harriman 1947). As concepts evolve progressively with experience, a person's ability to understand and deal with some domain may improve as well (Howard 1987).

A human subject has to identify relevant attributes, and then learn, develop, or apply a rule capable of manipulating these elements to formulate a concept. Human subjects also seek confirming information; they actively search their environment for appropriate exemplars to confirm or modify newly discovered concepts (Kristal 1981; Pollio 1974).

According to Rosch et al. (1976):

> *To categorize a stimulus means to consider it, for purposes of that categorization, not only equivalent to other stimuli in the same category but also different from stimuli not in that category.*

From this, two extremes can be formulated:

- First, it appears desirable for the categories to have many properties that distinguish them from other categories. This would lead to a large number of categories with the finest possible discrimination between them.
- On the other hand, an important purpose of categorization is to reduce the infinite differences among categories to *behaviorally and cognitively usable proportions*. Therefore, it seems advantageous not to differentiate when that differentiation is irrelevant to the task in hand.

According to Rosch (1977), the world contains *intrinsically separate things* that are so structured because of three principles. The first principle states that real-world attributes do not occur independently of one another.

Abstraction involves suppressing irrelevant detail and structuring hierarchical class levels. This premise forms the basis of the second principle, which states that objects of the world are structured. Therefore, there are many levels of abstraction at which any given thing can be classified. However, there is one basic level of abstraction at which the organism can obtain the most information with the least cognitive effort. Thus, there is (Rosch 1977):

- *one level with a lot of information with many properties. This therefore leads to the formation of a large number of categories with the finest possible discriminations between the categories;*
- *another level, which for the sake of reducing cognitive load, has a few classifications, a principle which would lead to the smallest number of the most abstract categories possible.*

A significant approach is to designate categories through the use of typical members or prototypes. The third principle states that categories become definitively structured because of this premise. Many experiments have shown that (Rosch 1977):

> *Categories are coded in the mind in terms of a prototype of a typical category member, and not by a list of each individual member of the category nor by means of a list of formal criteria necessary and sufficient for category membership.*

Thus, according to Rosch (1977), categories are not logical, bounded entities where membership requires all instances to possess the critical attributes. Instead, many natural categories are internally structured into a prototype of the category. Concepts can overlap and the boundaries can be fuzzy and irregular (Zhang 1990). As such, an item can be a definite or less definite member (or example) of a concept.

Concepts can be defined in terms of attributes, which in turn may be other concepts, and so forth (Pollio 1974). This is an obvious analogy to a hierarchical structure. Using this hierarchical principle in the organization of knowledge, it is possible to facilitate memory functions and the recognition of relationships and patterns (Anderson 1989). Concepts can thus be expressed as a set of defining features (both necessary and sufficient) that all instances of the concept share (Wiles 1987a). This is a simplification of human concepts, used as an underlying assumption to enable the modeling of some system. Anderson (1986) defines a concept as a mental representation or rule that picks out a class of objects or events. This definition is interesting because it states that there are two aspects of simple concept formation for humans; namely, the representation of a category by a prototype and the hierarchical structure of a concept.

The hierarchical structure or grouping of common features reduces redundancies (Wolff 1987) and has an impact on effectiveness and efficiency in human intelligence, from perception to creativity (Rendell 1987). To understand intelligence, one must work with units larger than a single response (Bruner et al. 1956). One must work with sequences of responses to understand the dynamic evolution of responses.

There are various models of concept representation in cognition. The definitional approach, or defining attribute model, uses rigid definitions for membership of an object in a category. Another model uses a fuzzy membership criterion. Here, a feature space proximity to a prototypical instance of a concept is the determining criterion for class membership (Rendell 1987).

Machine learning in AI has been based on the defining attribute model. Intermediate structures often form a useful bridge for learning between the large set of examples in the database and the final concise knowledge structures. Efficient and effective learning requires both symbolic structuring and statistical methods for noise immunity (Rendell 1987). As with any representional system, including the human mind, the degree of match between a representation formalism and reality can always be questioned (Boden 1989b).

Several studies (Bruner et al. 1956; Pollio 1974; Wolff 1987) indicate a need to group knowledge or categories to optimize performance. A range of data compression principles can be used to do this. These studies all suggest conjunctive (ANDing) and disjunctive (ORing) groupings. Wolff (1987) discusses further data compression principles, indicating that these principles, incorporated into a theory, can explain a wide range of phenomena in cognitive development.

In summary, concept learning, as modeled in AI, involves two sub-processes:

- identifying relevant attributes
- learning combinatorial rules.

6.4 Learning strategies

This section discusses the various learning strategies used by computer-based models of human learning. This discussion is not intended to provide a full description of the psychology of the learning strategies used by humans.

Learning strategies can be distinguished by the amount of inference the learner performs on the information provided. As this amount increases, the burden placed on the teacher or external environment decreases. It is much more difficult to teach a person by explaining each step in a complex task than by showing that person the way that similar tasks are usually handled. It is more difficult to program a computer to perform a complex task than it is to instruct a person; computer programs need explicit specifications of all of the details, whereas a person can use prior knowledge and common sense to fill in the most mundane details. The following taxonomy captures the trade-offs between these notions in the amount of effort required of the teacher and the learner (Carbonell et al. 1983).

- *Rote learning and direct implanting of new knowledge* — there is no inference or other transformation of the knowledge by the learner.
- *Learning by being told (i.e., by instruction)* — this case requires the learner to transform the knowledge from the input language to an internally usable representation. This knowledge can be obtained from a teacher or other written material, such as a textbook or manual. The new knowledge is integrated with prior knowledge for effective use. The learner is thus required to perform some inference, but a large fraction of the burden remains with the teacher. The teacher is required to organize knowledge in a way that incrementally augments the student's existing knowledge.
- *Learning by analogy* – this requires more inference on the part of the learner than does rote learning and learning by being told. Here, new facts and skills

are acquired by transforming and augmenting existing knowledge that bears a strong similarity to the desired new concept or skill. This transformed knowledge should be in a form that can be effectively used in the new situation.

- *Learning by example* — this type of learning has been used heavily for machine learning in AI. The basic premise is that, given a set of examples and counter-examples of a concept, the learner induces a general concept description of all the positive examples and none of the counter-examples. Here the learner is required to do a lot more inference, as the teacher provides no general concepts (as is the case in learning by being told) and no similar concepts from which a new concept can grow (as is the case in learning by analogy).

- *Learning by observation and discovery (i.e., unsupervised)* — this unsupervised learning requires the learner to perform more inference than any of the approaches described above, as this type of learning has no guidance from an external teacher. In this case, the learner is not provided with a set of instances that are the positive or negative examples of any given concept.

According to Boden (1987), it seems that learning a concept by meeting an example of it, is not only significantly different from learning it by hearsay, but is also somehow better. Learning by examples involves the development of descriptions representing the target domain. These descriptions are verified and refined through the use of examples and counter-examples. However, learning from examples involves gradual improvement of the representations of the world (Boden 1987). Several instances are required before significant learning can occur (Ohlsson 1987).

It is often impossible to avoid introducing more than one difference at a time. No concept learner that is forced to always assume that a linear conceptual model could possibly achieve the conceptual schemata possessed by people. However, for tractability, it is a reasonable first step to assume a linear conceptual model (Boden 1987).

The major weakness with these types of learning strategies is that they leave out the role of knowledge in learning. It seems obvious that the declarative knowledge of the objects, properties, and relations that are involved in a task domain should have some influence on the learning strategies for that domain (Ohlsson 1987).

6.5 Use of negative information for learning

The basic question discussed here is whether negative instances help in concept learning. If one is told that an item is not an example of some concept, does it or does it not help the person in figuring out what the concept might be (Pollio 1974)?

Pollio (1974) states that generally human subjects are less likely to use negative instances than positive ones in concept formation tasks. When negative instances are used, they often cause a good deal of difficulty to the subject performing the task. Defining an item as not being an example of a concept really provides the subject with little information as to what the concept may be. In this situation, unless the subject knows the relevant attributes of the concept, there is no way that the subject could know which attributes were ruled out by a given negative example. As pointed out by Pollio (1974), there is an infinite number of things that are not instances of a given concept. Also, humans almost never attempt to negate a hypothesis but instead prefer to confirm it. However, Pollio (1974) concludes that for now the inability to use negation for evaluating the adequacy of a hypothesis cannot be claimed as a general property of human processing. The extent to which humans do use negative information is highly dependent on the details of the examples and the learning situation.

The major problem with this work is that there is no indication of how negative the negative examples are. This requires clarification. Positive examples are positively correlated with a particular concept, while negative examples are negatively correlated or not correlated with the concept. However, the degree of correlation is dependent upon the amount of similarity between the example and the concept. Consider a few examples from the animal world:

- An elephant and a horse are strongly positively correlated. They are fairly similar since they are both mammals, have four legs, have one tail, and are large.
- An elephant and a mouse are positively correlated, but not as strongly or to the same degree as the correlation between an elephant and a horse. This is a partial positive correlation, as both animals are mammals, and have four legs and one tail, but a mouse is small compared with an elephant.
- An elephant and a bird are strongly negatively correlated. Apart from being classified as living creatures, they have no other similar features.
- The above animals and any non-living thing (such as a box) would have no or zero correlation, as they have no similar features at all.

Therefore, it is important to know the degree of negativity. Of course, if there is no correlation, then there would be an infinite number of things that an entity is not. However, if the example were partially correlated in either direction, then information could be extracted.

A well-known example of using negative instances to form concepts was provided by Winston's ARCH computer learning program (Winston 1984). The main purpose of this computer program was to develop a general description of an arch, given example data. This data included proper examples of an arch, and examples that were close to a proper arch. These latter examples were regarded as near misses and could be considered as negative examples, but only of a small degree. Thus, the near misses in this work were not fully negatively correlated; instead they were partially negative because they were considered to be *close* to what an arch should be. The result was that the proper examples generalized the concept description, while the near miss examples specialized the concept description. This work suggested that both positive and negative instances are essential to learning a given concept completely.

Ohlsson (1987) supports the view that both positive and negative examples are necessary for learning a concept. This underlies Ohlsson's theory of acquisition based on conjectures (positive) and refutations (negative). The acquisition process reflects the belief that the set of necessary conditions for an event to happen is unique. According to this theory, heuristic learning proceeds through two opposite processes. The first begins (Ohlsson 1987):

> *with a maximally restricted proposer, which is successively attenuated through the deletion of conditions found to be unnecessary for a good outcome.*

This leads to a large set of situations where each operator can be applied. Eventually some situations lead to errors. The second process is then applied, successively correcting the proposer by the creation of censors (Ohlsson 1987). For each operator, gradually more and more of the bad cases are correctly covered. The proportion of situations in which the problem solver has to fall back on trial and error search, as both of these processes proceed, becomes smaller. In the limit, there is no trial and error search and each operator is applied only in situations in which it is appropriate (Ohlsson 1987). Errors in this theory are an essential feature of the learning process. The theory also points out that direct formulation of every set of situations in which an operator is applicable would be difficult. However, according to Ohlsson (1987), an approximation is possible if performance is organized in terms of conjectures and refutations. A strong aspect of this work is that it uses the same mechanism to represent both the positive and negative aspects (i.e., strengths and weaknesses) of human learning. In summary (Ohlsson 1987):

> *The principle of conjectures and refutations describes a type of performance organization which allows systems at different organizational levels to make the most out of previous experience in the service of future action.*

6.6 Neuro-physiological considerations

In this section, various physiological aspects of the human brain are presented. The brain is the principal area where memories are stored and thoughts are conceived (Guyton 1984). It is impossible to present a complete survey of neuro-physiological aspects of the human brain here. Therefore, this discussion is slanted toward issues of importance to machine learning.

A fundamental assumption is that the brain comprises computational cells, called neurons, that interact in a variety of ways. These neurons, numbering about one hundred billion, conduct the signals in the nervous system (Guyton 1984). The major anatomical connections within the structured brain are specified genetically. Neurons are organized into well-defined and highly structured computational networks called (biological) neural networks. Neural networks are the principal computational systems of the brain. There are many types of these systems, including receptor networks and storage networks. Each neural network receives inputs through specific input pathways that are processed and responded to in some way. The response is sent through specific output pathways in a manner that depends on current and past inputs (Baron 1987).

It is believed that different neural networks perform different information processing tasks (Baron 1987). Thus, different areas of the cerebral cortex, such as the visual and auditory cortex, are specialized for processing information from different sensory modalities. However, Sejnowski (1986) states that all of these cortical areas have a similar internal anatomical organization. Therefore, the relatively uniform structure of the cerebral cortex suggests that it is capable of applying a general-purpose style of computation to many processing domains, from sensory processing to the most abstract reasoning. Whether the similarity between different areas of the cortex is merely superficial or extends to the computational level is an experimental question that depends on theoretical issues (Sejnowski 1986).

Any attempt to formulate a complete and detailed model of the brain is impossible at the present time. There is insufficient causal quantitative information about the interactions between the neurons to do so. Even if there were sufficient information (Baron 1987):

> *The computational difficulties of specifying the activity of 100 billion neurons with 100 trillion connections (i.e. synapses), their environment and entire history of inputs to the system, is simply not computationally feasible.*

However, a little is known about the computational processes of the brain, such as the way that visual images are processed, how experiences are recorded, and how communication is carried out via natural language (Baron 1987). Thus, it would be useful to build computational networks that perform the same processes as the brain and that use the neural networks as a guide to understand the computational logic of the brain (Baron 1987).

Biological neural networks are assumed to be constructed of neuron-like elements, interconnected with various links (Baron 1987). The typical neuron structure comprises four major parts, as shown in Figure 6.2, an adaptation from Guyton (1984). These parts are (Guyton 1984):

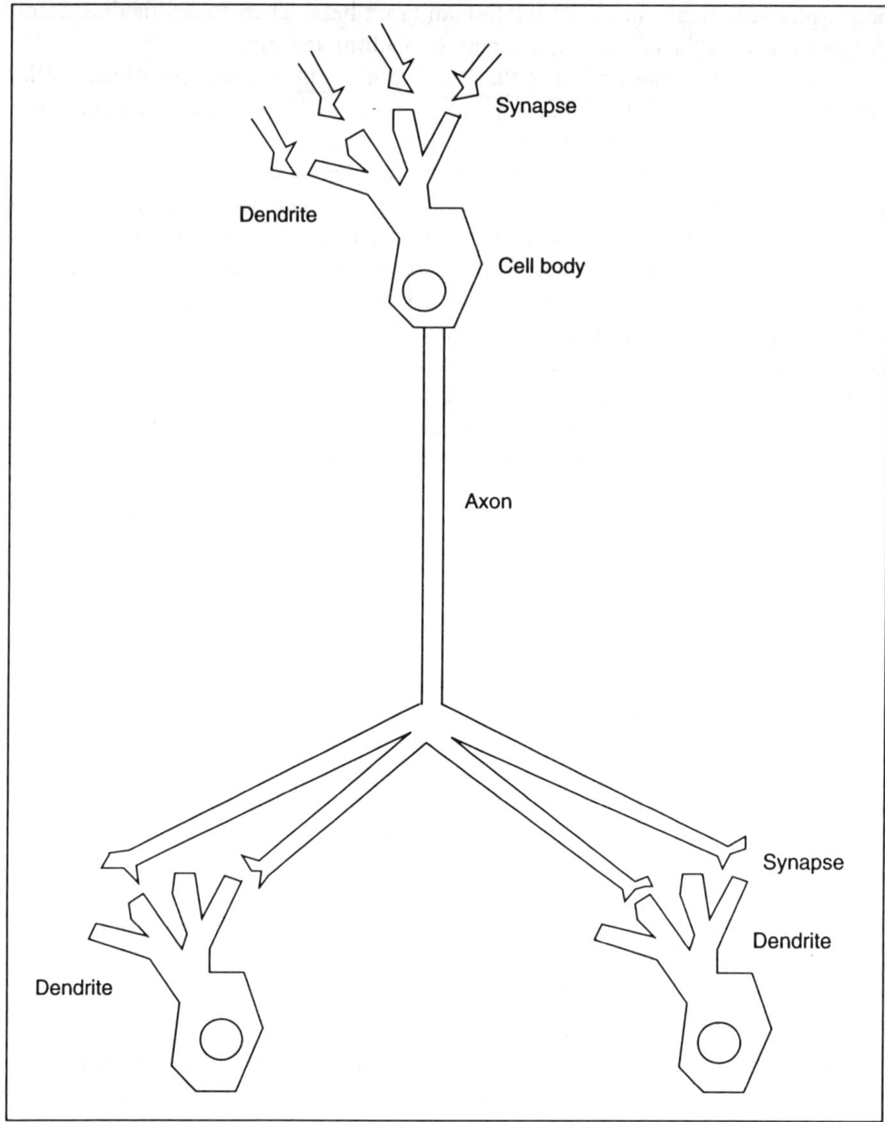

Figure 6.2   Schematic picture of the structure of a large neuron in the brain (Guyton 1984)

- *Cell body* — The other parts of the neuron grow from the cell body. Much of the nourishment that is required for maintaining the life of the entire neuron is contained in the cell body.

- *Dendrites* — There are several outgrowths branching from the cell body and these are known as dendrites. They are the main receptor portions of the neuron. Thus most signals that are to be transmitted by the neuron enter by way of the dendrites. However, some signals also enter directly through the surface of the cell body. The dendrites of each neuron usually receive signals from possibly thousands of contact points with other neurons. These contact points are called *synapses.*
- *Axon* — Each neuron has only one output that is known as an axon. It varies in size from only a few millimeters to as long as a meter. Axons carry the nerve signals to the next nerve cell or to muscles and glands in the peripheral parts of the body (Guyton 1984).
- *Synapses* — Each axon from the cell body branches many times, often thousands of times, at its end. At the end of each of these branches is a specialized axon terminal that, in the central nervous system, is called a synaptic knob because of its knob-like appearance (Guyton 1984). The synaptic knob connects to another neuron through the membrane surface of the dendrite or cell body. This connection or contact point between the knob end and the membrane is called a synapse. The signals transmitted from one neuron to the next are carried outward by the synapse. When stimulated, the synaptic knob releases a minute quantity of a hormone called a transmitter substance into the space between the knob and the membrane of the neuron. The transmitter substance then stimulates the neuron.

The functional parts of a typical neuron in the human body are the cell body of the neuron and the two types of projections, the dendrites and the axon. The many small fibers leading to the neuron terminate in synaptic knobs. These knobs lie on the surfaces of the cell body and dendrites. The synapse is the junction between the synaptic knob and the dendrite or cell body. The small fibers are the axons from other neurons (Guyton 1984).

Neurons are contacted by many, often thousands of, different cells at thousands of synapses. The fluctuations in the cell thus depend on the combined influence of all pre-synaptic cells. These fluctuations are dependent upon both the quantity and the type of neuro-transmitter released by the neuron (Baron 1987). In recent years it has been discovered that many different transmitters are secreted in various parts of the nervous system. These transmitters have different functions, such as providing prolonged or very rapid and brief stimulation of the neuron (Guyton 1984).

Signals are transmitted from one neuron to another through the synapse that has the capability of transmitting some signals and preventing the transmission of others. It is therefore a valuable tool of the nervous system for choosing which course of events to follow. The synapse is perhaps the most important single determinant of the central nervous system function owing to this variable transmission of signals (Guyton 1984). A transmitter substance is secreted by the synapses. This substance may be either excitatory or inhibitory, allowing the incoming signals to cause either excitation or suppression of the next neuron. A neuron can usually be excited only by the simultaneous firing of a large number of synapses, requiring signals from these synapses to combine before any action potential occurs in the stimulated neuron (Guyton 1984).

When two or more synaptic knobs are stimulated simultaneously, they each release the excitatory transmitter, causing a *summation* of the sodium that enters the cell body. This also causes a summation of the excitatory post-synaptic potential developed. The current flowing through the cell body becomes greater and greater as more and more knobs fire simultaneously, until finally it is *great enough to excite the axon.* If the post-synaptic potential increases still more, the rate of action potential firing also becomes faster and faster (Guyton 1984).

It is important to understand what is meant by *great enough to excite the axon.* When the excitatory post-synaptic potential becomes greater than a certain level, an action potential is generated in the axon that extends outward from the cell body of the neuron. The critical membrane potential at which an action potential occurs is called the threshold for excitation (Guyton 1984), or threshold firing rate (Baron 1987). Thus, as the post-synaptic potential becomes greater than this potential, the axon will fire repetitively. The firing will continue as long as the potential remains above the threshold. Subsequent stimulation of the neuron by inhibitory synaptic knobs will actually stop the firing of the neuron. Therefore, the inhibitory transmitter has an opposite effect on the synapse to that caused by the excitatory transmitter (Guyton 1984).

Hearst (1972) argues that both positive (excitatory) and negative (inhibitory) transmissions are used in the human body. However, Hearst states that there have been arguments and proposals that inhibition is merely reduced excitation. Those who deny the need for a concept of inhibition often argue that, since it is usually measured as a decrease in some excitation effect, the concept can be eliminated completely and an analysis of all effects accomplished in terms of positive and negative changes in only one factor (excitation). But as Hearst (1972) points out, this excitation approach ignores the physiological, anatomical, and biochemical data suggesting that both excitatory and inhibitory processes are involved in the nervous system action, and that these processes can be meaningfully and usefully separated. The separation of the two may provide an insight into the reasons why a stimulus is ineffective, as the properties of the various stimuli that produce an extremely low or zero level of response will be overlooked. Thus, a conceptual framework that includes both excitatory and inhibitory effects seems to encourage a deeper experimental and theoretical analysis of the reasons why a stimulus may be ineffective (Hearst 1972). More formal definitions of inhibitory and excitatory stimuli are provided by Hearst (1972):

- *An inhibitory stimulus is defined as a multi-dimensional environmental event that as a result of conditioning (in this case based on some negative correlation between presentation of the stimulus and subsequent occurrences of another event or outcome such as 'reinforcement') develops the capacity to decrease performance below the level occurring when that stimulus is absent. This definition includes both a decremental effect on behavior and an establishing (associative) operation.*
- *An excitatory stimulus refers to an event that as a result of conditioning (in this case based on some positive correlation between the presentation of the stimulus and subsequent occurrences of another event or outcome) develops the capacity to increase performance above the level occurring when that stimulus is absent.*

Baron (1987) distinguishes two possible types of information:

- *Static information* — a pattern, arrangement, or configuration of constituent units that encode the knowledge.
- *Dynamic information* — the signal impressed upon the input of the system is used to communicate the knowledge or event.

Within the brain, the dynamic patterns are the patterns of discharging neurons that convey signals from one network to another, while static patterns are memory traces encoded as spatial patterns of biochemical marker (Baron 1987). The smallest indivisible unit of information in the brain is the rate of firing of an individual neuron, but the fundamental unit of dynamic information is the set of firing rates of the neurons in a specific collection of neurons (Baron 1987). Baron (1987) explains that:

- a zero firing rate may represent the absence of an external signal;
- the maximum firing rate represents the maximum detectable value;
- an intermediate firing rate represents intermediate amounts of sensory signal;
- neural information is embedded in the interactions of the neurons;
- the rate of firing of the neurons rather than their states characterizes given patterns.

There are, in general, both spatial and time-varying patterns. According to Guyton (1984):

- *Spatial summation means that two or more synaptic knobs fire simultaneously, thereby adding their individual effects to the excitatory postsynaptic potential.*
- *Temporal summation, on the other hand, means that the same synaptic knobs fire two or more times in rapid succession, thus adding the effect of the second firing to that of the first, before the first effect is over.*

The central nervous system comprises excitatory neurons that secrete excitatory transmitters at their nerve endings, and inhibitory neurons that secrete inhibitory transmitters. Certain neuronal centers of the central nervous systems are composed entirely of excitatory neurons, others entirely of inhibitory neurons, and still others of both excitatory and inhibitory neurons. Therefore, the central nervous system has two modes of activity, either excitation or inhibition, instead of excitation alone (Guyton 1984).

The varying characteristics of the different neurons and their different connections in the nervous system allow the neurons in one portion of the nervous system to control one function of the body and those in another portion to control another function. The signals reaching the neuron by way of excitatory and inhibitory synapses are activated by neurons from other parts of the nervous system. If the resultant sum of all the excitatory and inhibitory effects is above the threshold for excitation, the neuron fires. From this, some of the neurons (Guyton 1984):

- fatigue rapidly, while others fatigue slowly
- have high thresholds, while others have low thresholds
- fire at rapid rates, while others fire at slow rates.

The varying characteristics of the neurons allow the sorting of signals to determine their meanings, the performance of special skilled motions, the thinking of specific thoughts, and the modification of these thoughts by signals arriving from other parts of the nervous system (Guyton 1984).

The model of a neuron used in some systems is greatly simplified. It assumes there are several dendrites that are usually branched and that receive information from other neurons. Also, the model assumes that there is a single axon that outputs the processed information, usually by the propagation of a spike or an action potential, and that this axon splits into various branches that make synapses onto the dendrites and cell bodies of other neurons. In the real human brain, complications arise due to (Crick & Asanuma 1986):

- a neuron having no obvious axon
- axons forming synapses on other axons
- dendrites forming synapses onto other dendrites.

Also, the following assertions are not justified by the available experimental evidence (Crick & Asanuma 1986):

- neurons excite some cells and inhibit others
- neurons that connect to all other cells are of the same type
- neurons with distinctive synapses do elaborate computations
- a neuron, by itself, can fire another cell (Sejnowski 1986).

A simplified model of the human brain consists of a representation that defines the behavior of a network in terms of excitatory and inhibitory processing elements, where each element sums its inputs and fires if a threshold is reached. According to this simplification, each neuron is assumed either to excite or inhibit another neuron. Also, the interconnections between the neurons are assumed initially to be random and, by experience or activity, the appropriate interconnections are formed (Stubbs 1990).

Finally, there are essential properties of human information processing that any such model must exhibit. Humans appear to work well in the face of ambiguity, incompleteness, and false information (Johnson-Laird 1989). The human system is not only robust, it is also flexible. Therefore, any model has to be able to work with descriptions rather than precise specifications, with partial information rather than complete information, and by competition among different interpretations (Norman 1986). Also, the model should provide graceful degradation of performance, relative insensitivity to missing or erroneous data, and an iterative retrieval process that works by descriptions rather than by more traditional search (Norman 1986).

6.7 Summary of these cognitive and neuro-physiological aspects

The preceding sections presented some aspects of human learning, as well as neuro-physiological considerations. These aspects were selected for their potential applicability to machine learning and, as such, do not constitute a complete survey of the work on human learning. Some of the major points made so far are listed below.

- The existing machine learning methodologies have not been used extensively in real-world knowledge acquisition. This indicates the need for another, more acceptable methodology.
- From neuro-physiological considerations, a simplified model of the human brain has been proposed. This model defines the behavior of a network in terms of excitatory and inhibitory processing elements, where each element sums its inputs and fires if a threshold is reached. According to this simplification, neurons are assumed either to excite or inhibit another neuron and the interconnections between the neurons are initially random. The appropriate interconnections are formed by experience or activity (Guyton 1984; Stubbs 1990).
- Humans appear to work well in the face of ambiguity, incompleteness, and false information. Any model should exhibit these features (Johnson-Laird 1989). The essential features of any such model are that it is robust and relatively insensitive to missing or erroneous data and to damage to its parts.
- Computer-based models inspired by this simplified model of the human brain are now being used as an alternative to the traditional AI approaches.
- For any type of learning, the use of knowledge is an important consideration.

Hence, the declarative knowledge of the objects involved in the domain should have some influence on the knowledge acquisition strategies for that domain (Ohlsson 1987).

- Concept learning, as modeled in AI, involves two sub-processes: identifying relevant attributes and learning combinatorial rules.
- Developing concepts or categories enables one to develop a hierarchy of the domain. This structure reduces redundancies and is more efficient and understandable (Wolff 1987).
- The use of compression principles improves the representation of data. Forming conjunctive and disjunctive groupings improves efficiency (Bruner et al. 1956; Pollio 1974; Wolff 1987).
- Using negative information aids in the process of learning, provided that there is some correlation.

6.8 Relationship between cognitive representations and physiological aspects

Anderson's ACT* theory (1983, 1990) claims that there is no contradiction between a rule-based system and the kind of neural system that has been found to be plausible. According to the ACT* framework, the focus of those who believe human behavior is not rule-like has been on the neural interactions that implement the rules. Thus they have not acknowledged the rules themselves. Anderson believes that both cognitive rules and neural aspects exist, and that rule organization plays an absolutely critical role in structuring the acquisition of complex cognitive skills. According to Anderson, it is unlikely that humans can have an accurate psychological theory without rules.

A number of computational approaches to learning fall predominantly into what might be called the *explicit rule formation* tradition, as Winston (1984) and the ACT* theory of Anderson represent. The underlying assumption is that the goal of learning is to formulate explicit rules that capture powerful generalizations in an adequate way (McClelland et al. 1986b).

However, the approach to developing models inspired by the neural structure of the brain has different motivations. First, there is no assumption that the goal of learning is the formation of explicit rules. Rather, it is the acquisition of connection strengths that allows a network of simple units to act as though it knew the rules (McClelland et al. 1986b). Second, the learning mechanism contains no powerful computational capabilities. Instead it alters the strengths of the connections between the units based on some mechanism. Some view this argument against explicit rules as an argument against the cognitive approach to psychology (Rumelhart & McClelland 1986). However, the underlying aim is to study mechanisms of cognition and, as such, the application of a rule is neither more nor less cognitive than the activation of the units in the models. As stated by Rumelhart and McClelland (1986):

> *The real character of cognitive science is the attempt to explain mental phenomena through an understanding of the mechanisms underlying those phenomena.*

According to Gallant (1988) it is important to distinguish between the process humans use for arriving at a conclusion and the process humans use for communicating sequentially (by language) as a justification for that conclusion. Humans seldom follow logical rules in daily life, even though they may construct such rules to justify or explain those conclusions to other humans (Gallant 1988). Kohonen (1988) also supports this when discussing decision-making. He argues that a subject may make some form of formal analysis (such as rules) in order to avoid bad decisions, but when it comes to the final strategy other reasons, based on hunches and intuitive insight into the situation, become more important.

Knowledge can be classified by the following three types:

* sub-symbolic (i.e., not symbolic)
* symbolic and non-formal
* symbolic and formal.

Clearly, the first representation falls into the area of direct neural processing, where information is learned and represented in a non-symbolic manner. This representation appears to employ the neural structures directly. The second representation includes natural language expressions, production rules, concepts, and concept hierarchies. Human beings seem to be good at using the first and second representations; that is, the sub-symbolic and the symbolic, yet informal approaches. This could support Anderson's viewpoint. The third representation, symbolic and formal, includes mathematical models and rigorous logical structures. It requires specialized training.

Consider the following illustration of the various representations. Suppose that, as a young child, Emily plays ball with her parents and from this learns some basic skills, such as catching a ball. When asked now to describe how she catches a ball, Emily finds it hard to articulate. However, she is able to recognize the patterns of the various throws of the ball and has developed a suitable pattern of response. This obviously constitutes knowledge, but it is sub-symbolic knowledge because she is unable to convert it into the symbolic form of natural language. This is direct neural processing. Suppose that, as a teenager, Emily joins an inter-school netball team with its own coach. The coach will teach Emily certain ways to catch and throw the ball in certain situations. In order to do this, the coach will teach her in symbolic terms, such as if *the ball is too high, step back*. This knowledge comprises rules that are in a symbolic and yet informal form. Suppose that, as an adult, Emily (a physicist) develops a computer-based mathematical simulation of netball games. Such a representation is symbolic and formal. This illustrates the three possible types of representations.

The interesting issue is whether there are analogs in the computer field to the neuro-physiological and cognitive aspects. The answer is *yes*.

- Neural networks or connectionist architectures, as discussed in Chapter 4, appear to be analogous to the neuro-physiological structures.
- High-level knowledge representations used in traditional AI, such as rules, frames, and semantic nets, are analogous to cognitive structures. The processing associated with these representations corresponds to the cognitive view of psychology.

From the three representations presented above, the computer field reflects the following divisions of knowledge:

- sub-symbolic representation — effectively carried out by neural networks in the computer field;
- symbolic and non-formal representation — effectively carried out by traditional AI representations;
- symbolic and formal representation — effectively carried out by computer algorithms, logic, and mathematical formulations.

It is interesting that humans seem to be able to move easily from the first representation to the second; that is, from the sub-symbolic to the symbolic but non-formal representations. Humans appear to require no special training to accomplish this. Hence the conjecture to be tested is whether the analogs in the computer field can similarly move from the first representation to the second; that is, from neuro-physiologically inspired neural networks to cognitive-based AI knowledge representations. In order to investigate this, the following sections probe further into the analogs in the computer field.

6.9 Computer-based analogs to cognitive aspects

6.9.1 Analogs to cognitive structures

In computer-based applications, the following knowledge representations could be considered analogous to human cognitive structures:

- production rules
- hierarchies, classes, and sub-classes
- frames, semantic networks, and objects to represent concepts.

As these representations are basically symbolic in nature, the various issues associated with symbolic representations are discussed next.

6.9.2 Symbolic paradigm — rules and rule-based behavior

Computers manipulate symbols. A symbol is an inherently meaningless cipher that becomes meaningful by having meaning assigned to it by a user who, thereafter, interprets the symbol in a particular way (Boden 1987). There is no need to have any intrinsic similarity between a symbol and what it represents. Intelligence, from this point of view, may be defined as the creative ability to manipulate symbols or process information, given the requirements of the task in hand. Efficient and effective learning demands both symbolic structuring and statistical methods for noise immunity (Rendell 1987).

According to Newell and Simon (1976):

> *The Physical Symbol System Hypothesis states that a physical symbol system has the necessary and sufficient means for general intelligent action.*

The evidence in support of this can be taken from various sources, including visual perception where it is more tempting to suspect the influence of non-symbolic processes (Rich 1983). However, Rich states that perhaps this hypothesis is only partially true, and perhaps only some aspects of human intelligence can be modeled by the physical symbol system, while others cannot. Regardless of this, the hypothesis forms the basis of the belief that it is possible to build programs to perform intelligent tasks that people now perform. Systems that use symbols are called *symbolic*.

Symbols are usually taken to represent something beyond themselves, and have some pre-defined semantic interpretation. Crucial questions are *what is a symbol designating* and *what uses it*. For example, in symbolic AI, a symbol such as an atom might designate a set of properties that describe an individual or class. Generally this representation is used by the author or user of the program and the interpretive processes that retrieve and operate on the properties. A classic confusion in AI is attributing understanding to the interpretive processes that, in reality, comprise an interface made by the author/user of the program (Rich 1983).

However, the physical symbol itself does not indicate content, similarity, and distribution. Thus in AI, symbols have no internal structure and mean very little; they are simply used as names or pointers to larger structures of symbols (Pollack 1988). Also, as stated by Chandrasekaran et al. (1988):

> *Symbols are types about which abstract rules of behavior are known and these rules can be brought into play. This distinction leads to symbols being labels that are interpreted during the process. Thus, a symbolic system can represent abstract forms.*

The symbolic paradigm believes that processes that interpret symbol systems provide a good basis for modeling human cognition. It does not restrict one to only serial computation or von Neumann computer architectures. Traditional AI is tied to the symbolic processing paradigm in that it assumes that any system exhibiting intelligence will be a symbol processing system (Wiles 1987b).

According to Winston (1984), knowledge representations in AI applications should be concise, complete, transparent, computationally efficient, detail suppressing, and computable. In AI, much work has been done with the standard IF-THEN rule. Rules represent different things to different people and to different areas. In AI, a rule usually refers to a production rule made up of symbols. A rule of this type specifies a transformation, defining the initial state and the next state without specifying the process by which the next state is attained. Rules consist of a finite set of symbolic descriptors that describe the relevant domain. Rules have to be explicit, but they are usually written in a different notation from the ones they manipulate. For example, a theorem prover could be written in LISP and the weights in a neural net.

Rules are a remarkably effective way of capturing knowledge about the reasoning behavior of experts. Even if such systems have captured only a fraction of the flexibility of the inferencing capabilities of humans, there seems to be a clear benefit in the formalization of such knowledge as rules. A rule-based representation is well supported by cognitive scientists and AI researchers for modeling higher-level symbolic reasoning tasks (Goodman et al. 1989). Also, the Disjunctive Normal Form of rules has been used because it is more intuitive to humans (Saito & Nakano 1990).

One could describe a system as having rule-based behavior, if one could provide a rule-based mechanism for explaining the evolution of this behavior. It is important, however, to distinguish between modeling this behavior using rules and asserting that the behavior is governed by rules. Just because it can be modeled through rules does not necessarily imply that it is governed by a knowledge base containing rules.

Symbolic systems learn top-down (Rich 1990). A symbolic system is given a set of generalizations, or rules, that are already formed. The rules are obtained directly or indirectly from a human expert in the field in which the system is to function. The system then applies these rules to the individual situations it deals with. According to Rich (1990), symbolic systems can:

- be told things explicitly, making a large amount of data unnecessary if the basic principles are known;
- be programmed modularly, making updating easy when individual facts change;
- generate explanations for their conclusions;
- explore multiple alternatives;
- manipulate very complex situations;

- interface with conventional symbolic databases;
- remember what they are told.

6.10 Computer-based analogs to physiological aspects

6.10.1 Analogs to physiology

Computer-based neural networks, as discussed in Chapter 4, were inspired by various mathematical theories and the architecture of the human brain. However, this representation is not equivalent to the human brain — it is a very simplified version of its architecture. This version is composed of nodes connected together with weighted links. As the information within the computer-based network is sub-symbolic, various aspects of sub-symbolism are discussed next.

6.10.2 Sub-symbolic paradigm — core aspects of connectionism

Computer-based neural networks are often said to involve a sub-symbolic level of computation because only numerically valued activation passes from unit to unit in the network (Jones & Hoskins 1987). This sub-symbolic paradigm reflects the fact that a formal description of cognition is only tractable at a lower level of description than the traditionally accepted conceptual level, and a large number of sub-symbolic features is used to define each semantic-level feature (Wiles 1987b).

There are two main factors relating to sub-symbolic systems. The first is that some units, particularly in distributed representations, may not cleanly correspond to natural concepts in the real world. The second factor is the great flexibility in many connectionist frameworks, such as content-addressable memories, in accessing representations from partial information about the content of the memory. Behavior of individual neurons in the brain may be, and most probably is, sub-symbolic.

Connectionist structures are ones in which the system's permanent memory is stored as a pattern of connections or connection strengths among the processing elements. Therefore, the knowledge directly determines how the processing elements interact, rather than sitting passively by in a memory, waiting to be looked at by the CPU. The term *connectionism* was first used to refer to the study of a certain class of massively parallel architectures for Artificial Intelligence (Fahlman & Hinton 1987).

The principle behind connectionism is that the totality of the connections defines the information content (Chandrasekaran et al. 1988). Connectionist architectures in the parallel distributive processing style share the following characteristics. The representation of information is in the form of weights of connections between processing units in a network. Information processing consists of the units transforming their input into some output, which is then modulated by the weights of connections to become input to other units. Thus, with connectionism, the computation of the system comes from the high connectivity between the nodes. The processing of the system is carried out via the interconnections between the nodes in the system.

Connectionist theories emphasize a form of learning in which the weights are adjusted continuously so that the network's output tends toward the desired output (Chandrasekaran et al. 1988; Jones & Hoskins 1987) in the case of supervised learning. The network learns from examples and therefore the knowledge acquisition problem of extracting knowledge or rules from an expert is not an issue. The knowledge acquisition obstacle generally found in expert system paradigms appears to be avoided effectively by neural networks, as they can be trained to respond appropriately by example. The training represents the most computationally intensive aspect of the development of a neural network (Dietz et al. 1988). The actual mapping process from the input to the outputs requires very little computational effort and is therefore suited to real-time applications. These networks are more resistant to noise.

According to Chandrasekaran et al. (1988):

> *The interesting characteristics of each solution come from the representational commitments the network makes, not from the symbolic/ non-symbolic nature of its architecture.*

Also, in connectionist schemes (Chandrasekaran et al. 1988):

- *A significant part of the abstractions needed are built into the architecture in the choice of input, feedback directions, allocation of sub-networks, and semantics that underlie the choice of layers.*
- *The representation medium has no internal labels that are interpreted and no abstract forms that are instantiated during processing.*

A neural network learns bottom-up (Rich 1990). It is trained on a large collection of experiences. From this, it attempts to form generalizations that characterize a larger universe of possibilities. A network develops the ability to interpolate between the data points it has seen. However, a neural network never looks up a specific fact in the database from which it was trained.

There are several contributions of connectionism to AI (Chandrasekaran et al. 1988; Rich 1990). The first of these is in the representation formalism. Connectionist formalisms allow noisy input mappings. They also create fault-tolerant systems and associative representations without pre-defined built-in associations. In the field of reasoning, large-scale knowledge systems can be reasoned with, and most importantly, this can proceed with partial or incomplete information. Finally, in the field of learning, connectionist methods of associated pattern learning without explicit pre-defined decision criteria form a new approach to the normal learning methodologies. From this, various new learning algorithms have been constructed.

6.11 Sub-symbolic versus symbolic representations

In conventional computing, the basic units of knowledge are symbols and processing is performed on symbols without regard for the entities they represent. In associative computing, the basic units of knowledge are concepts that have a sub-symbolic representation distributed over the processing units in the network (Wiles 1987b).

There is a large gap between numeric, low-level tasks (vision, speech) and symbolic, high-level tasks (object recognition, language, planning). Connectionism is beginning to build tools to bridge that gap. The principal contribution of connectionism to AI has been in opening up a whole new range of possibilities to model human-like behavior. The possibility of sub-symbolic approaches for the generation of intelligent behavior has been raised. This approach does not require explicit manipulation of symbolic representations of the intelligent agent's domain. Hence it is fundamentally different from traditional AI approaches.

According to Chandrasekaran et al. (1988):

- *Connectionism and symbolism both agree on the view of intelligence as information processing of representations. However, they disagree about the medium in which the representations reside and the corresponding processing mechanisms. These two paradigms are fundamentally different in terms of the representational commitments they make.*
- *The difference between the recognition schemes in the symbolic and connectionist paradigms is in how the evidence is represented. In the symbolic approach, the evidence is represented with labeled symbols which permit abstract rules of composition to be invoked and instantiated. In the connectionist approach, evidence is represented more directly and affects the processing without undergoing any interpretive process.*

The link between these two paradigms has already intrigued others. In the work carried out by Fozzard et al. (1989), the same data was applied to determine rules for an expert system and to train a multi-layered neural network. The data was incomplete and inaccurate, with numerous inconsistencies and noise, and as such required careful handling of rule strengths and certainty factors. However, dealing with this kind of data is the strength claimed for connectionist networks. Thus, if a connectionist network can perform the same task as a rule-based system, then a study of the internal representations constructed by the network may give some insights into the micro-structure of the reasoning processes occurring in the human brain, and these internal representations must be examined for any relationship between them and the symbolic representations (Fozzard et al. 1989). Without these interpretations, connectionist networks cannot easily offer the help and explanation facilities of traditional expert systems that are a consequence of the rule-writing process.

Fodor and Pylyshyn (1988) present arguments that methods used by connectionist approaches are incapable of exhibiting certain properties that are essential aspects of human cognition. These properties include the ability to compose, generalize, and systematize. The main point made by Fodor and Pylyshyn (1988) is that these involve operations that are at a higher level of abstraction than connectionism. In contrast, Hadley (1990) argues that humans do sometimes follow rules that are very rapidly assigned explicit internal representations, and that humans possess general mechanisms capable of interpreting such rules. These contradictory views indicate that constructing general-purpose, rule-following mechanisms in a connectionist architecture is still a major challenge in this field.

6.12 Recapitulation

A number of characteristics of the two paradigms, traditional symbolic AI and connectionist sub-symbolic AI, are listed below.

- Traditional AI with its symbolic representations has had some success in a number of areas where the knowledge is focused, concentrated, and available in a symbolic form. It has had less success where the knowledge is not available in an explicit form, is diffuse as in common sense reasoning, is fuzzy, or involves too many special cases likely to lead to a combinatorial explosion. One major weakness is the inability or limited ability of these systems to learn from primary case material or examples of decisions. A further disadvantage is the inability to improve their knowledge incrementally as more information becomes available.
- Connectionist architectures, on the other hand, are more able to deal with fuzzy and messy situations, and they can develop a representation directly from primary case material. However, the inability of these systems to provide explanations for these decisions creates suspicion among users. Another problem arises from this opaqueness of the representation to a cognitive analysis. Consider a financial analysis that is dependent on government regulations. If the regulations change, there is a time lag before sufficient case material is available to update the system. Thus, if there is a qualitative change in the

phenomenon being studied and not enough new case material is generated quickly, there is no simple way of altering the representation to cater for this new situation. A visible symbolic representation could be updated in a more timely fashion.

- Many people in this research area see that the future lies in the integration of the sub-symbolic processing of connectionism methods with the symbolic processing of traditional AI methods. It is felt that it is crucial to integrate the insights gained from the analysis and synthesis of present-day connectionist networks, along with the knowledge accumulated through several decades of conventional AI efforts, to build systems that exploit the strengths of both and, hopefully, suffer from the weaknesses of neither. Many people are in favor of mixing symbolic and connectionist methodologies (Pollack 1988). Recent work has also focused on developing hybrid systems that couple connectionist models of low-level processing directly with more traditional symbolic AI models (Khosla & Dillon 1992a–b, 1993a–d).
- Connectionism has been useful in refocusing attention on alternative models of computation. However, for much of AI and cognition, the supposed battle between connectionism and symbolism is *mere shadow-boxing*. Neither of the theories explains all intelligence or cognition. The power of intelligence comes as a result of the co-operation between different mechanisms and representations at different levels of description (Chandrasekaran et al. 1988). It is believed that the most significant progress on the outstanding problems of cognitive science and AI is most likely to come from combining connectionism and symbolic AI into systems quite different from their current implementations.

Considerable advantage in linking these two paradigms comes from the possibility of extracting knowledge from a trained neural network. If this can be achieved, the inherent learning process of training a neural network will be exploited. As stated, a neural network learns to give the correct answer by being trained by examples. The process of modeling the data is implicit in this training process. An attempt can then be made to extract information from this model of the data in a form suitable for human understanding, and that can be used by other knowledge-based systems, such as expert systems. The aim here is to harness the learning power of connectionist networks for expert system construction (Gallant 1988). The methods of Fu (1991), Gallant (1988), Sestito and Dillon (1989, 1990a–c, 1991a–b, 1992, 1993), and Towell and Shavlik (1992) are some of the first attempts at achieving this goal.

The important difference between the two paradigms is that symbolic learning systems produce results that are generally more *readable* than the collection of weights produced by connectionist systems (Mooney et al. 1989). The machine learning method, Building Representations for AI using Neural NEtworks (BRAINNE), is an attempt at linking the sub-symbolic neural network to symbolic rules and concepts. BRAINNE uses the computer-based model inspired by a simplified architecture of the human brain, to learn and store knowledge from example data. This model is then the basis for extracting knowledge in the form of rules and concepts, as shown in Figure 6.3. According to Norman (1986), computer-based artificial neural networks contain many of the essential human processing facilities, such as insensitivity to noise, graceful degradation, and being able to learn from example data. From the discussion in this chapter, there is a need for statistical methods for noise immunity, the use of negative information to aid the learning process, and the inclusion of knowledge in the learning. The need for grouping of information into both immediate and final structures in order to improve learning is also taken into account.

The next several chapters in this book describe the development of the BRAINNE approach, which uses neural networks to model the data. The main aim is to develop a knowledge acquisition tool. As a side effect of this, the inner workings of a trained neural network will also be explored. One of the greatest advantages of neural networks is their ability to handle noise and conflicting data effectively. Many automated knowledge acquisition methods have a problem dealing with such noise. This feature of a neural network is invaluable for a knowledge acquisition method, as it enables the actual knowledge in the data to be learned.

The next chapter describes the first attempt at developing an automated knowledge acquisition method using single-layered neural networks. Chapter 8 outlines the basis of BRAINNE. The first part of the chapter describes a technique for extracting one conjunctive rule for each output, using a multi-layered neural network. The extension to this, extracting several disjunctive rules defining the same output, is then presented in the second part of the

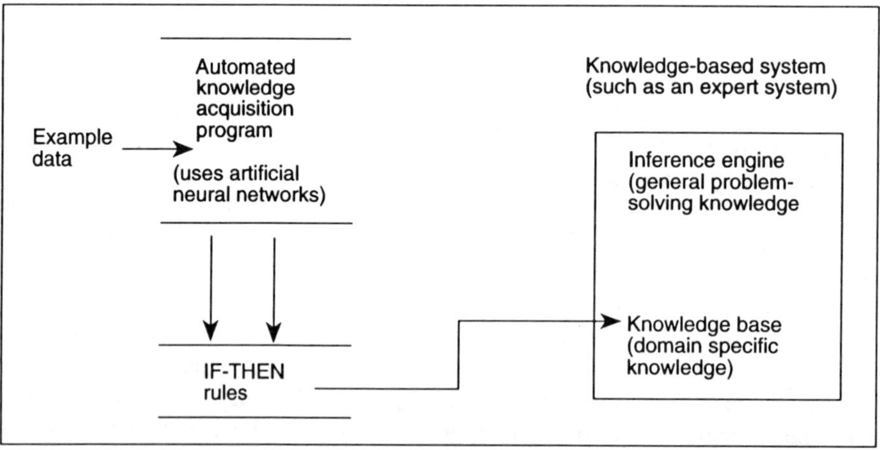

Figure 6.3   Basic ideas underlying the automated knowledge acquisition method known as BRAINNE

chapter. The modifications to the method, required so that knowledge acquisition can be performed in the presence of continuous-valued input attributes, are then discussed in the subsequent chapter. These latter two chapters, 8 and 9, comprise the automated knowledge acquisition method known as BRAINNE.

References

Anderson, J.A. 1986, *Concepts in Connectionist Models*, American Institute of Physics, pp. 17–22

Anderson, J.R. 1983, *The Architecture of Cognition*, Harvard University Press, Cambridge, Massachusetts

Anderson, J.R. 1988, "Acquisition of cognitive skill", in *Readings in Cognitive Science: A Perspective from Psychology and Artificial Intelligence*, eds A. Collins & E.E. Smith, Morgan Kaufmann, San Mateo, California, pp. 362–80

Anderson, J.R. 1989, "Features of advisory and expert systems", in *Intelligent Systems in a Human Context: Development, Implications, and Applications*, eds L.A. Murray & J.T.E. Richardson, Oxford University Press, Oxford, pp. 92–116

Anderson, J.R. 1990, "A theory of the origins of human knowledge", in *Readings in Machine Learning*, eds J. Shavlik & T. Dietterich, Morgan Kaufmann Publishers, San Francisco, California, pp. 664–83

Arbib, M.A. 1989, *The Metaphorical Brain 2: Neural Networks and Beyond*, Wiley, New York

Baron, R.J. 1987, *The Cerebral Computer: An Introduction to the Computational Structure of the Human Brain*, Erlbaum, Hillsdale, New Jersey

Boden, M.A. 1987, *Artificial Intelligence and Natural Man*, 2nd edition, Basic Books, New York

Boden, M.A. 1989a, "Artificial intelligence: opportunities and dangers", in *Intelligent Systems in a Human Context: Development, Implications, and Applications*, eds L.A. Murray & J.T.E. Richardson, Oxford University Press, Oxford, pp. 8–19

Boden, M.A. 1989b, "Meeting of man and machine", in *Intelligent Systems in a Human Context: Development, Implications, and Applications*, eds L.A. Murray & J.T.E. Richardson, Oxford University Press, Oxford, pp. 165–78

Bruner, J.S., Goodnow, J.J. & Austin, G.A. 1956, *A Study of Thinking*, Wiley, New York

Carbonell, J.G. 1989, "Introduction: Paradigms for machine learning", *Artificial Intelligence*, vol. 40, pp. 1–9

Carbonell, J.G., Michalski, R.S. & Mitchell, T.M. 1983, "An overview of machine learning", in *Machine Learning: An Artificial Intelligence Approach*, eds R.S. Michalski, J.G. Carbonell & T.M. Mitchell, Tioga Publishing, Palo Alto, California, pp. 3–23

Chandrasekaran, B., Goel, A. & Allemang, D. 1988, "Connectionism and information-processing abstractions", *AI Magazine*, vol. 9, no. 4, Winter, pp. 25–34, Copyright © 1988, American Association for Artificial Intelligence

Collins, A. & Smith, E.E. 1988, "A perspective on cognitive science", in *Readings in Cognitive Science: A Perspective from Psychology and Artificial Intelligence*, eds A. Collins & E.E. Smith, Morgan Kaufmann, San Mateo, California, pp. 1–4

Crick, F.H.C. & Asanuma, C. 1986, "Certain aspects of the anatomy and physiology of the cerebral cortex", in *Parallel Distributed Processing, Volume 2: Psychological and Biological Models,* J.L. McClelland, D.E. Rumelhart & the PDP Research Group, MIT Press, Cambridge, Massachusetts, pp. 333–71

Dietz, W.E., Kiech, E.L. & Ali, M. 1988, "Pattern-based fault diagnosis using neural networks", *The First International Conference on Industrial and Engineering Applications of Artificial Intelligence and Expert Systems (IEA/ AIE 88)*, vol. I, Tullahoma, Tennessee, pp. 13–23

Fahlman, S.E. & Hinton, G.E. 1987, "Connectionist architectures for artificial intelligence", *IEEE Computer*, January, pp. 100–9

Fodor, J.A. & Pylyshyn, Z.W. 1988, "Connectionism and cognitive architecture: A critical analysis", *Cognition*, vol. 28, pp. 3–71

Fozzard, R., Bradshaw, G. & Ceci, L. 1989, "A connectionist expert system that actually works", in *Neural Information Processing Systems (NIPS) 1*, ed. D.S. Touretzky, Morgan Kaufmann, San Mateo, California, pp. 248–55

Fu L. 1991, "Rule learning by searching on adapted nets", *Proceedings of the Ninth National Conference on Artificial Intelligence (AAAI-91),* Anaheim, California, pp. 590–5

Gallant, S. 1988, "Connectionist expert systems", *Communications of the ACM*, vol. 31, no. 2, February, pp. 152–69

Gennari, J., Langely, P. & Fisher, D. 1989, "Models of incremental concept formation", *Artificial Intelligence*, vol. 40, pp. 11–61

Goodman, R., Miller, J. & Smyth, P. 1989, "An information theoretic approach to rule-based connectionist expert systems", in *Neural Information Processing Systems (NIPS) 1*, ed. D.S. Touretzky, Morgan Kaufmann, San Mateo, California, pp. 256–63

Guyton, A.C. 1984, *Physiology of the Human Body*, 6th edition, Saunders College, Philadelphia

Hadley, R.F. 1990, "Connectionism, rule following and symbolic manipulation", *Proceedings of the American Association for Artificial Intelligence,* Boston, August

Harriman, P.L. 1947, *The New Dictionary of Psychology*, Philosophical Library, New York, p. 80

Hearst, E. 1972, "Some persistent problems in the analysis of conditioned inhibition", in *Inhibition and Learning*, eds R.A. Boakes & M.S. Halliday, Academic Press, London, pp. 3–59

Howard, R.W. 1987, *Concepts and Schemata: An Introduction*, Cassell Educational, Philadelphia

Johnson-Laird, P.N. 1989, "Human experts and expert systems", in *Intelligent Systems in a Human Context: Development, Implications, and Applications*, eds L.A. Murray & J.T.E. Richardson, Oxford University Press, Oxford, pp. 35–46

Jones, W.P. & Hoskins, J. 1987, "Back-propagation: A generalized delta learning rule", *Byte*, October, pp. 155–62

Khosla, R. & Dillon, T.S. 1992a, "An integrated neuro-expert system model for real-time systems", in *International Joint Conference on Neural Networks (IJCNN)*, vol. I, Beijing, China, November, pp. 154–9

Khosla, R. & Dillon, T.S. 1992b, "A generic neuro-expert system architecture with application to alarm processing in a power system control centre", *Fourth IEEE Conference on Tools with Artificial Intelligence*, Arlington, Virginia, pp. 471–2

Khosla, R. & Dillon, T.S. 1993a, "A neuro-expert system approach for power system problems", keynote paper, in *Proceedings of Expert System Application to Power Systems IV*, ed. T.S. Dillon, CRL Publishing, London, pp. 8–15

Khosla, R. & Dillon, T.S. 1993b, "Applying an integrated neuro-expert system model in a real-time alarm processing system", in *Applications of Artificial Intelligence 1993: Knowledge-Based Systems in Aerospace and Industry*, eds U.M. Fayyad & R. Uthurusamy, Proceedings of the International Society for Optical Engineering (SPIE), pp. 68–79

Khosla, R. & Dillon, T.S. 1993c, "A symbolic-connectionist model for time critical and diagnostic domains", *Proceedings of the Thirteenth Inter-national Conference on Artificial Intelligence, Expert Systems and Natural Language*, vol. 1, Avignon, France, May, pp. 233–42

Khosla, R. & Dillon, T.S. 1993d, "Task decomposition and competing expert system-artificial neural net objects for reliable and real time inference", *IEEE International Conference on Neural Networks*, vol. II, San Francisco, March, pp. 794–800

Klausmeier, H.J., Ghatala, E.S. & Frayer, D.A. 1974, *Conceptual Learning and Development: A Cognitive View*, Academic Press, New York

Kochen, M. 1974, "Representations and algorithms for cognitive learning", *Artificial Intelligence*, vol. 5, pp. 199–216

Kohonen, T. 1988, "An introduction to neural computing", *Neural Networks*, vol. 1, pp. 3–16

Kristal, L., ed. 1981, *ABC of Psychology*, Michael Joseph, London, pp. 56–7

McClelland, J.L. & Rumelhart, D.E. 1988, *Explorations in Parallel Distributed Processing: A Handbook of Models, Programs and Exercises*, MIT Press, Cambridge, Massachusetts, pp. 83–137

McClelland, J.L.; Rumelhart, D.E. & the PDP Research Group 1986a, *Parallel Distributed Processing, Volume 2: Psychological and Biological Models*, MIT Press, Cambridge, Massachusetts

McClelland, J.L., Rumelhart, D.E. & Hinton, G.E. 1986b, "Appeal of parallel distributed processing", in *Parallel Distributed Processing, Volume 1: Foundations*, D.E. Rumelhart, J.L. McClelland & the PDP Research Group, MIT Press, Cambridge, Massachusetts, pp. 3–44

Michalski, R.S. 1987, "Learning strategies and automated knowledge acquisition: An overview", in *Computational Models of Learning*, ed. L. Bolc, Springer-Verlag, Berlin, pp. 1–20

Mooney, R., Shavlik, J., Towell, G. & Gove, A. 1989, "An experimental comparison of symbolic and connectionist learning algorithms", *International Joint Conference on Artificial Intelligence (IJCAI-89)* Detroit, pp. 775–80

Newell, A. & Simon, H.A. 1976, "Computer science as empirical inquiry: Symbols and search", *Communications of the ACM*, vol. 19, no. 3. pp. 113–27

Norman, D.A. 1986, "Reflections on cognition and parallel distributed processing", in *Parallel Distributed Processing, Volume 2: Psychological and Biological Models,* J.L. McClelland, D.E. Rumelhart & the PDP
Research Group, MIT Press, Cambridge, Massachusetts, pp. 531–46

Ohlsson, S. 1987, "Transfer of training in procedural learning: A matter of conjectures and refutations?", in *Computational Models of Learning*, ed. L. Bolc, Springer-Verlag, Berlin, pp. 55–88

Patarnello, S. & Carnevali, P. 1989, "Learning capabilities of Boolean networks", in *Neural Computing Architectures: The Design of Brain-Like Machines,* ed. I. Aleksander, North Oxford Academic, London, pp. 117–32

Pollack, J. 1988, "Workshop report: High-level connectionist models", *AI Magazine*, vol. 9, no. 4, Winter, pp. 65–9

Pollio, H.R. 1974, *The Psychology of Symbolic Activity,* Addison-Wesley, Reading, Massachusetts

Rendell, L.A. 1987, "Conceptual knowledge acquisition in search", in *Computational Models of Learning*, ed. L. Bolc, Springer-Verlag, Berlin, pp. 89–160

Rich, E. 1983, *Artificial Intelligence*, McGraw-Hill, New York

Rich, E. 1990, "Expert systems and neural networks can work together: Interview of Elaine Rich by Ware Myers", *IEEE Expert*, October, pp. 5–7

Rosch, E. 1977, "Classification of real-world objects: Origins and representations in cognition", in *Thinking: Readings in Cognitive Science*, eds P.N. Johnson-Laird & P.C. Wason, Cambridge University Press, Cambridge, pp. 212–22

Rosch, R., Mervis, C.B., Gray, W.D., Johnson, D.M. & Boyes-Braem, P. 1976, "Basic objects in natural categories", *Cognitive Psychology,* vol. 8, pp. 382–439

Rumelhart, D.E. & McClelland, J.L. 1986, "PDP models and general issues in cognitive science", in *Parallel Distributed Processing, Volume 1: Foundations*, D.E. Rumelhart, J.L. McClelland & the PDP Research Group, MIT Press, Cambridge, Massachusetts, pp. 110–46

Rumelhart, D.E., McClelland, J.L. & the PDP Research Group 1986, *Parallel Distributed Processing, Volume 1: Foundations*, MIT Press, Cambridge, Massachusetts

Saito, K. & Nakano, R. 1990, "Rule extraction from facts and neural networks", *International Conference on Neural Networks (ICNN-90-PARIS)*, Paris, France, July, pp. 379–82

Sejnowski, T.J. 1986, "Open questions about computation in cerebral cortex", in *Parallel Distributed Processing, Volume 2: Psychological and Biological Models*, J.L. McClelland, D.E. Rumelhart & the PDP Research Group, MIT Press, Cambridge, Massachusetts, pp. 372–89

Sestito, S. & Dillon, T.S. 1989, "Using neural networks for the extraction of high level knowledge representation for machine learning", *Australian Artificial Intelligence Conference (AI '89)*, Melbourne, Australia, pp. 413–28

Sestito, S. & Dillon, T.S. 1990a, "Using sub-symbolic methods for machine learning of high level knowledge representation", keynote paper, *Finnish AI Symposium (STeP-'90)*, Oulu, Finland, pp. 27–49

Sestito, S. & Dillon, T.S. 1990b, "Using multi-layered neural networks for learning symbolic knowledge", *Australian Artificial Intelligence Conference (AI '90)*, Perth, Australia, November, pp. 249–62

Sestito, S. & Dillon, T.S. 1990c, "Machine learning using single-layered and multi-layered neural networks", *IEEE Conference on Tools for AI (TAI-90)*, Washington DC, November, pp. 269–75

Sestito, S. & Dillon, T.S. 1991a, "Using single-layered neural networks for the extraction of conjunctive rules and hierarchical classifications", *Journal of Applied Intelligence,* vol. 1, pp. 157–73

Sestito, S. & Dillon, T.S. 1991b, "The use of sub-symbolic methods for the automation of knowledge acquisition for expert systems", *Eleventh International Conference on Expert Systems & Their Applications (Avignon '91)*, Avignon, France, pp. 317–28

Sestito, S. & Dillon, T.S. 1992, "Automated knowledge acquisition of rules with continuously valued attributes", *Twelfth International Conference on Expert Systems and their Applications (Avignon '92)*, Avignon, France, pp. 645–56

Sestito, S. & Dillon, T.S. 1993, "Knowledge acquisition of conjunctive rules using multi-layered neural networks", *International Journal of Intelligent Systems*, vol. 8, no. 7, pp. 779–806

Sills, D.L., ed. 1968, *International Encyclopedia of the Social Sciences*, vols. 9 & 10, Macmillan & The Free Press, New York

Stubbs, D.F. 1990, *Neurocomputers*, Springer-Verlag

Tattersall, G. 1989, "Neural map applications", in *Neural Computing Architectures: The Design of Brain-Like Machines,* ed. I. Aleksander, North Oxford Academic, London, pp. 41–73

Towell, G. & Shavlik, J. 1992, *The Extraction of Refined Rules from Knowledge-based Neural Networks*, Machine Learning Research Group Working Paper 91-4, University of Wisconsin, Madison

Wiles, J. 1987a, *The Structure and Representation of Concepts in Parallel Distributed Associative Memory Models*, Technical Report No. 312, Basser Department of Computer Science, University of Sydney, Sydney, Australia, October

Wiles, J. 1987b, *A Comparison of Parallel Distributed Models of Memory*, Technical Report No. 313, Basser Department of Computer Science, University of Sydney, Sydney, Australia, October

Winston, P.H. 1984, *Artificial Intelligence*, Addison-Wesley, Reading, Massachusetts

Wolff, J.G. 1987, "Cognitive development as optimization", in *Computational Models of Learning*, ed. L. Bolc, Springer-Verlag, Berlin, pp. 161–206

Zhang, J. 1990, "A method that combines inductive learning with exemplar-based learning", *IEEE Conference on Tools for AI (TAI-90)*, Washington, DC, November, pp. 31–7

7

The extraction of rules and concepts using a single Hebbian neural network

7.1 Introduction

The theoretical considerations in the previous chapter suggested an automated knowledge acquisition method that uses neural networks to model the data. In this chapter we propose a knowledge acquisition method using single-layered neural networks as the basis for extracting high-level knowledge representations. Such single-layered neural networks are only able to model linearly separable problems successfully (McClelland & Rumelhart 1988; Rumelhart et al. 1986). However, the assumption of a linear conceptual model is a reasonable first step, even though it has limitations for modeling the conceptual schemata of people (Boden 1987). This represents the initial attempt to automate the process of knowledge acquisition by extracting knowledge from a neural network.

The symbolic knowledge representation extraction method consists of the following stages:

- training the network
- extracting the rules
- extracting higher-level concepts and concept hierarchies.

Chapter 4 presented methods for training a neural network. Here, techniques for extracting rules and higher-level concepts are discussed.

For this single-layered approach, once a network is trained a conjunctive rule defining each output is determined. From these rules, higher-level concepts are also extracted. These concepts are defined by the antecedents of those rules with the minimum number of contributory attributes. In the remaining set of rules, the attributes defining these concepts are replaced by the concept itself. Thus, new sets of rules are formed and different levels of abstraction are possible.

7.2 Extracting basic rules

Consider a domain of m inputs denoted by (a_1, a_2, ..., a_m) and n outputs denoted by (b_1, b_2, ..., b_n). The first stage in this method is to train the fully connected single-layered neural network shown in Figure 7.1, with Hebb's Rule, as described in Chapter 4. From Hebb's Rule, a matrix containing the weights of the links from all inputs to all outputs is produced.

The weights in the weight matrix represent the contribution each input

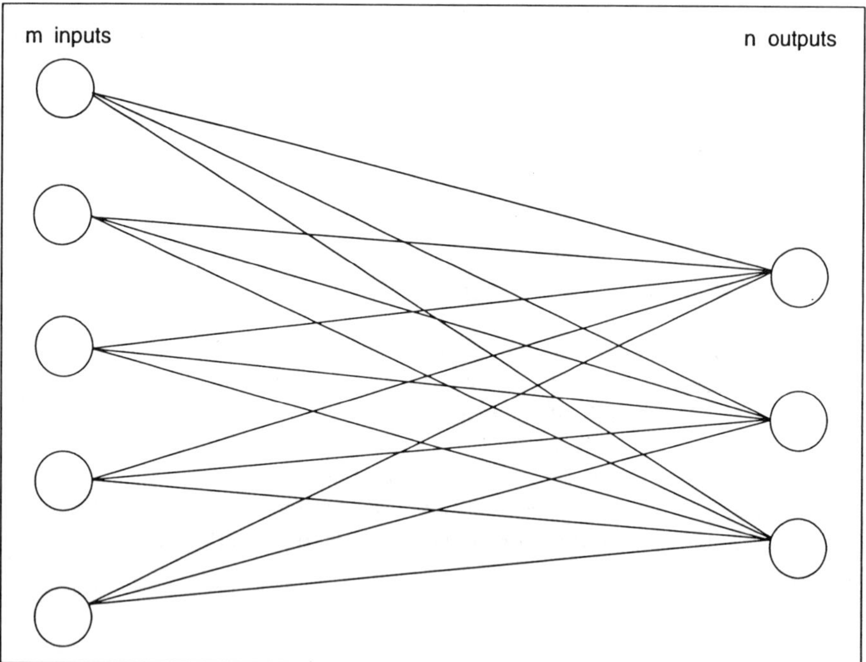

Figure 7.1   A typical single-layered neural network with m inputs and n outputs

makes to each output. For a given output, the input with the largest weighted connection makes the largest contribution to the output. The correlation between this input and the given output is thus higher than the correlation between any other input and the given output.

The rules defining the knowledge learned from the examples and represented in the weight matrix can be extracted. The first step is to determine the maximum weight contribution of all the inputs to any given output. For example, the maximum weight contribution of all the inputs to output b_k is the maximum of the following weights:

$$(w_{1k}, w_{2k}, ..., w_{mk}).$$

Any input is taken to be contributory to an output if its weighted link is within some range of this maximum weight. The size of the range is influenced by the noise that may be present in the data and is crucial for the generation of correct initial rules. The range determined by an error threshold is used for all the outputs. For the output b_k, the weights from all the links w_{1k}, w_{2k}, ..., w_{mk} that are within some range of the maximum weight are considered as the contributory weights to b_k. The corresponding inputs are the contributory inputs. For instance, if weight w_{4k} is within the given range, then the input a_4 is a contributory input.

The contributory inputs are joined together with the AND connective to form the antecedent of a conjunctive rule that has the associated output as its consequent. These rules contain the initial primitive attributes only. For example, if the contributory inputs for output b_k are a_1, a_4, and a_m, then the following rule would be constructed:

$$\text{IF } (a_1 \text{ AND } a_4 \text{ AND } a_m) \text{ THEN } (b_k).$$

An alternative notation for the preceding rule is:

$$(a_1 \text{ AND } a_4 \text{ AND } a_m) \Rightarrow (b_k).$$

This procedure is repeated for all outputs and a set of initial rules is produced.

The steps for extracting the initial rules for output b_k from the weight matrix for a domain with m inputs are summarized below:

- Determine the maximum weight contribution W_{max} for output b_k:

$$W_{max} = \max(w_{1k}, w_{2k}, ..., w_{mk}).$$

- Select all inputs a_i with an associated weight w_{ik} within a particular range of W_{max} to be contributory inputs of the output b_k. Thus, the weights w_{ik} satisfy:

$$w_{ik} \geq \beta W_{max}$$

  The constant β has a value between 0 and 1, inclusive. It can be regarded as the error threshold, reflecting the range of permissible values. For example,

if $\beta = 0.95$, then all inputs with weights equal to or greater than 95% of the maximum weight are selected as contributory inputs.
- Construct conjunctive rules from these contributory inputs:

$$(a_i \,[\text{AND } a_j]^*) \Rightarrow (b_k),$$

where []* denotes 0 or more repetitions.

7.3 Extracting higher-level concepts

A concept is an abstraction for representing a collection of real-world attributes. The permissible values of these attributes are used to define the necessary and sufficient conditions for describing a concept. In Dillon and Tan (1993), concepts are given both static and dynamic characteristics. However, only the static character of concepts is considered here. Concepts may be arranged in a hierarchy in which higher-level concepts represent generalizations and lower-level concepts represent specializations. Also, those concepts lower down in the hierarchy inherit properties of the higher-level concepts and have additional attributes or restrictions.

This section describes extracting concepts, defined as a specific combination of attributes, by examining all the generated rules. Those rules with the minimum number of attributes (i.e., contributory inputs) forming clauses in the antecedent are selected. The consequents of the selected rules are taken to be concepts. By choosing the minimum number of attributes to define the concept, the most generalized concept in the concept hierarchy is initially selected. Lower-lying concepts in the hierarchy are specializations of these, designated by the values associated with the additional attributes.

The combination of attributes implying a concept can occur in any other rule in the rule base. These are replaced with the concept itself. A new set of rules is thus obtained. New concepts are then determined, and with these new concepts yet another set of rules is formulated. This process is continued until all the rules are reduced to tautologies; that is, the concepts implying themselves. Eventually, everything is defined as a concept, as illustrated below.

Consider the following example of a rule base:

$$(a_1 \text{ AND } a_2 \text{ AND } a_4) \Rightarrow (b_1)$$
$$(a_1 \text{ AND } a_5) \Rightarrow (b_2)$$
$$(a_1 \text{ AND } a_3 \text{ AND } a_5) \Rightarrow (b_3)$$
$$(a_2 \text{ AND } a_3 \text{ AND } a_5) \Rightarrow (b_4)$$
$$(a_1 \text{ AND } a_2) \Rightarrow (b_5).$$

The second and fifth rules, $(a_1 \text{ AND } a_5) \Rightarrow (b_2)$ and $(a_1 \text{ AND } a_2) \Rightarrow (b_5)$, are taken to represent concepts since they both contain the least number of defining attributes (i.e., 2). Hence, the concept labels are b_2 and b_5, and the defining attributes are a_1 and a_5, and a_1 and a_2, respectively. That is:

$$\text{Concept 0: } (a_1 \text{ AND } a_5) \Rightarrow (b_2)$$
$$\text{Concept 1: } (a_1 \text{ AND } a_2) \Rightarrow (b_5).$$

The initial rules can now be modified to incorporate these concepts. If any of the rules contain all the attributes defining a particular concept, these attributes are removed from the list of contributory inputs and replaced by the associated concept. The rules are reworked using the determined concepts as attributes. For the rule base just described, the resulting new rules after the introduction of Concept 0 and Concept 1 are:

$$(b_5 \text{ AND } a_4) \Rightarrow (b_1)$$
$$(b_2) \Rightarrow (b_2)$$
$$(b_2 \text{ AND } a_3) \Rightarrow (b_3)$$
$$(a2 \text{ AND } a_3 \text{ AND } a_5) \Rightarrow (b_4)$$
$$(b_5) \Rightarrow (b_5).$$

The rules that do not contain all of the defining attributes for a concept are unchanged, and the original rules defining the concepts are replaced by tautological statements with the same input implying the same output; that is, $(b_2) \Rightarrow (b_2)$ and $(b_5) \Rightarrow (b_5)$. This process can be repeated, giving new rules, and therefore new concepts, after each pass. Concepts are always constructed by determining the minimum number of attributes defining a rule, and replacing these attributes by the new concept in all rules containing all the defining attributes. Thus at each step at least one new concept is formed. This entails specialization of an existing concept by requiring the presence of additional attributes. A class hierarchy evolves with lower-level concepts as subclasses of the higher-level concepts. The process terminates when each input tautologically implies its output; that is, the only rules left are tautologies.

In summary, the extraction of these concepts and their use in refining the set of rules enable the construction of a hierarchy of the domain, if it exists. By requiring that additional attributes be present, the concepts lower down in the hierarchy consist of specializations of a higher-lying concept.

7.4 Summary of the method

The following steps can be taken to determine a conjunctive rule for each output, using a single-layered neural network:

- Train a single-layered neural network using Hebb's Rule.
- For each output, determine the maximum weight of the links between it and all the inputs.

- Select those inputs that are within some range (determined by an error threshold) of the maximum weight.
- Form a conjunctive rule using the contributory inputs as the antecedent and the output as the consequent.

From this set of conjunctive rules, high-level concepts can be extracted. The following steps are repeated until all rules are reduced to tautologies:

- Select the rules with the least number of contributory attributes.
- Insert these concepts into the rule base by replacing all combinations of the attributes that define a concept by the concept itself, in any of the remaining rules.

This method produces a different set of rules after each pass. The first set contains rules with antecedents that are conjunctions of the initial (i.e., primitive) inputs, while the last is a set of tautologies. In between, various levels of abstractions, related to the determined concepts, are possible. A hierarchical structure of the domain, if present, is thus determined. This knowledge may then be placed into a frame-like structure, if required.

7.5   Illustrative applications

7.5.1 Animal world domain example

To illustrate in detail the method described in Section 7.4, it was applied to a subset of the animal world. This data is an artificial, noise-free set of binary attributes used only for demonstration purposes.

The training set consisted of 109 examples, described by 29 inputs and 27 outputs, as listed in Tables 7.1 and 7.2, respectively. For example, input 3 is a binary-valued variable indicating the presence (1) or absence (0) of Egglaying. A portion of the weight matrix produced by applying Hebb's Rule with a learning parameter of 0.1 is given in Table 7.3.

The initial primitive rules for each output, as shown in Table 7.4, were determined. An error threshold of 0.00 was used to select the contributory inputs, as the data is known to be free of noise. Consider the production of the initial conjunctive rule for the MARSUPIAL output. The associated weighted links for this output from Table 7.3 are re-stated below:

$$2 \mid \begin{array}{cccccccccccccccc} 0.6 & 0.6 & 0.0 & 0.0 & 0.6 & 0.0 & 0.0 & 0.0 & 0.0 & 0.0 & 0.0 & 0.0 & 0.0 & 0.0 & 0.0 \\ 0.0 & 0.0 & 0.0 & 0.0 & 0.0 & 0.0 & 0.0 & 0.0 & 0.0 & 0.0 & 0.0 & 0.0 & 0.0 & 0.0 \end{array}$$

The maximum weighted link of all the inputs to this MARSUPIAL output is 0.6. Thus, any input with an associated weight of 0.6 is considered a contributory

0	Hair	1	Milk	2	Feathers
3	Egglaying	4	Pouches	5	Placenta
6	Oceanic	7	Land	8	Tree
9	Field-mead	10	Lake-river	11	Large
12	Medium	13	Fly	14	Fly-short-d
15	Fly-long-d	16	Five-digit	17	Claws
18	Hoofs	19	Odd-toed	20	Even-toed
21	Herbivore	22	Sturdy-feet	23	Web-feet
24	Tail	25	Trunk	26	Slit-eyes
27	Black-stripe	28	Bird-o-prey		

Table 7.1   Input attributes for the animal domain

0	MAMMAL	1	MONOTREMES	2	MARSUPIAL
3	BAT	4	MARINE-M	5	LAND-M
6	APE	7	MONKEY	8	BEAR
9	CAT	10	DOG	11	UNGULATE
12	ELEPHANT	13	ZEBRA	14	HORSE
15	EVEN-TOED	16	BIRD	17	RUN-BIRD
18	LAND-BIRD	19	WEBBED-B	20	FLY-BIRD
21	FOWL	22	LAKE-RIV-B	23	SEA-BIRD
24	PER-B-PREY	25	PER-B-NO-PREY	26	FIELD-B

Table 7.2   Output attributes for the animal domain

	0	1	2	3	4	5	6	7	8	9	10	11	12	13	14	15	16	17	18	19	20	21	22	23	24	25	26	27	28
0	6.1	6.1	0.0	0.2	0.6	5.3	0.6	4.4	0.0	0.0	0.0	0.0	1.4	0.3	0.0	0.0	0.8	2.0	1.6	0.8	0.8	0.3	0.0	0.0	0.4	0.2	0.8	0.3	0.0
1	0.2	0.2	0.0	0.2	0.0	0.0	0.0	0.0	0.0	0.0	0.0	0.0	0.0	0.0	0.0	0.0	0.0	0.0	0.0	0.0	0.0	0.0	0.0	0.0	0.0	0.0	0.0	0.0	0.0
2	0.6	0.6	0.0	0.0	0.6	0.0	0.0	0.0	0.0	0.0	0.0	0.0	0.0	0.0	0.0	0.0	0.0	0.0	0.0	0.0	0.0	0.0	0.0	0.0	0.0	0.0	0.0	0.0	0.0
3	0.3	0.3	0.0	0.0	0.0	0.3	0.0	0.0	0.0	0.0	0.0	0.0	0.0	0.3	0.0	0.0	0.0	0.0	0.0	0.0	0.0	0.0	0.0	0.0	0.0	0.0	0.0	0.0	0.0
4	0.6	0.6	0.0	0.0	0.0	0.6	0.6	0.0	0.0	0.0	0.0	0.0	0.0	0.0	0.0	0.0	0.0	0.0	0.0	0.0	0.0	0.0	0.0	0.0	0.0	0.0	0.0	0.0	0.0
5	4.4	4.4	0.0	0.0	0.0	4.4	0.0	4.4	0.0	0.0	0.0	1.0	1.4	0.0	0.0	0.0	0.8	2.0	1.6	0.8	0.8	0.3	0.0	0.0	0.4	0.2	0.8	0.3	0.0

Table 7.3   A portion of the weighted links from the inputs (across) to the outputs (down) produced by Hebb's Rule for the animal data

---

(Hair AND Milk) ⇒ (MAMMAL)
(Hair AND Milk AND Egglaying) ⇒ (MONOTREMES)
(Hair AND Milk AND Pouches) ⇒ (MARSUPIAL)
(Hair AND Milk AND Placenta AND Fly) ⇒ (BAT)
(Hair AND Milk AND Placenta AND Oceanic) ⇒ (MARINE-M)
(Hair AND Milk AND Placenta AND Land) ⇒ (LAND-M)
(Hair AND Milk AND Placenta AND Land AND Large AND Five-digit) ⇒
    (APE)
(Hair AND Milk AND Placenta AND Land AND Five-digit AND Tail) ⇒
    (MONKEY)
(Hair AND Milk AND Placenta AND Land AND Large AND Claws) ⇒
    (BEAR)
(Hair AND Milk AND Placenta AND Land AND Claws AND Slit-eyes) ⇒
    (CAT)
(Hair AND Milk AND Placenta AND Land AND Claws AND Medium) ⇒
    (DOG)
(Hair AND Milk AND Placenta AND Land AND Hoofs) ⇒ (UNGULATE)
(Hair AND Milk AND Placenta AND Land AND Hoofs AND Odd-toed
    AND Trunk) ⇒ (ELEPHANT)
(Hair AND Milk AND Placenta AND Land AND Hoofs AND Odd-toed
    AND Medium AND Black-stripe) ⇒ (ZEBRA)
(Hair AND Milk AND Placenta AND Land AND Hoofs AND Odd-toed
    AND Medium AND Herbivore) ⇒ (HORSE)
(Hair AND Milk AND Placenta AND Land AND Hoofs AND Even-toed)
    ⇒ (EVEN-TOED-U)
(Feathers AND Egglaying) ⇒ (BIRD)
(Feathers AND Egglaying AND Land) ⇒ (RUN-BIRD)
(Feathers AND Egglaying AND Land AND Sturdy-feet) ⇒ (LAND-B)
(Feathers AND Egglaying AND Land AND Web-feet) ⇒ (WEBBED-B)
(Feathers AND Egglaying AND Fly) ⇒ (FLY-BIRD)
(Feathers AND Egglaying AND Fly AND Fly-short-d AND Claws) ⇒ (FOWL)
(Feathers AND Egglaying AND Fly AND Fly-short-d AND Lake-river) ⇒
    (LAKE-RIV-B)
(Feathers AND Egglaying AND Fly AND Fly-long-d AND Oceanic) ⇒
    (SEA-BIRD)
(Feathers AND Egglaying AND Fly AND Fly-long-d AND Tree AND Bird-
    o-prey) ⇒ (PER-B-PREY)
(Feathers AND Egglaying, Fly AND Fly-long-d AND Tree AND Claws) ⇒
    (PER-B-NO-PREY)
(Feathers AND Egglaying AND Fly AND Fly-long-d AND Field-mead) ⇒
    (FIELD-B)

Table 7.4   Rules after the first pass of the animal data

input to the output MARSUPIAL. The contributory inputs of Hair, Milk, and Pouches (i.e., inputs 0, 1, and 4) form the antecedent of the rule:

(Hair AND Milk AND Pouches) $\Rightarrow$ (MARSUPIAL).

As another example, consider the land mammal output labeled LAND-M. The weights for this output from Table 7.3 are re-stated below:

$$5 \mid \begin{array}{ccccccccccccccc} 4.4 & 4.4 & 0.0 & 0.0 & 0.0 & 4.4 & 0.0 & 4.4 & 0.0 & 0.0 & 0.0 & 1.0 & 1.4 & 0.0 & 0.0 \\ 0.0 & 0.8 & 2.0 & 1.6 & 0.8 & 0.8 & 0.3 & 0.0 & 0.0 & 0.4 & 0.2 & 0.8 & 0.3 & 0.0 \end{array}$$

The maximum weighted link of all the inputs to the LAND-M output is 4.4. Any input with an associated weight of 4.4 is thus considered a contributory input to the output LAND-M. The contributory inputs of Hair, Milk, Placenta, and Land (i.e., inputs 0, 1, 5, and 7) form the antecedent of the rule:

(Hair AND Milk AND Placenta AND Land) $\Rightarrow$ (LAND-M).

Unlike the MARSUPIAL example, the other weights are not all zero. This indicates that all LAND-M have the attributes Hair, Milk, Placenta, and Land, and some, but not all, have other attributes such as Large (input 11) or Claws (input 17). The maximum weight is used to select the contributory inputs, rather than those weights within some range of the maximum weight. This approach is only taken with data that is known to be free of noise.

The process of extracting higher-level concepts from the initial primitive rules begins with selecting the rule(s) with the minimum number of contributory attributes. For the animal data, these are:

(Hair AND Milk) $\Rightarrow$ (MAMMAL)
(Feathers AND Egglaying) $\Rightarrow$ (BIRD) .

Thus, MAMMAL and BIRD are the initial concepts extracted, with their associated defining attributes, as shown in Table 7.5.

These concepts are now incorporated into the initial rule base to give the rules listed in Table 7.6. These new rules result from all combinations of the attributes that define the MAMMAL or BIRD concepts being replaced by the concept itself. For instance, the rule defining the MARSUPIAL output has both the attributes Hair and Milk in its antecedent. These attributes are replaced by MAMMAL to form the new rule:

(MAMMAL AND Pouches) $\Rightarrow$ (MARSUPIAL).

As expected, the MAMMAL and BIRD inputs tautologically imply their outputs:

(MAMMAL) $\Rightarrow$ (MAMMAL)
(BIRD) $\Rightarrow$ (BIRD).

The concepts extracted from the new rules are given at the end of Table

(Hair AND Milk) $\Rightarrow$ (MAMMAL)
(Hair AND Milk AND Egglaying) $\Rightarrow$ (MONOTREMES)
(Hair AND Milk AND Pouches) $\Rightarrow$ (MARSUPIAL)
(Hair AND Milk AND Placenta AND Fly) $\Rightarrow$ (BAT)
(Hair AND Milk AND Placenta AND Oceanic) $\Rightarrow$ (MARINE-M)
(Hair AND Milk AND Placenta AND Land) $\Rightarrow$ (LAND-M)
(Hair AND Milk AND Placenta AND Land AND Large AND Five-digit) $\Rightarrow$
    (APE)
(Hair AND Milk AND Placenta AND Land AND Five-digit AND Tail) $\Rightarrow$
    (MONKEY)
(Hair AND Milk AND Placenta AND Land AND Large AND Claws) $\Rightarrow$
    (BEAR)
(Hair AND Milk AND Placenta AND Land AND Claws AND Slit-eyes) $\Rightarrow$
    (CAT)
(Hair AND Milk AND Placenta AND Land AND Claws AND Medium) $\Rightarrow$
    (DOG)
(Hair AND Milk AND Placenta AND Land AND Hoofs) $\Rightarrow$ (UNGULATE)
(Hair AND Milk AND Placenta AND Land AND Hoofs AND Odd-toed
    AND Trunk) $\Rightarrow$ (ELEPHANT)
(Hair AND Milk AND Placenta AND Land AND Hoofs AND Odd-toed
    AND Medium AND Black-stripe) $\Rightarrow$ (ZEBRA)
(Hair AND Milk AND Placenta AND Land AND Hoofs AND Odd-toed
    AND Medium AND Herbivore) $\Rightarrow$ (HORSE)
(Hair AND Milk AND Placenta AND Land AND Hoofs AND Even-toed)
    $\Rightarrow$ (EVEN-TOED-U)
(Feathers AND Egglaying) $\Rightarrow$ (BIRD)
(Feathers AND Egglaying AND Land) $\Rightarrow$ (RUN-BIRD)
(Feathers AND Egglaying AND Land AND Sturdy-feet) $\Rightarrow$ (LAND-B)
(Feathers AND Egglaying AND Land AND Web-feet) $\Rightarrow$ (WEBBED-B)
(Feathers AND Egglaying AND Fly) $\Rightarrow$ (FLY-BIRD)
(Feathers AND Egglaying AND Fly AND Fly-short-d AND Claws) $\Rightarrow$ (FOWL)
(Feathers AND Egglaying AND Fly AND Fly-short-d AND Lake-river) $\Rightarrow$
    (LAKE-RIV-B)
(Feathers AND Egglaying AND Fly AND Fly-long-d AND Oceanic) $\Rightarrow$
    (SEA-BIRD)
(Feathers AND Egglaying AND Fly AND Fly-long-d AND Tree AND Bird-
    o-prey) $\Rightarrow$ (PER-B-PREY)
(Feathers AND Egglaying AND Fly AND Fly-long-d AND Tree AND Claws)
    $\Rightarrow$ (PER-B-NO-PREY)
(Feathers AND Egglaying AND Fly AND Fly-long-d AND Field-mead) $\Rightarrow$
    (FIELD-B)

Concept 0: (Hair AND Milk) $\Rightarrow$ (MAMMAL)
Concept 1: (Feathers AND Egglaying) $\Rightarrow$ (BIRD)

Table 7.5   Rules and concepts after the first pass of the animal data

(MAMMAL) $\Rightarrow$ (MAMMAL)
(MAMMAL AND Egglaying) $\Rightarrow$ (MONOTREMES)
(MAMMAL AND Pouches) $\Rightarrow$ (MARSUPIAL)
(MAMMAL AND Placenta AND Fly) $\Rightarrow$ (BAT)
(MAMMAL AND Placenta AND Oceanic) $\Rightarrow$ (MARINE-M)
(MAMMAL AND Placenta AND Land) $\Rightarrow$ (LAND-M)
(MAMMAL AND Placenta AND Land AND Large AND Five-digit) $\Rightarrow$ (APE)
(MAMMAL AND Placenta AND Land AND Five-digit AND Tail) $\Rightarrow$ (MONKEY)
(MAMMAL AND Placenta AND Land AND Large AND Claws) $\Rightarrow$ (BEAR)
(MAMMAL AND Placenta AND Land AND Claws AND Slit-eyes) $\Rightarrow$ (CAT)
(MAMMAL AND Placenta AND Land AND Claws AND Medium) $\Rightarrow$ (DOG)
(MAMMAL AND Placenta AND Land AND Hoofs) $\Rightarrow$ (UNGULATE)
(MAMMAL AND Placenta AND Land AND Hoofs AND Odd-toed AND Trunk) $\Rightarrow$ (ELEPHANT)
(MAMMAL AND Placenta AND Land AND Hoofs AND Odd-toed AND Medium AND Black-stripe) $\Rightarrow$ (ZEBRA)
(MAMMAL AND Placenta AND Land AND Hoofs AND Odd-toed AND Medium AND Herbivore) $\Rightarrow$ (HORSE)
(MAMMAL AND Placenta AND Land AND Hoofs AND Even-toed) $\Rightarrow$ (EVEN-TOED-U)
(BIRD) $\Rightarrow$ (BIRD)
(BIRD AND Land) $\Rightarrow$ (RUN-BIRD)
(BIRD AND Land AND Sturdy-feet) $\Rightarrow$ (LAND-B)
(BIRD AND Land AND Web-feet) $\Rightarrow$ (WEBBED-B)
(BIRD AND Fly) $\Rightarrow$ (FLY-BIRD)
(BIRD AND Fly AND Fly-short-d AND Claws) $\Rightarrow$ (FOWL)
(BIRD AND Fly AND Fly-short-d AND Lake-river) $\Rightarrow$ (LAKE-RIV-B)
(BIRD AND Fly AND Fly-long-d AND Oceanic) $\Rightarrow$ (SEA-BIRD)
(BIRD AND Fly AND Fly-long-d AND Tree AND Bird-o-prey) $\Rightarrow$ (PER-B-PREY)
(BIRD AND Fly AND Fly-long-d AND Tree AND Claws) $\Rightarrow$ (PER-B-NO-PREY)
(BIRD AND Fly AND Fly-long-d AND Field-mead) $\Rightarrow$ (FIELD-B)

Concept 0: (MAMMAL AND Egglaying) $\Rightarrow$ (MONOTREMES)
Concept 1: (MAMMAL AND Pouches) $\Rightarrow$ (MARSUPIAL)
Concept 2: (BIRD AND Land) $\Rightarrow$ (RUN-BIRD)
Concept 3: (BIRD AND Fly) $\Rightarrow$ (FLY-BIRD)

Table 7.6   Rules and concepts after the second pass of the animal data

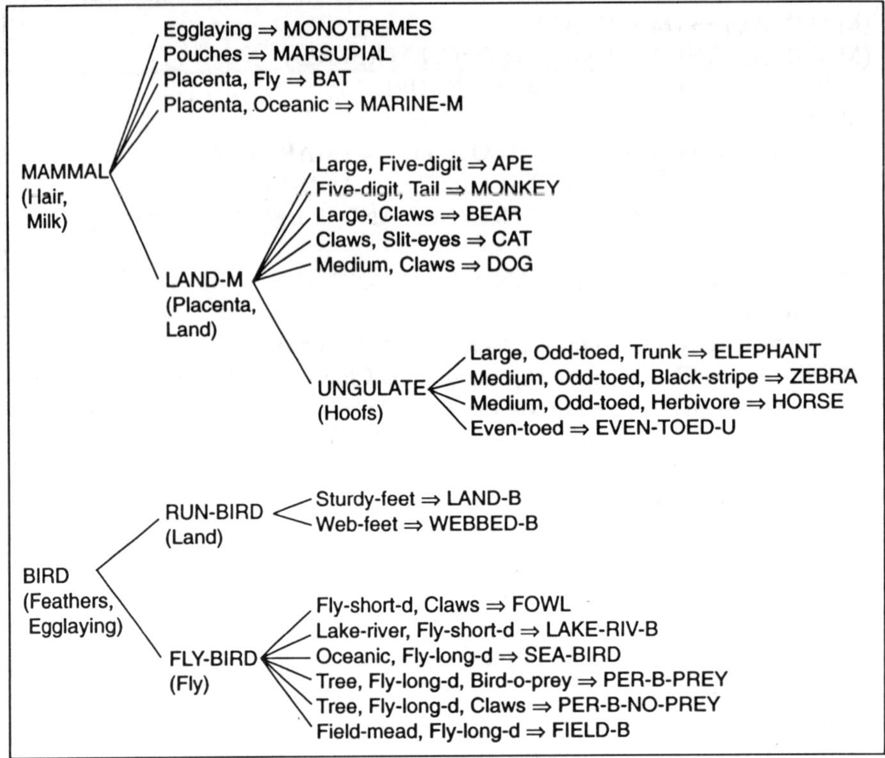

Figure 7.2　Final hierarchy of rules produced for the animal data

7.6. Note that the four new concepts formed at this stage represent 2 specializations of MAMMAL and 2 specializations of BIRD. The higher-level concepts of MAMMAL and BIRD therefore constitute classes, with the concepts MONOTREMES and MARSUPIAL as subclasses of MAMMAL, and the concepts RUN-BIRD and FLY-BIRD as subclasses of BIRD. The procedure of determining concepts and reforming rules is repeated until all the rules are reduced to tautologies. Figure 7.2 contains the final rules, reflecting the structure of the class hierarchy.

7.5.2 LED digit domain example

This example domain contains data defining the 10 decimal digits used on LED displays. The data consists of 3000 randomly generated examples, each described in terms of 7 binary attributes and 10 equiprobable classes. Seven elements are used to configure each decimal digit found on a LED display, as shown in Figure 2.7. Each input element of the data was subjected to a 10% random error; that is, a probability of 0.1 that an input element has its correct

	Up-center	Up-left	Up-right	Mid-center	Down-left	Down-right	Down-center
ZERO	13.35	13.15	13.05	1.40	12.90	13.65	13.20
ONE	1.90	1.85	14.15	1.80	1.70	13.85	1.40
TWO	13.60	1.40	13.35	13.80	13.40	1.85	13.55
THREE	12.50	1.40	12.25	12.25	1.20	11.75	11.85
FOUR	1.10	12.90	13.30	13.05	1.20	12.45	1.15
FIVE	14.75	14.90	1.65	14.65	1.75	14.40	14.60
SIX	13.30	13.60	1.70	13.60	13.10	13.70	13.00
SEVEN	13.55	1.55	13.55	1.35	1.30	13.45	1.15
EIGHT	13.80	13.50	13.35	13.00	13.30	12.9	13.50
NINE	13.85	13.90	13.70	14.05	2.05	14.20	13.95

Table 7.7   The weighted links from the inputs (across) to the outputs (down) produced by Hebb's Rule for the LED data

status inverted (Breiman et al. 1984; Quinlan 1987). The example set allows evaluation of this method on a noisy domain.

A subset of 500 examples was used to train a single-layered neural network comprising 7 inputs (for the 7 LED elements in the different positions of the display) and 10 outputs (for the 10 digits 0 to 9). Table 7.7 contains the weights determined by Hebb's Rule with a learning parameter of 0.05. Using an error threshold of 10% (reflecting the random error in the data), all the initial rules produced were correct. These primitive rules are given in Table 7.8.

For this same data set, the original ID3 algorithm discussed in Chapter 2 produced the very complicated decision tree given in Figure 2.8. ID3 is very inefficient on this noisy data, and improvements to ID3 have been implemented in C4.5, as detailed in Chapter 2.

In contrast, the method proposed in this chapter produced only 10 rules and they reflected a correct representation of the domain. One of the strengths of neural networks is the ability to deal with noise. A neural network effectively filters out the noise in the data. For the LED domain, the rules produced were correct, straightforward, and understandable to a human user.

By extracting specific combinations of attributes, the hierarchical structure for this domain evolves, as given in Figure 7.3. From this hierarchy, the following equivalent rules defining the decimal digit 3 can be extracted:

(Up-right AND Down-right AND Up-center AND Mid-center AND Down-center) $\Rightarrow$ (THREE)
(ONE AND Up-center AND Mid-center AND Down-center) $\Rightarrow$ (THREE)
(SEVEN AND Mid-center AND Down-center) $\Rightarrow$ (THREE).

((Up-center = On) AND (Up-left = On) AND (Up-right = On) AND (Down-left = On) AND (Down-right = On) AND (Down-center = On)) $\Rightarrow$ (ZERO)
(Up-right = On) AND (Down-right = On)) $\Rightarrow$ (ONE)
((Up-center = On) AND (Up-right = On)) $\Rightarrow$ (Mid-center = On) AND (Down-left = On) AND (Down-center = On)) $\Rightarrow$ ((TWO)
((Up-center = On) AND (Up-right = On) AND (Mid-center = On) AND (Down-right = On) AND (Down-center = On)) $\Rightarrow$ (THREE)
((Up-left = On) AND (Up-right = On) AND (Mid-center = On) AND (Down-Right = On)) $\Rightarrow$ (FOUR)
((Up-center = On) AND (Up-left = On) AND (Mid-center = On) AND (Down-right = On) AND (Down-center = On)) $\Rightarrow$ (FIVE)
((Up-Center = On) AND (Up-left = On) AND (Mid-center = On) AND (Down-left = On) AND (Down-right = On) AND (Down-center = On)) $\Rightarrow$ (SIX)
((Up-center = On) AND (Up-right = On) AND (Down-right = On)) $\Rightarrow$ (SEVEN)
((Up-center = On) AND (Up-left = On) AND (Up-right = On) AND (Mid-center = On) AND (Down-left = On) AND (Down-right = On) AND (Down-center = On)) $\Rightarrow$ (EIGHT)
((Up-center = On) AND (Up-left = On) AND (Up-right = On) AND (Mid-center = On) AND (Down-right = On) AND (Down-center = On)) $\Rightarrow$ (NINE)

Table 7.8   Initial rules produced for the LED data

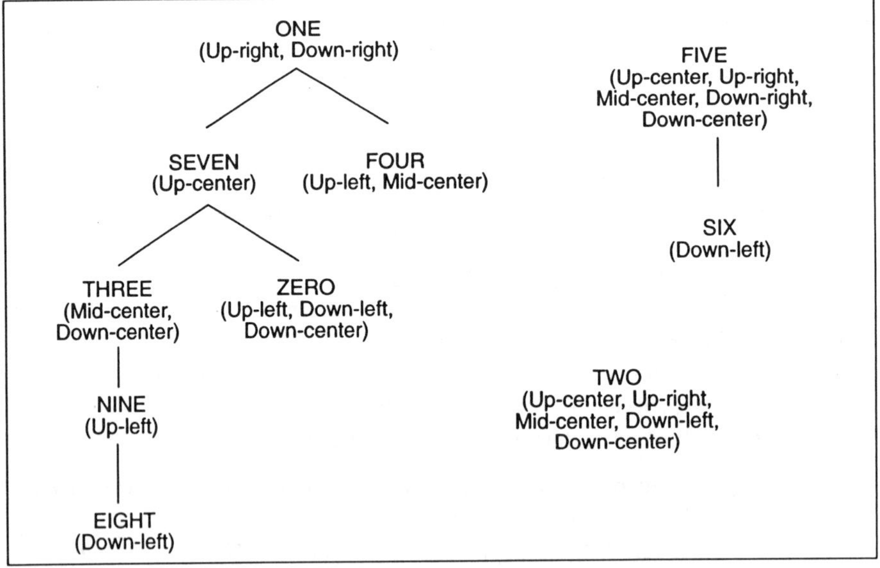

Figure 7.3   Final hierarchy produced for the LED data

7.6 Problems with the method

The method presented in this chapter provides a technique for the automatic generation of high-level knowledge representations from the low-level representations used by a single-layered neural network. The formation of intermediate concepts in this technique enables this method to produce different levels of abstraction.

One of the weaknesses of the method is the use of Hebb's Rule to train the neural network. Hebb's Rule determines the direct correlation values between the inputs and the outputs. The use of this training rule allowed the construction of linear models of the test domains, and with these linear models the selection of the contributory attributes was fairly straightforward. However, the direct correlation feature of Hebb's Rule enabled the determination of the correct results. Even though it is well known that single-layered networks cannot model complex, non-linear data accurately, the single-layered network contained enough knowledge of the domain for the method to generate the rules for the simple test domains successfully.

Another problem with this method is that the rules produced are conjunctive rules. The determined contributory inputs are linked in the antecedent with the AND connective and the consequent is the associated output. Hence, only one rule can be produced for each output. This is not feasible in real-world domains where different situations may lead to the same action or conclusion. For instance, there may be two distinct rules for MAMMAL:

$$(\text{Hair AND Milk}) \Rightarrow (\text{MAMMAL}), \text{ and}$$
$$(\text{Animal AND Warm-blooded}) \Rightarrow (\text{MAMMAL}).$$

These two rules represent two different areas of the input space that map onto the same point in output space, as shown in Figure 7.4.

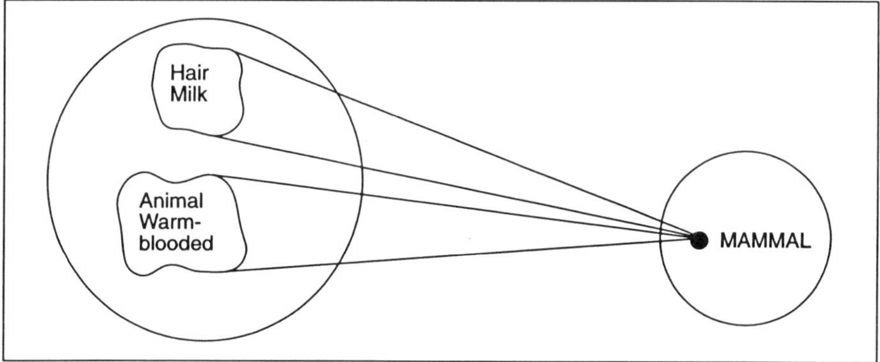

Figure 7.4   Two distinct areas of input space being mapped to the same area of output space

7.7 Recapitulation

To address these problems, the next chapter explores the use of multi-layered neural networks that have the advantage of being able to model most problem domains correctly (McClelland & Rumelhart 1988; Rumelhart et al. 1986). A technique is described that extracts conjunctive rules using both a single-layered and a multi-layered neural network. It forms the basis of the method known as BRAINNE. This method also allows the construction of disjunctive rules that provide for more than one conjunctive rule defining the same output. In addition, an extension to BRAINNE effectively deals with continuous data.

References

Boden, M.A. 1987, *Artificial Intelligence and Natural Man*, 2nd edition, Basic Books, New York

Breiman, L., Friedman, J.H., Olshen, R.A. & Stone, C.J. 1984, *Classification and Regression Trees*, Wadsworth International Group, Belmont, California

Dillon, T.S. & Tan, P.L. 1993, *Object-Oriented Conceptual Modeling*, Prentice Hall, Sydney, Australia

McClelland, J.L. & Rumelhart, D.E. 1988, *Explorations in Parallel Distributed Processing: A Handbook of Models, Programs, and Exercises*, MIT Press, Cambridge, Massachusetts

Quinlan, J.R. 1987, "Simplifying decision trees", *International Journal of Man-Machine Studies*, 27, pp. 221–34

Rumelhart, D.E., McClelland, J.L. & the PDP Research Group 1986, *Parallel Distributed Processing, Volume 1: Foundations*, MIT Press, Cambridge, Massachusetts

8

BRAINNE – automated knowledge acquisition using multi-layered neural networks

8.1 Introduction

The previous chapter presented a method that could extract rules from a single-layered neural network. This method is deficient for the following reasons: a single-layered neural network could not model complex non-linear domains; Hebb's Rule was used to train the network; and only one rule could be produced for each output.

To overcome these difficulties, we present in this chapter an alternative solution to the problem of automated knowledge acquisition using neural networks. This solution uses the excitatory aspects of a multi-layered neural network to model the problem domains. In addition, a single-layered neural network is used to model the inhibitory effects of the problem domains. The multi-layered neural network structure has the advantage that most problem domains can be successfully modeled, as discussed in Chapter 4 (Funahashi 1989; Hornik et al. 1989; McClelland & Rumelhart 1988; McClelland et al. 1986; Rumelhart et al. 1986; Sontag 1990). The first part of this chapter presents a technique that allows the construction of conjunctive rules for each output. This technique provides the foundation for the BRAINNE (Building Representations for AI using Neural NEtworks) method. The second part of this chapter discusses the extensions to BRAINNE that allow the detection and then extraction of multiple rules defining the same output.

Extracting information from a multi-layered neural network is not as straightforward as extracting information from a single-layered neural network. There are more layers to deal with in a multi-layered neural network and the information stored within the links is more distributed across the network. Tracing the contribution of any one input to any one output is not simple.

Consider a common, multi-layered network configuration with one hidden layer of units. As shown in Figure 8.1, input a has links to all the units in the hidden layer, and all these hidden units have links to output b. Thus, determining the contribution of input a to output b is fairly complex. However, some measure of the contributions from the various inputs to the various outputs is needed.

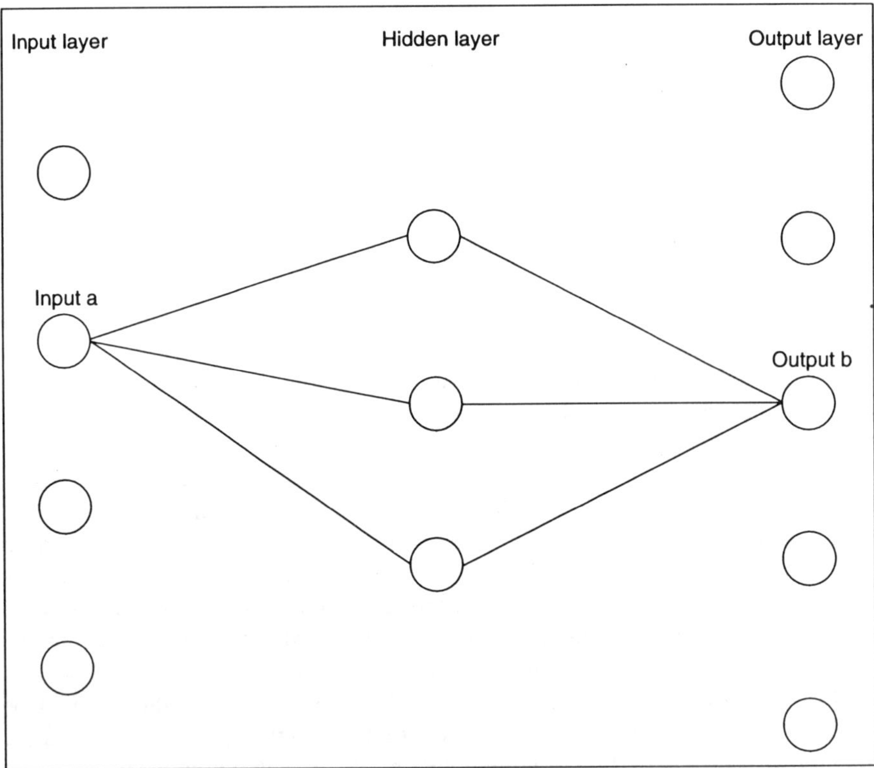

Figure 8.1   Tracing the links between input a and output b

8.2 Training a modified multi-layered network with Back-propagation

Let the original network configuration consist of m inputs, n outputs, and one hidden layer containing s hidden units, as shown in Figure 8.2. To have some means of determining the associations between the inputs and the desired outputs (targets), it was decided to extend the input set to include all the desired outputs; that is, the desired outputs are used as additional inputs. Now, the new network configuration, illustrated in Figure 8.3, consists of (m + n) inputs, n outputs, and s hidden units. Since the inputs and the desired outputs are now at the same level (i.e., at the input level), they can be directly compared without going through the hidden layers. Of course, there is a direct association between the additional inputs and the respective outputs.

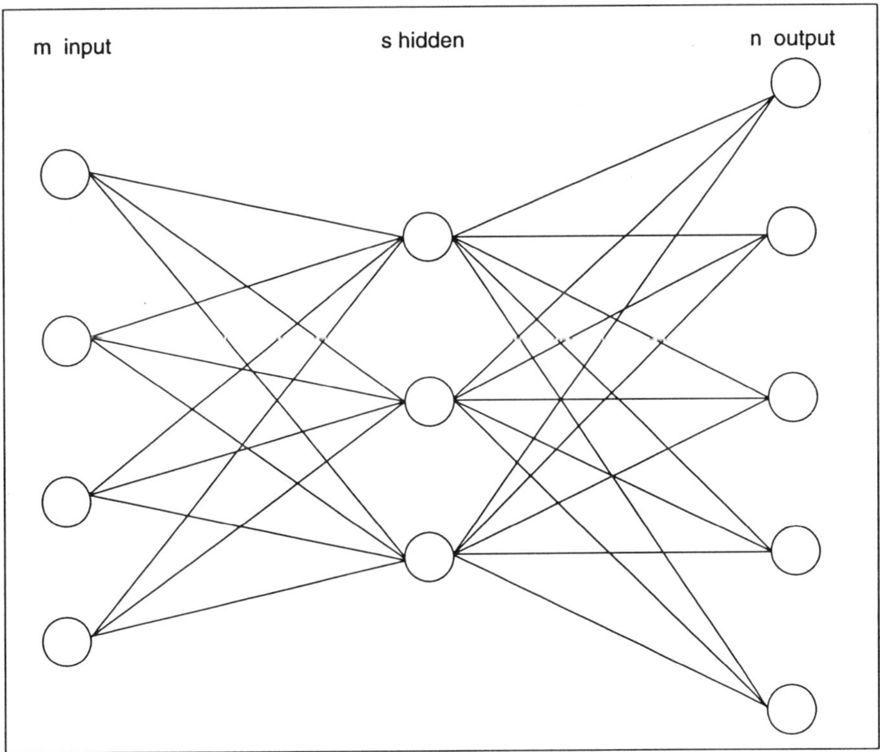

Figure 8.2 A neural network consisting of m inputs, n outputs, and s hidden units

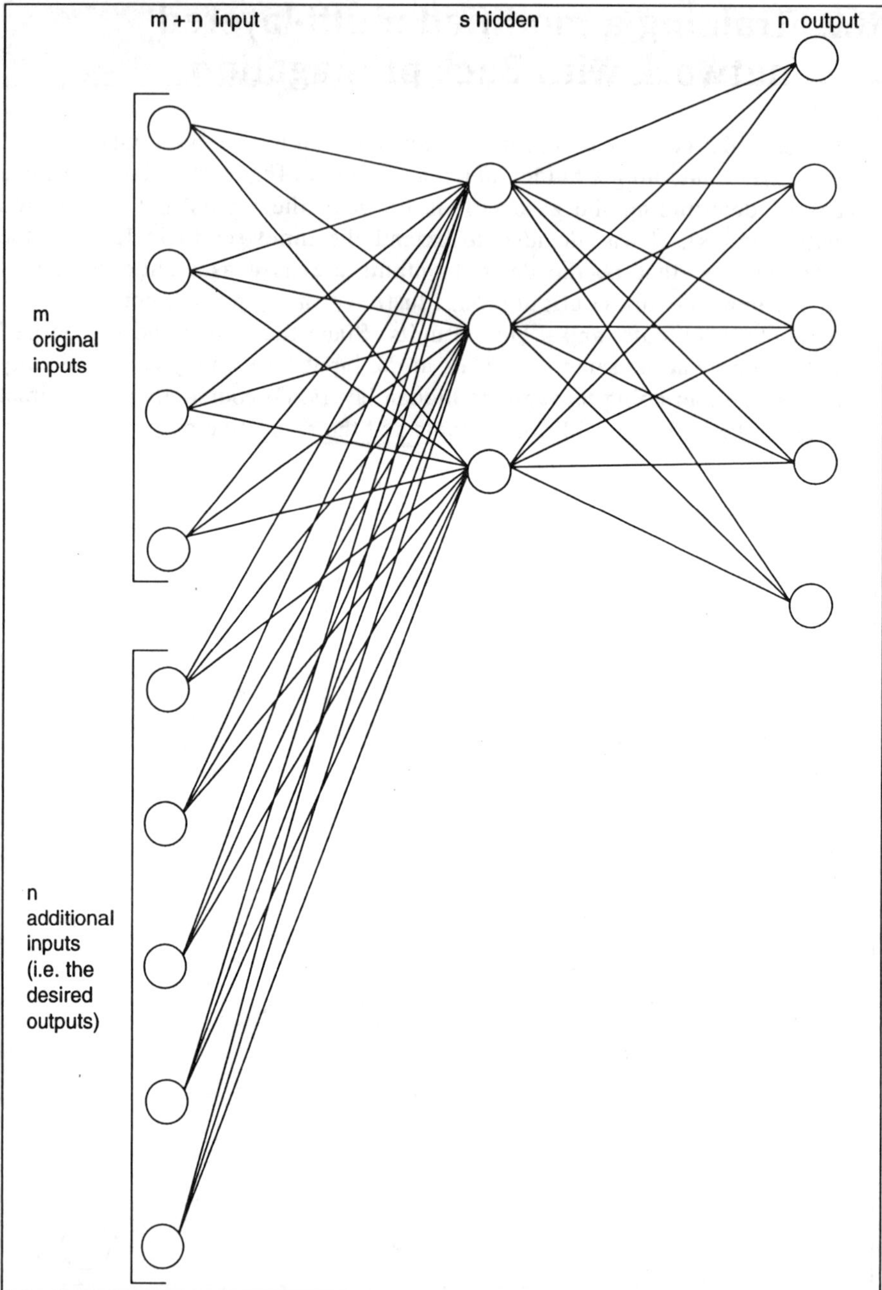

Figure 8.3   The new network configuration, using the desired outputs as additional inputs

As discussed previously, the use of knowledge is an important consideration in learning. Ohlsson (1987) stated that the declarative knowledge of objects involved in the domain should have some influence on the acquisition of the strategies (rules) for that domain. By using the desired outputs as additional inputs, this requirement has been fulfilled as further information is being utilized at the input level.

This new neural network configuration can now be trained using an appropriate learning technique such as Back-propagation, as described in Chapter 4. Once the network has stabilized to a reasonable solution, the various links can be examined in order to determine the contribution of an input to an output.

8.3 Sum of Squares Error (SSE) measurements

If the weights from an original input and one of the additional inputs (i.e., a desired output) to the hidden units are similar or identical, it is likely that there is a close association between the two. If one input is directly associated with an output, these weights are identical. Generally, however, the weights are not the same; there may be combinations of inputs required, or errors (noise) in the data. Hence, a Sum of Squares Error (SSE) criterion is adopted for determining the closeness between the weights from the original inputs and the weights from the additional inputs to the hidden units.

To measure the contribution of input a to desired output b (i.e., an additional input), a SSE measurement between the two attributes is used. The first step in this calculation is to determine the difference between a's contribution to hidden unit j and b's contribution to hidden unit j. In each case, the contribution is simply the numeric value of the weighted link. The difference between these values is then squared. Once this calculation is done for all of the hidden units, its sum determines the total difference between a and b. Figure 8.4 illustrates the links involved in this process.

For a more formal definition of the SSE measurement, let the value of the link between input a and hidden unit j be W_{aj}, and the link between desired output b and hidden unit j be W_{bj}. The SSE between a and b is defined as:

$$SSE_{ab} = \sum_{j} (W_{bj} - W_{aj})^2$$

where j is the number of the hidden unit. A smaller value of SSE indicates that the attributes are more closely related as the weights are closer to each other. If an input is directly associated with a particular output, its SSE measurement equals zero.

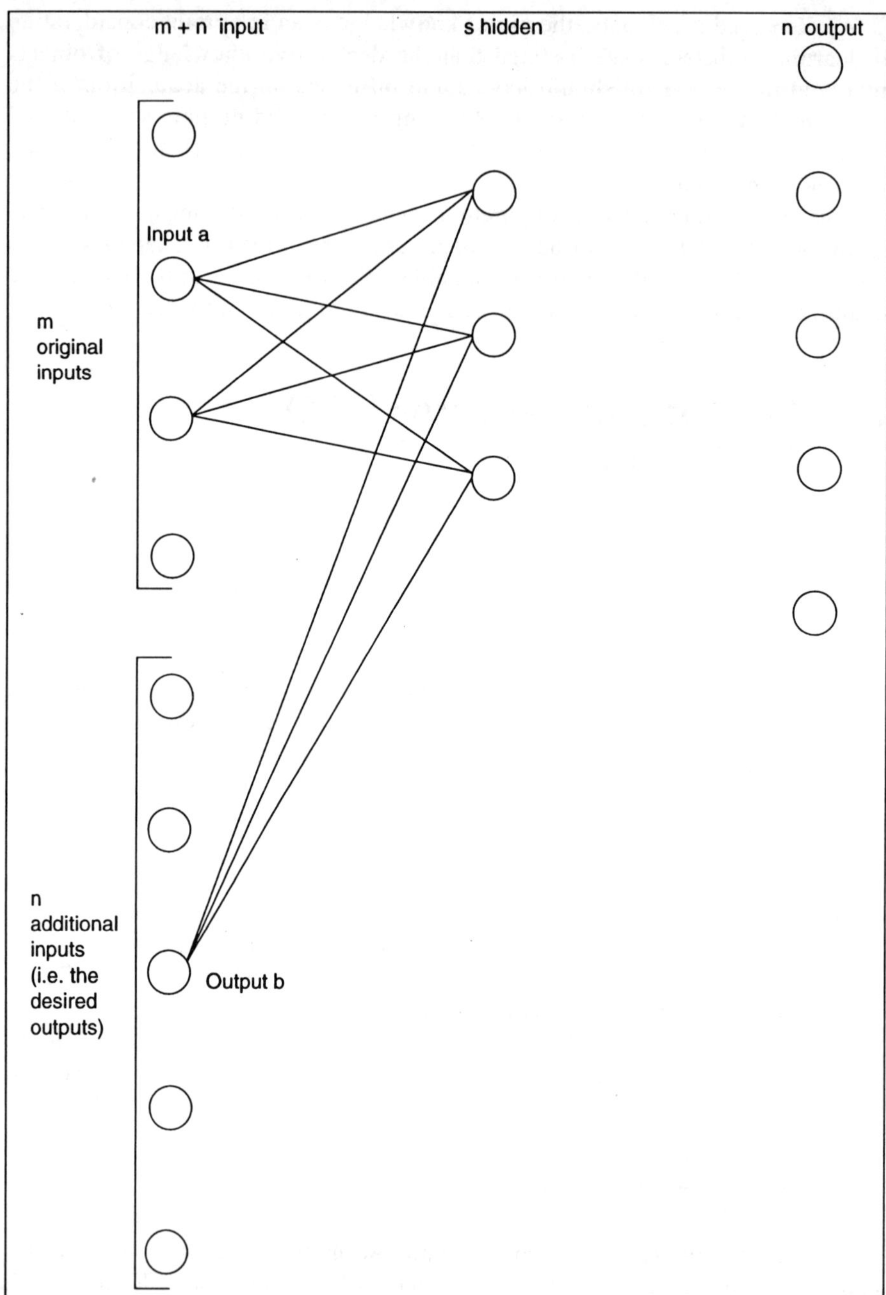

Figure 8.4   The links used to determine the SSE measurement between input a and output b

It is important to include statistical methods for noise immunity (Rendell 1987). As the degree of match can always be questioned, it is essential to use approximation instead of rigid equality. The SSE measure, the sum of the differences squared, provides this immunity. Squaring the differences diminishes the measure for small differences and accentuates larger differences.

However, if there is only a small number of examples of one desired output, problems can arise with these measurements, particularly with noisy data. The resulting SSE measurements do not seem to reflect the correct distribution of the information. Some of the SSE measurements could be small for inputs not related at all to the given desired output. In such cases involving only a few examples of a particular output, it could be useful to know the number of times that the particular input is activated and the output is not. The use of inhibitory links, as described in the next section, helps to obtain a measure of this type. The fact that knowledge is distributed across the whole network may be another drawback to using only an SSE measurement. A particular input may contribute to several outputs and it is the relevant combination of inputs that gives the correct results. Using inhibitory links also helps identify this more effectively.

8.4   Training a single-layered network with Hebb's Rule to determine inhibitory links

Inhibitory links between the original inputs and the original outputs help characterize:

- cases with few examples in the data set
- widely distributed contributions from a single input to several outputs.

The need to consider both positive and negative effects when learning is supported by neuro-physiological findings (Guyton 1984), as described in Chapter 6. The work of Hearst (1972), Ohlsson (1987), and Winston (1984) also supports this from a cognitive perspective. The use of inhibitory links seeks to implement these effects. The weighted inhibitory links reflect those input attributes that are not related to the outputs.

One way of obtaining the necessary examples to train the inhibitory links is to negate the input attributes, while keeping the output attributes constant for each example in the original training set. For instance, if the original training set contains the example:

$$(1, 0, 1) \Rightarrow (1, 0)$$

then the corresponding inhibitory example is:

$$(0, 1, 0) \Rightarrow (1, 0).$$

Thus a new set of example data can be formulated to reflect the irrelevance of the various attributes. Formally, the original activation levels of the input attributes are actually subtracted from 1 (assuming either binary or normalized continuous input values). Since the purpose here is not to model the excitatory effects of the domain, which is carried out by the multi-layered network, but rather to obtain a measure of the irrelevance of a particular input to a given output, the correlation between the inputs and outputs is considered sufficient.

These inhibitory links are directly trained using Hebb's Rule. Since Hebb's Rule provides the direct correlation values between the negated inputs and the outputs, these values can be used as an additional controlling factor for the attributes. The larger the correlation between the negated input and the output, the stronger the likelihood that the existence of the input implies the non-occurrence of the output. Hence, smaller inhibitory values indicate that the original attributes are more closely related to the output.

8.5 The products of the inhibitory links and the SSE measurements

The technique given in this section combines the modeling of both the excitatory and inhibitory effects. To extract a rule defining an output, the products of the inhibitory links (determined from Hebb's Rule) and the SSE measurements (determined from Back-propagation) between all the inputs and the output are taken. The resulting products indicate which of the inputs are associated with the output under consideration. These products are close to or equal to zero for those inputs that are directly associated with the output. Thus, the input attributes that have a small or zero product are taken to be the attributes defining the particular output. These input attributes form part of the antecedent and the output becomes the consequent of a conjunctive IF-THEN rule. Repeating this for each output produces one conjunctive rule for each output.

Stated formally, the products for all combinations of the inputs a and the outputs b are:

$$\text{Product}_{ab} = \text{Weight}_{ab} * \text{SSE}_{ab}$$

where Weight_{ab} is the weight of the inhibitory link between a and b determined by Hebb's Rule, and SSE_{ab} is the SSE measurement between a and b determined from the weights produced by Back-propagation. If the product value is zero for any combination, then the attributes are directly associated. By taking the product of the 2 measures, the 2 effects are combined into a single statistic. This statistic measures the relevance between an input and an output.

8.6 Selection of the defining attributes for a conjunctive rule

The list of the products for all the inputs and a particular output is used to select the defining attributes of the output. In this list (sorted from maximum to minimum), there may be a distinct cut-off point determining which input attributes should be used to define the output and which should not. Such a definite cut-off usually occurs where two consecutive products of the sorted list are at least two to three times different in magnitude. For example, let the following sorted list represent the input attributes and their associated products defining a particular output:

$$((B\ 5.1)\ (C\ 3.15)\ (E\ 2.23)\ (D\ 0.72)\ (A\ 0.65)).$$

Here, the cut-off point is clearly at attribute E with a product of 2.23. Therefore, all of the attributes with products below 2.23 (D and A) are taken to be the attributes defining that particular output.

The inputs (a's) selected in this manner are then grouped together in the antecedent with the AND connective, and the appropriate output (b) is taken to be the consequent of the rule. Thus the conjunctive rule, (a [AND a]*) $\Rightarrow$ (b), is produced for each output, where []* denotes 0 or more repetitions. If the above example has a consequent of OUTPUT 1 then the following is formed:

$$(D\ AND\ A) \Rightarrow (OUTPUT\ 1).$$

8.7 Extracting higher-level concepts

If the training data has inbuilt concepts, the rules produced will reflect this. Here, concepts are defined as a specific combination of attributes. Thus, as well as containing the original input attributes, the resulting rules will also contain any concepts.

To state this formally, let the attributes x and y define the concept Z. If the data has inbuilt concepts, then the following types of rules will be extracted:

$$(x\ AND\ y\ AND\ Z) \Rightarrow (Z)$$
$$(x\ AND\ y\ AND\ Z\ AND\ a1\ AND\ a2\ AND\ B1) \Rightarrow (B1).$$

Z and B1 appear in the antecedents as well, as they are additional inputs. It then follows that:

$$(Z \text{ AND } a1 \text{ AND } a2) \Rightarrow (B1)$$

where $(x \text{ AND } y) \Rightarrow (Z)$.

Different levels of abstraction are thus possible. Also, the detection of these concepts or regular features allows the formation of a class hierarchical structure of the domain, if this is possible. The approach for extracting concepts is explained in Section 7.3, and illustrated in Section 8.9.

The use of intermediate knowledge structures can facilitate learning (Rendell 1987). The construction of concepts or categories enables the development of a class hierarchy of the domain. This hierarchical structure reduces redundancy and is more efficient and understandable (Wolff 1987).

8.8 Summary of BRAINNE for conjunctive rules

The following steps need to be taken to extract information in the form of conjunctive rules for each output using both a multi-layered and an inhibitory single-layered neural network.

- Extend the input set by using the desired outputs as additional inputs. Set up a multi-layered network using the extended input set, the original output set, and one hidden layer. Train the multi-layered neural network using Back-propagation.

- Calculate the Sum of Squares Errors (SSE) between all the original inputs and all additional inputs (i.e., desired outputs).

$$SSE_{ab} = \sum_{j}(W_{bj} - W_{aj})^2$$

  where a is an input attribute, b is an additional input (i.e., a desired output), and W_{aj} and W_{bj} are the values of the links between a and hidden unit j, and b and hidden unit j, respectively. This value provides a measure of the closeness between the input a and the additional input (desired output) b. A smaller SSE reflects a greater contribution of the attribute to the output.

- Determine inhibitory links between the negated inputs and the outputs of a single-layered neural network using Hebb's Rule. This provides direct correlation values between the attributes and is, in fact, a measure of the irrelevance between the inputs and outputs. This measure is used as an additional controlling factor. The smaller the value, the more closely related the two attributes are.

- Calculate the product of the inhibitory weight values and the SSE measurements between all combinations of the inputs a and the outputs b.

$$Product_{ab} = Weight_{ab} * SSE_{ab}$$

where $Weight_{ab}$ is the weight of the inhibitory link between a and b determined by Hebb's Rule, and SSE_{ab} is the SSE measurement between a and b determined from the weights produced by Back-propagation.

- Sort the product list for a particular output from maximum to minimum. Select those input attributes that are below some clear cut-off point in the product list. This cut-off point usually occurs where two consecutive products are at least two to three times different in magnitude.
- Use the method for extracting concepts, as described in Section 7.3, if required.

8.9 Illustrative applications for conjunctive rules

The technique described in this chapter was applied to the same test domains used in the previous chapter — that is, the animal and LED domains. These results are presented next.

8.9.1 Animal world domain example

This example domain was chosen because the taxonomy of the animal world is well known. The data from 109 animals is a clean, noise-free subset of the animal world.

The 109 animals were used to train a multi-layered neural network comprising 29 inputs, 27 outputs, and one hidden layer containing 16 hidden units. After determining the SSE values and the inhibitory links, the resulting products and the appropriate cut-off points were determined. Table 8.1 contains some of these products. Note that as this domain is noise-free, the attributes chosen to be relevant to the output have a product equal to zero. The 27 rules produced were consistent with the expected taxonomy. A complete listing of these rules is given in Table 8.2.

Consider the portion of the product measurements for the MARSUPIAL output listed in Table 8.1 and re-stated below:

OUTPUT 2 = MARSUPIAL

....

$3.006 \Rightarrow$ Tree	$2.973 \Rightarrow$ Web-feet	$2.902 \Rightarrow$ Feathers
$2.777 \Rightarrow$ Lake-river	$2.753 \Rightarrow$ Bird-o-prey	$2.680 \Rightarrow$ Odd-toed
$2.551 \Rightarrow$ Trunk	$0.000 \Rightarrow$ Pouches	$0.000 \Rightarrow$ Milk
$0.000 \Rightarrow$ Hair	$0.000 \Rightarrow$ MAMMAL	$0.000 \Rightarrow$ MARSUPIAL

```
OUTPUT 0 = MAMMAL
..........
22.071 ⇒ Field-mead    20.836 ⇒ Lake-river    20.836 ⇒ Pouches
18.524 ⇒ Tree          12.764 ⇒ Land           2.327 ⇒ Placenta
 0.000 ⇒ Milk           0.000 ⇒ Hair            0.000 ⇒ MAMMAL

OUTPUT 2 = MARSUPIAL
..........
 3.006 ⇒ Tree           2.973 ⇒ Web-feet        2.902 ⇒ Feathers
 2.777 ⇒ Lake-river     2.753 ⇒ Bird-o-prey     2.680 ⇒ Odd-toed
 2.551 ⇒ Trunk          0.000 ⇒ Pouches         0.000 ⇒ Milk
 0.000 ⇒ Hair           0.000 ⇒ MAMMAL          0.000 ⇒ MARSUPIAL

OUTPUT 5 = LAND-M
..........
18.363 ⇒ Hoofs         18.145 ⇒ Lake-river     17.816 ⇒ Tail
17.311 ⇒ Slit-eyes     15.166 ⇒ Medium         13.820 ⇒ Five-digit
 0.000 ⇒ Land           0.000 ⇒ Placenta        0.000 ⇒ Milk
 0.000 ⇒ Hair           0.000 ⇒ MAMMAL          0.000 ⇒ LAND-M

OUTPUT 13 = ZEBRA
..........
 1.026 ⇒ Lake-river     1.001 ⇒ Five-digit      0.808 ⇒ Trunk
 0.000 ⇒ Black-stripe   0.000 ⇒ Odd-toed        0.000 ⇒ Hoofs
 0.000 ⇒ Medium         0.000 ⇒ Land            0.000 ⇒ Placenta
 0.000 ⇒ Milk           0.000 ⇒ Hair            0.000 ⇒ MAMMAL
 0.000 ⇒ LAND-M         0.000 ⇒ UNGULATE        0.000 ⇒ ZEBRA

OUTPUT 16 = BIRD
..........
16.564 ⇒ Lake-river    15.964 ⇒ Bird-o-prey    15.913 ⇒ Sturdy-feet
10.551 ⇒ Tree           4.973 ⇒ Fly-long-d      2.122 ⇒ Fly
 0.000 ⇒ Egglaying      0.000 ⇒ Feathers        0.000 ⇒ BIRD

OUTPUT 23 = SEA-BIRD
..........
 1.921 ⇒ Large          1.811 ⇒ Black-stripe    1.601 ⇒ Trunk
 1.576 ⇒ Slit-eyes      0.000 ⇒ Fly-long-d      0.000 ⇒ Fly
 0.000 ⇒ Oceanic        0.000 ⇒ Egglaying        0.000 ⇒ Feathers
 0.000 ⇒ BIRD           0.000 ⇒ FLY-BIRD         0.000 ⇒ SEA-BIRD
```

Table 8.1   Portion of the resulting products for the animal data

(Hair AND Milk) ⇒ (MAMMAL)
(Hair AND Milk AND Egglaying) ⇒ (MONOTREMES)
(Hair AND Milk AND Pouches) ⇒ (MARSUPIAL)
(Hair AND Milk AND Placenta AND Fly) ⇒ (BAT)
(Hair AND Milk AND Placenta) ⇒ (MARINE-M)
(Hair AND Milk AND Placenta AND Land) ⇒ (LAND-M)
(Hair AND Milk AND Placenta AND Land AND Large AND Five-digit)
   ⇒ (APE)
(Hair AND Milk AND Placenta AND Land AND Five-digit AND Tail) ⇒
   (MONKEY)
(Hair AND Milk AND Placenta AND Land AND Large AND Claws) ⇒
   (BEAR)
(Hair AND Milk AND Placenta AND Land AND Claws AND Slit-eyes) ⇒
   (CAT)
(Hair AND Milk AND Placenta AND Land AND Claws AND Medium) ⇒
   (DOG)
(Hair AND Milk AND Placenta AND Land AND Hoofs) ⇒ (UNGULATE)
(Hair AND Milk AND Placenta AND Land AND Hoofs AND Odd-toed
   AND Trunk) ⇒ (ELEPHANT)
(Hair AND Milk AND Placenta AND Land AND Hoofs AND Odd-toed
   AND Medium AND Black-stripe) ⇒ (ZEBRA)
(Hair AND Milk AND Placenta AND Land AND Hoofs AND Odd-toed
   AND Medium AND Herbivore) ⇒ (HORSE)
(Hair AND Milk AND Placenta AND Land AND Hoofs AND Even-toed)
   ⇒ (EVEN-TOED-U)
(Feathers AND Egglaying) ⇒ (BIRD)
(Feathers AND Egglaying AND Land) ⇒ (RUN-BIRD)
(Feathers AND Egglaying AND Land AND Sturdy-feet) ⇒ (LAND-B)
(Feathers AND Egglaying AND Land AND Web-feet) ⇒ (WEBBED-B)
(Feathers AND Egglaying AND Fly) ⇒ (FLY-BIRD)
(Feathers AND Egglaying AND Fly AND Fly-short-d AND Claws) ⇒ (FOWL)
(Feathers AND Egglaying AND Fly AND Fly-short-d AND Lake-river) ⇒
   (LAKE-RIV-B)
(Feathers AND Egglaying AND Fly AND Fly-long-d AND Oceanic) ⇒
   (SEA-BIRD)
(Feathers AND Egglaying AND Fly AND Fly-long-d AND Tree AND Bird-
   o-prey) ⇒ (PER-B-PREY)
(Feathers AND Egglaying AND Fly AND Fly-long-d AND Tree AND Claws)
   ⇒ (PER-B-NO-PREY)
(Feathers AND Egglaying AND Fly AND Fly-long-d AND Field-mead) ⇒
   (FIELD-B)

Table 8.2   Rules produced for the animal data

The products have already been sorted from maximum to minimum. As the data is noise-free, only those attributes with a zero product measurement are taken to be part of a conjunctive rule defining a MARSUPIAL. Thus, from the above list, the original input attributes of Pouches, Milk, and Hair, and the additional inputs (desired outputs) of MAMMAL and MARSUPIAL are determined to be the important contributory attributes for the output MARSUPIAL. These attributes, joined by the AND connective, form the antecedent of the resulting rule:

$$(\text{Hair AND Milk AND MAMMAL AND Pouches AND MARSUPIAL}) \Rightarrow (\text{MARSUPIAL}).$$

The concepts of MAMMAL and MARSUPIAL (as expected) contribute to MARSUPIAL. As the example data has these inbuilt higher concepts, the resulting rules reflect this. Hence, the rule defining a MARSUPIAL could be expressed using:

- original inputs only:

    $$(\text{Hair AND Milk AND Pouches}) \Rightarrow (\text{MARSUPIAL})$$

- original inputs and additional inputs:

    $$(\text{Hair AND Milk AND MAMMAL AND Pouches AND} \\ \text{MARSUPIAL}) \Rightarrow (\text{MARSUPIAL})$$

- higher-level concepts:

    $$(\text{MAMMAL AND Pouches}) \Rightarrow (\text{MARSUPIAL}) \\ \text{where (Hair AND Milk)} \Rightarrow (\text{MAMMAL}).$$

Other rules similarly produced from Table 8.1 are:

$$(\text{Hair AND Milk AND MAMMAL}) \Rightarrow (\text{MAMMAL})$$
$$(\text{Hair AND Milk AND MAMMAL AND Land AND Placenta}) \\ \Rightarrow (\text{LAND-M})$$
$$(\text{Hair AND Milk AND MAMMAL AND Land AND Placenta AND} \\ \text{LAND-M AND Hoofs AND UNGULATE AND Medium AND} \\ \text{Odd-toed AND Black-stripe AND ZEBRA}) \Rightarrow (\text{ZEBRA})$$
$$(\text{Feathers AND Egglaying AND BIRD}) \Rightarrow (\text{BIRD})$$
$$(\text{Feathers AND Egglaying AND BIRD AND Fly AND FLY-BIRD} \\ \text{AND Fly-long-d AND Oceanic}) \Rightarrow (\text{SEA-BIRD}).$$

The class hierarchy of this domain is given in Figure 7.2.

8.9.2 LED digit domain example

This example domain contains data representing the decimal digits commonly found on LED displays. As stated in Chapters 2 and 7, the data consists of 3000 randomly generated examples, each described in terms of 7 binary attributes and 10 equiprobable classes. Note that each input element of the data was subjected to a 10% random error; that is, a probability of 0.1 that an input element has its correct status inverted (Breiman et al. 1984; Quinlan 1987). A test example set containing 500 examples from this noisy data set was used to evaluate BRAINNE on a noisy domain.

A multi-layered neural network consisting of 7 inputs (defining the On/Off status of the seven positions on the LED display), 10 outputs (defining the ten digits 0–9), and one hidden layer containing 8 hidden units was trained using Back-propagation. After determining the products and detecting the appropriate cut-off points, all the rules produced were correct. Table 8.3 contains some of the resulting products and Table 8.4 lists the rules determined.

Consider the portion of the products for output TWO, listed in Table 8.3 and re-stated below:

```
OUTPUT 2 = TWO
169.776 ⇒ ONE          144.921 ⇒ FOUR        144.467 ⇒ THREE
142.812 ⇒ NINE         124.103 ⇒ SIX         123.949 ⇒ FIVE
 84.488 ⇒ SEVEN         61.751 ⇒ ZERO         40.288 ⇒ Up-left
 37.353 ⇒ Down-right    23.960 ⇒ EIGHT         4.907 ⇒ Mid-center
  2.953 ⇒ Up-right       2.942 ⇒ Down-left      0.982 ⇒ Up-center
  0.981 ⇒ Down-center    0.000 ⇒ TWO
```

Once again, the products are first sorted from maximum to minimum. However, as the data is not noise-free, the contributory inputs do not necessarily have a product measurement equal to zero. Note that an assumption of noise-free data should never be made. Hence, a distinct cut-off point in the magnitude of consecutive products in the list is sought. Starting from the maximum product and going toward the minimum product, there is no distinct break in the numbers until the consecutive product values of 23.960 for EIGHT and 4.907 for Mid-center. The ratio between these two products is approximately 5 to 1. Thus, the attributes below the EIGHT attribute are selected to be part of the antecedent of the following rule defining the output TWO:

(Mid-center AND Up-right AND Down-left AND Up-center AND Down-center) ⇒ (TWO).

OUTPUT 0 = ZERO

316.571 ⇒ SIX	168.821 ⇒ FOUR	157.729 ⇒ NINE
137.831 ⇒ THREE	101.820 ⇒ SEVEN	98.947 ⇒ FIVE
90.963 ⇒ ONE	69.985 ⇒ TWO	56.636 ⇒ EIGHT
52.290 ⇒ Mid-center	10.929 ⇒ Down-left	8.744 ⇒ Up-left
6.596 ⇒ Up-center	5.498 ⇒ Down-right	5.469 ⇒ Down-center
4.370 ⇒ Up-right	0.000 ⇒ ZERO	

OUTPUT 1 = ONE

331.311 ⇒ SIX	226.368 ⇒ TWO	223.783 ⇒ EIGHT
128.455 ⇒ SEVEN	115.724 ⇒ THREE	107.016 ⇒ ZERO
104.148 ⇒ NINE	89.869 ⇒ FIVE	59.287 ⇒ Mid-center
58.402 ⇒ Down-left	57.395 ⇒ FOUR	56.297 ⇒ Down-center
56.287 ⇒ Up-center	54.004 ⇒ Up-left	7.403 ⇒ Up-right
5.305 ⇒ Down-right	0.000 ⇒ ONE	

OUTPUT 2 = TWO

169.776 ⇒ ONE	144.921 ⇒ FOUR	144.467 ⇒ THREE
142.812 ⇒ NINE	124.103 ⇒ SIX	123.949 ⇒ FIVE
84.488 ⇒ SEVEN	61.751 ⇒ ZERO	40.288 ⇒ Up-left
37.353 ⇒ Down-right	23.960 ⇒ EIGHT	4.907 ⇒ Mid-center
2.953 ⇒ Up-right	2.942 ⇒ Down-left	0.982 ⇒ Up-center
0.981 ⇒ Down-center	0.000 ⇒ TWO	

....

OUTPUT 7 = SEVEN

217.134 ⇒ NINE	203.471 ⇒ SIX	169.970 ⇒ EIGHT
150.203 ⇒ THREE	104.905 ⇒ ONE	97.827 ⇒ ZERO
97.044 ⇒ FIVE	93.960 ⇒ FOUR	91.998 ⇒ TWO
58.261 ⇒ Down-center	57.173 ⇒ Up-left	55.891 ⇒ Mid-center
54.593 ⇒ Down-left	9.950 ⇒ Up-right	2.475 ⇒ Down-right
2.464 ⇒ Up-center	0.000 ⇒ SEVEN	

OUTPUT 8 = EIGHT

200.974 ⇒ FOUR	200.700 ⇒ SIX	193.945 ⇒ ONE
184.359 ⇒ FIVE	180.376 ⇒ SEVEN	143.353 ⇒ THREE
124.101 ⇒ NINE	57.747 ⇒ ZERO	27.687 ⇒ TWO
8.697 ⇒ Down-left	7.459 ⇒ Down-center	6.221 ⇒ Up-right
5.000 ⇒ Down-right	4.968 ⇒ Mid-center	2.489 ⇒ Up-left
1.251 ⇒ Up-center	0.000 ⇒ EIGHT	

Table 8.3   Portion of the resulting products for the LED data

---

((Up-center = On) AND (Up-left = On) AND (Up-right = On) AND (Down-left = On) AND (Down-right = On) AND (Down-center = On)) $\Rightarrow$ (ZERO)

((Up-right = On) AND (Down-right = On)) $\Rightarrow$ (ONE)

((Up-center = On) AND (Up-right = On) AND (Mid-center = On) AND (Down-left = On) AND (Down-center = On)) $\Rightarrow$ (TWO)

((Up-center = On) AND (Up-right = On) AND (Mid-center = On) AND (Down-right = On) AND (Down-center = On)) $\Rightarrow$ (THREE)

((Up-left = On) AND (Up-right = On) AND (Mid-center = On) AND (Down-right = On)) $\Rightarrow$ (FOUR)

((Up-center = On) AND (Up-left = On) AND (Mid-center = On) AND (Down-right = On) AND (Down-center = On)) $\Rightarrow$ (FIVE)

((Up-center = On) AND (Up-left = On) AND (Mid-center = On) AND (Down-left = On) AND (Down-right = On) AND (Down-center = On)) $\Rightarrow$ (SIX)

((Up-center = On) AND (Up-right = On) AND (Down-right = On)) $\Rightarrow$ (SEVEN)

((Up-center = On) AND (Up-left = On) AND (Up-right = On) AND (Mid-center = On) AND (Down-left = On) AND (Down-right = On) AND (Down-center = On)) $\Rightarrow$ (EIGHT)

((Up-center = On) AND (Up-left = On) AND (Up-right = On) AND (Mid-center = On) AND (Down-right = On) AND (Down-center = On)) $\Rightarrow$ (NINE)

Table 8.4   Rules produced for the LED data

Although the resulting product measurements of contributory inputs are not equal to zero for noisy data, a clear cut-off point in the sorted product list exists at the correct position for the various outputs. Additional comments made in Chapter 7 on this domain are relevant here.

8.10   The need for and detection of disjunctive rules

In the first part of this chapter we presented a technique to extract conjunctive rules for each output. In this approach, the relevant attributes are determined and then joined with the AND connective to form the antecedent part of a conjunctive rule. Therefore, there is one rule produced for each output.

In the real world, there are numerous examples where different situations result in the same action. For instance, if you are bored you may decide to go to the movies, but the same action of going to the movies may occur simply because a friend asks you to go. In a disjunctive form, this becomes:

IF bored OR asked by a friend THEN go to the movies.

Forming both conjunctive (attributes linked by ANDs) and disjunctive (attributes linked by ORs) groupings improves efficiency (Bruner et al. 1956; Pollio 1974; Wolff 1987). Hence, a method must be able to produce disjunctive rules to be complete and more realistic. The rest of this chapter describes the BRAINNE technique for detecting and then extracting such rules.

From the products list (sorted from maximum to minimum), the extraction of the appropriate attributes relies on the magnitude of the products determined. The cut-off is taken at the distinct point where the numeric value of one product is at least two to three times as large as the value of the next product in the sorted list. For example, let the following list represent the attributes defining a particular output and their associated products:

((Dots 5.1) (Stripes 3.15) (Glass 2.23) (Square 0.72) (Red 0.65)).

Here the cut-off point is clearly at attribute Glass with a product of 2.23. Hence, all the attributes with a product below 2.23 (i.e., Square and Red) are ANDed together to form a conjunctive rule defining that particular output.

It is postulated that if there is no distinct cut-off point, then there may be more than one rule for that output. In some test domains experienced, it was found that there is no definite cut-off point. However, it is interesting that a cut-off point is *almost* present, but not quite. If the product cut-off is defined as the point where 2 consecutive products are 1½ times different in magnitude, then a cut-off point could be established. This is highlighted in the following example where the cut-off could almost be taken at Glass:

((Dots 5.1) (Stripes 3.15) (Glass 1.50) (Square 0.72) (Red 0.65)).

As with most real-world problems, this domain is noisy because, in a clean domain, the products determined are zero for all defining attributes.

8.11 Overview of the methodology

To extract disjunctive rules, the data must be broken up into disjoint subsets so that each subset can be dealt with separately. The strategy is that each subset may represent one conjunctive rule that uniquely identifies the decision-making process associated with that subset. The combination of these conjunctive rules then produces a set of disjunctive rules for an output.

A formal description of this process follows. Let a training set of examples, A, consist of m possible outputs. Let A_1, A_2, ..., A_m represent m subsets of the training set A, where each subset covers one output, as illustrated in Figure 8.5. Thus:

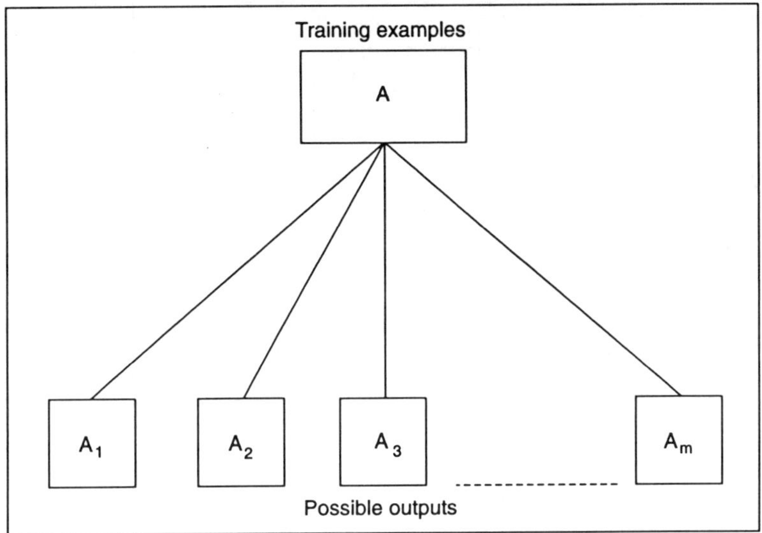

Figure 8.5   The example set A subdivided into m subsets, A_1, A_2, ..., A_m

$$A = A_1 \cup A_2 \cup ... \cup A_m \text{ and}$$
$$A_1 \subseteq A, A_2 \subseteq A, ..., A_m \subseteq A.$$

The subsets A_i can be overlapping, as an example can have more than one output and therefore be covered by more than one subset. For instance, an animal may have Hair, give Milk, and have a Pouch. This animal could be defined as both a MAMMAL and a MARSUPIAL and, as such, would be included in both the MAMMAL and MARSUPIAL subsets.

Initially, consider subset A_1 of A. First, two subsets of the example data covered by A_1 are constructed by considering the presence or absence of a particular attribute X. The resulting subsets, B_{11} and B_{12}, have the following properties:

- subset B_{11} contains the example data of A_1 with attribute X present
- subset B_{12} contains the example data of A_1 with attribute X absent.

Thus:

$$A_1 = B_{11} \cup B_{12}$$
$$B_{11} \subseteq A_1, B_{12} \subseteq A_1$$
$$B_{11} \cap B_{12} = \{\}.$$

Hence, the two subsets B_{11} and B_{12}, shown in Figure 8.6, are mutually exclusive and independent.

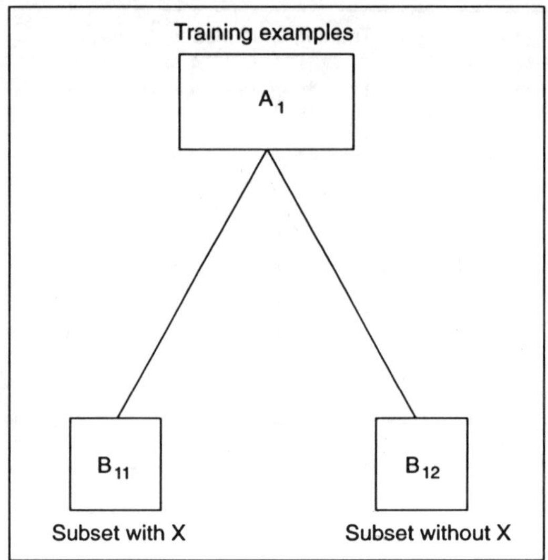

Figure 8.6   The two disjoint subsets, B$_{11}$ and B$_{12}$, formed from A$_1$

The obvious rules for these two subsets are:

For subset B$_{11}$:

Rule 11: $(X) \Rightarrow (A_1)$

For subset B$_{12}$:

Rule 12: $(NOT\ X) \Rightarrow (A_1)$

A problem arises if these rules are applicable to any examples of the other outputs A_2, A_3, ..., A_m. Hence, the pertinent question is whether Rule 11 and Rule 12 uniquely identify output A_1. Thus, two possibilities can occur:

- Each rule uniquely identifies the corresponding subset, and so no further subdivision of the subset is required.
- Each rule does not uniquely identify the corresponding subset, and so further subdivision of the subset is required by expanding the rule.

A rule is unique if it covers examples in the output class and does not cover any examples in any other class. As an illustration, let e_1 and e_2 denote two examples in the training set that have outputs of A_1 and A_2, respectively. Hence, $e_1 \in A_1$ and $e_2 \in A_2$. Let the attribute X be present in both examples e_1 and e_2. Applying Rule 11: $(X) \Rightarrow (A_1)$ to the entire training set A results in the following two cases:

- Rule 11 covers example e_1 because X is present in e_1. Therefore, the output of this example should be A_1. As $e_1 \in A_1$, the rule is specific enough and correct for example e_1.
- Rule 11 also covers example e_2 because X is present in e_2. Therefore, the output of this example should be A_1. But $e_2 \in A_2$, indicating that the rule is not correct or specific enough to classify example e_2.

In the case where the rule is not specific enough to identify only the relevant examples, the subset should be further subdivided into subsets C_{111} and C_{112} on the basis of the presence or absence of attribute Y. Figure 8.7 shows this process of expanding subset B_{11} because it misclassifies some examples of the other outputs.

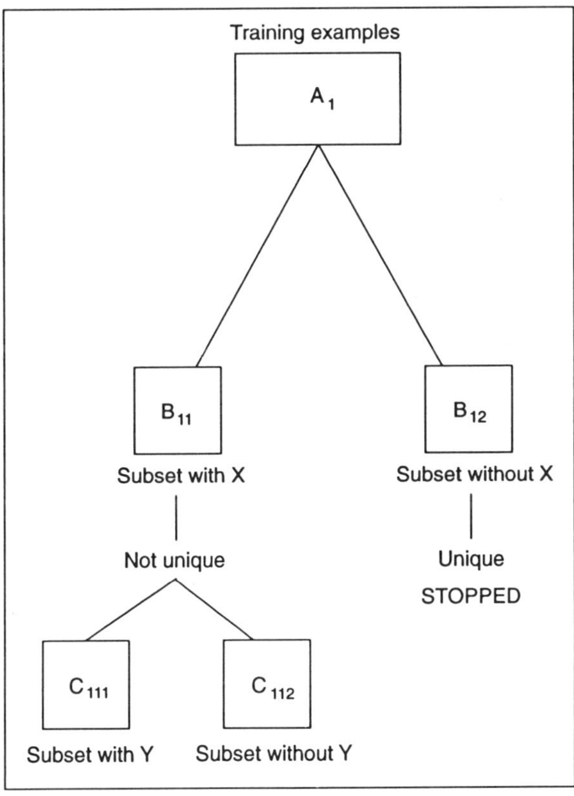

Figure 8.7   Subset B_{11} is further specialized, as the rule describing the subset misclassifies some examples

The subset B_{11} can be regarded as an unfinished subset requiring further division so that a unique rule identifying B_{11} can be determined. The rules now representing subsets C_{111} and C_{112} are:

For subset C_{111}:

Rule 111:　$(X \text{ AND } Y) \Rightarrow (A_1)$

For subset C_{112}:

Rule 112:　$(X \text{ AND NOT } Y) \Rightarrow (A_1)$

If subset B_{12} had required further division, the Xs in the above rules would be replaced by NOT Xs.

The subdivision of a subset can also be stopped by the selection of an attribute that does not discriminate further. This results in non-unique rules. In the previous example, the attribute Y determined the subsets C_{111} and C_{112} with the given associated rules. However, if $X = Y$ then C_{111} and C_{112} give no further useful information. To explain this, the associated rules become:

For subset C_{111}:

Rule 111:　$(X \text{ AND } X) \Rightarrow (A_1)$

For subset C_{112}:

Rule 112:　$(X \text{ AND NOT } X) \Rightarrow (A_1)$

Rule 111 for C_{111} reduces to $(X) \Rightarrow (A_1)$ (the same as Rule 11), whereas Rule 112 for C_{112} is an empty set. This is an illustration of the selection of a non-discriminatory attribute. It indicates that the subset B_{11} cannot be usefully split any further. This means that there may not be enough discriminatory information in the input attributes to distinguish some examples uniquely.

Subdivision is continued until all of the rules uniquely identify the corresponding subsets or only a small portion of examples are misclassified. The whole procedure is repeated for each subset A_2, ..., A_m of the training set A.

8.12　Starting the process to extract disjunctive rules

The methodology provided in the previous section is further explained here. The overall aim is to divide the training set into subsets that can be uniquely described by one conjunctive rule. A part of that process is shown in Figure 8.8.

First, a method of splitting the data into subsets is required. BRAINNE proposes the most used attribute or a group of the most used attributes as the

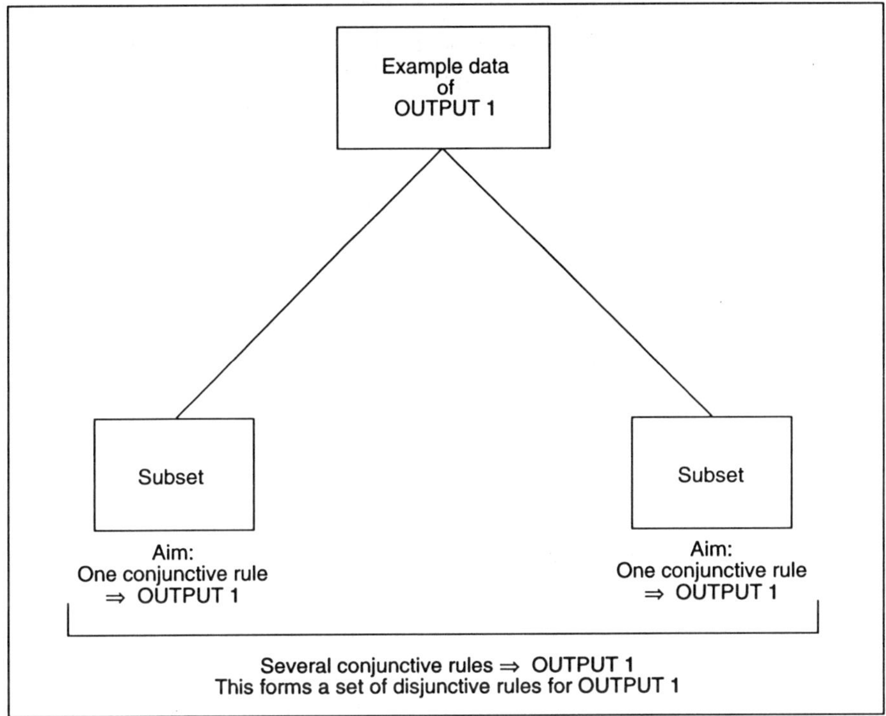

Figure 8.8   Dividing the data into subsets that may each represent one conjunctive rule

initial focal point. These attributes are determined from the product values. Consider the following set of examples:

(Red, Square, Wood) ⇒ (OUTPUT 1)
(Red, Square, Glass, Stripes) ⇒ (OUTPUT 1)
(Red, Square, Glass, Dots) ⇒ (OUTPUT 1).

Within the sorted products list for OUTPUT 1, attributes Red and Square have the smallest (and closest) products, and the Glass attribute has the next smallest product value. This results from the products reflecting the number of times that an attribute occurs in the examples. It is important to remember that the frequency of an attribute is dependent upon the amount of noise.

The attribute with the lowest product value is then chosen and two rules are formed. The first rule comprises the selected attribute, while the second comprises the absence of this attribute. For example, if the attribute Red has the smallest product for OUTPUT 1, then the following two rules are produced, as illustrated in Figure 8.9:

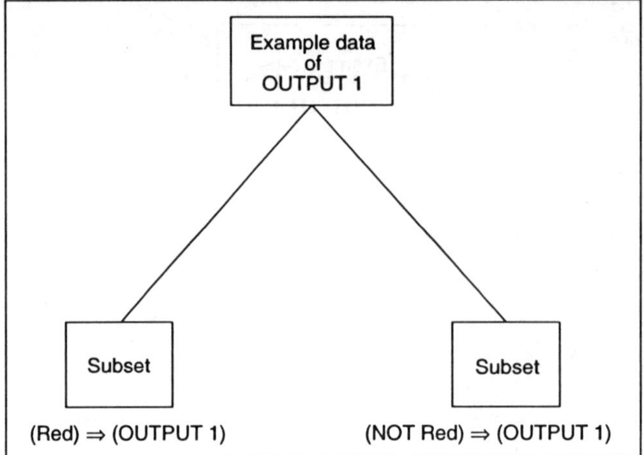

Figure 8.9   The formation of two subsets

> Rule 1: (Red) ⇒ (OUTPUT 1)
> Rule 2: (NOT Red) ⇒ (OUTPUT 1).

The negation (NOT Red) in Rule 2 means that the Red attribute should not be present.

In some cases, there may be a group of attributes (such as Red and Square) with similar low product values. This group can be selected as the initial focal point instead of a single attribute. Here, the first rule formed is the conjunction of the attributes in the group plus the next attribute in the sorted products list. The second rule comprises the group attributes and the negation of that next attribute. So, if Glass is the next attribute in the list after Red and Square, then the following two rules are produced:

> Rule 1: (Red AND Square AND Glass) ⇒ (OUTPUT 1)
> Rule 2: (Red AND Square AND NOT Glass) ⇒ (OUTPUT 1).

If it is unclear whether more than one attribute should be initially selected, it is better to select the single attribute with the smallest product.

Of course, any attributes with a zero product value are uniquely related to the corresponding output and should be part of any defining rule. If Red has a product value of zero and the next attribute, Square, does not, then the following two rules are produced:

> Rule 1: (Red AND Square) ⇒ (OUTPUT 1)
> Rule 2: (Red AND NOT Square) ⇒ (OUTPUT 1).

The initial state of the network is represented in Figure 8.10.

With the construction of these initial (and subsequent) rules, it is assumed

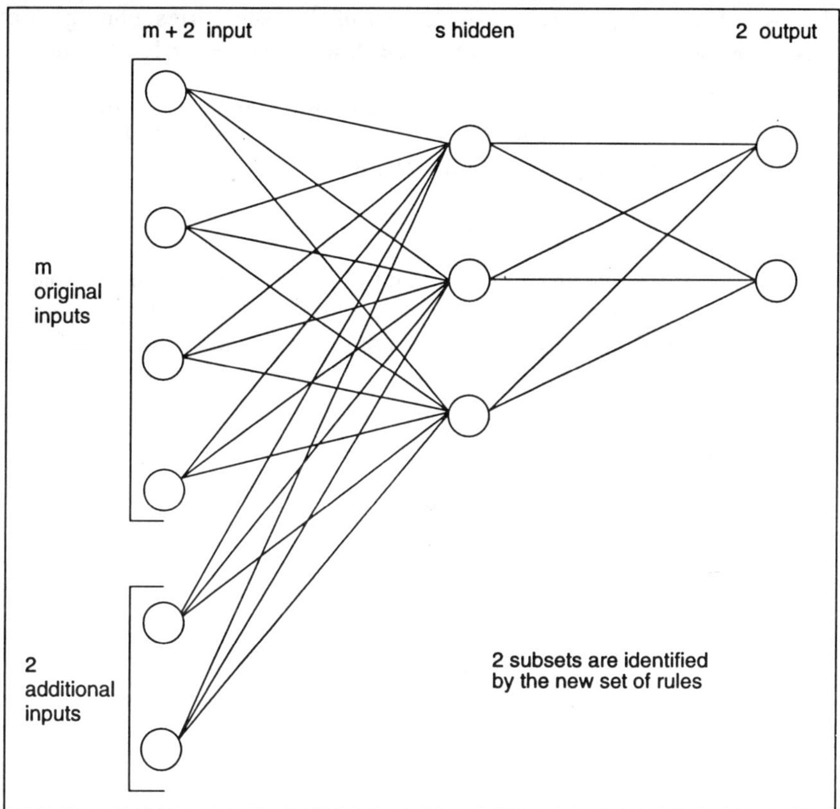

Figure 8.10   The initial state of the net with the outputs as additional inputs

that all the attributes in the domain are distinctly present or absent. While only binary attributes are considered in the explanations for simplicity, BRAINNE can be applied to any number of discrete attributes. Also, the extension of BRAINNE to deal with continuously valued attributes is discussed in the next chapter.

8.13 The steps in the full process

As stated, the initial aim is to construct one conjunctive rule for each subset, uniquely classifying that subset. The major steps in this procedure are as follows:

1. Let example data set A consist of m possible outputs.

2. Let A_1, A_2, ..., A_m represent m subsets of A, each corresponding to one output. Repeat the following for each set $S = A_i$, where $i = 1, 2, ..., m$:

   2.1. Select an attribute from the appropriate products list on which to subdivide the set S into two subsets B_{i1} and B_{i2}, such that $B_{i1} \cap B_{i2} = \{\}$. For each of the sets B_{ij} where $j = 1, 2$:

- Form one conjunctive rule describing B_{ij} by collating the list of attributes selected so far.
- Does the rule uniquely describe B_{ij}? If *Yes*, stop the further expansion of this rule and process the next subset at Step 2.1 or go to Step 2.
- If *No*, does the rule select a non-discriminatory attribute for B_{ij}? If *Yes*, stop the further expansion of this rule and process the next subset at Step 2.1 or go to Step 2.
- If *No*, further specialize this subset B_{ij} by letting $S = B_{ij}$ and repeating Step 2.1.

When this process terminates, each rule has been stopped from further expansion.

We next discuss the relationship of the conjunctive rules to the final set of disjunctive rules. Let the set of conjunctive rules determined for each subset be:

$$(\text{Antecedent } 1) \Rightarrow (\text{OUTPUT } 1)$$
$$(\text{Antecedent } 2) \Rightarrow (\text{OUTPUT } 1)$$

$$..................$$

$$(\text{Antecedent } n) \Rightarrow (\text{OUTPUT } 1)$$

This set of rules is equivalent to linking the rules with the OR connective:

$$((\text{Antecedent } 1) \Rightarrow (\text{OUTPUT } 1)) \text{ OR}$$
$$((\text{Antecedent } 2) \Rightarrow (\text{OUTPUT } 1)) \text{ OR}$$

$$..................$$

$$((\text{Antecedent } n) \Rightarrow (\text{OUTPUT } 1))$$

which reduces to:

$$((\text{Antecedent } 1) \text{ OR } (\text{Antecedent } 2) \text{ OR } ... \text{ OR } (\text{Antecedent } n))$$
$$\Rightarrow (\text{OUTPUT } 1).$$

8.14 Extracting disjunctive rules in detail

A guided generate-and-test methodology is used to construct possible rules from the product list and determine their validity. If a rule is retained (i.e., it covers a portion of the examples) then different stopping criteria are used to determine whether the associated subset should be further split by specializing the rule. The stopping criteria include the selection of a non-discriminatory or contradictory attribute and the uniqueness of a rule, where a unique rule covers no examples of another output. These stopping criteria may generate rules that cover only one or two examples. Such rules may reflect either noise or exceptions in the data. If necessary, the generation of these rules can be eliminated by removing a subset and its corresponding rule, if the rule covers only a small portion of the examples.

8.14.1 Determining the number of examples covered by each rule

A rule covers an example when the attributes in the antecedent of the rule all occur in the example. The first step in extracting rules that uniquely identify a subset is to determine the number of examples covered by the current set of rules. This is accomplished by determining whether the attributes defining a particular rule are present or absent, as appropriate, in an example. To illustrate this, let Rule 1 be defined by the attribute Red and Rule 2 be defined by NOT Red. Let example 1 be defined by Triangle and Red.

- Rule 1 covers example 1 as the example contains all the attributes defining Rule 1.
- However, Rule 2 does not cover example 1 as the example contains none of the attributes defining Rule 2.

A rule covers or accounts for an example if, and only if, the example contains *all* of the attributes defining that rule.

The number of the total examples covered by the rule can be determined. If a rule covers no examples, it is removed from the list. Otherwise it is retained.

8.14.2 Using all rules as additional inputs

The second step in the guided generate-and-test procedure is to use all the rules that so far identify the subsets as the outputs of the system. Therefore, these rules can also be used as additional inputs. Figure 8.11 illustrates the current state of the net.

From this neural network configuration, a new list of the product measurements described earlier is determined. The defining attributes of a rule have a zero product in the resulting list for that particular rule or output. For instance, for a rule:

$$(\text{Red AND Triangle}) \Rightarrow (\text{OUTPUT 1})$$

the corresponding list of product measurements could be:

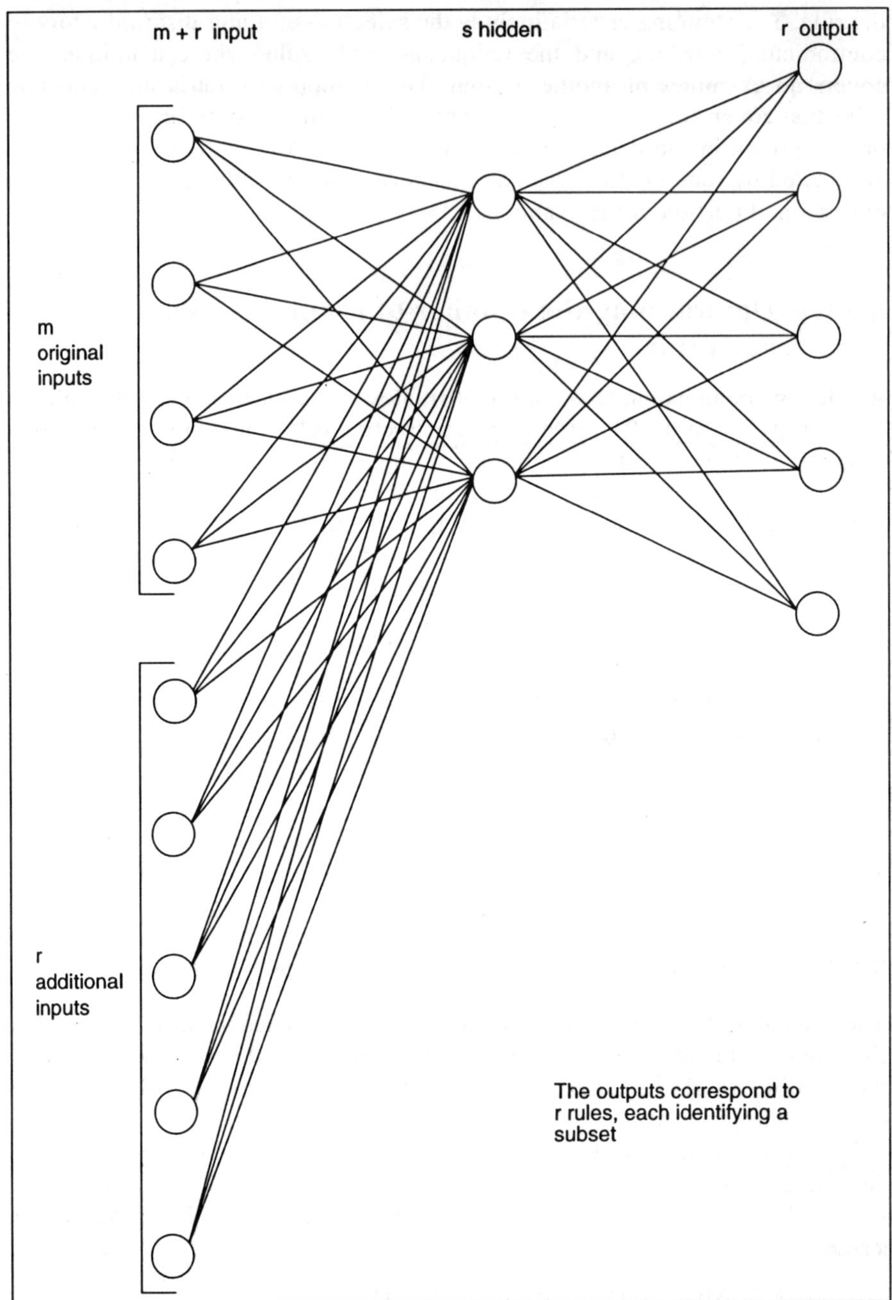

Figure 8.11 The current state of the net with the outputs as additional inputs

Attribute	Product
Square	4.5
Blue	2.3
Triangle	0
Red	0

Note that the defining attributes, Red and Triangle, have a product measurement of zero.

8.14.3 The uniqueness stopping criterion

At this stage, the aim of obtaining one conjunctive rule for each subset has been met. However, a rule may cover examples of another output. Two cases must be thus considered for each rule:

- no misclassification occurs — the rule can be stopped from any further expansion, or
- misclassification occurs — the rule needs to be further expanded by specialization.

To highlight these possibilities, let Rule 1 be:

$$(\text{Red AND NOT Square}) \Rightarrow (M)$$

and let examples 1 and 2 be:

$$(\text{Red, Triangle, Brick}) \Rightarrow (M)$$
$$(\text{Red, Triangle, Glass}) \Rightarrow (N).$$

Example 1 is covered by Rule 1, and the rule and the example both have the same output M. This implies that the rule does not need further specialization. However, example 2 is also covered by Rule 1, but the rule and the example have different outputs of M and N respectively. This implies that the rule does require further specialization. As Rule 1 would misclassify example 2, it must be specialized so that this does not occur. When the example domain has several outputs, this is an extremely important consideration.

8.14.4 The non-discriminatory or contradictory attribute stopping criterion

A rule is specialized by selecting an attribute on which to split the data further. The next available attribute with the smallest, non-zero product measurement in the list of product measurements for that rule is chosen. However, a contradiction can occur at this point. For instance, if Rule 1 is defined by Red and NOT Square and the next available attribute (i.e., the attribute with the smallest, non-zero product) to specialize Rule 1 is Triangle, then no contradiction occurs. On the other hand, if Square is the next available attribute then a contradiction does occur. The expanded rule would have Square and NOT Square joined by AND as part of its antecedent. In this latter case, Rule 1 cannot be further expanded because of the selection of this contradictory (non-discriminatory) attribute. Note that the stopped rule could still misclassify a portion of the examples. This indicates that the attributes do not have enough discriminatory information to specialize the rule further.

8.14.5 Forming new rules

Two new rules are formed from each rule if the rule has not been stopped from participating in further expansion. The first rule consists of the attributes defining the original rule plus the next available attribute determined from the product list. The second rule contains the initial defining attributes and the negation of that next available attribute. For example, if Rule 1 is defined by Red and NOT Square and the next attribute selected from the product list is Triangle, then the antecedents of the two new rules formed are defined by:

> (Red, NOT Square, Triangle)
> (Red, NOT Square, NOT Triangle).

8.14.6 Testing new rules

The number of examples in the total training set covered by the same combination of attributes defining each of the new rules is determined. If any of these totals equals zero then the corresponding rule is discarded. This indicates that the rule is not relevant to any of the examples in the training set.

8.14.7 Terminating the process

This process is repeated from the second step (using rules as additional inputs) until only final rules (rules stopped from further expansion) are left and/or only a small number (preferably zero) of examples is misclassified. The steps require that:

- all remaining rules are used as outputs (and hence as additional inputs) and the new products (from newly determined SSE measurements and inhibitory links) are determined;
- these products are checked and two new rules are formed for each rule that has not been stopped from further expansion;
- the number of examples that each rule covers is checked;
- the process is repeated until only final rules remain and/or misclassifications are small.

It is imperative that a generated rule does not misclassify a large portion of the examples. If it does, the rule must be made more specific by selecting more attributes for the antecedent. Once the rule produced does not cover any (or only a small portion) of the examples of another output, the generate-and-test process for that rule is stopped.

The final set of rules can now be pruned. If the total number of examples covered by a rule is less than some threshold ω then the rule could be discarded. However, such a rule may be retained to reflect any exceptions and/or noise in the data.

8.15 A simplified illustrative example trace

To provide a full understanding of this process, an example trace is now given in Figure 8.12. The task is to determine the disjunctive rule for output X.

Let a simple training set consist of the following examples:

> Example 1: (a, b, c) $\Rightarrow$ (X)
> Example 2: (a, e, f) $\Rightarrow$ (X)
> Example 3: (g) $\Rightarrow$ (X)
> Example 4: (a, d, e) $\Rightarrow$ (Y).

Assume that attribute a has the smallest initial product for output X. The following temporary rules are therefore constructed:

> Rule 1: (a) $\Rightarrow$ (X_1)
> Rule 2: (NOT a) $\Rightarrow$ (X_2)

where $X_1 \Rightarrow X$ and $X_2 \Rightarrow X$.

These two conjunctive rules, both implying output X, form two branches of a tree containing the defining attributes.

Next, the number of examples covered by the same combination of attributes is extracted. There are three examples covered by Rule 1 and one example covered by Rule 2. In this simple case both rules are kept but, in a training set of a more realistic size, the second rule may be terminated owing to the small number of covered examples. On checking now for misclassification, Rule 1 correctly classifies examples 1 and 2 with outputs of X, but the covered example 4 has an output of Y. As example 4 is incorrectly classified, Rule 1 requires further expansion. On the other hand, Rule 2, which correctly classifies example 3 as an example of output X, is stopped from further expansion. Hence, it is a final rule.

New products must now be calculated with Rule 1 and Rule 2 as the outputs and additional inputs. When an example is presented to the network,

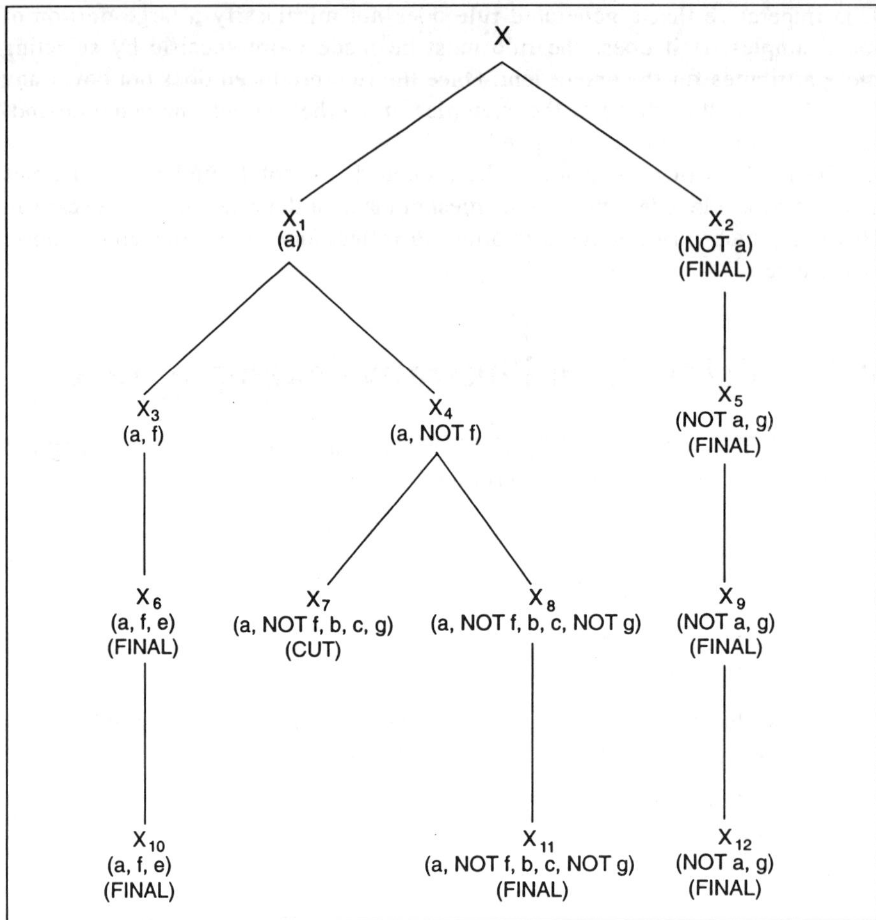

Figure 8.12 A trace of the steps to determine the disjunctive rules defining output X

the value of each rule is set to 0 or 1. A value of 1 indicates that the example satisfies the rule. If the rule does not cover the example its value is 0.

After recalculating the products, the next available attribute can be selected to specialize Rule 1, which covers examples 1, 2, and 4. The next attribute with the smallest, non-zero product is f. The following list of rules results:

$$\text{Rule 11:} \quad (a \text{ AND } f) \Rightarrow (X_3)$$
$$\text{Rule 12:} \quad (a \text{ AND NOT } f) \Rightarrow (X_4)$$
$$\text{Rule 2:} \quad (\text{NOT } a \text{ AND } g) \Rightarrow (X_5) \text{ (FINAL)}$$

where $X_3 \Rightarrow X$, $X_4 \Rightarrow X$, and $X_5 \Rightarrow X$.

For the final Rule 2, the attribute g is automatically selected, as the product value for this attribute is zero at this point. A count of the examples reveals that there is one example of Rule 11, two examples of Rule 12, and one example of Rule 2. Rules 11 and 2 cause no misclassifications and are therefore regarded as final rules. However, Rule 12 still misclassifies example 4, and so it must be further specialized. Once again, the next attribute selected for Rule 12 is g, determined by calculating the products. The following list of rules results:

$$
\begin{array}{lll}
\text{Rule 11:} & \text{(a AND f AND e)} \Rightarrow (X_6) \text{ (FINAL)} \\
\text{Rule 121:} & \text{(a AND NOT f AND b AND c AND g)} \Rightarrow (X_7) \\
\text{Rule 122:} & \text{(a AND NOT f AND b AND c AND NOT g)} \Rightarrow (X_8) \\
\text{Rule 2:} & \text{(NOT a AND g)} \Rightarrow (X_9) \text{ (FINAL)}
\end{array}
$$

where $X_6 \Rightarrow X$, $X_7 \Rightarrow X$, $X_8 \Rightarrow X$, and $X_9 \Rightarrow X$.

For Rule 11 the attribute e is an automatic selection because the product of this attribute is zero at this point. This also occurs with the attributes b and c for Rule 12. Counting reveals that Rule 121 covers no examples with output X, and so it is removed from the list of generated rules.

In summary:

$$
\begin{array}{ll}
\text{Rule 11:} & \text{(a AND f AND e)} \Rightarrow (X_{10}) \text{ (FINAL)} \\
& \text{covers example 2;} \\
\text{Rule 122:} & \text{(a AND NOT f AND b AND c AND NOT g)} \Rightarrow (X_{11}) \\
& \text{(FINAL)} \\
& \text{covers example 1;} \\
\text{Rule 2:} & \text{(NOT a AND g)} \Rightarrow (X_{12}) \text{ (FINAL)} \\
& \text{covers example 3,}
\end{array}
$$

where $X_{10} \Rightarrow X$, $X_{11} \Rightarrow X$, and $X_{12} \Rightarrow X$.

The number of examples covered and the number of misclassifications are determined and, as no rule covers zero examples and no misclassification occurs, all these rules are established as final rules for the output X. Hence, the disjunctive rule for output X is:

(a AND f AND e) OR (a AND NOT f AND b AND c AND NOT g)
OR (NOT a AND g) $\Rightarrow$ (X).

This illustration is very simple because the final rules are a direct reflection of the original examples. Three rules were produced, each one describing one positive example of the output. In real applications, each rule will cover a group of examples with the same characteristics. However, rules covering exceptions (i.e., only a few examples) can also be determined.

8.16 Summary of BRAINNE for disjunctive rules

In the second part of this chapter, BRAINNE was extended to extract multiple rules defining an output. Initial product measurements are produced for each output, as described earlier. If there is no clear cut-off point or the rule constructed from the cut-off is not unique, then two initial rules are generated for that output. If an initial rule covers no examples, it is discarded.

Follow these steps for each output:

- Use all the rules as additional inputs and thus produce a new list of product measurements. Sort the list from maximum to minimum.
- Select the next attribute to be the attribute with the smallest non-zero product value.
- If a contradiction occurs or the attribute is non-discriminating, do not expand the current rule any further.
- Form two new rules for each existing rule (if expansion of the rule has not been terminated).
- If the rule does not misclassify any examples, do not expand the new rule any further.
- Count the number of examples covered by each rule. If these totals are equal to zero, eliminate the rule.
- If any remaining rule requires expansion, return to the first step. Otherwise, as only a small (preferably zero) number of misclassifications still exists, the guided generate-and-test procedure is finished.

This technique can be used to form a hierarchy of the data and thus detect classes, subclasses, and specific instances. As a neural network effectively filters out noise in the data, it is an invaluable representation for modeling real-world domains. Understandable rules are determined using the weighted links of trained neural networks. The rules produced contain attributes that are either present or negated. These rules can then be used in other knowledge-based systems, such as expert systems.

8.17 Illustrative applications for disjunctive rules

8.17.1 Modified animal world domain example

To test this procedure, the animal domain used previously was modified so that all the MAMMALS were grouped into one class (one output), and all the

BIRDS were grouped into another. Thus, the entire animal data is equivalent to the total training set A, while the subsets of BIRDS and MAMMALS are equivalent to A_1 and A_2 respectively.

First, the product measurements were calculated for the BIRD subset. These can be found in Table 8.5. As the input attributes of Feathers and Egglaying have zero product measurements, they must be included in any rule or rules defining a BIRD. Therefore, before proceeding, it is important to test whether a rule containing only these 2 attributes uniquely identifies the BIRD examples. For this simple problem data:

Rule 1: (Feathers AND Egglaying) $\Rightarrow$ (BIRD)

correctly and uniquely classifies all the BIRD examples. It must be remembered that this data is noise-free and, therefore, is not indicative of real-world problem domains.

However, if this uniqueness stopping criterion is relaxed, and the only possible termination of a rule is by the selection of a contradictory attribute, a

---

Total number of examples 48
Number of inputs 30
Number of hidden units 12
Total concepts 1
Total Sum of errors Squared 0.000001
(TSS from Back-propagation)

Products for output BIRD

0.000460	$\Rightarrow$ Black-stripe	0.000458	$\Rightarrow$ Slit-eyes
0.000455	$\Rightarrow$ Trunk	0.000452	$\Rightarrow$ Tail
0.000444	$\Rightarrow$ Herbivore	0.000442	$\Rightarrow$ Even-toed
0.000439	$\Rightarrow$ Odd-toed	0.000437	$\Rightarrow$ Hoofs
0.000431	$\Rightarrow$ Five-digit	0.000421	$\Rightarrow$ Medium
0.000419	$\Rightarrow$ Large	0.000404	$\Rightarrow$ Placenta
0.000401	$\Rightarrow$ Pouches	0.000394	$\Rightarrow$ Milk
0.000391	$\Rightarrow$ Hair	0.000359	$\Rightarrow$ Field-mead
0.000355	$\Rightarrow$ Web-feet	0.000316	$\Rightarrow$ Tree
0.000314	$\Rightarrow$ Bird-o-prey	0.000285	$\Rightarrow$ Sturdy-feet
0.000272	$\Rightarrow$ Lake-river	0.000222	$\Rightarrow$ Oceanic
0.000190	$\Rightarrow$ Land	0.000122	$\Rightarrow$ Claws
0.000117	$\Rightarrow$ Fly-long-d	0.000030	$\Rightarrow$ Fly-short-d
0.000002	$\Rightarrow$ Fly	0.000000	$\Rightarrow$ Egglaying
0.000000	$\Rightarrow$ Feathers		

Table 8.5 Initial products for the grouped output representing a BIRD in the animal data

different situation occurs. From Table 8.5, the following 2 rules are constructed
and used to start the guided generate-and-test procedure:

> Rule 11: (Feathers AND Egglaying AND Fly) $\Rightarrow$ (BIRD)
> Rule 12: (Feathers AND Egglaying AND NOT Fly) $\Rightarrow$ (BIRD).

From this starting point, the rules determined to be final using the guided
generate-and-test procedure are equivalent to the rules defining the various
original BIRD outputs. In other words, the resulting rules represent each individual
type of BIRD in the animal domain.

This is illustrated in Figure 8.13, which is a trace of the partitioning of the
BIRD examples. The starting rule for this portion of the trace of the guided
generate-and-test procedure is Rule 12, as defined above. Rule 12 partitions
the examples by defining a subset satisfying:

> (Feathers AND Egglaying AND NOT Fly) $\Rightarrow$ (BIRD).

From the products determined for this subtree, the attribute Sturdy-feet is
selected as the next attribute on which to branch. The Land attribute with a
product measurement equal to zero is automatically selected. Thus the following
two rules result:

> (Feathers AND Egglaying AND NOT Fly AND Land AND
>   Sturdy-feet) $\Rightarrow$ (BIRD)
> (Feathers AND Egglaying AND NOT Fly AND Land AND
>   NOT Sturdy-feet) $\Rightarrow$ (BIRD).

Once again, considering only the rightmost subset defined by:

> (Feathers AND Egglaying AND NOT Fly AND Land AND
>   NOT Sturdy-feet) $\Rightarrow$ (BIRD)

the next attribute on which to branch is the Fly-short-d input attribute. The
attribute Web-feet is automatically extracted for the rightmost subset as its
product measurement is zero. Thus the subsets defined by the following two
rules are determined:

> (Feathers AND Egglaying AND NOT Fly AND Land AND NOT
>   Sturdy-feet AND Fly-short-d) $\Rightarrow$ (BIRD)
> (Feathers AND Egglaying AND NOT Fly AND Land AND NOT
>   Sturdy-feet AND NOT Fly-short-d AND Web-feet) $\Rightarrow$ (BIRD).

The first rule:

> (Feathers AND Egglaying AND NOT Fly AND Land AND NOT
>   Sturdy-feet AND Fly-short-d) $\Rightarrow$ (BIRD)

is deleted since it covers no examples. This is indicated by CUT in Figure

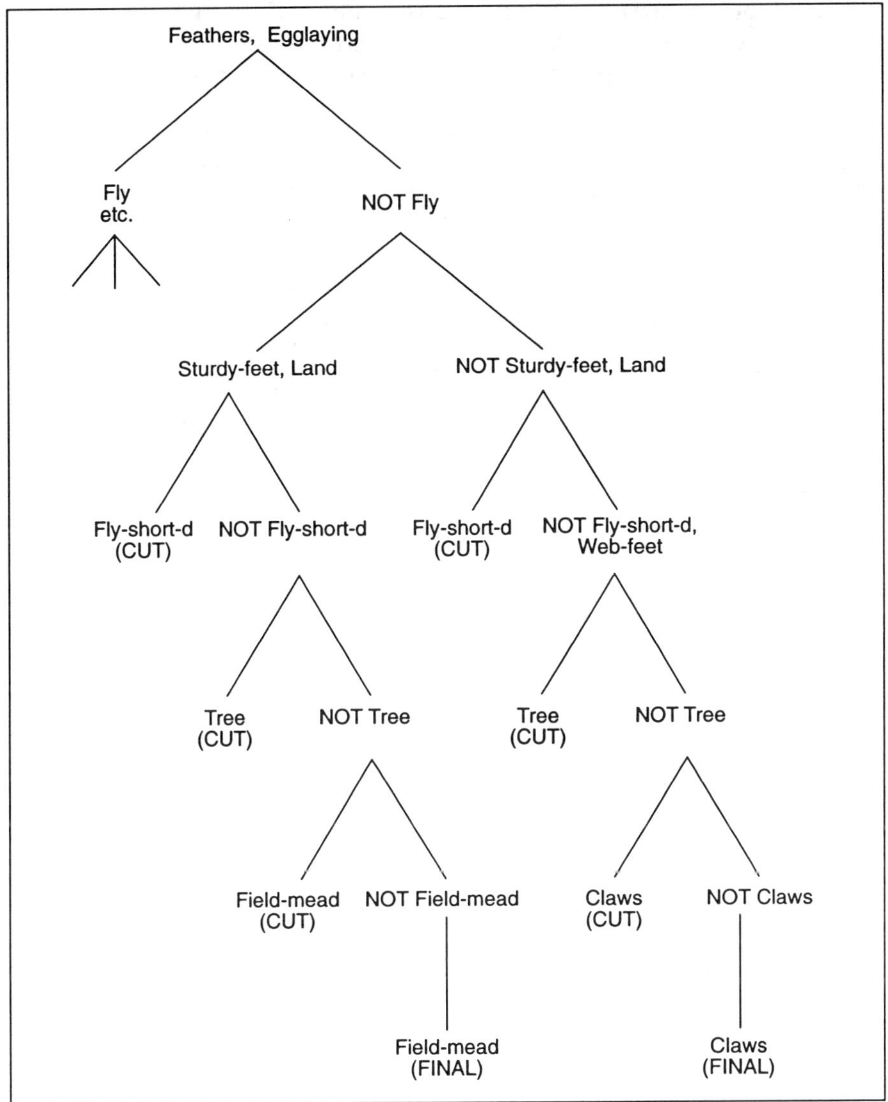

Figure 8.13 A partial trace of the partitioning of the BIRD examples into the various subsets

8.13. The next attribute selected for the remaining subset is Tree. The first rule constructed with this attribute is deleted because it covers no examples. Similarly, the first rule constructed with the next chosen attribute of Claws is deleted. At this stage, the following rule represents the rightmost subset:

(Feathers AND Egglaying AND NOT Fly AND Land AND
NOT Sturdy-feet AND NOT Fly-short-d AND
Web-feet AND NOT Tree AND NOT Claw) $\Rightarrow$ (BIRD).

Now, the next attribute selected for the subset is Claws. However, this attribute cannot be used for this subset as NOT Claws is already part of the rule. It represents the selection of a contradictory attribute that causes the termination of the rule. This is indicated by FINAL in Figure 8.13. The final rule is equivalent to the WEBBED-B (birds with webbed feet) output of the original unmodified data set. The other individual BIRD rules and the rules pertaining to the other subset of MAMMAL examples are similarly constructed.

8.17.2 Modified LED digit domain example

The LED example data used previously was also modified to produce the following groupings:

Actual digit output	New output
0	0
1	1
4	2
7	3
2, 3, 5, 6, 8, 9	4

Thus, the original digit outputs of 0, 1, 4, and 7 remain distinct, while the outputs of 2, 3, 5, 6, 8, and 9 are grouped into one output. The resulting lists of product measurements are given in Table 8.6.

As before, there is a distinct break in the product lists for the single digit outputs and thus one conjunctive rule is formed for each of these outputs. However, these rules are not unique since they cover some examples of the other outputs. As an illustration, consider the attributes extracted from Table 8.6 to define the outputs 1 and 3:

(Up-right AND Down-right) $\Rightarrow$ (OUTPUT 1)   {the digit 1}
(Up-right AND Down-right AND Up-center)
    $\Rightarrow$ (OUTPUT 3)   {the digit 7}

As we see from these rules, the attributes defining OUTPUT 1 are a subset of the attributes defining OUTPUT 3. Therefore, additional information is necessary to make these rules unique. Using the guided generate-and-test method, the unique rules listed in Table 8.7 result for these outputs. Note that rules covering less than a threshold $\omega = 10\%$ of the examples are deleted as the data is known to be noisy.

Total number of examples 500
Number of inputs 7
Number of hidden units 12
Total concepts 5
Total Sum of errors Squared 3.943003
(TSS from Back-propagation)

OUTPUT 0 covers 51 examples
OUTPUT 1 covers 60 examples
OUTPUT 2 covers 35 examples
OUTPUT 3 covers 49 examples
OUTPUT 4 covers 305 examples

Products for OUTPUT 0   {the digit 0}
37.091 $\Rightarrow$ Mid-center   6.439 $\Rightarrow$ Down-left   5.363 $\Rightarrow$ Up-left
3.973 $\Rightarrow$ Up-center   3.570 $\Rightarrow$ Down-right   3.260 $\Rightarrow$ Down-center
2.723 $\Rightarrow$ Up-right

Products for OUTPUT 1   {the digit 1}
109.121 $\Rightarrow$ Down-left   104.903 $\Rightarrow$ Up-center   104.261 $\Rightarrow$ Mid-center
103.844 $\Rightarrow$ Down-center   95.034 $\Rightarrow$ Up-left   11.906 $\Rightarrow$ Up-right
8.590 $\Rightarrow$ Down-right

Products for OUTPUT 2   {the digit 4}
25.077 $\Rightarrow$ Down-left   24.816 $\Rightarrow$ Up-center   23.503 $\Rightarrow$ Down-center
5.124 $\Rightarrow$ Down-right   1.654 $\Rightarrow$ Up-right   1.033 $\Rightarrow$ Up-left
0.462 $\Rightarrow$ Mid-center

Products for OUTPUT 3   {the digit 7}
39.512 $\Rightarrow$ Mid-center   38.447 $\Rightarrow$ Down-center   36.911 $\Rightarrow$ Up-left
35.497 $\Rightarrow$ Down-left   6.004 $\Rightarrow$ Up-right   1.384 $\Rightarrow$ Down-right
1.323 $\Rightarrow$ Up-center

Products for OUTPUT 4   {the digits 2, 3, 5, 6, 8, 9}
342.248 $\Rightarrow$ Down-left   289.018 $\Rightarrow$ Up-right   248.424 $\Rightarrow$ Up-left
152.978 $\Rightarrow$ Down-right   75.644 $\Rightarrow$ Mid-center   65.105 $\Rightarrow$ Up-center
63.036 $\Rightarrow$ Down-center

Table 8.6   Initial products for the modified LED data

Consider the product measurements determined for the grouped output (OUTPUT 4). From Table 8.6, there is no distinct break in the numbers. However, the products of the common features of the digits in the output (i.e., the three center positions Up-center, Mid-center, and Down-center) are close, with the attribute Down-right having the next smallest product value.

(Up-right AND Down-right AND Up-center AND Up-left AND
   Down-left AND Down-center AND NOT Mid-center)
   ⇒ (OUTPUT 0)   {the digit 0}
(Up-right AND Down-right AND NOT Up-center AND NOT Up-left AND
   NOT Mid-center AND NOT Down-left AND NOT Down-center)
   ⇒ (OUTPUT 1)   {the digit 1}
(Up-left AND Up-right AND Mid-center AND Down-right AND
   NOT Up-center AND NOT Down-left AND NOT Down-center)
   ⇒ (OUTPUT 2)   {the digit 4}
(Up-center AND Up-right AND Down-right AND NOT Down-left AND
   NOT Mid-center AND NOT Down-center AND NOT Up-left)
   ⇒ (OUTPUT 3)   {the digit 7}

Table 8.7   Unique rules for the single digit outputs for the LED data

The first step is to determine whether the combination of (Up-center AND
Mid-center AND Down-center) uniquely identifies the grouped output. If the
10% inherent error in the data is considered, this rule succeeds in uniquely
identifying all of the examples of the grouped output. However, as the amount
of erroneous data is not known in advance in a real-world situation, the guided
generate-and-test procedure is used. From Table 8.6, the initial rules consist of:

> Rule 1: (Up-center AND Mid-center AND Down-center AND
>   Down-right) ⇒ (OUTPUT 4)
> Rule 2: (Up-center AND Mid-center AND Down-center AND
>   NOT Down-right) ⇒ (OUTPUT 4).

Note that if this common grouping is not apparent, then two rules are formed
from Down-center as it is the attribute with the lowest product value. The
same results will be produced.

This procedure generates 16 rules. Only five of these rules cover a significant
portion of the examples, but they are not the six expected rules for this combined
output. The expected rules are those generated for the original single digit
outputs 2, 3, 5, 6, 8, and 9. However, the antecedents of the five rules, listed
in Table 8.8, are still correct. Rules 1, 2, 4, and 5 cover the examples of the
digits 8, 9, 3, and 2 respectively. However, Rule 3 covers the examples of
both digits 5 and 6. Each antecedent of these rules represents one conjunctive
rule implying the grouped output. These antecedents, combined with the OR
connective, form the disjunctive rule implying the grouped output.

The guided generate-and-test method can construct the expected rules by
relaxing the uniqueness stopping criterion. Hence, a rule is not stopped merely
because it is unique, but continued until a contradiction occurs. The resulting
trace, represented by the associated LED display, is given in Figure 8.14.

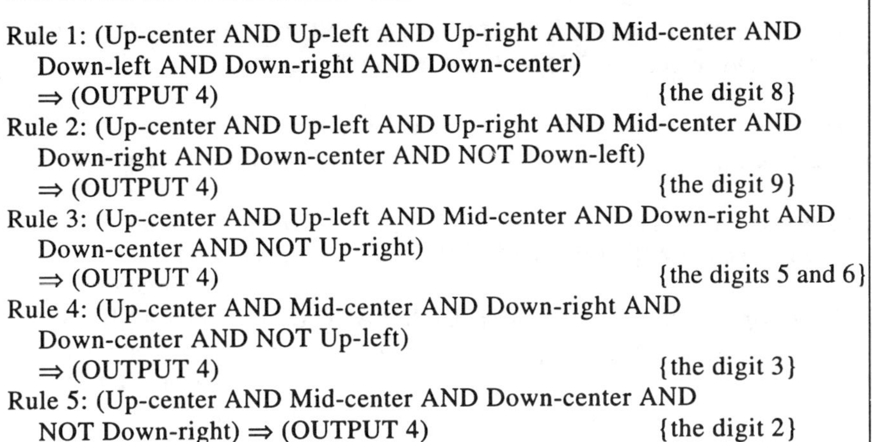

Rule 1: (Up-center AND Up-left AND Up-right AND Mid-center AND
    Down-left AND Down-right AND Down-center)
    ⇒ (OUTPUT 4)   {the digit 8}
Rule 2: (Up-center AND Up-left AND Up-right AND Mid-center AND
    Down-right AND Down-center AND NOT Down-left)
    ⇒ (OUTPUT 4)   {the digit 9}
Rule 3: (Up-center AND Up-left AND Mid-center AND Down-right AND
    Down-center AND NOT Up-right)
    ⇒ (OUTPUT 4)   {the digits 5 and 6}
Rule 4: (Up-center AND Mid-center AND Down-right AND
    Down-center AND NOT Up-left)
    ⇒ (OUTPUT 4)   {the digit 3}
Rule 5: (Up-center AND Mid-center AND Down-center AND
    NOT Down-right) ⇒ (OUTPUT 4)   {the digit 2}

Table 8.8   Rules produced from the guided generate-and-test procedure for the grouped output of the LED data

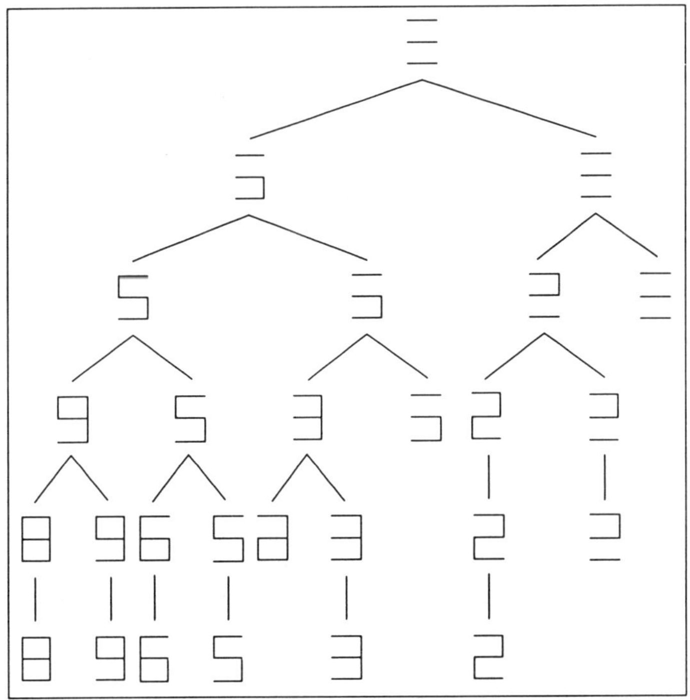

Figure 8.14 Tracing of the steps to determine the retained individual rules for the grouped output in the LED data

(Up-right AND Down-right AND Up-center AND Up-left AND Down-left
    AND Down-center AND Mid-center) ⇒ (Output 4)
{the digit 8}
(Up-right AND Down-right AND Up-center AND Up-left AND
    Down-center AND Mid-center AND NOT Down-left) ⇒ (Output 4)
{the digit 9}
(Down-left AND Down-right AND Up-center AND Up-left AND
    Down-center AND Mid-center AND NOT Up-right) ⇒ (Output 4)
{the digit 6}
(Down-right AND Up-center AND Up-left AND Down-center AND
    Mid-center AND NOT Up-right AND NOT Down-left) ⇒ (Output 4)
{the digit 5}
(Down-right AND Up-center AND Up-right AND Down-center AND Mid-
center AND NOT Up-left AND NOT Down-left) ⇒ (Output 4)
{the digit 3}
(Down-left AND Up-center AND Up-right AND Down-center AND
    Mid-center AND NOT Up-left AND NOT Down-right) ⇒ (Output 4)
{the digit 2}

Table 8.9   The expected rules from the guided generate-and-test procedure
for the grouped output of the LED data

Note that rules covering only a few examples (using a threshold $\omega = 10\%$) are
not shown on this trace. The resulting retained rules, which are more in line
with a human's understanding of how the digit should be defined, are listed in
Table 8.9.

8.17.3 The stopping criteria reconsidered

The two criteria for stopping the expansion of a rule are the selection of a
contradictory attribute and the uniqueness of a rule. A contradictory attribute
is the negation of an attribute already in the antecedent of a rule. A unique
rule is one that does not cover examples of another output. Generally, a rule is
stopped when either of the criteria is met. However, in the previous two
example domains, the stopping criteria needed to be relaxed to obtain the
expected rules. A stopping criterion of the selection of a contradictory attribute
can lead to more informative rules than stopping once a rule is unique. In
other words, in some cases the generation of a rule could continue as much as
possible, even though it may be unique. This extracts the maximum possible
information. Note that in real-world domains where there are no preconceived
expectations, the stopping criteria are usually not relaxed.

8.18 Recapitulation

This chapter has described a learning method known as BRAINNE (Building Representations for AI using Neural NEtworks). BRAINNE uses both a single-layered and a multi-layered neural network to model the inhibitory and excitatory aspects of a problem domain, respectively.

When a new problem domain is encountered, the first step is to use the technique discussed in the first part of this chapter to determine a list of products for each input and output pair. Then for each output, a cut-off point indicating the relevance of the input attributes is determined. If a distinct cut-off point is detected, then a conjunctive rule can be established for that output. The uniqueness of the conjunctive rule must be checked. On the other hand, if there is no distinct cut-off point or the rule constructed is not unique, then the technique described in the second part of this chapter to construct disjunctive rules is followed. If there is doubt about a cut-off point, it is better to assume that there is no cut-off and use the technique described to generate the appropriate rules. This technique extracts multiple rules, if necessary, for each output. The antecedent of a rule contains attributes or their negations. The applicability of BRAINNE to real-world problems is highlighted in Chapter 10.

An important extension to BRAINNE allows the automatic determination of symbolic rules where the input attributes are continuously valued. The next chapter describes Continuously BRAINNE, which allows the efficient and effective handling of continuous-valued input attributes.

References

Breiman, L., Friedman, J.H., Olshen, R.A. & Stone, C.J. 1984, *Classification and Regression Trees*, Wadsworth International Group, Belmont, California

Bruner, J.S., Goodnow, J.J. & Austin, G.A. 1956, *A Study of Thinking*, Wiley, New York

Funahashi, K. 1989, "On the approximate realization of continuous mappings by neural networks", *Neural Networks*, vol. 2, pp. 183–92

Guyton, A.C. 1984, *Physiology of the Human Body*, 6th edition, Saunders College, Philadelphia

Hearst, E. 1972, "Some persistent problems in the analysis of conditioned inhibition", in *Inhibition and Learning*, eds R.A. Boakes & M.S. Halliday, Academic Press, London, pp. 3–59

Hornik, K., Stinchcombe, M. & White, H. 1989, "Multilayer feedforward networks are universal approximators", *Neural Networks*, vol. 2, pp. 359–66

McClelland, J.L. & Rumelhart, D.E. 1988, *Explorations in Parallel Distributed Processing: A Handbook of Models, Programs, and Exercises*, MIT Press, Cambridge, Massachusetts

McClelland, J.L., Rumelhart, D.E. & the PDP Research Group 1986, *Parallel Distributed Processing, Volume 2: Psychological and Biological Models*, MIT Press, Cambridge, Massachusetts

Ohlsson, S. 1987, "Transfer of training in procedural learning: A matter of conjectures and refutations?", in *Computational Models of Learning*, ed. L. Bolc, Springer Verlag, Berlin, pp. 55–88

Pollio, H.R. 1974, *The Psychology of Symbolic Activity*, Addison-Wesley, Reading, Massachusetts

Quinlan, J.R. 1987, "Simplifying decision trees", *International Journal of Man-Machine Studies*, 27, pp. 221–34

Rendell, L.A. 1987, "Conceptual knowledge acquisition in search", in *Computational Models of Learning*, ed. L. Bolc, Springer-Verlag, Berlin, pp. 89–160

Rumelhart, D.E., McClelland, J.L. & the PDP Research Group 1986, *Parallel Distributed Processing, Volume 1: Foundations*, MIT Press, Cambridge, Massachusetts

Sontag, E.D. 1990, *Feedback Stabilization using Two Hidden Layer Nets*, Report SYCON-90-11, Rutgers Center for Systems and Control

Winston, P.H. 1984, *Artificial Intelligence*, Addison-Wesley, Reading, Massachusetts

Wolff, J.G. 1987, "Cognitive development as optimisation", in *Computational Models of Learning*, ed. L. Bolc, Springer-Verlag, Berlin, pp. 161–206

9

Continuously BRAINNE — automated knowledge acquisition using continuous data

9.1 Introduction

In the previous chapter we presented the BRAINNE method, which extracts knowledge in the form of IF-THEN rules. Both a multi-layered and a single-layered neural network are used in the process. BRAINNE derives conjunctive and disjunctive rules, and it is capable of determining concept hierarchies.

The BRAINNE method so far described is only applicable to discrete-valued input attributes. However, a number of real-world problem domains involve continuous-valued attributes. This chapter therefore presents an extension to BRAINNE that is able to handle continuous-valued inputs.

As stated in Chapter 1, it is possible to distinguish several different types of input data, including (DARPA 1988):

- binary-valued (only 2 possible values)
- discrete-valued (a larger number of fixed values)
- analog or continuous-valued (a continuous range of values).

As binary-valued data can be regarded as discrete-valued data with only two values, binary and discrete values are both cases of the discrete.

An integral part of BRAINNE is the ability to determine whether an example is covered by a particular rule or a particular concept. This enables BRAINNE to determine the number of examples each rule covers. If not enough examples are covered by a rule, then that rule can be removed or deleted from the list of the possible rules. When dealing with discrete data, this coverage check is straightforward because of the distinct presence or absence of a particular attribute. However, this approach cannot be used with continuous data, where the input attributes of an example are defined by numerical values and not by the presence or absence of the attributes. This chapter offers a solution to this problem. First, the manner in which BRAINNE deals with discrete data is outlined, followed by the reasons why this solution is not viable when dealing with continuous data. An approach for dealing with continuous data is then presented.

9.2 Dealing with discrete data

The rules determined in BRAINNE are defined as a list of attributes. In the discrete case, where each input attribute is defined by the presence or absence of a particular value, it is easy to determine whether an example is covered by a rule or a concept. The following simple assertions are made:

- If all of the attributes defining a rule are present in an example, then this example is covered by the rule.
- If all of the attributes defining a rule are not present in an example, then this example is not covered by the rule.

As an illustration, let Rule X be defined by the attributes Red and Round, and let examples 1 and 2 be defined by (Red, Round, Big) and (Red, Square, Big), respectively.

- Example 1 is covered by Rule X, as both Red and Round are present in the example.
- Example 2 is not covered by Rule X. Even though Red is present in the example, Round is not.

The more specific rules are checked before the more general rules. For instance, if Rule Y consists only of attribute Red, then at the end of the counting procedure, example 1 is considered as an example of Rule X, and not of Rule Y. This occurs because Rule X is more specific than Rule Y and therefore it is checked first. Example 2 is an example of Rule Y.

In Chapter 8, a combination of the input attributes was defined to be a particular rule or concept. These new concepts were used as new outputs of the network and thus as additional inputs in the augmented net. The product measurements produced by BRAINNE equal zero for those attributes defining the output. So, using Rule X determined above, the product measurements of the input attributes Red and Round will be zero, while all the other product measurements will be non-zero. If the product measurements for any other input attributes are zero, then those attributes should also be used to define the rule.

BRAINNE needs to know the number of examples covered by a generated rule. This determines whether the extracted rule is viable or not. For data consisting only of discrete attributes, the presence or absence of an attribute determines whether the example is covered, or accounted for, by the rule.

9.3 Existing solutions using continuous data

A variable X is said to be continuous if its set of possible values is an entire interval of numbers; that is, for some $A < B$, any number between A and B is a valid value. Thus there is an infinite number of possible values for a continuous input attribute.

A common way of dealing with continuous data is to convert it into discrete data. Two approaches are used to accomplish this. The first approach picks some threshold value and then determines whether a particular value is above or below this threshold. Hence, the data is broken up into two discrete classes. If a variable X is bounded by A and B (where $A < B$), this approach selects a threshold T, such that:

$$A < T \text{ and } T < B.$$

Here (A, B) is considered to be an open interval. The two resulting intervals (A, T] (A excluded, T included) and (T, B) (T and B excluded) represent two bins or regions for the continuous attribute X. The underlying problem with this approach is that the actual value of the data within the interval is not truly reflected. For instance, suppose that a threshold value of 75° is chosen for a Temperature attribute. Then, an example with a Temperature value of 65° is put into the first bin, defined as all temperatures below 75°. However, another example with a Temperature value of $-10°$ also belongs in the same bin, even though it is dramatically smaller than the example of 65°. An additional problem, of course, is how to determine the threshold value for the attribute.

The second approach solves these two problems by grouping the data into several classes. Once again, if a variable is bounded by A and B (where $A < B$), then several values, $T_1, T_2, ..., T_n$, are selected such that:

$$A < T_1, T_1 < T_2, ..., T_n < B.$$

Here, n+1 intervals or bins are determined, each representing a different class.

The resulting intervals are usually, but not necessarily, the same size. For example, the Temperature attribute could be grouped into several bins defined by various temperature ranges, such as 0°–9° for class 1, 10°–19° for class 2, and so on. Picking these groupings may be difficult in certain areas. However, a more fundamental problem is that this solution greatly increases the number of inputs to consider. For example, if the input attributes of Temperature, Humidity, and Wind-velocity each have 10 defined ranges, then a total of 30 input attributes have to be considered instead of the original 3. This could have serious repercussions in large problem domains.

Both of these approaches break up the data into 2 or more bins. Thus the membership of a particular bin relies upon the precision and accuracy of the numerical value. However, the precision and accuracy of values are affected by noise, which is common in real-world domains. Another problem is that arbitrary ranges not arising from the data are imposed upon the continuous attributes. For instance, a range of 10°–20° may be selected for a Temperature attribute, when a more important or relevant distribution is the 15°–25° range. There is a need to automate the process of selecting the ranges of the continuous attributes. It is advantageous if these ranges can be determined directly from the raw data.

9.4 How neural networks handle the various types of data

A useful feature of neural networks is their ability to deal with both discrete and continuous data. If the data is discrete or has been broken up into two or more bins by one of the approaches mentioned above, then the input attributes of the network are used as binary units. This means that if an example has a particular value for an attribute, then the value of the corresponding input attribute is set to 1. For instance, if an example is defined by Red and Round and the input attributes of the network are Red, Blue, Square, and Round, then the values of the input attributes are set to 1 for Red and Round, and 0 for Blue and Square. In the case of a continuous attribute value falling within a particular bin, the input attribute associated with that bin is set to 1.

Continuous data can be handled directly by a neural network with the actual value of the attribute used as the value of the input. If an example has a Temperature value of 65°, then the value of the Temperature input attribute is set to 65, or some corresponding normalized value. Normalized attribute values have been mapped into the range 0–1. This is a distinct advantage over the previous approaches because no pre-processing is required to break up the continuous data. Also, more importantly, the values themselves are used to determine the solution.

The neural networks used in BRAINNE deal with the continuous data directly; that is, they assign the actual (but normalized) numeric value to be the input. To determine if a rule is valid or not, it is necessary for BRAINNE to know whether an example is covered by the rule. In the continuous case, different representation schemes are used to depict the information; that is, a rule is defined by a list of attributes, while an example is defined by a group of numbers. In the next section we present the approach developed to address the use of continuous data.

9.5 BRAINNE and continuous data

9.5.1 Purpose

The aim of this section is to develop a technique to determine whether a continuous example is covered by a rule or not. Each rule produced in BRAINNE covers a subset of the training set. Consider a continuous example X and let Rule R cover a subset S of the training set. The following question must be answered:

- Is the example X in subset S,

    that is, $X \in S$?

- In other words, does the Rule R cover example X?

Two different representations are being used to denote an example and a rule. An example is represented by a list of real numbers, while a rule is represented by a list of attributes that are present or negated. A comparable representation is required to determine whether a continuous example is covered by a rule. To achieve this, a rule must be constructed that restricts the possible values of the continuous attributes. This requires the restriction of the range of the continuous variables. These restricted variables can then be placed into a clause of the antecedent of a rule. From this representation, the question of whether the rule covers an example can be answered. For instance:

- Let Rule 1 be defined by (attrA) $\Rightarrow$ (Output 1).
- Let input attribute attrA be bounded by MinA and MaxA, where MinA < MaxA.
- Hence, the following construction:

    $$(MinA \leq attrA \leq MaxA)$$

    is used as a clause in the antecedent.
- Rule 1 becomes:

    $$(MinA \leq attrA \leq MaxA) \Rightarrow (Output\ 1).$$

- Now, let a1 be a particular value of input attribute, attrA.
- If (MinA $\leq$ a1 $\leq$ MaxA) is true, then the clause is true and Rule 1 is applicable.
- However, if (MinA $\leq$ a1 $\leq$ MaxA) is false, then the clause is false and Rule 1 is not applicable.

The manner in which the restriction is generated must not be arbitrary, but must arise from the method itself.

The rest of this section describes in detail a technique to construct the clauses restricting the range of continuous attributes. The continuous attributes contributing to a particular rule are then reflected in clauses of the form:

$$(MinA \leq attrA \leq MaxA)$$

where attrA is the continuous contributory variable, and MinA and MaxA are the values that delimit that variable, attrA. The method of clause construction has 3 steps:

- Determine the closeness of an example to a rule.
- Dynamically choose a threshold to determine whether an example is covered by the rule or not.
- Calculate the actual boundaries (MinA and MaxA) for each attribute.

9.5.2 The nature of examples and rules

As explained in Section 9.4, the actual values of the continuous variables (normalized in the range of 0–1) are used as the values for the inputs of the neural network. Thus, unlike the binary numbers used in the discrete case, an example is now defined as a list of real numbers:

$$(a_1, b_1, c_1, ..., n_1)$$

where $a_1, b_1, c_1, ..., n_1$ are the normalized values of the input attributes a, b, c, ..., n.

A rule, on the other hand, is defined by a list of attributes that are present or negated. Thus, the antecedent of a rule is defined by:

$$(attr1 \text{ AND } attr2 \text{ AND } ... \text{ AND } attrk)$$

where attr1, attr2, ..., attrk represent the attributes that must be either present or negated for the rule to be applicable. When dealing with continuous-valued attributes, *negated* refers to those attributes with a low value in the defining rule. In other words, the attribute is still present (in the discrete sense), but it has a low value. This highlights that for some attributes, low values are more important than high values for a particular rule to apply.

The rule definition requires that the value of the attributes present in the rule are set to 1.0, while the value of the attributes negated in the rule are set to 0.0. Here, the continuous data is assumed to have been normalized, resulting in:

- the antecedent of a rule defined by (attr1 AND attr2 AND ... AND attrk), and
- the possible values of the attributes in the rule given by (1.0/0.0, 1.0/0.0, ..., 1.0/0.0), where 1.0/0.0 means either 1.0 or 0.0.

If the attribute is present in the antecedent of the rule, then the value in the rule is 1.0; if the attribute is negated, the value is 0.0. For example, if the antecedent of Rule 1 is defined by:

(a AND b AND NOT d)

then the corresponding values for the antecedent of Rule 1 are:

(1.0, 1.0, 0.0).

9.5.3 Coverage of a continuous example by a rule

To determine whether an example is covered by a particular rule, a statistical measure is adopted to calculate the closeness of the example to the rule. First, the difference between the value of an attribute in the defining rule and the actual value of the corresponding attribute in the example is determined. This provides an error measure between a rule and an example for a particular attribute. Squaring and summing this error measure over all of the attributes defining the rule results in a global measure of the closeness between an example and a rule. In a formal way, this sum of the differences is defined by:

$$\text{SumDifference} = \sum_i (R{:}act{:}attr_i - E{:}act{:}attr_i)^2$$

where   i ranges over the total number of attributes defining a rule,
         $attr_i$ is the attribute currently being considered,
         $R{:}act{:}attr_i$ is the value of the attribute in the rule, and
         $E{:}act{:}attr_i$ is the value of the attribute in the example.

For instance, let Rule 1 be defined by (a AND b AND NOT d) and example 1 be defined by (a_1, b_1, c_1, d_1).

- The corresponding values for the antecedent of the rule are:

(1.0, 1.0, 0.0).

- The SumDifference between example 1 and Rule 1 is:

$$(1.0 - a_1)^2 + (1.0 - b_1)^2 + (0.0 - d_1)^2.$$

As the SumDifference indicates how well an example is covered by a rule, it is a measure of closeness between an example and the subset representing the rule. A threshold, t, is now chosen to delineate whether the example is covered by the rule or not. If the SumDifference is below or equals this threshold, then the corresponding example is considered to be covered by that rule; otherwise it is not. Let the SumDifference between Rule 1 and example 1 be SD1, and let t be the threshold for the rule.

- If SD1 $\leq$ t then example 1 is covered by Rule 1.
- If SD1 $>$ t then example 1 is not covered by Rule 1.

Assuming a threshold value of t = 0.2, consider the following:

- Let Rule X be defined by Temperature, Humidity, and NOT Wind-velocity, resulting in values of 1.0, 1.0, and 0.0 respectively for the attributes in the antecedent of the rule. The NOT refers to low values.

- Let example 1 be defined by (0.75, 0.85, 0.45, 0.20), corresponding to the normalized values of the input attributes of Temperature, Humidity, Air-pressure, and Wind-velocity. The SumDifference between Rule X and example 1 is:

$$(1.0 - 0.75)^2 + (1.0 - 0.85)^2 + (0.0 - 0.20)^2 = 0.1250.$$

As this value is less than the threshold value of 0.2, example 1 is considered to be covered by Rule X.

- Let example 2 be defined by (0.75, 0.85, 0.45, 0.80), corresponding to the normalized values of the input attributes of Temperature, Humidity, Air-pressure, and Wind-velocity. Note that only the Wind-velocity value of example 1 has changed from 0.2 to 0.8. The SumDifference between Rule X and example 2 is:

$$(1.0 - 0.75)^2 + (1.0 - 0.85)^2 + (0.0 - 0.80)^2 = 0.7250.$$

As this value is greater than the threshold value of 0.2, example 2 is considered not to be covered by Rule X.

9.5.4 The dynamic selection of the threshold

The selection of the threshold is obviously a crucial consideration. In Continuously BRAINNE, this threshold is dynamically chosen. To clarify this, consider the following. As the rules grow (i.e., become more specific with the addition of new attributes), more attribute values need to be considered when calculating the SumDifference. If the threshold is too small, some of the examples will not be covered by the rules because of the number of attributes contributing to the SumDifference. Thus, as the rules grow, it is important that the threshold be increased to classify the examples correctly. To highlight this issue:

- Let Rule 1 have a threshold t, and let the SumDifference between example 1 and Rule 1 be SD1.
- Assume SD1 $\leq$ t and therefore conclude that Rule 1 covers example 1.
- Construct two new rules from Rule 1:

$$\text{Rule } 11 = \text{Rule } 1 + \text{new-attr}$$

$$\text{Rule } 12 = \text{Rule } 1 + \text{NOT new-attr}$$

and let these rules have the same threshold t.
- Let the SumDifference between example 1 and Rule 11 be SD11, and let the SumDifference between example 1 and Rule 12 be SD12.
- As the examples covered by Rule 1 have been split into two disjoint subsets — one covered by Rule 11 and one by Rule 12 — then example 1 must be a member of one of those subsets. Hence, it is expected that:

$$\text{SD11} \leq t \quad \text{or} \quad \text{SD12} \leq t.$$

If one inequality is true, but not both, then example 1 is still covered. This corresponds to Figure 9.1, since the new attribute partitions the original set.

If both inequalities are true (because of the size of the threshold), example 1 is considered covered by the rule that is checked first (Rule 11) and not by Rule 12.

If neither inequality is true, then example 1 is not covered by Rule 11 or Rule 12, as shown in Figure 9.2. This is not possible since the example belonged to the original set. In this case, the threshold t must be increased so that the example is covered once again.

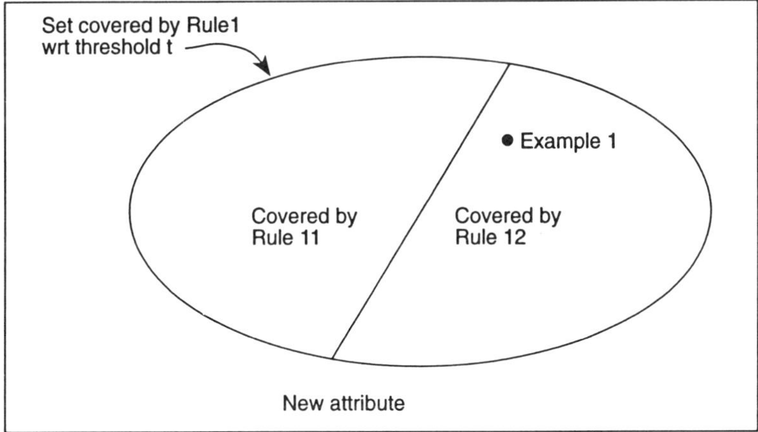

Figure 9.1   Example 1 covered by one of the rules with an appropriately chosen threshold

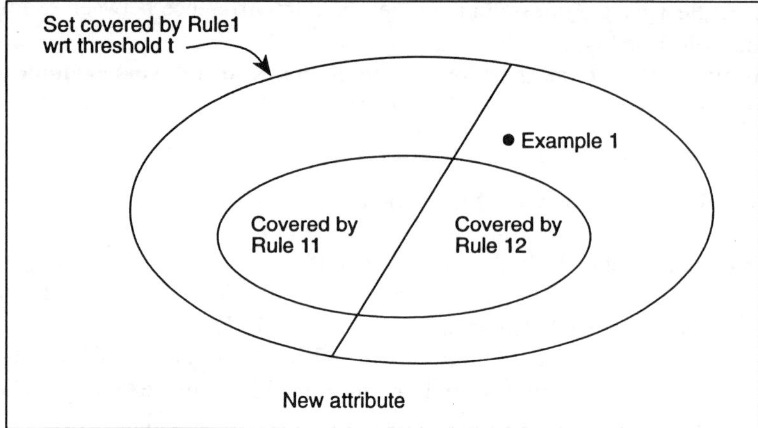

Figure 9.2   Example 1 not covered by at least one of the rules, as the chosen threshold is too small

In Continuously BRAINNE, the threshold is dynamically checked and increased, if necessary, after the division of the subsets. A division of a subset entails the creation of two new rules from the one rule that covered the original subset. After all such divisions occur, the examples are first classified using the same threshold (say 0.2) that applied to the original undivided subsets. From here, two cases can arise:

- If a sufficiently large number of examples is covered by the new set of rules, then there is no change in the value of the threshold.
- On the other hand, if a sufficiently large number of examples is not covered by the new set of rules, then the threshold is increased (say to 0.3) and reclassification of the examples takes place.

The latter process, if required, is continued until all (or a sufficiently large number) of the original examples are covered. Thus, the threshold t is selected such that:

$$\text{NumExsCov} = \text{ActualNumExs},$$

where NumExsCov and ActualNumExs are the total number of covered examples and actual examples, respectively.

Consider the following illustration:

- From before, let Rule X be defined by Temperature, Humidity, and NOT Wind-velocity, and let the initial threshold be 0.2. Also, let example 1 be defined by (0.75, 0.85, 0.45, 0.20), corresponding to the normalized values of the input attributes of Temperature, Humidity, Air-pressure, and Wind-velocity. Example 1, with a SumDifference of 0.1250, is covered by Rule X as the SumDifference is less than the threshold (i.e., $0.1250 < 0.2$).

- Let the next attribute chosen for Rule X be Air-pressure. Therefore, the antecedents of the two new rules are:

  Rule X1 : (Temperature AND Humidity AND NOT Wind-velocity AND Air-pressure)

  Rule X2 : (Temperature AND Humidity AND NOT Wind-velocity AND NOT Air-pressure).

- The SumDifferences of example 1 for the two rules are:

  Rule X1: $(1.0 - 0.75)^2 + (1.0 - 0.85)^2 + (0.0 - 0.20)^2 + (1.0 - 0.45)^2$
             $= 0.4275$

  Rule X2: $(1.0 - 0.75)^2 + (1.0 - 0.85)^2 + (0.0 - 0.20)^2 + (0.0 - 0.45)^2$
             $= 0.3275.$

- Using these SumDifferences and a threshold of 0.2, example 1 cannot be classified as an example of Rule X1 or Rule X2. This is obviously not correct, as example 1 was covered by the original rule. The threshold is hence too restrictive. To overcome this problem the threshold is dynamically chosen so that all (or most) of the examples are covered by the rules determined.

9.5.5 The ranges of the continuous attributes

The next step determines the magnitude of the continuous attributes. The technique so far described extracts the relevant contributory attributes, but it does not give the magnitude of the attributes in the rule necessary for a solution. This requires the following process. First, the SumDifference is used to determine whether a rule covers a particular example. From this, the minimum and maximum values of the attributes defining the rule are obtained from the set of examples covered by that rule. The two steps to determine the ranges of the continuous contributory inputs of a rule follow:

- Loop through all the examples and determine which examples are covered by Rule X by calculating the SumDifferences. Let the set S comprise the examples covered by Rule X.

- For all the examples covered by Rule X, determine the minimum and maximum values for each attribute attrA defining Rule X, by examining the values for that attribute in set S.

The minimum and maximum values represent a range or interval for the corresponding continuous attribute. Both the minimum and maximum values are determined because this accurately restricts the values of the attributes to a closed interval. From these bounds the form of each clause in the antecedent of the conjunctive rule is:

$$(MinA \leq attrA \leq MaxA),$$

where attrA is a contributory attribute of the rule, and MinA and MaxA are the minimum and maximum values respectively, for attrA in the examples covered by the rule.

For instance, let Rule X be defined by a and NOT c and let the examples listed below (defined by the values for the attributes a, b, and c) be covered by Rule X:

> Example 1: (0.90, 0.51, 0.20)
> Example 2: (0.80, 0.68, 0.10)
> Example 3: (0.85, 0.75, 0.25)

Now, the minimum and maximum values for attribute a are 0.80 and 0.90, respectively. Attribute c has minimum and maximum values of 0.10 and 0.25, in that order. Hence, the following clauses are determined for the antecedent of Rule X:

$$(0.80 \leq a \leq 0.90) \text{ AND } (0.10 \leq c \leq 0.25).$$

BRAINNE thus determines the appropriate ranges of the defining attributes of the rules dynamically. Once the ranges are calculated for the individual attributes in the rule, the examples are reclassified according to these restrictions instead of the threshold value. It is an obvious advantage that these ranges come directly from the data and not from the user, who may have no understanding of the actual range or distribution of the input attribute. Another advantage is that these ranges are determined separately for each rule. This allows an attribute to have different ranges in different rules.

9.5.6 Final classification of the examples

The examples are finally classified according to the determined ranges and not according to the arbitrary threshold that was dynamically chosen previously. In fact, the distribution of the examples using the threshold is not necessarily the same as the distribution obtained from the ranges. However, the threshold classification is necessary to calculate the ranges of the particular attributes defining the various rules. These rules enable BRAINNE to create groups of examples that can be classified together.

More importantly, the actual ranges of the continuous attributes are obtained directly and automatically from the example data. There are no preconceived notions placed on the expected ranges of the continuous attributes. These determined ranges can then be included in the antecedent of a rule, in order to restrict the permissible values of the continuous attributes. From this form of the rule, it is easy to determine whether an example is covered by the rule.

9.6 Improving the generalization of the final set of rules

To allow for the fact that the selected examples from which learning is done may not contain values at the extreme boundaries of the attribute range, the range can be extended. Consider the following final rule:

$$(a_1 \leq \text{attrA} \leq a_2) \Rightarrow \text{OUTPUT1}.$$

The bounds a_1 and a_2 can be modified according to the equations:

$$a_1 = a_1 - (a_2 - a_1) * \theta$$
$$a_2 = a_2 + (a_2 - a_1) * \theta$$

Here, θ is chosen for the particular domain of interest. It is normally a small fraction, varying for different domains and associated noise. If this modification is required, each clause in each rule is adjusted separately. The process is invoked when the test data is inadequately classified by the rules obtained from the training data.

9.7 Illustrative applications of Continuously BRAINNE

9.7.1 Modified LED domain

To test this procedure, the previous LED example domain was again used. This data was modified in two important ways. First, as used in Chapter 8, instead of the original 10 possible outputs, the perspective was modified so that there were only 5 outputs, as shown in Table 9.1. Thus the original outputs for 0, 1, 4, and 7 remained unchanged (with output labels of 0–3, respectively), while the actual digit outputs of 2, 3, 5, 6, 8, and 9 were grouped together into one output (labeled OUTPUT 4).

Output number	Actual digit output
0	0
1	1
2	4
3	7
4	2, 3, 5, 6, 8, 9

Table 9.1   First modification to the LED domain

Second, in order to convert the inputs into continuous-valued attributes (instead of the original discrete values), each On was given a value randomly set between 0.8 and 1.0, instead of the original 1. Similarly, each Off was given a value randomly set between 0.0 and 0.2, instead of the original 0. This is summarized in Table 9.2.

Original value	Original input	Modified input
On	1.0	0.8–1.0
Off	0.0	0.0–0.2

Table 9.2   Modifications to the values of the input attributes for the LED domain

A multi-layered neural network configuration of 7 original inputs (corresponding to the segments of the LED display), 5 outputs, and one hidden layer of 10 units was used. The initial products generated for this data are given in Table 9.3. From this table, there is a distinct break in the product measurements for each of the outputs 0, 1, 2, and 3. However, to obtain the appropriate

---

OUTPUT 0   {the digit 0}
  32.76 ⇒ Mid-center   7.61 ⇒ Down-left   7.09 ⇒ Up-left
  5.06 ⇒ Up-right   5.04 ⇒ Down-right   4.94 ⇒ Up-center
  4.79 ⇒ Down-center

OUTPUT 1   {the digit 1}
  84.22 ⇒ Up-center   83.44 ⇒ Down-left   81.01 ⇒ Down-center
  79.26 ⇒ Mid-center   72.34 ⇒ Up-left   16.43 ⇒ Down-right
  16.306 ⇒ Up-right

OUTPUT 2   {the digit 4}
  22.08 ⇒ Up-center   21.36 ⇒ Down-left   20.96 ⇒ Down-center
  5.82 ⇒ Down-right   3.71 ⇒ Up-right   2.29 ⇒ Up-left
  1.97 ⇒ Mid-center

OUTPUT 3   {the digit 7}
  34.78 ⇒ Down-center   33.75 ⇒ Mid-center   31.16 ⇒ Up-left
  30.26 ⇒ Down-left   8.54 ⇒ Up-right   3.82 ⇒ Down-right
  3.49 ⇒ Up-center

OUTPUT 4   {the digits 2, 3, 5, 6, 8, 9}
  332.73 ⇒ Down-left   282.85 ⇒ Up-right   259.16 ⇒ Up-left
  181.27 ⇒ Down-right   120.48 ⇒ Mid-center   109.21 ⇒ Up-center
  103.51 ⇒ Down-center

Table 9.3   Initial products for the modified continuous-valued LED domain

ranges and make the rules unique, the guided generate-and-test procedure was used on all of the outputs.

Using the modified LED domain, Continuously BRAINNE produced the rules found in Table 9.4 (by relaxing the stopping criterion for the grouped output as described in Chapter 8, discarding rules covering few examples according to the threshold $\omega = 10\%$ arising from the noise level in the data, and using a value of $\theta = 0$). For instance, consider the rule produced for OUTPUT 3, which represents the decimal digit 7:

$((0.8000 \leq$ Up-center $\leq 0.9900)$ AND $(0.8040 \leq$ Up-right $\leq 0.9970)$ AND
$(0.8000 \leq$ Down-right $\leq 0.9990)$ AND $(0.0000 \leq$ Up-left $\leq 0.1950)$ AND
$(0.0000 \leq$ Mid-center $\leq 0.1990)$ AND $(0.0000 \leq$ Down-left $\leq 0.1970)$ AND
$(0.0000 \leq$ Down-center $\leq 0.1900)) \Rightarrow$ (OUTPUT 3)   {digit 7}

Here, the values of Up-center, Up-right, and Down-right must be in the high range (from 0.8 to 1.0), while the other attributes must be in the low range (from 0.0 to 0.2). This reflects the constraints a human would expect. Six disjunctive rules were also produced for the grouped OUTPUT 4 (representing the six decimal digits 2, 3, 5, 6, 8, and 9), as given in Table 9.4. Continuously BRAINNE has thus successfully modeled the domain.

9.7.2 A real-world domain

In real-world applications, the percentage of errors or noise is usually unknown. Therefore, the dynamic selection of the threshold should be enforced, even though many rules covering only a few examples may be generated. These rules are easily pruned later using an appropriate value for the threshold ω, if required.

A real-world example domain is briefly discussed to illustrate the application of Continuously BRAINNE further. This example domain, comprising data obtained from a submarine sonar, is fully detailed in Chapter 10. A brief trace for the MINES output is presented in Figure 9.3. The comments on the left of the figure reflect the major steps of BRAINNE, with those in italics referring to Continuously BRAINNE alone.

In this domain, the dynamic selection of the threshold and ranges was enforced, a value of $q = 0$ was used, and the stopping criteria for a rule considered both misclassifications and the selection of a non-discriminatory attribute. The procedure used to generate the rules is exactly the same as that described in Chapter 8, with the addition of the dynamic selection of the threshold and the ranges for the continuous variables. Two of the resulting rules for the MINES output are given in Table 9.5. In these rules, each continuous, contributory attribute has a range indicating the permissible values of the attribute.

((0.8080 ≤ Up-center ≤ 0.9990) AND (0.8000 ≤ Up-left ≤ 0.9950) AND
 (0.8000 ≤ Up-right ≤ 0.9990) AND (0.8000 ≤ Down-left ≤ 0.9900) AND
 (0.8420 ≤ Down-right ≤ 0.9960) AND (0.8000 ≤ Down-center ≤ 0.9990) AND
 (0.0010 ≤ Mid-center ≤ 0.2000)) ⇒ (OUTPUT 0)   {the digit 0}
((0.8000 ≤ Up-right ≤ 0.9940) AND (0.8000 ≤ Down-right ≤ 0.9990) AND
 (0.0000 ≤ Down-center ≤ 0.1990) AND (0.0000 ≤ Up-center ≤ 0.1990) AND
 (0.0020 ≤ Up-left ≤ 0.1950) AND (0.0000 ≤ Down-left ≤ 0.1860) AND
 (0.0050 ≤ Mid-center ≤ 0.1940) ⇒ (OUTPUT 1)   {the digit 1}
((0.8020 ≤ Up-left ≤ 0.9980) AND (0.8000 ≤ Up-right ≤ 0.9960) AND
 (0.8000 ≤ Mid-center ≤ 0.9740) AND (0.8000 ≤ Down-right ≤ 0.9900) AND
 (0.0010 ≤ Up-center ≤ 0.1840) AND (0.0210 ≤ Down-left ≤ 0.1930) AND
 (0.0170 ≤ Down-center ≤ 0.1740)) ⇒ (OUTPUT 2)   {the digit 4}
((0.8000 ≤ Up-center ≤ 0.9900) AND (0.8040 ≤ Up-right ≤ 0.9970) AND
 (0.8000 ≤ Down-right ≤ 0.9990) AND (0.0000 ≤ Up-left ≤ 0.1950) AND
 (0.0000 ≤ Mid-center ≤ 0.1990) AND (0.0000 ≤ Down-left ≤ 0.1970) AND
 (0.0000 ≤ Down-center ≤ 0.1900)) ⇒ (OUTPUT 3)   {the digit 7}
((0.8000 ≤ Up-center ≤ 0.9990) AND (0.8000 ≤ Up-left ≤ 0.9990) AND
 (0.8000 ≤ Up-right ≤ 0.9900) AND (0.8000 ≤ Mid-center ≤ 0.9740) AND
 (0.8000 ≤ Down-left ≤ 0.9980) AND (0.8000 ≤ Down-right ≤ 0.9990) AND
 (0.8000 ≤ Down-center ≤ 0.9990)) ⇒ (OUTPUT 4)   {the digit 8}
((0.8010 ≤ Up-center ≤ 0.9970) AND (0.8000 ≤ Up-left ≤ 0.9980) AND
 (0.8010 ≤ Up-right ≤ 0.9990) AND (0.8000 ≤ Mid-center ≤ 0.9930) AND
 (0.8000 ≤ Down-right ≤ 0.9980) AND (0.8000 ≤ Down-center ≤ 0.9980) AND
 (0.0000 ≤ Down-left ≤ 0.1970)) ⇒ (OUTPUT 4)   {the digit 9}
((0.8000 ≤ Up-center ≤ 0.9930) AND (0.8000 ≤ Up-left ≤ 0.9930) AND
 (0.8000 ≤ Mid-center ≤ 0.9960) AND (0.8000 ≤ Down-left ≤ 0.9990) AND
 (0.8000 ≤ Down-right ≤ 0.9990) AND (0.8000 ≤ Down-center ≤ 0.9960) AND
 (0.0000 ≤ Up-right ≤ 0.2000)) ⇒ (OUTPUT 4)   {the digit 6}
((0.8000 ≤ Up-center ≤ 0.9940) AND (0.8140 ≤ Up-left ≤ 0.9990) AND
 (0.8020 ≤ Mid-center ≤ 0.9990) AND (0.8000 ≤ Down-right ≤ 0.9840) AND
 (0.8000 ≤ Down-center ≤ 0.9900) AND (0.0000 ≤ Up-right ≤ 0.1910) AND
 (0.0000 ≤ Down-left ≤ 0.1980)) ⇒ (OUTPUT 4)   {the digit 5}
((0.8000 ≤ Up-center ≤ 0.9980) AND (0.8000 ≤ Up-right ≤ 0.9990) AND
 (0.8000 ≤ Mid-center ≤ 0.9920) AND (0.8000 ≤ Down-right ≤ 0.9940) AND
 (0.8010 ≤ Down-center ≤ 0.9880) AND (0.0000 ≤ Up-left ≤ 0.1960) AND
 (0.0000 ≤ Down-left ≤ 0.1960)) ⇒ (OUTPUT 4)   {the digit 3}
((0.8000 ≤ Up-center ≤ 0.9890) AND (0.8000 ≤ Up-right ≤ 0.9870) AND
 (0.8000 ≤ Mid-center ≤ 0.9970) AND (0.8000 ≤ Down-left ≤ 0.9990) AND
 (0.8000 ≤ Down-center ≤ 0.9910) AND (0.0000 ≤ Down-right ≤ 0.1920) AND
 (0.0000 ≤ Up-left ≤ 0.1980)) ⇒ (OUTPUT 4)   {the digit 2}

Table 9.4   Rules produced by Continuously BRAINNE for the modified LED
domain with continuous-valued inputs

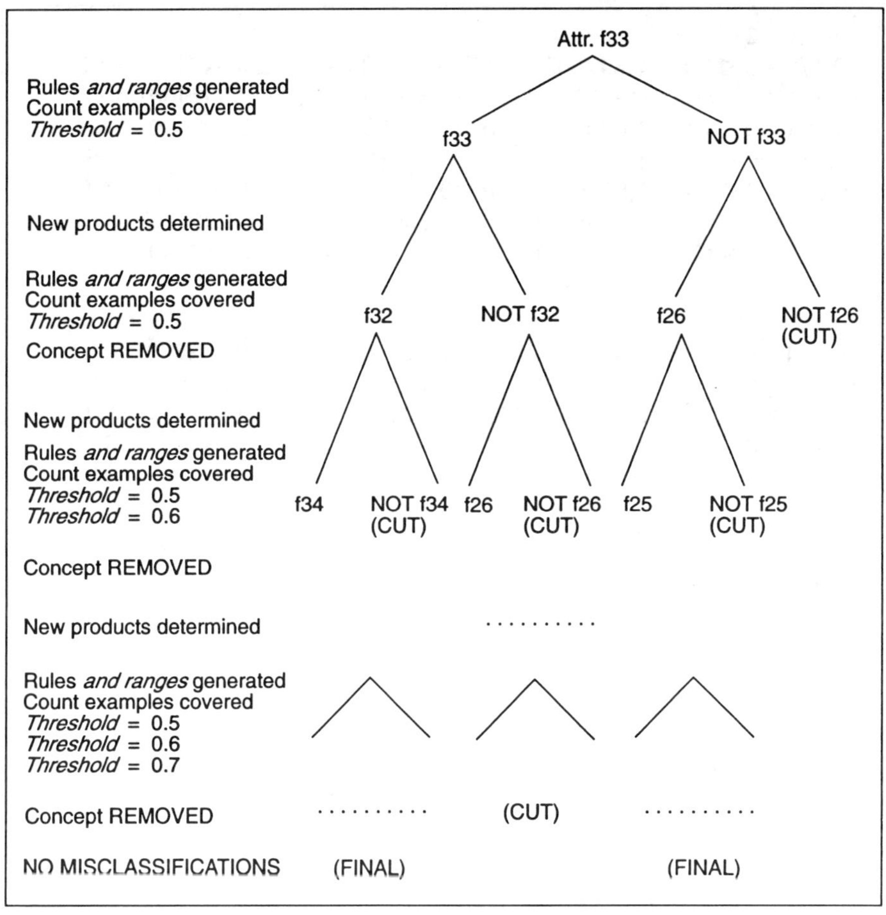

Figure 9.3 A portion of the trace for the MINES output from the submarine sonar data

9.8 Recapitulation

There are two important points when dealing with continuously valued input attributes. First, the technique presented in this chapter enables BRAINNE to use the raw (but normalized) continuous values of any real-world example data directly. There is no need to break up the values of any continuous attributes arbitrarily into two or more discrete classes. This has the obvious advantage that the raw data itself is used, making the rules reflect the true nature of the data. Second, the ranges determined for the continuous attributes

---

Rule No. 27
((0.476500 ≤ f16 ≤ 0.842600) AND (0.582300 ≤ f17 ≤ 0.847600) AND
(0.604100 ≤ f18 ≤ 0.903300) AND (0.674900 ≤ f19 ≤ 0.958400) AND
(0.708400 ≤ f20 ≤ 1.000000) AND (0.789000 ≤ f21 ≤ 1.000000) AND
(0.870500 ≤ f22 ≤ 1.000000) AND (0.640300 ≤ f23 ≤ 1.000000) AND
(0.506700 ≤ f24 ≤ 1.000000) AND (0.539500 ≤ f25 ≤ 1.000000) AND
(0.693400 ≤ f26 ≤ 0.989600) AND (0.660000 ≤ f27 ≤ 0.995600) AND
(0.551200 ≤ f28 ≤ 0.896200) AND (0.401600 ≤ f29 ≤ 0.719600))
⇒ MINES

Rule No. 28
((0.334500 ≤ f17 ≤ 0.464600) AND (0.523300 ≤ f18 ≤ 0.648700) AND
(0.626000 ≤ f19 ≤ 0.726500) AND (0.742000 ≤ f20 ≤ 0.834600) AND
(0.745200 ≤ f21 ≤ 0.826800) AND (0.794000 ≤ f22 ≤ 0.879300) AND
(0.840000 ≤ f23 ≤ 1.000000) AND (0.881000 ≤ f24 ≤ 0.986500) AND
(0.881400 ≤ f25 ≤ 0.994500) AND (0.930100 ≤ f26 ≤ 1.000000) AND
(0.931500 ≤ f27 ≤ 1.000000) AND (0.823700 ≤ f28 ≤ 0.903600) AND
(0.606900 ≤ f29 ≤ 0.640900) AND (0.229800 ≤ f16 ≤ 0.368500))
⇒ MINES

Table 9.5   Two of the rules defining MINES generated from the submarine sonar data

of the rules are obtained directly from the data. This avoids applying the ranges arbitrarily before or during any processing. The ranges determined enable BRAINNE to construct the conditions necessary for restricting the values of the continuous attributes. Also, the ranges of the attributes are constructed separately for each rule, giving the considerable advantage that an attribute can have different ranges in different rules.

The generalization capability of a set of rules is a measure of the ability to classify unseen examples correctly. To enhance this capability, the range of each contributory attribute can be manually increased. This heuristic is demonstrated in Chapter 10.

Finally, it should be emphasized that in unknown domains the dynamic selection of the threshold and the ranges should be enforced. The termination of the expansion of a rule should consider both misclassifications and the selection of a contradictory attribute. In noisy domains, the dynamic selection of the threshold and the ranges may produce rules that cover only a few examples. However, if required, such rules can be easily pruned.

Further examples of the successful application of BRAINNE are given in Chapter 10. The example domains contain both discrete and continuous-valued attributes. For the continuous data, the extensions to BRAINNE that constitute

Continuously BRAINNE must be invoked. Domains containing only discrete data use the BRAINNE methodology described in Chapter 8. However, Continuously BRAINNE must be applied to domains with a mixture of data types.

References

DARPA (Defense Advanced Research Project Agency) 1988, *Neural Network Study*, AFCEA International Press, Fairfax, Virginia

10

BRAINNE
in the real world

10.1 Introduction

This chapter presents the results of the BRAINNE method applied to various real-world problem domains. These include the well-known machine learning domains of the mushroom and soya bean data. Example domains consisting primarily of continuous-valued attributes, such as the submarine sonar data, are also used. Most of this data can be obtained from the UCI (University of California, Irvine) repository of machine learning databases. The databases are accessed via the anonymous ftp site *ics.uci.edu,* under the subdirectory of /pub/machine-learning-databases.

10.2 BRAINNE in summary

The following steps were taken with each problem domain:

- Using the outputs as additional inputs, train a multi-layered neural network using Back-propagation.

280

- Determine the Sum of Squares Errors (SSE) between all the original inputs and all additional inputs (i.e., the original outputs).
- Use Hebb's Rule to determine the correlation between the negated inputs and the outputs to learn the inhibitory links. The example data for this is obtained by negating the values of the input attributes and leaving unchanged the values of the desired outputs, for each original example.
- Determine the product between the SSE measurement and the weight of the inhibitory link between each input and additional input (i.e., desired output) combination.
- Sort the products in decreasing order for each output.
- Select the attributes in each sorted list with values below some cut-off point. This cut-off is defined as the point where two consecutive products are at least two to three times different in magnitude.
- If a clear cut-off exists, form a conjunctive IF-THEN rule. The antecedent of the rule contains the selected input attributes joined with the AND connective, and the consequent is the appropriate output. This is described in the first part of Chapter 8.
- If no clear cut-off exists or the conjunctive rule produced is not unique, then loop through the guided generate-and-test procedure to determine the disjunctive rule defining the output. This is described in the second part of Chapter 8.
- If any of the input attributes are continuously valued, then use the method discussed in Chapter 9. This method includes the dynamic selection of a threshold and the ranges bounding the continuous variables.

10.3 Exclusive OR problem

The eXclusive OR (XOR) Boolean function has been widely used to investigate the feasibility of various connectionist models. To demonstrate the applicability of the BRAINNE method, 500 examples of the XOR function were produced. Each example consisted of one of the following input/output combinations:

X_1	X_2	XOR
0	0	0
0	1	1
1	0	1
1	1	0

A rule defining the positive output (XOR = 1) was sought. Note that when XOR is used as an output in BRAINNE; it means XOR = 1. The multi-layered neural network configuration comprised 2 original inputs, 1 output, and one hidden layer with 2 hidden units. As shown in Table 10.1, the initial products contained no clear cut-off point as there is no distinct jump in the magnitude of the products.

Total number of examples 247
Number of inputs 3
Number of hidden units 2
Total concepts 1
Total Sum of errors Squared 0.007443
(TSS from Back-propagation)

XOR covers 247 examples

Products for XOR
$137.2516 \Rightarrow X_2$ $133.6483 \Rightarrow X_1$ $0.0000 \Rightarrow XOR$

Table 10.1   Initial products for the Exclusive OR problem data for XOR = 1

Owing to the absence of a cut-off point, the guided generate-and-test procedure was invoked to determine the unique conjunctive rule or the disjunctive rule defining the output. The attribute with the smallest product is X_1, resulting in the following two initial rules for the generation process:

Rule 1: $(X_1) \Rightarrow (XOR)$
Rule 2: $(NOT\ X_1) \Rightarrow (XOR)$.

The antecedents of the final rules resulting from this guided generate-and-test procedure:

$(X_1\ AND\ NOT\ X_2) \Rightarrow (XOR)$
$(NOT\ X_1\ AND\ X_2) \Rightarrow (XOR)$

can be combined with the OR connective to form the required disjunctive rule:

$(X_1\ AND\ NOT\ X_2)\ OR\ (NOT\ X_1\ AND\ X_2) \Rightarrow (XOR)$.

The demonstration on this simple, yet not linearly separable, problem was further extended by using 3 original inputs, instead of 2. As $(X_1\ XOR\ X_2\ XOR\ X_3) = ((X_1\ XOR\ X_2)\ XOR\ X_3)$, the defining examples are:

X_1	X_2	X_3	XOR
0	0	0	0
0	0	1	1
0	1	0	1
0	1	1	0
1	0	0	1
1	0	1	0
1	1	0	0
1	1	1	1

Once again, the initial products contained no clear cut-off point. Hence, using the guided generate-and-test procedure, the following rules were produced:

$$(X_1 \text{ AND NOT } X_2 \text{ AND NOT } X_3) \Rightarrow (\text{XOR})$$
$$(\text{NOT } X_1 \text{ AND } X_2 \text{ AND NOT } X_3) \Rightarrow (\text{XOR})$$
$$(\text{NOT } X_1 \text{ AND NOT } X_2 \text{ AND } X_3) \Rightarrow (\text{XOR})$$
$$(X_1 \text{ AND } X_2 \text{ AND } X_3) \Rightarrow (\text{XOR}).$$

BRAINNE was therefore successful in obtaining the rules defining the positive output of the XOR function. If it is unclear whether a cut-off exists, it is always safer to assume that there is no cut-off. The guided generate-and-test procedure can then be applied to determine the unique rules defining the corresponding output.

10.4 U.S.A. Congressional Voting data

The 1984 U. S. A. Congressional Voting Records database (*Congressional Quarterly Almanac*, 98th Congress, 2nd session 1984, Volume XL) was obtained via ftp from the Irvine database. This data set includes the votes from each

Label	Attribute	Values
X_0	Handicapped-infants	Yes No
X_1	Water-project-cost-sharing	Yes No
X_2	Adoption-of-the-budget-resolution	Yes No
X_3	Physician-fee-freeze	Yes No
X_4	El-salvador-aid	Yes No
X_5	Religious-groups-in-schools	Yes No
X_6	Anti-satellite-test-ban	Yes No
X_7	Aid-to-nicaraguan-contras	Yes No
X_8	Mx-missile	Yes No
X_9	Immigration	Yes No
X_{10}	Synfuels-corporation-cutback	Yes No
X_{11}	Education-spending	Yes No
X_{12}	Superfund-right-to-sue	Yes No
X_{13}	Crime	Yes No
X_{14}	Duty-free-exports	Yes No
X_{15}	Export-administration-act-south-africa	Yes No
OUT	REPUBLICAN DEMOCRAT	

Table 10.2 Congressional Voting attributes

member of Congress on 16 key issues (i.e., the input attributes) identified by the *Congressional Quarterly Almanac* (CQA). The CQA lists 9 different types of votes: *voted for, paired for,* and *announced for* simplified to *Yes*; *voted against, paired against,* and *announced against* simplified to *No*; *voted present, voted present to avoid conflict of interest,* and *did not vote or otherwise make a position known* simplified to a *?*, indicating an uncommitted position. There are 435 examples in the data set, 168 Republicans and 267 Democrats. Each example is defined by the 16 input attributes and 2 outputs listed in Table 10.2.

For training and testing purposes, 80% of the data was used to learn the rules and 20% was used to check the generated rules. Thus the training set contained a total of 348 examples with 133 (of the original 167) REPUBLICAN examples and 215 (of the original 267) DEMOCRAT examples. A multi-layered neural network configuration of 16 original inputs, 2 outputs, and one hidden layer with 4 units was used. The initial products produced for the 2 outputs are listed in Table 10.3.

First, consider OUTPUT 0, which consists of 133 examples defined as REPUBLICAN voters. From the initial product list, input attribute X_3 (Physician-

---

Total number of examples 348
Number of inputs 18
Number of hidden units 4
Total concepts 2
Total Sum of errors Squared 0.233428
(TSS from Back-propagation)

OUTPUT 0 covers 133 examples
OUTPUT 1 covers 215 examples

Products for OUTPUT 0 = REPUBLICAN

$91.2330 \Rightarrow X_{10}$	$77.8663 \Rightarrow X_8$	$70.2758 \Rightarrow X_{14}$	$66.7815 \Rightarrow X_2$
$59.5468 \Rightarrow X_0$	$59.2444 \Rightarrow X_7$	$53.8112 \Rightarrow X_6$	$42.6616 \Rightarrow X_1$
$21.9473 \Rightarrow X_{15}$	$18.8919 \Rightarrow X_9$	$15.7295 \Rightarrow X_{12}$	$12.3082 \Rightarrow X_{11}$
$7.7094 \Rightarrow X_5$	$4.2163 \Rightarrow X_4$	$3.0971 \Rightarrow X_{13}$	$0.6725 \Rightarrow X_3$

Products for OUTPUT 1 = DEMOCRAT

$192.4016 \Rightarrow X_3$	$108.2819 \Rightarrow X_{11}$	$89.6996 \Rightarrow X_4$	$81.2998 \Rightarrow X_9$
$77.2310 \Rightarrow X_{13}$	$72.8739 \Rightarrow X_{12}$	$55.9089 \Rightarrow X_1$	$49.4154 \Rightarrow X_5$
$43.5388 \Rightarrow X_{15}$	$43.0394 \Rightarrow X_0$	$39.1876 \Rightarrow X_{14}$	$33.5827 \Rightarrow X_{10}$
$26.5571 \Rightarrow X_6$	$24.7756 \Rightarrow X_8$	$19.7665 \Rightarrow X_7$	$13.3700 \Rightarrow X_2$

Table 10.3   Initial products determined for the Congressional Voting data (X_0 to X_{15} are the labels listed in Table 10.2)

fee-freeze) could be selected as the only important attribute, giving the following rule:

Rule 1: (Physician-fee-freeze = Yes) $\Rightarrow$ (REPUBLICAN).

The accuracy of this rule was then tested by considering all of the original examples from both the training and test sets. The number of correct and incorrect classifications made by applying Rule 1 were:

- correct classifications (REPUBLICAN):

number classified	= 163
REPUBLICAN examples	= 167
percentage correct	= 163/167
	= 97.0%

- incorrect classifications (DEMOCRAT):

number classified	= 14
DEMOCRAT examples	= 267
percentage incorrect	= 14/267
	= 5.2%

If these tolerances are acceptable, Rule 1 is the only rule defining a REPUBLICAN voter. However, if these tolerances are not acceptable, then the guided generate-and-test procedure should be invoked to determine the defining disjunctive rule for this output. Taking the attribute with the smallest product (i.e., X_3), the following 2 initial rules were used in the guided generate-and-test procedure for the output:

Rule 0: (Physician-fee-freeze = Yes) $\Rightarrow$ (REPUBLICAN)

Rule 1: (Physician-fee-freeze = No) $\Rightarrow$ (REPUBLICAN).

The process was continued until the final disjunctive rules for the output REPUBLICAN were obtained. The resulting rules are not much better, since the same number of REPUBLICAN examples are covered and incorrect classifications are down only slightly to 9 examples or 3.37%.

For OUTPUT 1, consisting of 215 examples defined as DEMOCRAT voters, there is no clear cut-off point. Therefore, using the attribute with the smallest product value (i.e., X_2), the following 2 initial rules were used in the guided generate-and-test procedure:

Rule 0: (Adoption-of-the-budget-resolution = Yes) $\Rightarrow$ (DEMOCRAT)

Rule 1: (Adoption-of-the-budget-resolution = No) $\Rightarrow$ (DEMOCRAT).

In total, 48 rules were determined for this output and a portion of these are given in Table 10.4.

Rule 0 (covers 19 examples)
((Handicapped-infants = Yes) AND
   (Adoption-of-the-budget-resolution = Yes) AND (Anti-satellite-ban = Yes)
   AND (Aid-to-nicaraguan-contras = Yes) AND (Mx-missile = Yes) AND
   (Immigration = Yes) AND (Duty-free-exports = Yes) AND
   (Export-administration-act-south-africa = Yes))
⇒ (DEMOCRAT)

Rule 3 (covers 35 examples)
((Adoption-of-the-budget-resolution = Yes) AND (Anti-satellite-ban = Yes)
   AND (Aid-to-nicaraguan-contras = Yes) AND (Mx-missile = Yes) AND
   (Duty-free-exports = Yes) AND
   (Export-administration-act-south-africa = Yes) AND
   (Immigration = No))
⇒ (DEMOCRAT)

Rule 11 (covers 46 examples)
((Adoption-of-the-budget-resolution = Yes) AND (Anti-satellite-ban = Yes)
   AND (Aid-to-nicaraguan-contras = Yes) AND (Mx-missile = Yes) AND
   (Export-administration-act-south-africa = No))
⇒ (DEMOCRAT)

Rule 19 (covers 11 examples)
((Adoption-of-the-budget-resolution = Yes) AND (El-salvador = Yes) AND
   (Religious-groups-in-school = Yes) AND (Superfund-right-to-sue = Yes)
   AND (Crime = Yes) AND (Aid-to-nicaraguan-contras = No) AND
   (Education-spending = No))
⇒ (DEMOCRAT)

Rule 42 (covers 1 example)
((Handicapped-infants = Yes) AND (Water-project-cost-sharing = Yes)
   AND (Religious-groups-in-school = Yes) AND
   (Synfuels-corporation-cutback = Yes) AND (Superfund-right-to-sue =
   Yes) AND (Export-administration-act-south-africa = Yes) AND
   (Adoption-of-the-budget-resolution = No) AND (Crime = No) AND
   (Duty-free-exports = No))
⇒ (DEMOCRAT)

Table 10.4   Portion of the rules produced for the DEMOCRAT output

Rule 17 (covers 1 REPUBLICAN and 3 DEMOCRAT examples)
((Adoption-of-the-budget-resolution = Yes) AND (El-salvador = Yes) AND
   (Religious-groups-in-school = Yes) AND (Immigration = Yes) AND
   (Synfuels-corporation-cutback = Yes) AND (Education-spending = Yes)
   AND (Superfund-right-to-sue = Yes) AND (Crime = Yes) AND
   (Aid-to-nicaraguan-contras = No))
⇒ (DEMOCRAT)
Rule 29 (covers 3 REPUBLICAN and 1 DEMOCRAT examples)
((Water-project-cost-sharing = Yes) AND (Physician-fee-freeze = Yes)
   AND (El-salvador = Yes) AND (Religious-groups-in-school = Yes) AND
   (Synfuels-corporation-cutback = Yes) AND (Education-spending = Yes)
   AND (Crime = Yes) AND (Adoption-of-the-budget-resolution = No)
   AND (Mx-missile = No) AND (Handicapped-infants = No) AND
   (Immigration = No))
⇒ (DEMOCRAT)
Rule 31 (covers 3 REPUBLICAN and 1 DEMOCRAT examples)
((Physician-fee-freeze = Yes) AND (El-salvador = Yes) AND
   (Religious-groups-in-school = Yes) AND
   (Synfuels-corporation-cutback = Yes) AND (Education-spending = Yes)
   AND (Superfund-right-to-sue = Yes) AND (Crime = Yes)
   AND (Adoption-of-the-budget-resolution = No) AND (Mx-missile = No)
   AND (Water-project-cost-sharing = No) AND (Aid-to-nicaraguan-contras
   = No))
⇒ (DEMOCRAT)
Rule 35 (covers 1 REPUBLICAN and 1 DEMOCRAT examples)
((Handicapped-infants = Yes) AND (Water-project-cost-sharing = Yes)
   AND (Physician-fee-freeze = Yes) AND (El-salvador = Yes) AND
   (Religious-groups-in-school = Yes) AND
   (Synfuels-corporation-cutback = Yes) AND (Superfund-right-to-sue =
   Yes) AND (Crime = Yes) AND (Adoption-of-the-budget-resolution =
   No) AND (Mx-missile = No) AND (Education-spending = No)
   AND (Duty-free-exports = No) AND (Immigration = No))
⇒ (DEMOCRAT)

Table 10.5   Rules incorrectly classifying some REPUBLICAN examples for the
DEMOCRAT output

In total, 257 examples out of the original 268 (96%) DEMOCRAT examples are correctly classified using these rules, and 8 REPUBLICAN examples are incorrectly classified (8/167 = 4.8%). The DEMOCRAT rules misclassifying some of the REPUBLICAN examples are listed in Table 10.5. It appears that there is not sufficient discriminatory information to distinguish between some examples of the different outputs. However, as less than 5% of the REPUBLICAN examples are misclassified, no further analysis is done.

Some of the rules generated cover only 1 example. Such rules arise from noise and/or exceptions in the data that do not fit the more general rules. The resulting list of rules generated for the DEMOCRAT voters has a total of 22 such rules covering only 1 example.

In summary, using the generated rules, 420 DEMOCRAT and REPUBLICAN examples were correctly classified. This gives an accuracy of 97% (420/435 original examples). Exceptions to the more general rules were easily obtained.

Label	Attribute	Values
0–5	Cap-shape	b c x f k s
6–9	Cap-surface	f g y s
10–19	Cap-color	n b c g r p u e w y
20–21	Bruises	t f
22–30	Odor	a l c y f m n p s
31–34	Gill-attachment	a d f n
35–37	Gill-spacing	c w d
38–39	Gill-size	b n
40–51	Gill-color	k n b h g r o p u e w y
52–53	Stalk-shape	e t
54–59	Stalk-root	b c u e z r
60–63	Stalk-surface-above-ring	f y k s
64–67	Stalk-surface-below-ring	f y k s
68–76	Stalk-color-above-ring	n b c g o p e w y
77–85	Stalk-color-below-ring	n b c g o p e w y
86–87	Veil-type	p u
88–91	Veil-color	n o w y
92–94	Ring-number	n o t
95–102	Ring-type	c e f l n p s z
103–111	Spore-print-color	k n b h r o u w y
112–117	Population	a c n s v y
118–124	Habitat	g l m p u w d
OUT	POISONOUS EDIBLE	

Table 10.6   Mushroom attributes and their possible values

Also, a few of the rules were unable to distinguish between some examples of different outputs. These examples do not have enough discriminatory information to be partitioned. However, as their number is small, they can be regarded as noise.

10.5 Mushroom data

This data, also from the Irvine database, consists of 8124 examples described by various characteristics of mushrooms and indicating whether the mushroom is poisonous or not. As information is distributed throughout the entire set of examples, the first 70 examples of every 100 formed the training set, while the remaining 30 examples were used to check the results. Thus the training set consisted of 5609 examples, with 2689 POISONOUS mushroom examples and 2920 EDIBLE mushroom examples.

Total number of examples 5609
Number of inputs 127
Number of hidden units 10
Total concepts 2
Total Sum of errors Squared 0.813738
(TSS from Back-propagation)

OUTPUT 0 covers 2689 examples
OUTPUT 1 covers 2920 examples

Some products for OUTPUT 0

$1072.072 \Rightarrow 84$	$1063.604 \Rightarrow 75$	$1055.533 \Rightarrow 106$	$1044.766 \Rightarrow 110$
$1013.316 \Rightarrow 08$	$994.991 \Rightarrow 02$	$949.519 \Rightarrow 42$	$943.633 \Rightarrow 96$
$901.790 \Rightarrow 53$	$851.617 \Rightarrow 52$	$811.731 \Rightarrow 66$	$804.275 \Rightarrow 54$
$741.178 \Rightarrow 62$	$692.229 \Rightarrow 29$	$688.107 \Rightarrow 26$	$613.259 \Rightarrow 39$
$526.125 \Rightarrow 116$	$310.685 \Rightarrow 21$	$50.201 \Rightarrow 93$	$46.241 \Rightarrow 35$
$8.359 \Rightarrow 33$	$3.341 \Rightarrow 90$	$0.000 \Rightarrow 86$	

Some products for OUTPUT 1

$1156.667 \Rightarrow 08$	$1140.358 \Rightarrow 21$	$1133.034 \Rightarrow 03$	$1059.753 \Rightarrow 23$
$1049.250 \Rightarrow 22$	$1043.956 \Rightarrow 103$	$1019.725 \Rightarrow 02$	$1015.945 \Rightarrow 124$
$991.439 \Rightarrow 104$	$711.279 \Rightarrow 20$	$684.170 \Rightarrow 53$	$632.709 \Rightarrow 84$
$608.454 \Rightarrow 35$	$604.386 \Rightarrow 75$	$457.479 \Rightarrow 100$	$33.214 \Rightarrow 67$
$241.148 \Rightarrow 93$	$240.394 \Rightarrow 63$	$147.122 \Rightarrow 28$	$97.518 \Rightarrow 38$
$93.139 \Rightarrow 33$	$89.603 \Rightarrow 90$	$0.000 \Rightarrow 86$	

Table 10.7 Portion of the initial products for the mushroom data (using the labels listed in Table 10.6)

There are 22 original input variables defined by the 125 discrete values listed in Table 10.6. Hence, there are 125 input attributes indicating whether a mushroom is POISONOUS or EDIBLE. A multi-layered neural network configuration consisting of 125 original inputs, 2 outputs, and one hidden layer of 10 units was used. Some of the initial products determined from the training examples are given in Table 10.7.

Interestingly, the three smallest products for both the outputs, POISONOUS and EDIBLE, are from the same input attributes. The attribute labeled 86 has a zero product value for both outputs, with the next 2 attributes on the sorted lists having labels of 90 and 33. A quick scan of the input data confirms that the values of these attributes are the same for most (if not all) of the examples. The labels 86, 90, and 33 correspond to the following variables and their values:

$$
\begin{array}{lll}
\text{Label} & 86: & \text{Veil-type} = \text{p} \\
& 90: & \text{Veil-color} = \text{w} \\
& 33: & \text{Gill-attachment} = \text{f.}
\end{array}
$$

A cut-off point could be selected for each output, but the rules generated misclassify a large portion of the examples. This occurs because outputs have the same attributes at the low end of their respective sorted product lists.

Thus, to determine the unique rules for each of the outputs, the guided generate-and-test procedure was used. The following antecedents were used in the initial rules for both outputs, as the same attributes gave the lowest products in each sorted list:

$$
\begin{array}{l}
86 \text{ AND } 90 \\
86 \text{ AND NOT } 90.
\end{array}
$$

The attribute labeled 86 is automatically selected as a part of all defining rules because its product value is zero for both outputs.

In total, 46 rules were generated for this data: 29 for the EDIBLE output and 17 for the POISONOUS output. Some of these values are listed in Table 10.8. A final check was made of all the original (i.e., both training and test) examples. The statistics in Table 10.9 indicate that all of the 8124 original examples are covered by the rules determined. Thus, all examples are correctly classified, representing 100% accuracy.

The large number of conditions in the resulting rules were extracted after only 8 passes of the guided generate-and-test procedure. More than one attribute can be extracted at each pass when the product value of an attribute is zero. All of the examples, without exception, are correctly classified using the rules determined. The success of BRAINNE on this problem data indicates the suitability of this method for real-world problems.

Rule 0
((Cap-surface = y) AND (Bruises = t) AND (Odor = n) AND (Gill-attachment = f) AND
  (Gill-spacing = c) AND (Gill-size = b) AND (Stalk-shape = t) AND
  (Stalk-root = b) AND (Stalk-surface-above-ring = s) AND
  (Stalk-surface-below-ring = s) AND (Veil-type = p) AND (Veil-color = w) AND
  (Ring-number = o) AND (Ring-type = p) AND (Habitat = d))
⇒ (EDIBLE)

Rule 1
((Cap-surface = f) AND (Bruises = t) AND (Odor = n) AND (Gill-attachment = f) AND
  (Gill-spacing = c) AND (Gill-size = b) AND (Stalk-shape = t) AND
  (Stalk-root = b) AND (Stalk-surface-above-ring = s) AND
  (Stalk-surface-below-ring = s) AND (Veil-type = p) AND (Veil-color = w) AND
  (Ring-number = o) AND (Ring-type = p) AND (Habitat = d) AND
  (Cap-surface != y))
⇒ (EDIBLE)

Rule 2
((Bruises = t) AND (Gill-attachment = f) AND (Gill-spacing = c) AND
  (Gill-size = b) AND (Stalk-shape = e) AND (Stalk-root = c) AND
  (Stalk-surface-above-ring = s) AND (Stalk-surface-below-ring = s) AND
  (Stalk-color-above-ring = w) AND (Stalk-color-below-ring = w) AND
  (Veil-type = p)(Veil-color = w) AND (Ring-number = o) AND (Ring-type = p) AND
  (Stalk-root != b))
⇒ (EDIBLE)

Rule 29
((Bruises = f) AND (Gill-attachment = f) AND (Gill-spacing = c) AND
  (Gill-size = n) AND (Veil-type = p) AND (Veil-color = w) AND
  (Ring-number = o) AND (Ring-type = e) AND (Spore-pint-color = w) AND
  (Population = v))
⇒ (POISONOUS)

Rule 30
((Cap-shape = x) AND (Bruises = f) AND (Odor = c) AND (Gill-attachment = f) AND
  (Gill-spacing = c) AND (Gill-size = n) AND (Stalk-shape = e) AND
  (Stalk-root = b) AND (Stalk-surface-above-ring = s) AND
  (Stalk-surface-below-ring = s) AND (Stalk-color-above-ring = w) AND
  (Stalk-color-below-ring = w) AND (Veil-type = p) AND (Veil-color = w) AND
  (Ring-number = o) AND (Ring-type = p) AND (Population = v) AND
  (Habitat = d) AND (Ring-type != e) AND (Population != c))
⇒ (POISONOUS)

Table 10.8   Portion of the rules determined for the mushroom data
(!= means not equal)

Rule No.	P exs	E exs	Rule No.	P exs	E exs
0	0	864	1	0	864
2	0	512	3	0	192
4	0	96	5	0	96
6	0	96	7	0	48
8	0	48	9	0	296
10	0	72	11	0	528
12	0	16	13	0	24
14	0	24	15	0	24
16	0	24	17	0	24
18	0	24	19	0	24
20	0	24	21	0	24
22	0	24	23	0	12
24	0	12	25	0	12
26	0	12	27	0	96
28	0	96	29	1760	0
30	48	0	31	648	0
32	648	0	33	48	0
34	288	0	35	64	0
38	64	0	39	96	0
40	8	0	41	72	0
42	9	0	43	9	0
44	18	0	45	8	0

Totals	Original	Covered	Not covered
POISONOUS	3916	3916	0
EDIBLE	4208	4208	0

Table 10.9   Final statistics showing the number of POISONOUS (P) and EDIBLE (E) examples covered by the rules for the mushroom data

10.6 Soya bean data

Soya bean data consisting of 302 examples was also obtained from the Irvine database. The 35 original input attributes are listed in Table 10.10 with their possible values. In the actual data file, the values of the input attributes were encoded numerically. The first value of each attribute is encoded as 0, the second as 1, and so on. This resulted in 83 distinct possible input values. Only 17 of the 19 original outputs associated with the soya beans were used and these are listed in Table 10.11. No examples existed for the 2 ignored outputs. All examples were used in the training set as the number of examples was small. A multi-layered neural network configuration of 83 original inputs, 17 outputs, and one hidden layer with 10 units was used.

No.	Attribute	Values
1	Date	April May June July August September October ?
2	Plant-stand	Normal Lt-normal ?
3	Precip	Lt-norm Norm Gt-norm ?
4	Temp	Lt-norm Norm Gt-norm ?
5	Hail	Yes No ?
6	Crop-hist	Diff-lst-year Same-lst-yr Same-lst-two-yrs Same-lst-sev-yrs ?
7	Area-damaged	Scattered Low-areas Upper-areas Whole-field ?
8	Severity	Minor Pot-severe Severe ?
9	Seed-tmt	None Fungicide Other ?
10	Germination	90-100per 80-89per Lt-80per ?
11	Plant-growth	Norm Abnorm ?
12	Leaves	Norm Abnorm ?
13	Leafspots-halo	Absent Yellow-halos No-yellow-halos ?
14	Leafspots-marg	W-s-marg No-w-s-marg Dna ?
15	Leafspot-size	Lt-1/8 Gt-1/8 Dna ?
16	Leaf-shread	Absent Present ?
17	Leaf-malf	Absent Present ?
18	Leaf-mild	Absent Upper-surf Lower-surf ?
19	Stem	Norm Abnorm ?
20	Lodging	Yes No ?
21	Stem-cankers	Absent Below-soil Above-soil Above-sec-nde ?
22	Canker-lesion	Dna Brown Dk-brown-blk Tan ?
23	Fruiting-bodies	Absent Present ?
24	External-decay	Absent Firm-and-dry Watery ?
25	Mycelium	Absent Present ?
26	Int-discolor	None Brown Black ?
27	Sclerotia	Absent Present ?
28	Fruit-pods	Norm Diseased Few-present Dna ?
29	Fruit-spots	Absent Colored Brown-w/blk-specks Distort Dna ?
30	Seed	Norm Abnorm ?
31	Mold-growth	Absent Present ?
32	Seed-discolor	Absent Present ?
33	Seed-size	Norm Lt-norm ?
34	Shriveling	Absent Present ?
35	Roots	Norm Rotted Galls-cysts ?

Table 10.10 Soya bean input attributes and their values

No.	Output name	Total exs
0	DIAPORTHE-STEM-CANKER	10
1	CHARCOAL-ROT	10
2	RHIZOCTONIA-ROOT-ROT	10
3	PHYTOPHTHORA-ROT	40
4	BROWN-STEM-ROT	20
5	POWDERY-MILDEW	10
6	DOWNY-MILDEW	10
7	BROWN-SPOT	40
8	BACTERIAL-BLIGHT	10
9	BACTERIAL-PUSTULE	10
10	PURPLE-SEED-STAIN	10
11	ANTHRACNOSE	20
12	PHYLLOSTICTA-LEAF-SPOT	10
13	ALTERNARIALEAF-SPOT	40
14	FROG-EYE-LEAF-SPOT	40
15	DIAPORTHE-POD-AND-STEM-BLIGHT	6
16	CYST-NEMATODE	6
		302

Table 10.11   Soya bean outputs

The initial products were determined for all of the outputs. The product list for each output contained some input attributes with a zero product measurement. These inputs are automatically identified with the corresponding output. A check was made to determine if the conjunction of the extracted input attributes with products of zero uniquely identified the corresponding output. For each of the following 10 outputs, the associated conjunctive rule was sufficient:

Output No.	Output name
0	DIAPORTHE-STEM-CANKER
1	CHARCOAL-ROT
2	RHIZOCTONIA-ROOT-ROT
3	PHYTOPHTHORA-ROT
4	BROWN-STEM-ROT
5	POWDERY-MILDEW
6	DOWNY-MILDEW
10	PURPLE-SEED-STAIN
15	DIAPORTHE-POD-AND-STEM-BLIGHT
16	CYST-NEMATODE

For outputs 8, 9, 11, and 12 (BACTERIAL-BLIGHT, BACTERIAL-PUSTULE, ANTHRACNOSE, and PHYLLOSTICTA-LEAF-SPOT) the guided generate-and-test procedure determined the appropriate unique disjunctive rules.

So far, a set of 28 conjunctive rules fully account for 14 of the outputs. Table 10.12 contains a sample of the resulting rules. Those covering 1 or 2 examples could be regarded as exceptions and/or noise. Table 10.13 lists the number of examples covered and the output for each of the 28 rules.

Rule 0 (covers 10 examples)
((Precip = 2) AND (Temp = 1) AND (Plant-growth = 1) AND (Leaves = 1) AND
    (Leafspot-marg= 2) AND (Leafspot-size = 2) AND (Stem = 1) AND
    (Stem-cankers = 3) AND (Fruiting-bodies = 1) AND (External-decay = 1) AND
    (Fruit-spots = 4))
⇒ (DIAPORTHE-STEM-CANKER)

Rule 3 (covers 40 examples)
((Plant-stand = 1) AND (Area-damaged = 1) AND (Plant-growth = 1) AND
    (Leaves = 1) AND (Stem = 1) AND (Canker-lesion = 2))
⇒ (PHYTOPHTHORA-ROT)

Rule 14 (covers 8 examples)
((Leaves = 1) AND (Leafspot-marg = 1))
⇒ (BACTERIAL-PUSTULE)

Rule 15 (covers 1 example)
((Date = 4) AND (Plant-stand = 1) AND (Precip = 2) AND (Temp = 1) AND
    (Crop-hist = 3) AND (Severity = 1) AND (Germination = 2) AND (Leaves = 1)
    AND
    (Leafspot-halo = 1) AND (Leaf-shread = 1) AND (Leaf-malf = 1) AND
    (Seed-size = 1) AND (Roots = 1) AND (Leafspot-marg != 1) AND
    (Roots != 3))
⇒ (BACTERIAL-PUSTULE)

Rule 17 (covers 17 examples)
((Precip = 2) AND (Leafspot-marg = 2) AND (Leafspot-size = 2) AND
    (Stem = 1) AND (Stem-cankers = 3) AND (Fruit-pods = 1) AND
    (Fruit-spots = 2))
⇒ (ANTHRACNOSE)

Rule 18 (covers 2 examples)
((Precip = 2) AND (Severity = 1) AND (Plant-growth = 1) AND (Leaves = 1) AND
    (Leafspot-marg = 2) AND (Leafspot-size = 2) AND (Stem = 1) AND
    (Stem-cankers = 2) AND (External-decay = 1) AND (Seed-tmt = 1) AND
    (Fruit-spots != 2))
⇒ (ANTHRACNOSE)

Table 10.12   Portion of the rules produced for the soya bean outputs (!= means not equal)

Rule No.	Exs covered	Output No. and name
0	10	0 DIAPORTHE-STEM-CANKER
1	10	1 CHARCOAL-ROT
2	10	2 RHIZOCTONIA-ROOT-ROT
3	40	3 PHYTOPHTHORA-ROT
4	20	4 BROWN-STEM-ROT
5	10	5 POWDERY-MILDEW
6	10	6 DOWNY-MILDEW
7	1	8 BACTERIAL-BLIGHT
8	2	8 BACTERIAL-BLIGHT
9	2	8 BACTERIAL-BLIGHT
10	2	8 BACTERIAL-BLIGHT
11	1	8 BACTERIAL-BLIGHT
12	1	8 BACTERIAL-BLIGHT
13	1	8 BACTERIAL-BLIGHT
14	9	9 BACTERIAL-PUSTULE
15	1	9 BACTERIAL-PUSTULE
16	10	10 PURPLE-SEED-STAIN
17	17	11 ANTHRACNOSE
18	2	11 ANTHRACNOSE
19	1	11 ANTHRACNOSE
20	2	12 PHYLLOSTICTA-LEAF-SPOT
21	2	12 PHYLLOSTICTA-LEAF-SPOT
22	1	12 PHYLLOSTICTA-LEAF-SPOT
23	1	12 PHYLLOSTICTA-LEAF-SPOT
24	3	12 PHYLLOSTICTA-LEAF-SPOT
25	1	12 PHYLLOSTICTA-LEAF-SPOT
26	6	15 DIAPORTHE-POD-AND-STEM-BLIGHT
27	6	16 CYST-NEMATODE

Table 10.13 Statistics on the first 28 rules produced for the soya bean data

The remaining three outputs 7, 13, and 14 (BROWN-SPOT, ALTERNARIALEAF-SPOT, and FROG-EYE-LEAF-SPOT) are closely related. For each output, the initial products for inputs 33, 35, and 40 were zero, with input 9 producing the next smallest product. In total, 46 rules were produced for these three outputs. As many of these rules cover only 1 or 2 examples, they may represent exceptions.

The rules 35, 40, 44, 45, and 56 misclassify some examples. This suggests that there was not enough discriminatory information in the attributes to separate some examples of different outputs clearly. As only a small number of examples is involved, the incorrect classifications can be regarded as noise.

This problem domain has once again highlighted the applicability of BRAINNE. First, if there is only one conjunctive rule defining an output, it is easily obtained. Second, if one or more unique rules define an output, then these are also easily determined using the guided generate-and-test procedure.

10.7 Submarine sonar data

A submarine sonar was used by Gorman and Sejnowski (1988a, 1988b) to study the application of neural networks to sonar target classification problems. The data demonstrates the success of neural networks in classifying complex continuous-valued signals for target discrimination (Gorman & Sejnowski 1988a, 1988b).

Two distinct groups are described in the data. The first group, consisting of 97 examples, is data identified as rocks, while the second group, consisting of 111 examples, is data identified as metal cylinders. The different aspect angle (Gorman & Sejnowski 1988a) for each example is disregarded in this analysis. Each example is defined by 60 original inputs denoted by f00 to f59. These inputs are a measure of the waveform of the sonar return at various intervals, pre-processed and normalized in the range of 0.0 to 1.0.

All of the input attributes in this data are continuous. Hence, this data set allows the testing of the extensions to BRAINNE that constitute Continuously BRAINNE. As stated in Chapter 9, Continuously BRAINNE directly considers the original 60 inputs. Other methods need to break up the continuous data into input classes. The threshold approach would result in 120 such input classes, whereas 600 classes would emerge from dividing each attribute into 10 ranges.

Both groups of data were placed into one data set of 208 examples, with the first 97 examples being ROCKS and the last 111 examples being MINES. This data set was then used to train the appropriate neural networks. The multi-layered network configuration consisted of 60 original inputs, 2 outputs, and one hidden layer with 6 hidden units. The initial products, as listed in Table 10.14, contained no clear cut-off point.

The guided generate-and-test procedure was required to determine the disjunctive rules for both the ROCKS and MINES outputs. For the ROCKS output, the attribute initially selected was f25, while attribute f27 began the process for the MINES output. Important aspects of Continuously BRAINNE's approach to continuous-valued attributes, such as the dynamic selection of the threshold and ranges for the various attributes, were enforced.

In total, 55 rules were determined (with $\theta = 0$ as discussed in Section 9.6) for this data: 27 defining the ROCKS output and 28 defining the MINES output. Some of these are listed in Table 10.15. There is a total of 14 rules

<table>
<tr><td colspan="3">
Total number of examples 208
Number of inputs 62
Number of hidden units 12
Total concepts 2
Total Sum of errors Squared 0.002929
(TSS from Back-propagation after 100 iterations)

OUTPUT 0 covers 97 examples
OUTPUT 1 covers 111 examples
</td></tr>
<tr><td colspan="3">
Some products for OUTPUT 0 = ROCKS
</td></tr>
<tr><td>56.665203 $\Rightarrow$ f13</td><td>54.376213 $\Rightarrow$ f38</td><td>53.190418 $\Rightarrow$ f37</td></tr>
<tr><td>52.518269 $\Rightarrow$ f14</td><td>52.506863 $\Rightarrow$ f39</td><td>47.140064 $\Rightarrow$ f15</td></tr>
<tr><td>45.904106 $\Rightarrow$ f36</td><td>45.264610 $\Rightarrow$ f16</td><td>44.754177 $\Rightarrow$ f17</td></tr>
<tr><td>44.282322 $\Rightarrow$ f32</td><td>44.123604 $\Rightarrow$ f18</td><td>43.780624 $\Rightarrow$ f31</td></tr>
<tr><td>43.349323 $\Rightarrow$ f34</td><td>42.973454 $\Rightarrow$ f33</td><td>41.321663 $\Rightarrow$ f35</td></tr>
<tr><td>40.213902 $\Rightarrow$ f19</td><td>36.312084 $\Rightarrow$ f20</td><td>35.346249 $\Rightarrow$ f30</td></tr>
<tr><td>35.190472 $\Rightarrow$ f21</td><td>34.083210 $\Rightarrow$ f29</td><td>31.620903 $\Rightarrow$ f22</td></tr>
<tr><td>29.196617 $\Rightarrow$ f28</td><td>27.967281 $\Rightarrow$ f23</td><td>26.335901 $\Rightarrow$ f24</td></tr>
<tr><td>25.961283 $\Rightarrow$ f27</td><td>24.206312 $\Rightarrow$ f26</td><td>23.666739 $\Rightarrow$ f25</td></tr>
<tr><td colspan="3">
Some products for OUTPUT 1 = MINES
</td></tr>
<tr><td>51.339863 $\Rightarrow$ f42</td><td>51.055347 $\Rightarrow$ f41</td><td>49.915173 $\Rightarrow$ f12</td></tr>
<tr><td>49.765480 $\Rightarrow$ f38</td><td>49.411346 $\Rightarrow$ f34</td><td>49.165798 $\Rightarrow$ f10</td></tr>
<tr><td>48.985374 $\Rightarrow$ f11</td><td>48.884819 $\Rightarrow$ f15</td><td>48.671833 $\Rightarrow$ f33</td></tr>
<tr><td>48.440441 $\Rightarrow$ f37</td><td>45.273731 $\Rightarrow$ f32</td><td>44.838913 $\Rightarrow$ f16</td></tr>
<tr><td>42.532089 $\Rightarrow$ f31</td><td>41.066536 $\Rightarrow$ f30</td><td>39.751701 $\Rightarrow$ f17</td></tr>
<tr><td>32.989300 $\Rightarrow$ f18</td><td>30.541697 $\Rightarrow$ f29</td><td>28.164150 $\Rightarrow$ f19</td></tr>
<tr><td>26.132879 $\Rightarrow$ f28</td><td>24.905298 $\Rightarrow$ f20</td><td>23.811323 $\Rightarrow$ f24</td></tr>
<tr><td>23.742918 $\Rightarrow$ f21</td><td>23.427261 $\Rightarrow$ f22</td><td>22.815380 $\Rightarrow$ f23</td></tr>
<tr><td>22.724586 $\Rightarrow$ f25</td><td>21.904711 $\Rightarrow$ f26</td><td>21.518208 $\Rightarrow$ f27</td></tr>
</table>

Table 10.14 Portion of the initial products for the sonar data

that cover only 1 example. A final check was made of all the examples. The statistics in Table 10.16 indicate that the 208 original examples are covered by the rules, with no misclassifications. In other words, all of the examples, without exception, are correctly classified by the determined rules, representing 100% accuracy.

The generalization capability of a set of rules is a measure of the ability to classify unseen examples correctly. To evaluate this generalization capability of the rules obtained by BRAINNE, 80% (167) of the examples were used to generate the rules. All of the 208 examples were used to test the rules. Using

Rule No. 0
$((0.432600 \leq f21 \leq 0.879300)$ AND $(0.554400 \leq f22 \leq 1.000000)$ AND
$(0.617300 \leq f23 \leq 0.936400)$ AND $(0.690500 \leq f24 \leq 0.928200)$ AND
$(0.693700 \leq f25 \leq 1.000000)$ AND $(0.567400 \leq f26 \leq 1.000000)$ AND
$(0.654000 \leq f27 \leq 0.985800)$ AND $(0.742300 \leq f28 \leq 1.000000)$ AND
$(0.661600 \leq f29 \leq 0.961900)$ AND $(0.492400 \leq f31 \leq 0.890300)$ AND
$(0.456300 \leq f32 \leq 0.970800)$ AND $(0.519700 \leq f34 \leq 0.991900))$
$\Rightarrow$ ROCKS

Rule No. 1
$((0.390300 \leq f21 \leq 0.765200)$ AND $(0.638400 \leq f22 \leq 0.920300)$ AND
$(0.747600 \leq f23 \leq 0.971900)$ AND $(0.702600 \leq f24 \leq 0.920700)$ AND
$(0.687400 \leq f25 \leq 0.940500)$ AND $(0.699700 \leq f26 \leq 1.000000)$ AND
$(0.855800 \leq f27 \leq 0.978500)$ AND $(0.730900 \leq f28 \leq 1.000000)$ AND
$(0.689600 \leq f29 \leq 0.962100)$ AND $(0.493500 \leq f31 \leq 0.757500)$ AND
$(0.310100 \leq f32 \leq 0.690200)$ AND $(0.024400 \leq f34 \leq 0.439600))$
$\Rightarrow$ ROCKS

Rule No. 27
$((0.476500 \leq f16 \leq 0.842600)$ AND $(0.582300 \leq f17 \leq 0.847600)$ AND
$(0.604100 \leq f18 \leq 0.903300)$ AND $(0.674900 \leq f19 \leq 0.958400)$ AND
$(0.708400 \leq f20 \leq 1.000000)$ AND $(0.789000 \leq f21 \leq 1.000000)$ AND
$(0.870500 \leq f22 \leq 1.000000)$ AND $(0.640300 \leq f23 \leq 1.000000)$ AND
$(0.506700 \leq f24 \leq 1.000000)$ AND $(0.539500 \leq f25 \leq 1.000000)$ AND
$(0.693400 \leq f26 \leq 0.989600)$ AND $(0.660000 \leq f27 \leq 0.995600)$ AND
$(0.551200 \leq f28 \leq 0.896200)$ AND $(0.401600 \leq f29 \leq 0.719600))$
$\Rightarrow$ MINES

Rule No. 28
$((0.334500 \leq f17 \leq 0.464600)$ AND $(0.523300 \leq f18 \leq 0.648700)$ AND
$(0.626000 \leq f19 \leq 0.726500)$ AND $(0.742000 \leq f20 \leq 0.834600)$ AND
$(0.745200 \leq f21 \leq 0.826800)$ AND $(0.794000 \leq f22 \leq 0.879300)$ AND
$(0.840000 \leq f23 \leq 1.000000)$ AND $(0.881000 \leq f24 \leq 0.986500)$ AND
$(0.881400 \leq f25 \leq 0.994500)$ AND $(0.930100 \leq f26 \leq 1.000000)$ AND
$(0.931500 \leq f27 \leq 1.000000)$ AND $(0.823700 \leq f28 \leq 0.903600)$ AND
$(0.606900 \leq f29 \leq 0.640900)$ AND $(0.229800 \leq f16 \leq 0.368500))$
$\Rightarrow$ MINES

Table 10.15 Portion of rules defining the sonar returns

the training set of 167 examples, a total of 46 rules were generated, with 11
rules covering only 1 example. The 46 rules uniquely cover the training set.
These rules were used to test the training set of 167 examples plus the 41
unseen examples with the ranges of the attributes as determined in the rules.
The range of each contributory attribute was then manually altered by reducing

Rule No.	ROCKS exs	MINES exs	Rule No.	ROCKS exs	MINES exs
0	12	0	1	3	0
2	3	0	3	1	0
4	4	0	5	1	0
6	7	0	7	6	0
8	3	0	9	3	0
10	7	0	11	1	0
12	10	0	13	1	0
14	4	0	15	4	0
16	1	0	17	5	0
18	3	0	19	2	0
20	5	0	21	2	0
22	1	0	23	5	0
24	3	0	25	2	0
26	1	0	27	0	12
28	0	6	29	0	10
30	0	1	31	0	2
32	0	3	33	0	5
34	0	6	35	0	1
36	0	4	37	0	2
38	0	8	39	0	1
40	0	2	41	0	2
42	0	4	43	0	8
44	0	3	45	0	2
46	0	5	47	0	2
48	0	6	49	0	1
50	0	1	51	0	4
52	0	7	53	0	2
54	0	1			

Totals	Original	Covered	Not covered
ROCKS output	97	97	0
MINES output	111	111	0

Table 10.16 Final statistics showing the number of examples covered by the rules for the sonar data

the minimum and increasing the maximum value of an attribute by the amount (max − min) * θ, where $\theta = 0.02$ (2%) and 0.05 (5%). The results were:

- 0% — in total 167 training + 10 unseen = 177 examples covered, including 2 incorrectly;
- 2% — in total 167 training + 19 unseen = 186 examples covered, including 12 incorrectly;

- 5% — in total 167 training + 26 unseen = 193 examples covered, including 17 incorrectly.

This example highlights the effectiveness of BRAINNE on continuous data where no pre-processing is necessary as the raw continuous signal had values in the range 0.0 to 1.0. Only after BRAINNE determines the contributory attributes for a rule is a technique used to determine the ranges of those attributes. The sonar data, containing only continuous-valued input attributes, illustrates the success of BRAINNE in domains with continuous real-world variables.

10.8 Iris plant data

This data, containing examples of 3 different types of Iris plant, was also obtained from the Irvine machine learning database. The 150 examples are each described by 4 numeric input attributes, as shown in Table 10.17.

Input No.	Name	Output No.	Name
0	Sepal-length (cm)	0	IRIS SETOSA
1	Sepal-width (cm)	1	IRIS VERSICOLOR
2	Petal-length (cm)	2	IRIS VIRGINICA
3	Petal-width (cm)		

Table 10.17 Inputs and outputs describing the Iris plants

First, the values of each of the input attributes were mapped into the range 0.0 to 1.0 using the following:

$$\text{Normalized Value} = \frac{\text{Actual Value} - \text{Min}}{\text{Max} - \text{Min}}$$

where Actual Value is the given original attribute value, and Min and Max are the minimum and maximum original values of the same attribute. The values that were used to normalize the input attributes are given in Table 10.18.

Input No.	Min	Max
0	4.3	7.9
1	2.0	4.4
2	1.0	6.9
3	0.1	2.5

Table 10.18 Maximum and minimum values for the original input attributes of the Iris plant domain

RULE 0
$((3.2 \leq$ Sepal-width $\leq 4.4)$ AND $(4.4 \leq$ Sepal-length $\leq 5.8))$
$\Rightarrow$ (IRIS SETOSA)
RULE 1
$((2.3 \leq$ Sepal-width $\leq 3.2)$ AND $(1.1 \leq$ Petal-length $\leq 1.6))$
$\Rightarrow$ (IRIS SETOSA)
RULE 2
$((6.3 \leq$ Sepal-length $\leq 7.0)$ AND $(3.0 \leq$ Sepal-width $\leq 3.3)$ AND
$(4.7 \leq$ Petal-length $\leq 5.0)$ AND $(1.4 \leq$ Petal-width $\leq 1.7))$
$\Rightarrow$ (IRIS VERSICOLOR)
RULE 3
$((6.0 \leq$ Sepal-length $\leq 6.9)$ AND $(4.4 \leq$ Petal-length $\leq 5.1)$ AND
$(1.3 \leq$ Petal-width $\leq 1.7)$ AND $(2.2 \leq$ Sepal-width $\leq 3.1))$
$\Rightarrow$ (IRIS VERSICOLOR)
RULE 4
$((5.8 \leq$ Sepal-length $\leq 7.0)$ AND $(4.0 \leq$ Petal-length $\leq 4.9)$ AND
$(1.0 \leq$ Petal-width $\leq 1.5))$
$\Rightarrow$ (IRIS VERSICOLOR)
RULE 5
$((3.2 \leq$ Sepal-width $\leq 3.546)$ AND $(4.5 \leq$ Petal-length $\leq 5.179)$ AND
$(1.3 \leq$ Petal-width $\leq 1.8)$ AND $(5.9 \leq$ Sepal-length $\leq 6.0))$
$\Rightarrow$ (IRIS VERSICOLOR)
RULE 6
$((3.9 \leq$ Petal-length $\leq 5.1)$ AND $(1.2 \leq$ Petal-width $\leq 1.6)$ AND
$(5.2 \leq$ Sepal-length $\leq 6.0)$ AND $(2.3 \leq$ Sepal-width $\leq 3.0))$
$\Rightarrow$ (IRIS VERSICOLOR)
RULE 7
$((3.0 \leq$ Petal-length $\leq 4.5)$ AND $(4.9 \leq$ Sepal-length $\leq 6.0)$ AND
$(1.0 \leq$ Petal-width $\leq 1.5))$
$\Rightarrow$ (IRIS VERSICOLOR)
RULE 8
$((6.2 \leq$ Sepal-length $\leq 7.9)$ AND $(5.1 \leq$ Petal-length $\leq 6.9)$ AND
$(1.6 \leq$ Petal-width $\leq 2.5)$ AND $(2.6 \leq$ Sepal-width $\leq 3.8))$
$\Rightarrow$ (IRIS VIRGINICA)
RULE 9
$((5.7 \leq$ Sepal-length $\leq 6.7)$ AND $(4.8 \leq$ Petal-length $\leq 5.8)$ AND
$(1.4 \leq$ Petal-width $\leq 2.4)$ AND $(2.2 \leq$ Sepal-width $\leq 3.0))$
$\Rightarrow$ (IRIS VIRGINICA)
RULE 10
$((4.5 \leq$ Petal-length $\leq 5.1)$ AND $(1.7 \leq$ Petal-width $\leq 2.0)$ AND
$(4.9 \leq$ Sepal-length $\leq 6.0)$ AND $(2.5 \leq$ Sepal-width $\leq 3.0))$
$\Rightarrow$ (IRIS VIRGINICA)

Table 10.19 Rules generated for the Iris plant database

The initial products determined for this domain contained no clear cut-off point. Therefore, the guided generate-and-test procedure was applied, with the extensions described in Chapter 9 to deal with continuous attributes. The 11 rules generated from this method with $\theta = 0$ are listed in Table 10.19. Table 10.20 contains the final classifications of the examples. Only Rule 3 incorrectly classifies any examples, and as only 2 examples in total are involved, these misclassifications can be regarded as noise.

Rule No.	Exs correctly classified	Exs misclassified
0	37	0
1	13	0
2	5	0
3	12	2
4	9	0
5	2	0
6	13	0
7	9	0
8	34	0
9	12	0
10	2	0
	148	2

Table 10.20   Final statistics for the rules generated for the Iris plant database

10.9 Engine diagnosis data

Engine diagnostics, consisting of a series of consecutive readings of steady-state data for an engine in which faults had been induced, were obtained from the Aeropropulsion Division of the Aeronautical Research Laboratory, Melbourne, Australia. The data was subjected to some initial smoothing, and mean and median filters were applied to remote outliers. As required by BRAINNE, the initial values were normalized.

There were 8 input attributes and 1 output associated with each of the 3738 examples. The data on the 16 possible subfaults was grouped to reflect generic faults. This resulted in a total of 7 generic faults. The input attributes and the outputs associated with the engine diagnostics are listed in Table 10.21.

A hidden layer with 6 hidden units gave the fastest convergence for Back-propagation training of the multi-layered neural network configuration. Some of the 16 rules produced for the subfaults are given in Table 10.22. Each of the resulting symbolic rules correctly classified the example data and produced no misclassifications.

No.	Input attributes
0	Low-pressure-spool-speed
1	High-pressure-spool-speed
2	Compressor-exit-pressure
3	Compressor-exit-temperature
4	Engine-pressure-ratio
5	Exhaust-gas-temperature
6	Fuel-flow
7	Exhaust-nozzle-area

No.	Subfaults	No.	Generic outputs
0	NFE	0	NO FAULT
1–3	CVG14 CVG28 CVG41	1	COMPRESSOR VARIABLE GEOMETRY FAULT
4–5	SGF55 SGF86	2	FUEL SPECIFIC GRAVITY FAULT
6–8	FVG51 FVG65 FVG83	3	FAN VARIABLE GEOMETRY FAULT
9–10	CBG14 CBG83	4	COMPRESSOR BLEED FAULT
11–12	A8H16 A8H45	5	EXHAUST NOZZLE FAULT
13–15	ECU30 ECU43 ECU60	6	ELECTRICAL CONTROL UNIT FAULT

Table 10.21 Inputs and outputs for the engine diagnosis data

This classification process was then abstracted further by seeking generic rules for the subfaults. The training data was grouped into generic faults by associating related subfaults. For example, subfaults A8H16 and A8H45, containing 75 and 187 examples respectively, were grouped into the one generic output of EXHAUST NOZZLE FAULT, with 75 + 187 = 262 examples.

For 4 of the 7 generic faults, unique rules were extracted covering all of the examples in the associated subgroups. Some of these rules are listed in Table 10.23. For the remaining 3 generic faults, the resulting rules correctly classified all of the relevant examples, but portions of the other faults were also covered. As these rules used most or all of the input attributes in their antecedents, there is not enough discriminatory information in the input attributes to distinguish between the faults. One of these rules is given in Table 10.24.

In some cases, an interesting relationship exists between the ranges of the contributory input attributes in the subfault rules and the ranges of the same attributes in the generic rules. Remember that all ranges are determined by BRAINNE, with no user input. The range in the generic rule for a particular attribute is the same as the combination of the ranges for the same attribute in the subfault rules. For instance:

RULE 0 (covers 75 correct examples, 0 incorrect examples)
((0.65 $\leq$ High-pressure-spool-area $\leq$ 0.80) AND
 (0.82 $\leq$ Compressor-exit-pressure $\leq$ 0.86) AND
 (0.70 $\leq$ Engine-pressure-ratio $\leq$ 0.87) AND
 (0.59 $\leq$ Exhaust-gas-temperature $\leq$ 0.61) AND (0.78 $\leq$ Fuel-flow $\leq$ 0.84)
AND (0.67 $\leq$ Exhaust-nozzle-area $\leq$ 0.89) AND
 (0.53 $\leq$ Compressor-exit-temperature $\leq$ 0.54))
$\Rightarrow$ (A8H16)   {exhaust nozzle fault}

RULE 1 (covers 187 correct examples, 0 incorrect examples)
((0.61 $\leq$ High-pressure-spool-area $\leq$ 0.75) AND
 (0.78 $\leq$ Compressor-exit-pressure $\leq$ 0.82) AND
 (0.62 $\leq$ Engine-pressure-ratio $\leq$ 0.77) AND (0.76 $\leq$ Fuel-flow $\leq$ 0.83) AND
 (0.68 $\leq$ Exhaust-nozzle-area $\leq$ 0.93) AND (0.66 $\leq$ Exhaust-gas-temperature
$\leq$ 0.70))
$\Rightarrow$ (A8H45)   {exhaust nozzle fault}

RULE 7 (covers 175 correct examples, 0 incorrect examples)
((0.92 $\leq$ Low-pressure-spool-area $\leq$ 1.00))
$\Rightarrow$ (ECU30)   {electrical control fault}

RULE 8 (covers 106 correct examples, 0 incorrect examples)

((0.85 $\leq$ Compressor-exit-pressure $\leq$ 0.88) AND
 (0.69 $\leq$ Engine-pressure-ratio $\leq$ 0.88) AND (0.79 $\leq$ Fuel-flow $\leq$ 0.86) AND
 (0.68 $\leq$ Exhaust-nozzle-area $\leq$ 0.97) AND
 (0.65 $\leq$ Compressor-exit-temperature $\leq$ 0.66))
$\Rightarrow$ (ECU43)   {electrical control fault}

Table 10.22 Portion of the rules produced by BRAINNE for the subfaults in the
engine diagnosis domain

- The clause involving the High-pressure-spool-area input from the rules for
  the 2 subfaults of EXHAUST NOZZLE FAULT are:

  RULE 0 (covers 75 correct examples, 0 incorrect examples)
  (0.65 $\leq$ High-pressure-spool-area $\leq$ 0.80)

  . . . . .

  $\Rightarrow$ (A8H16)   {exhaust nozzle fault}
  RULE 1 (covers 187 correct examples, 0 incorrect examples)
  (0.61 $\leq$ High-pressure-spool-area $\leq$ 0.75)

  . . . . .

  $\Rightarrow$ (A8H45)   {exhaust nozzle fault}

RULE 0 (covers 262 correct examples, 0 incorrect examples)
((0.61 ≤ High-pressure-spool-area ≤ 0.80) AND
 (0.78 ≤ Compressor-exit-pressure ≤ 0.86) AND
 (0.62 ≤ Engine-pressure-ratio ≤ 0.87) AND
 (0.59 ≤ Exhaust-gas-temperature ≤ 0.70) AND (0.76 ≤ Fuel-flow ≤ 0.84)
AND (0.67 ≤ Exhaust-nozzle-area ≤ 0.93) AND
 (0.49 ≤ Compressor-exit-temperature ≤ 0.54))
⇒ (EXHAUST NOZZLE FAULT)

RULE 9 (covers 561 correct examples, 0 incorrect examples)
((0.40 ≤ Low-pressure-spool-area ≤ 0.86) AND
 (0.66 ≤ High-pressure-spool-area ≤ 0.91) AND
 (0.60 ≤ Compressor-exit-pressure ≤ 0.91) AND
 (0.60 ≤ Compressor-exit-temperature ≤ 0.90) AND
 (0.58 ≤ Engine-pressure-ratio ≤ 0.90) AND
 (0.58 ≤ Exhaust-gas-temperature ≤ 0.89) AND (0.64 ≤ Fuel-flow ≤ 1.00)
AND (0.40 ≤ Exhaust-nozzle-area ≤ 1.00))
⇒ (FUEL SPECIFIC GRAVITY FAULT)

RULE 10 (covers 71 correct examples, 0 incorrect examples)
((0.60 ≤ High-pressure-spool-area ≤ 0.83) AND
 (0.85 ≤ Compressor-exit-pressure ≤ 0.86) AND
 (0.59 ≤ Compressor-exit-temperature ≤ 0.63) AND
 (0.70 ≤ Engine-pressure-ratio ≤ 0.87) AND
 (0.56 ≤ Exhaust-gas-temperature ≤ 0.66) AND (0.80 ≤ Fuel-flow ≤ 0.89)
AND (0.73 ≤ Exhaust-nozzle-area ≤ 1.00) AND
(0.40 ≤ Low-pressure-spool-area ≤ 0.46))
⇒ (FUEL SPECIFIC GRAVITY FAULT)

Table 10.23 Generic rules determined by BRAINNE for the engine diagnosis
domain

RULE 3 (covers 381 correct examples, 39 incorrect examples)
((0.71 ≤ High-pressure-spool-area ≤ 0.98) AND
 (0.67 ≤ Compressor-exit-pressure ≤ 0.87) AND
 (0.57 ≤ Engine-pressure-ratio ≤ 0.87) AND (0.58 ≤ Fuel-flow ≤ 0.81) AND
 (0.74 ≤ Exhaust-nozzle-area ≤ 0.93) AND
 (0.25 ≤ Compressor-exit-temperature ≤ 0.69))
⇒ (COMPRESSOR VARIABLE GEOMETRY FAULT)

Table 10.24 A generic rule that is not unique

- The clause involving the High-pressure-spool-area input from the generic rule defining EXHAUST NOZZLE FAULT is:

  RULE 0 (covers 262 correct examples, 0 incorrect examples)
  (0.61 ≤ High-pressure-spool-area ≤ 0.80)

  . . . . .

  ⇒ (EXHAUST NOZZLE FAULT)

  Hence, the ranges for High-pressure-spool-area from the subfault rules have been combined to give the range for the same attribute in the associated generic rule.

In order to evaluate the generalization ability of the rules obtained from Continuously BRAINNE, further testing was done. In total, 70% (2618) of the examples were used as a training set. Once again, 16 unique rules were produced. The coverage by these rules of the training set and the remaining unseen 30% (1119) of the examples was then determined for $\theta = 0$, giving:

(3672 examples covered)/(3737 tested examples) = 98.3%.

This generalization capability can be improved by adding a small threshold to each of the ranges of the continuous attributes in the determined rules. Manually reducing the minimum and increasing the maximum values of an attribute by the amount (max − min) * θ where $\theta = 0.1$ (10%) gave:

(3727 examples covered)/(3737 tested examples) = 99.7%.

In summary, BRAINNE was able to construct unique rules for the individual subfaults. In addition, rules covering the generic faults were produced for some cases. BRAINNE's ability to obtain rules for these higher abstractions is a useful facility as it increases the comprehensibility of the rules.

10.10 Recapitulation

This chapter has illustrated the successful application of BRAINNE in many diverse domains, including symbolic problem domains with discrete data and numeric domains with continuous-valued data. The rules generated by BRAINNE are understandable to humans, and can be used in other knowledge-based systems or for data reduction. These rules can also be employed in explanation-type reasoning for a neural network, in a manner similar to an expert system. The results reported in the chapter show that BRAINNE is versatile and capable in real-world domains.

All of the rules generated by BRAINNE do not require expert input. In other words, BRAINNE is totally automated. Thus, the rules determined may not be those produced or used by an expert, particularly with regard to the ranges of the continuous attributes. However, the labels generally employed by an expert can be incorporated into BRAINNE with appropriate pre-processing. The resulting rules will then contain terms familiar to the expert.

References

Gorman, R.P. & Sejnowski, T.J. 1988a, "Analysis of hidden units in a layered network trained to classify sonar targets", *Neural Networks*, vol. 1, pp. 75–89

Gorman, R.P. & Sejnowski, T.J. 1988b, "Learned classification of sonar targets using a massively parallel network", *IEEE Transactions on Acoustics, Speech, and Signal Processing (ASSP)*, vol. 36, no. 7, July, pp. 1135–40

11

Unsupervised BRAINNE — automated knowledge acquisition using unsupervised learning

11.1 Introduction

Several previously developed methods for automated knowledge acquisition have been discussed in the preceding chapters. These include methods based on decision trees, as described in Chapter 2 (Breiman et al. 1984; Quinlan 1986, 1987a–b; Zhou & Dillon 1988, 1989, 1991a–b), progressive rule generation, as described in Chapter 3 (Michalski 1983; Michalski et al. 1986), and supervised neural networks, as described in Chapters 8, 9, and 10 (Sestito & Dillon 1989, 1990a–c, 1991a–b, 1992, 1993). One striking similarity between these methods is the nature of the data set they use during learning. In the data set, each example is always composed of the input values or attributes and the corresponding target output value. This type of learning, called supervised learning, is commonly described as learning with a teacher, since the desired output of a given input vector is known and used during the learning process.

However, in some real-world situations, supervised learning is not possible. There are many cases where only the input vector is known and the corresponding target output vector is not known. Indeed, in some cases the possible output classes themselves are not known. Clearly the previous methods presented are not applicable in these situations. One approach to dealing with such data is given in Stepp III and Michalski (1986). In this chapter, a method based on neural networks is presented that learns symbolic knowledge representations using unsupervised learning.

11.2 Supervised and unsupervised learning

The process of learning can be categorized into supervised and unsupervised learning. Supervised learning requires a training set composed of input patterns with associated target or desired outputs. The target output acts like an external *teacher* to the network, evaluating its behavior and directing its subsequent modifications. The situation is analogous to being given a mathematics problem, as well as the solution. This is illustrated in Figure 11.1.

In unsupervised learning the training set consists solely of input patterns. Hence, during learning no comparison with predetermined desired responses on which to base subsequent modifications can be performed by the learning algorithm. There is therefore no external teacher in the sense described earlier. This situation is similar to being given a mathematics problem without the solution to guide the learning. Two cases can be distinguished in unsupervised learning:

- the possible outputs or clusters are known in advance even though the mappings of the input points to these are not given in the training data set, as shown in Figure 11.2(a);
- the possible outputs or clusters are not known in advance, as shown in Figure 11.2(b).

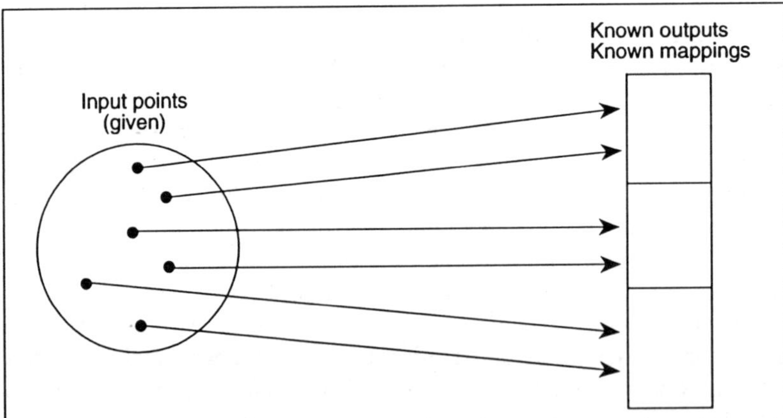

Figure 11.1 A training set for supervised learning

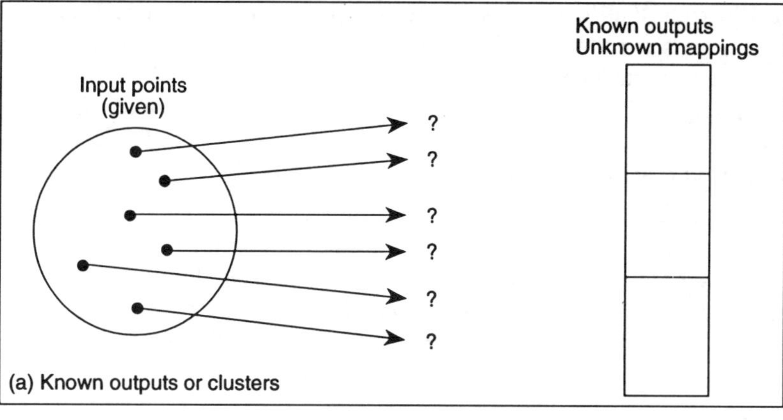

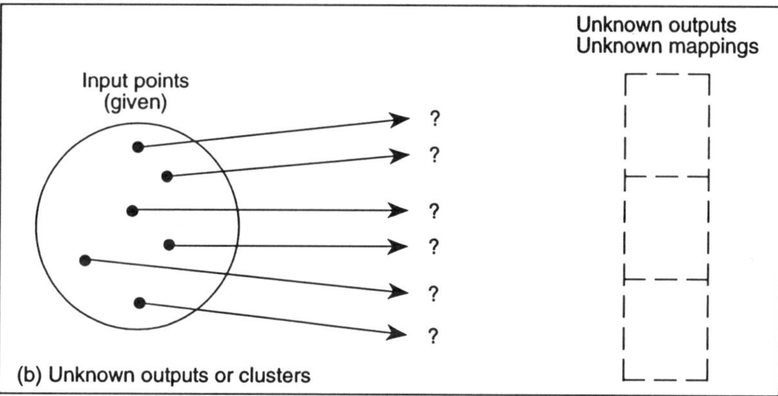

Figure 11.2 Training sets for unsupervised learning

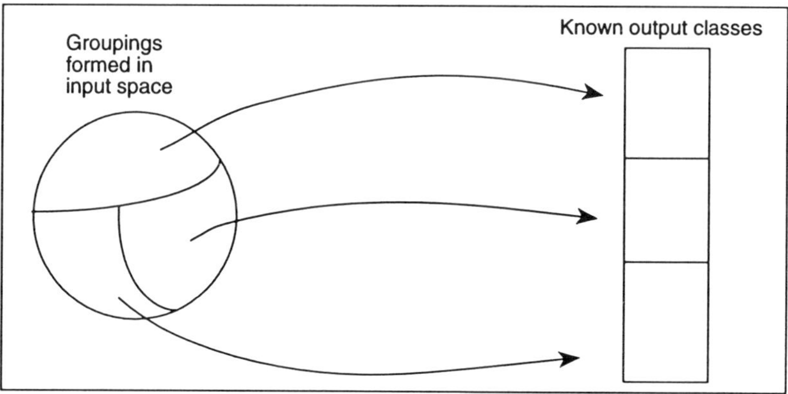

Figure 11.3 Partitions developed and the mapping determined in supervised learning

To illustrate the differences between supervised and unsupervised training data sets, consider the training set in Table 11.1. A corresponding version of this data set for unsupervised training is given in Tables 11.2(a) and 11.2(b). The mapping of the input space to the known outputs after supervised learning is shown in Figure 11.3. In contrast, the partitions of the input space developed after unsupervised learning are shown in Figure 11.4.

example 1	(Hair, Milk, Gray, Medium) $\Rightarrow$ (KANGAROO)
example 2	(Feathers, Egglaying, White, Medium) $\Rightarrow$ (PELICAN)
example 3	(Swims, Medium, Black) $\Rightarrow$ (TUNA)
example 4	(Swims, Large, Gray) $\Rightarrow$ (DOLPHIN)
example 5	(Swims, Large, White) $\Rightarrow$ (WHALE)

Table 11.1   A training set of example data

example 1	(Hair, Milk, Gray, Medium) $\Rightarrow$?
example 2	(Feathers, Egglaying, White, Medium) $\Rightarrow$?
example 3	(Swims, Medium, Black) $\Rightarrow$?
example 4	(Swims, Large, Gray) $\Rightarrow$?
example 5	(Swims, Large, White) $\Rightarrow$?
Possible outputs or clusters	KANGAROO, PELICAN, TUNA, DOLPHIN, WHALE

Table 11.2   (a)   Unsupervised training set with known outputs or clusters for the examples

example 1	(Hair, Milk, Gray, Medium) $\Rightarrow$?
example 2	(Feathers, Egglaying, White, Medium) $\Rightarrow$?
example 3	(Swims, Medium, Black) $\Rightarrow$?
example 4	(Swims, Large, Gray) $\Rightarrow$?
example 5	(Swims, Large, White) $\Rightarrow$?
Possible outputs or clusters	Unknown

Table 11.2   (b)   Unsupervised training set with unknown outputs or clusters for the examples

Consider the unsupervised learning case, illustrated in Figure 11.2(a) and Table 11.2(a), in which there are known clusters or outputs. However, no prior knowledge is available regarding an input's membership of a particular class. Gradually detected commonality between certain patterns is used to assist the learning method in defining possible boundaries within the input space that correspond to particular clusters. The similarity of input patterns

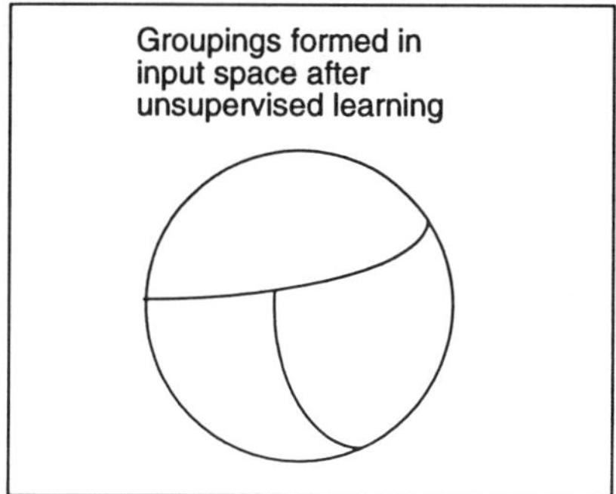

Figure 11.4 Partitions developed in unsupervised learning

can be used as the criterion for clustering the input data. The Euclidean distance between two patterns provides a measure of this similarity (Suing 1992; Zurada 1992).

The Euclidean distance between the two input patterns X and X_i, where X_i is known to belong to cluster i, is defined as:

$$|X - X_i| = [(X - X_i)^t (X - X_i)]^{1/2}$$

where $(X - X_i)^t$ is the transpose of the vector $(X - X_i)$. A threshold distance T is chosen to be the maximum permissible distance between two patterns in the same cluster. Thus if $|X - X_i| \leq T$, then X and X_i belong to the same cluster i. There are other alternative measures that could be used. The final situation after unsupervised learning with known clusters is depicted in Figure 11.5.

Unsupervised learning can also be used to carry out cluster discovery when

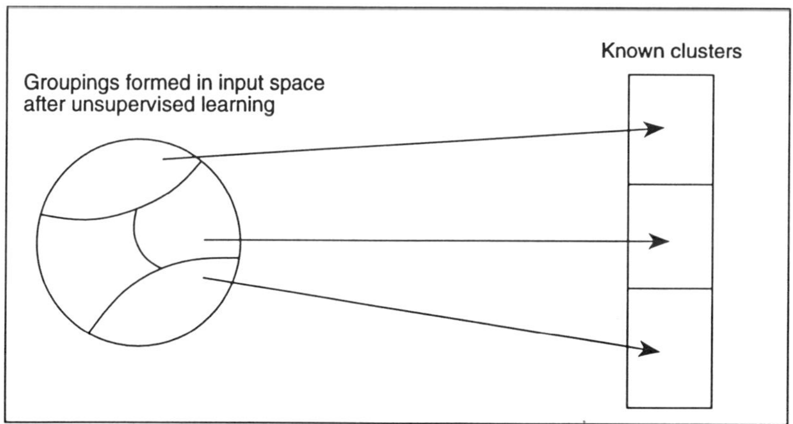

Figure 11.5 Partitions developed and the mapping allocated of the input space to the known clusters after unsupervised learning

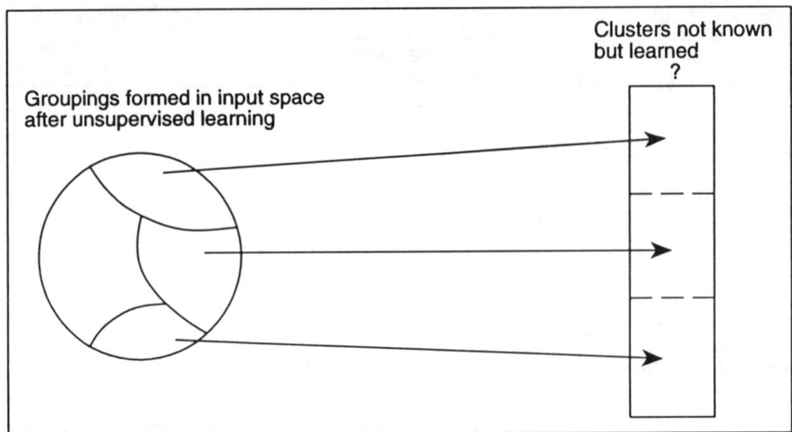

Figure 11.6 Identification of formed clusters

the clusters are not known in advance, as in Figure 11.2(b) and Table 11.2(b). The learning method determines the clusters by itself, without prior information about the possible number and nature of clusters. Essentially the learning method *follows the leader* after it designates the first cluster based on the first input pattern processed. It next examines other patterns, treating each as follows:

- If the Euclidean distance between the input pattern under consideration and a pattern from one of the existing identified clusters is less than a certain threshold, the input pattern is assigned to that existing cluster.
- If the Euclidean distance exceeds this threshold for all existing clusters, another cluster is defined.

This process of pattern inspection involves the learning method computing the measure of similarity of the present input to the previously determined clusters. The final clustering information about the patterns or features is stored, as depicted in Figure 11.6. If possible, the formed clusters may be given a physical interpretation in the real world. Otherwise they are abstractions that are given symbolic labels.

11.3 Unsupervised learning of symbolic knowledge structures

11.3.1 The problem outlined

The objective is to determine symbolic knowledge structures that characterize a problem domain from a given set of input patterns not labeled with an output class. No information is available that links a given input pattern to a target output class. Indeed, the output classes (or clusters) and their nature or number may not be known in advance. After the knowledge acquisition phase is completed:

- the output classes are determined
- a set of symbolic knowledge structures (such as production rules) that classify a given input according to these output classes is obtained.

This is illustrated in Figure 11.7. In this chapter, data sets containing only discrete attributes are considered. The input values are always normalized to the range 0 to 1 inclusive.

11.3.2 The network chosen

In unsupervised learning, a method able to learn from a data set containing no target output patterns associated with each example is needed. Several classes of neural networks have been successful in learning from such data sets. For the reasons given in Chapter 6, it is worthwhile to explore whether one of these could form the basis of a method for extracting symbolic knowledge representations that characterize such a data set. Among the neural networks that can perform unsupervised learning are:

- Kohonen nets (Kohonen 1982, 1984, 1988, 1990)
- ART nets (Carpenter & Grossberg 1988)
- Neocognitron (Fukushima 1980).

Of these, the Kohonen network is chosen as the most suitable for this study (Dillon et al. 1993; Suing 1992). Unlike some of the other neural networks, the Kohonen network is simple in structure, with no hidden layers or complex feedback to complicate the nature of the network's configuration. Its learning algorithm is straightforward and no tedious computations are needed. It also offers the ability to find clusters in the data and performs an ordered or topology preserving mapping that reveals existing similarities in the input vectors.

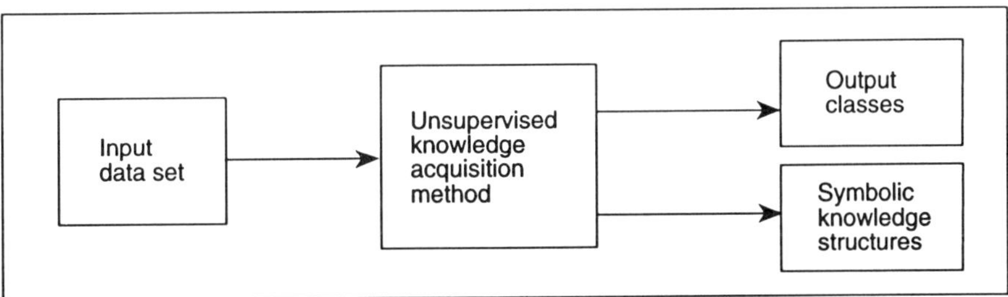

Figure 11.7 Unsupervised knowledge acquisition

11.4 Kohonen networks

11.4.1 Structure

The Kohonen net, first developed by Teuvo Kohonen over the period 1979–1982, is a self-organizing network. It forms abstractions by mapping high-dimensional input patterns into a lower-dimensional set of output clusters (Zeidenberg 1990).

In a typical Kohonen network, output units are arranged in a two-dimensional grid. However, it is possible to use one or more dimensions. This grid of output units is usually referred to as a Kohonen layer. All units in the input layer are fully connected to the units in the Kohonen layer. Feedback is restricted to lateral interconnections with immediately neighboring units in the Kohonen layer, as illustrated in Figure 11.8. The network structure in this figure is used in the discussion in the rest of this chapter.

11.4.2   Clustering

Each link between an input and an output has an associated weight. The net input into each neuron in the Kohonen layer is equal to the weighted sum of the inputs. Learning proceeds by modifying these weights from an assumed initial distribution with the presentation of each input pattern vector. The final weight matrix is the end product of this learning. This process identifies

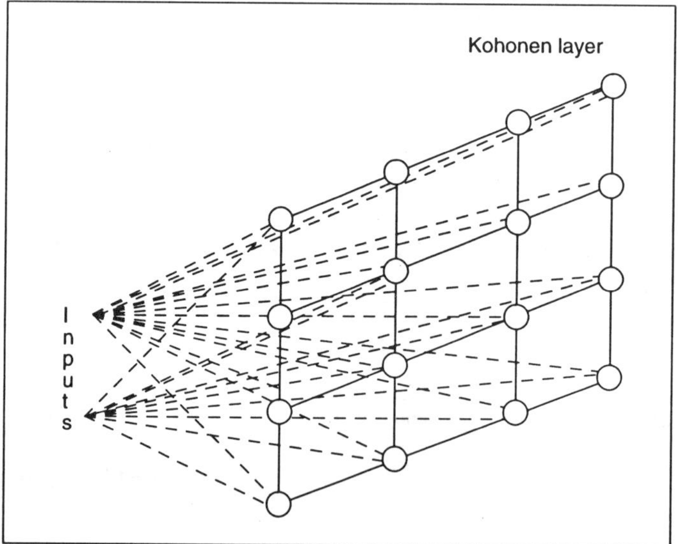

Figure 11.8 Structure of a typical Kohonen network

groups of nodes in the output layer that are close to each other and respond in a similar manner. A particular group of units together forms an output cluster. Thus, each output cluster is identified not necessarily with only one node, but with a group of nodes, as shown in Figure 11.9. Such a system is said to be topologically organized. The mappings to the clusters reflect the existing similarities in the inputs. This is sometimes referred to as a topology preserving mapping (Kohonen 1984), as it captures any regularities and statistical features, and models the probability distributions present in the input data.

11.4.3 Competitive learning

A central aspect of a Kohonen network is that it uses *competitive learning*. When an input pattern is imposed on the network, an output node is selected from among all the output nodes as having the *best response* according to some criterion. This output unit is declared the winner in the competition among all the neurons in the output layer. Only the winning neuron generates an output signal from the output layer. All the other neurons have a zero output signal, as Figure 11.10 illustrates. The notion of *best response* in a Kohonen net can be determined by the Euclidean distance. The winner is the neuron with the smallest Euclidean distance between the presented input vector pattern and its weight vector. The output neuron with a weight vector *closest* to the prescribed input vector pattern thus becomes the winner.

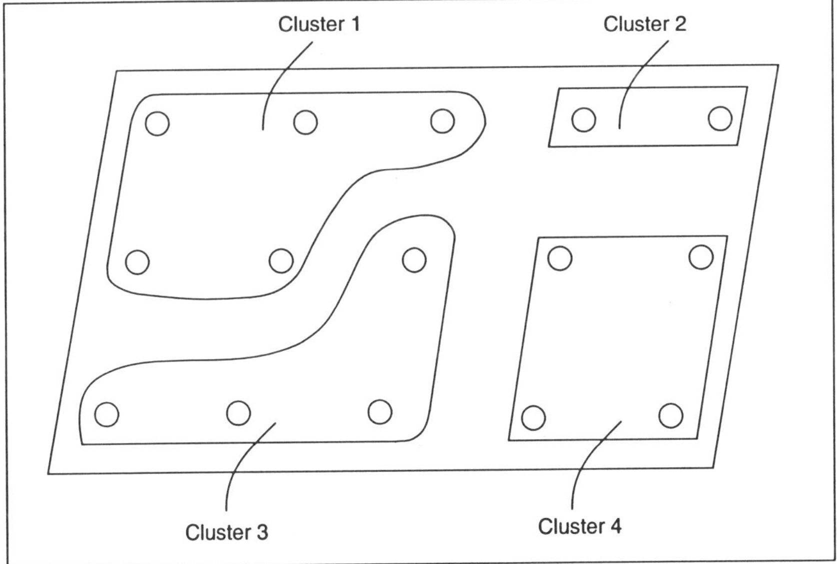

Figure 11.9 Illustrative cluster structure developed in the Kohonen layer

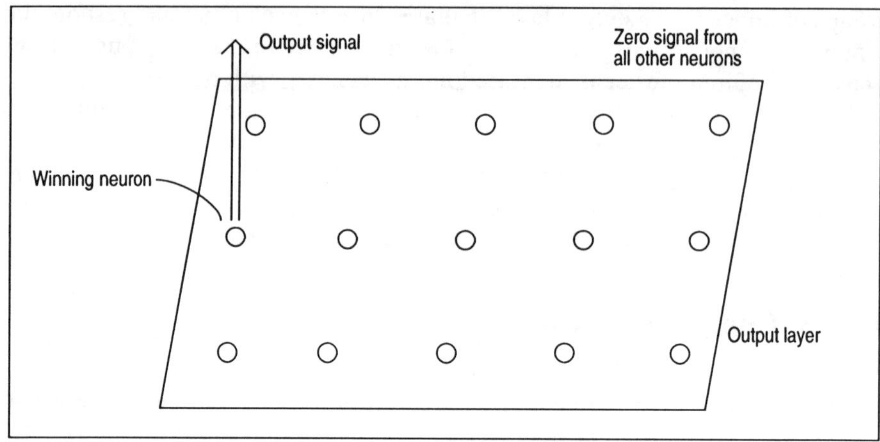

Figure 11.10 Winning neuron only outputs a signal

The input and weight vectors are usually normalized in a Kohonen net. Consider a normalized set of weight vectors $\hat{W}j$ lying around a unit circle, with the normalized input vector $\hat{X}$ displayed graphically on the same circle (Caudill 1987), as shown in Figure 11.11. If the dot products between the input and weight vectors are determined, the neuron with the largest dot product (i.e., the one with the smallest Euclidean distance) is declared to be the winner. Thus the winner is the vector obtained from the expression:

$$\max_{j} (\hat{X}^{t}\hat{W}_{j}).$$

As learning involves adjustment of weight vectors, the importance of determining the winner resides in the fact that only the neurons within a small region around the winner are allowed to learn with this particular input pattern. Learning for the nodes in this region is carried out by adjusting their weights closer to the input vector, as shown in Figure 11.12. This region around the winner is referred to as the neighborhood of the winning neuron. The neighborhood is defined by physical proximity of the neurons to the winning neuron. The size of the neighborhood is initially chosen to be fairly large, and may include all units in the Kohonen layer. Hence, a large number of neurons have their weights adjusted at the start. However, as learning proceeds, the size of the neighborhood is progressively reduced to a pre-defined limit, as shown in Figure 11.13. Thus during the latter stages, fewer neurons have their weights adjusted closer to the input vector. Lateral inhibition of weight vectors that are distant from a particular input pattern may also be carried out, as shown in Figure 11.14.

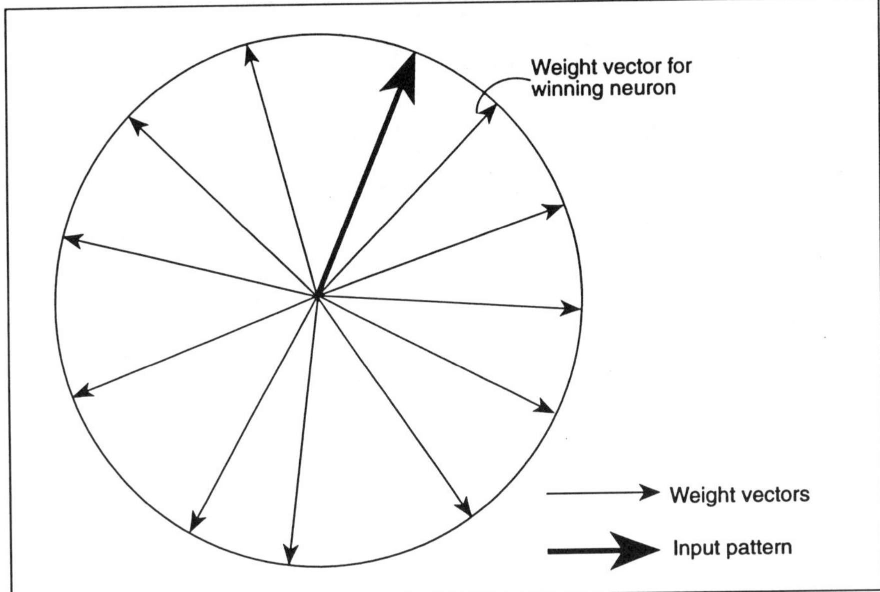

Figure 11.11 Graphical representation of competition between neurons

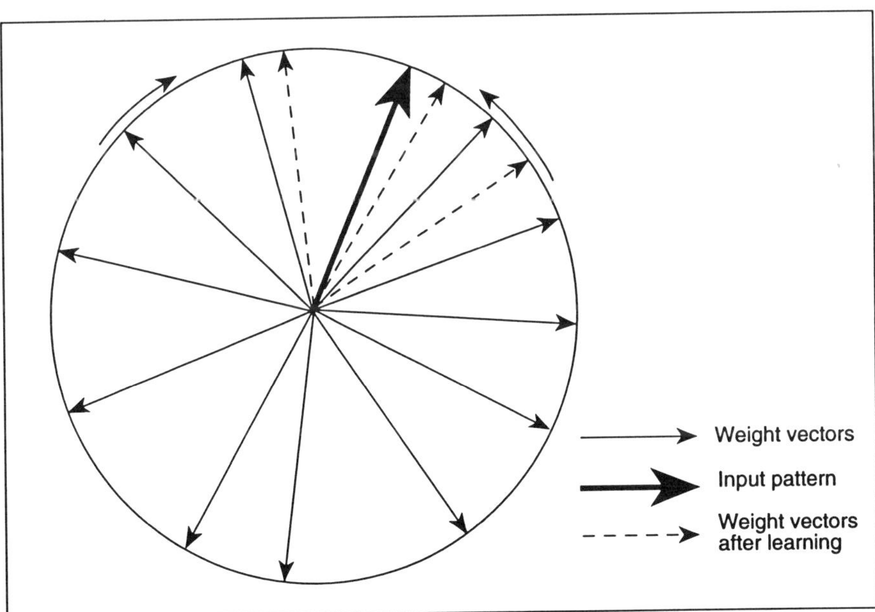

Figure 11.12 Learning adjustment of weight vectors in the neighborhood of the winning neuron

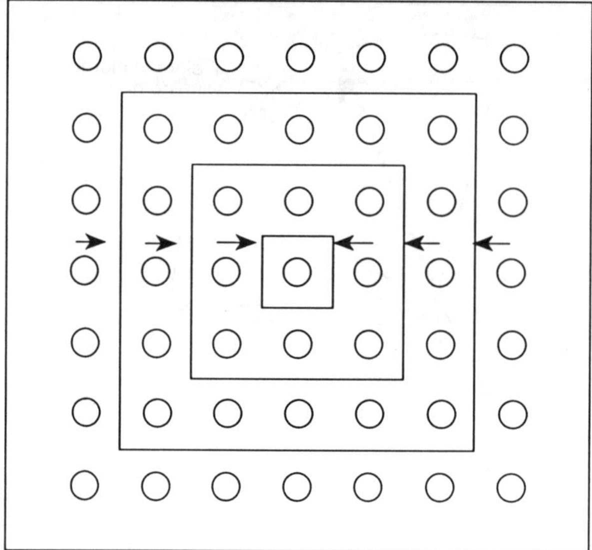

Figure 11.13 The changing size of the neighborhood

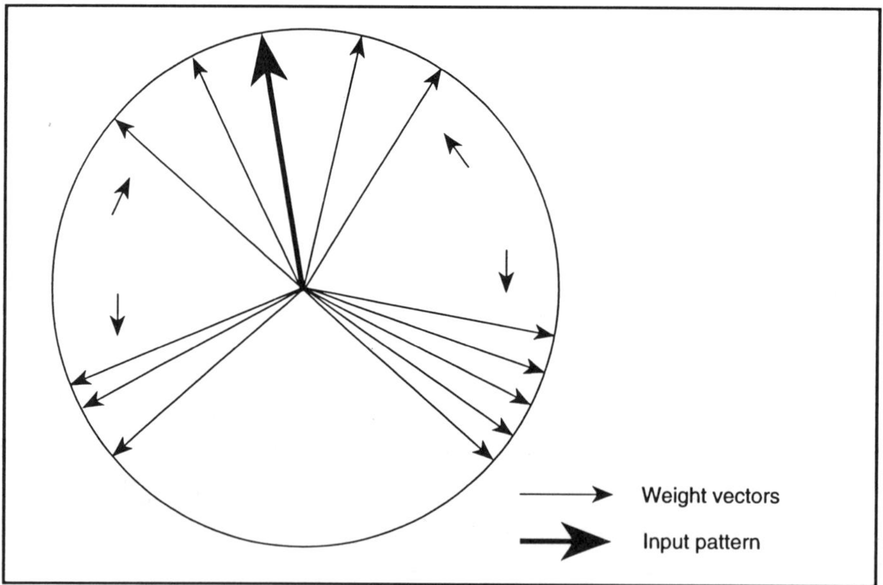

Figure 11.14 Illustrating lateral inhibition

Beale and Jackson (1990) provide the following formula for updating the weights of the winning node j* and the nodes within its neighborhood of size $N_{j*}(t)$, where $W_{ij}(t)$ is the weight from input i to node j:

$$W_{ij}(t+1) = W_{ij}(t) + \eta(t)(X_i(t) - W_{ij}(t))$$

For j in $N_{j*}(t)$, $0 \leq i \leq n-1$

The term $\eta(t)$ is a gain term $(0 < \eta(t) < 1)$ that decreases in time, so slowing the weight adaption. Notice that the neighbourhood $N_{j*}(t)$ decreases in size as time goes on, thus localising the area of maximum activity.

There is existing anatomical and physiological evidence that lateral interaction between cells in the brain can be one of the following types (Kohonen 1982):

- short-range lateral excitation in a small region
- inhibitory action surrounding the excitatory area
- weaker excitatory action surrounding the inhibitory area.

The Mexican hat function given in Figure 11.15 is a plausible model of the effect of the lateral interconnections described above. Kohonen introduced the concept of topological neighborhoods in his system in an attempt to implement these types of inhibitory and excitatory interconnections in his network.

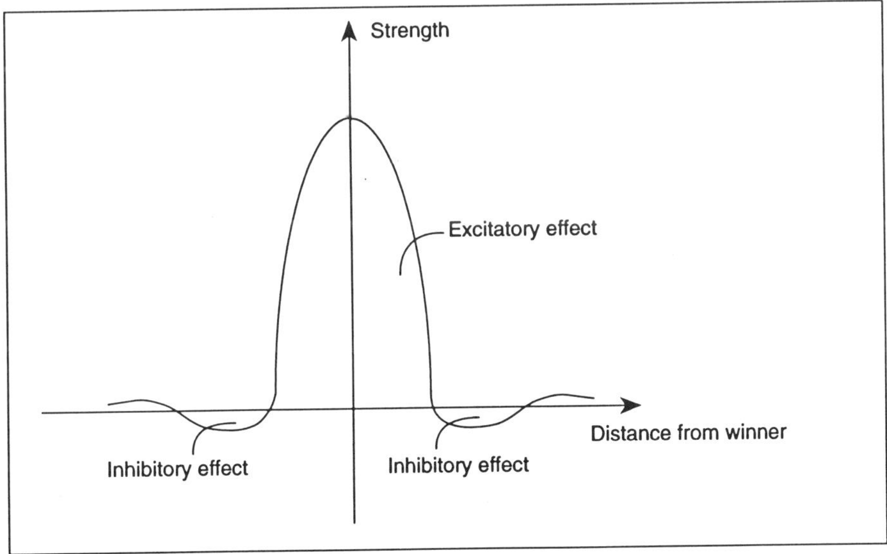

Figure 11.15 Mexican hat function

11.4.4 Learning algorithm

The basic function that the learning algorithm performs is to organize the units in the grid into local neighborhoods that act as feature classifiers on the input vectors. As the learning is unsupervised, no training response is specified for any training input. Therefore, from a randomly organized set of units the grid settles into a feature map that has local representation and is self-organized (Beale & Jackson 1990).

A general algorithm for the Kohonen net follows:

1. Initialize weights to small random values and set the initial neighborhood to be large.
2. Stimulate the net with a given input vector.
3. Calculate the Euclidean distance between the input and each output node and select the output with the minimum distance.
4. Update weights for the selected node and the nodes within its neighborhood.
5. Repeat from 2.

Step 1 involves suitable initialization of the weight vectors. One approach is to set each weight vector equal to an input vector pattern. This is acceptable when there are more training input patterns than output units. When there are equal numbers of output units and training input patterns, the units simply memorize each pattern. Hence this approach performs best with very large networks and training sets. In the algorithm used in Unsupervised BRAINNE, the weight vectors are initialized using normalized input patterns so that every vector component lies in the range 0 to 1 inclusive.

Another important issue is the normalization of the weight and input vectors. According to Caudill (1988), modeling correct statistical features requires normalization procedures that are appropriate for those features. Simple Euclidean normalization may not extract the desired statistics. Unsupervised BRAINNE uses weight vector and input vector components that are normalized to values between 0 and 1 inclusive. If necessary, the input vectors can be translated to ensure every component has a value in the required range.

Kohonen (1982) reports some *special effects* that have been experienced in particular implementations. These include:

- *Boundary Effects* caused by one-sided interaction of the boundary nodes;
- *Pinch Phenomenon* where the distribution of weight vectors falls in a ring-like structure instead of a planar configuration;
- *Collapse Phenomenon* where the final vectors have roughly the same value;
- *Focusing Phenomenon* where one or two units dominate the learning process.

11.5 Extraction of symbolic knowledge

As with the supervised learning techniques in Chapters 7 to 10, the symbolic knowledge to be extracted from the Kohonen net is in the form of:

- production rules
- concepts and a related concept hierarchy.

The first stage of processing consists of deleting all irrelevant attributes included in the training data set that have no influence on distinguishing between any output nodes. The weight components from an irrelevant input to all the output nodes are all zero. These inputs and their corresponding attributes are not considered further in the analysis.

The next stage of the process consists of extraction of a set of rules that map the input nodes into output nodes. Through this, clusters of output nodes are designated. If there is a real-world significance for each of these clusters, they are given a label expressing these semantics. This process assigns an output node to a particular output class. If, however, a particular cluster has no real-world meaning, a virtual cluster name can be used.

The output classes or clusters are concepts in the sense described in Chapter 7; that is, collections of attributes and their values that constitute the definition or intension of the concept. The antecedents of the rules that define these concepts consist of *contributory inputs* and *inhibitory inputs*. Rules that have all the possible inputs represented as contributory or inhibitory in the antecedent are taken as production rules belonging to the lowest-level concepts in a concept hierarchy. Any rules with *don't care* designations for certain inputs, in addition to the contributory and inhibitory inputs, are explored further to determine if they are higher-level concepts in the hierarchy. The inputs that are not contributory or inhibitory are taken to be *don't care*.

The set of rules containing *don't cares*, hereafter called the *set with don't cares,* is initially re-stated with contributory inputs only in the antecedents. Contributory inputs alone are considered when exploring common features in lower-level concepts. This avoids the problem that the negation of an input may arise from too few examples of a lower sub-concept. Using the approach outlined in Chapter 7, the concepts can be arranged into a ISA hierarchy, where concepts lower in the hierarchy represent specializations of higher-lying concepts. The concepts in the *set with don't cares* that are found to be higher-level concepts are retained in their re-stated form; that is, with contributory inputs only in the antecedents. However, the concepts in the *set with don't cares* that are not higher-lying concepts have their inhibitory inputs restored to the antecedents. These concepts are then examined to determine if they correspond to lowest-level concepts in the domain. If not, they are treated as unidentified boundary nodes between clusters and are processed no further.

At this stage, a large number of the output nodes are allocated to particular output classes or clusters, a set of production rules is defined, and a concept hierarchy is identified. Note that only those nodes allocated to clusters have been examined. Any remaining single nodes are unexplored and unclassified. They may represent intermediate concepts (if they have *don't care* inputs), not explicitly known when the initial allocation of clusters was labeled. If that is the case, these unclassified nodes are labeled as new concepts and inserted at the appropriate place in the hierarchy. Otherwise, they are treated as boundary nodes between clusters that cannot be classified, a phenomenon that sometimes occurs with Kohonen nets (Kohonen 1990). If the number of unidentified nodes is too large, the granularity of the output nodes may not be high enough. The unsupervised learning with the Kohonen net is then repeated with different output grid dimensions.

11.5.1 Extraction of production rules

Production rules consist of condition/action pairs of the form:

IF A THEN B.

The condition part could be a compound form consisting of a number of predicates joined together with connectives. In this section we discuss two different approaches for extracting conjunctive rules from the Kohonen network. These techniques are referred to as:

- the Threshold technique
- the Breakpoint technique.

Threshold technique

In a Kohonen network, each output node is connected to every input node, with the strength of the interconnection reflected in the associated weight vector. The larger the weight vector associated with a link, the greater is the contribution of the corresponding input node to the output node. The input with the largest weight link makes the largest contribution to the output node. Therefore, the one or more largest components of the weight vector associated with a particular output can be taken as contributory to that output. However, as explained in Chapter 7, with problems such as noise inherent in real-world domains, the component weights within a certain limit of the maximum value should be considered.

To determine the *contributory inputs* from the N input nodes, the maximum weight component in the weight vector associated with the output unit j is first found by:

$$W_{maxj} = \max(W_{1j}, W_{2j}, ..., W_{Nj})$$

where $W_{maxj} > \varepsilon$, for ε a positive number between 0 and 1. If the largest weight component is less than the designated ε, none of the inputs is considered to be contributory to the output node. All inputs i are included as contributory inputs in the antecedent of the rule for output node j if:

$$|W_{maxj} - W_{ij}| < T$$

where the threshold T is a positive number between 0 and 1. This procedure is repeated in turn for each of the output nodes. T is usually chosen to reflect the noise in the data and a value of about 10% is frequently acceptable. These contributory inputs are joined by the AND connective in the antecedent.

In addition to determining those inputs with an excitatory effect on an output, it is useful to characterize the inputs with a strong inhibitory effect for the reasons given in Section 6.5. These *inhibitory inputs* have weight vector components that are close to zero. A small threshold near zero delineates the group of inhibitory inputs. Each inhibitory input is treated by ANDing its negation in the associated antecedent. Hence, all inputs i such that $W_{ij} < T_{inh}$, where T_{inh} is the inhibitory threshold value, are negated in the antecedent. The inputs that are not selected as either contributory or negated inputs are treated as *don't care* in the related rule.

Consider the weight vector from the seven inputs A, B, C, D, E, F, and G to an output node j below:

$$\begin{aligned} W_{maxj} &= \max(W_{Aj}, W_{Bj}, W_{Cj}, W_{Dj}, W_{Ej}, W_{Fj}, W_{Gj}) \\ &= \max(0.430, 0.430, 0.430, 0.000, 0.420, 0.430, 0.200) \\ &= 0.430 \end{aligned}$$

Assuming $\varepsilon = 0.2$, $T = 0.1$, and $T_{inh} = 0.05$, the inputs A, B, C, E, and F are considered contributory to the output node j, and input D is considered inhibitory. The input G is a *don't care* input attribute. The resulting antecedent for the rule associated with the output node j is:

A AND B AND C AND E AND F AND NOT D.

Breakpoint technique

First the components of the weight vector associated with a particular output are sorted in descending order. Then the existence of a clear breakpoint in this sorted list, such that one component is at least β times larger than the next component, is investigated. Normally β is chosen to be equal to 2 or 3. If such a breakpoint exists, those inputs with weight components greater than or equal to the breakpoint are the *contributory inputs* in the antecedent for the relevant production rule. In summary, for output node j:

- Sort $\quad W_j \quad = (W_{1j}, W_{2j}, ..., W_{Nj})$
  into a list $\quad W_{sortj} = [W_{.j}^2, W_{.j}^2, ..., W_{.j}^k, W_{.j}^{k+1}, ..., W_{.j}^N]$
  such that $\quad W_{.j}^{k+1} \leq W_{.j}^k$ for $k = 1, ..., N$.
- Determine a breakpoint k' such that $W_{.j}^{k'}/W_{.j}^{k'+1} \geq \beta$.
- The contributory inputs in the antecedent of the rule are the inputs i corresponding to all $k \leq k'$.
- The *inhibitory inputs* that are negated in the antecedent of the rule and the *don't care inputs* are determined as for the Threshold technique.

For the same example used by the Threshold technique above, the sorted list is:

$$W_{sortj} = [0.430, 0.430, 0.430, 0.430, 0.420, 0.200, 0.000]$$
$$= [W_{Aj}, W_{Bj}, W_{Cj}, W_{Fj}, W_{Ej}, W_{Gj}, W_{Dj}].$$

For $\beta = 2$, the breakpoint occurs at $W_{Ej} = 0.420$. Thus components A, B, C, E, and F are contributory inputs and for $T_{inh} = 0.05$, component D is an inhibitory input in the antecedent of the production rule. The antecedent has the form:

$$A \text{ AND } B \text{ AND } C \text{ AND } E \text{ AND } F \text{ AND NOT } D.$$

If there is no clear breakpoint in the sorted list, one of the following three distinct cases applies:

- All the weights are considerably larger than zero and of a similar size; that is, $1 > W_{ij} \gg 0$ for all i and $W_{kj} \cong W_{(k+1)j}$ for $k = 1, ..., N-1$. Thus, all the inputs i can be considered as contributory inputs and all inputs are included in the antecedent. The output nodes corresponding to the digit 8 in the LED example presented later in this chapter illustrate this case.
- All the weights are small and of a similar size; that is, $0 < W_{ij} < \gamma$ (where γ is a small positive constant) for all i and $W_{kj} \cong W_{(k+1)j}$ for $k = 1, ..., N-1$. In this case, none of the inputs are considered to be contributory to the particular output node. If all the weights are less than T_{inh}, then all the inputs are considered inhibitory and are negated in the antecedent.
- There is a spread of weight component values in the range of 0 to 1, but there is no sharply defined break. Consider the weight vector:

$$W_j \quad = (0.430, 0.430, 0.187, 0.430, 0.430, 0.243, 0.360)$$

with the corresponding sorted list:

$$W_{sortj} = [0.430, 0.430, 0.430, 0.430, 0.360, 0.243, 0.187].$$

If $\beta = 2$, it is not possible to determine a breakpoint, and if $T_{inh} = 0.05$, no input is inhibitory. Thus, the Threshold technique is required for this particular output node. In the illustrative examples considered later in this chapter, no case of this type was encountered.

11.5.2 Identification of clusters

Once the antecedents for the production rules corresponding to the different output nodes are known, they are used to determine the cluster in which each output node belongs. The output nodes associated with production rules that have the same antecedent are grouped in the same cluster.

Consider a net with a 4X4 Kohonen output layer, where the nodes are designated (row no., col. no.), as shown in Figure 11.16. Assume that nodes (0,0), (0,1), (1,0), (1,1), (2,0), and (2,1) all have the following antecedent in their production rules:

A AND B AND C AND E AND F,

and that nodes (3,1), (0,2), (0,3), (1,2), (1,3), (2,2), (2,3), (3,2), and (3,3) have production rules with the antecedent:

A AND D AND G.

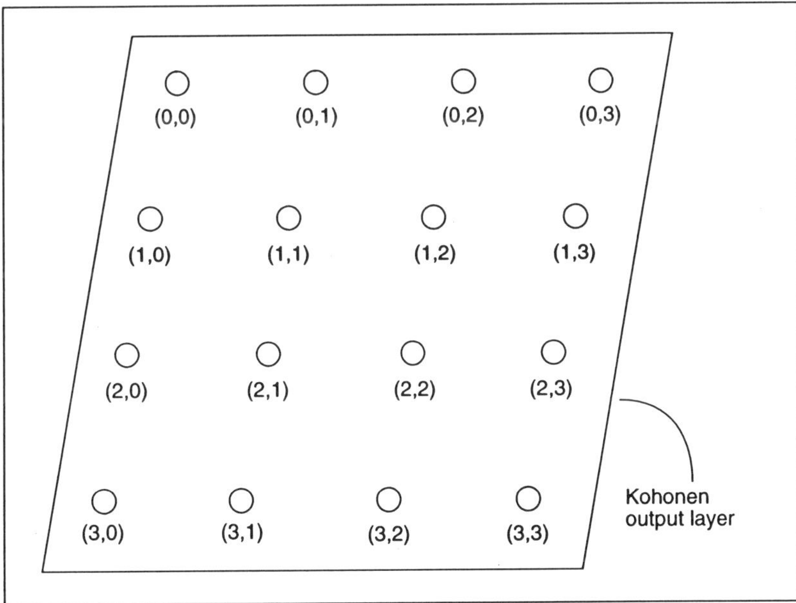

Figure 11.16 4X4 Kohonen output layer

Hence, two different clusters can be defined in the net, as shown in Figure 11.17.

From the two distinct clusters, two production rules can be derived for the data:

$$(A \text{ AND } B \text{ AND } C \text{ AND } E \text{ AND } F) \Rightarrow (CLUSTER\ 1)$$
$$(A \text{ AND } D \text{ AND } G) \Rightarrow (CLUSTER\ 2).$$

It may be possible to assign a real-world significance to CLUSTER 1 and CLUSTER 2 from the nature of the domain. For instance, CLUSTER 1 may correspond to MAMMAL and CLUSTER 2 to BIRD, giving the production rules:

$$(A \text{ AND } B \text{ AND } C \text{ AND } E \text{ AND } F) \Rightarrow (MAMMAL)$$
$$(A \text{ AND } D \text{ AND } G) \Rightarrow (BIRD).$$

If no real-world significance is apparent, the labeling could be left as CLUSTER 1 and CLUSTER 2.

Note that if CLUSTER 1 and CLUSTER 2 represent MAMMAL and BIRD, respectively, they are considered to be concepts with defining attributes given by the terms in the antecedents. By the method given in Chapter 7, these concepts can be ordered into a hierarchy.

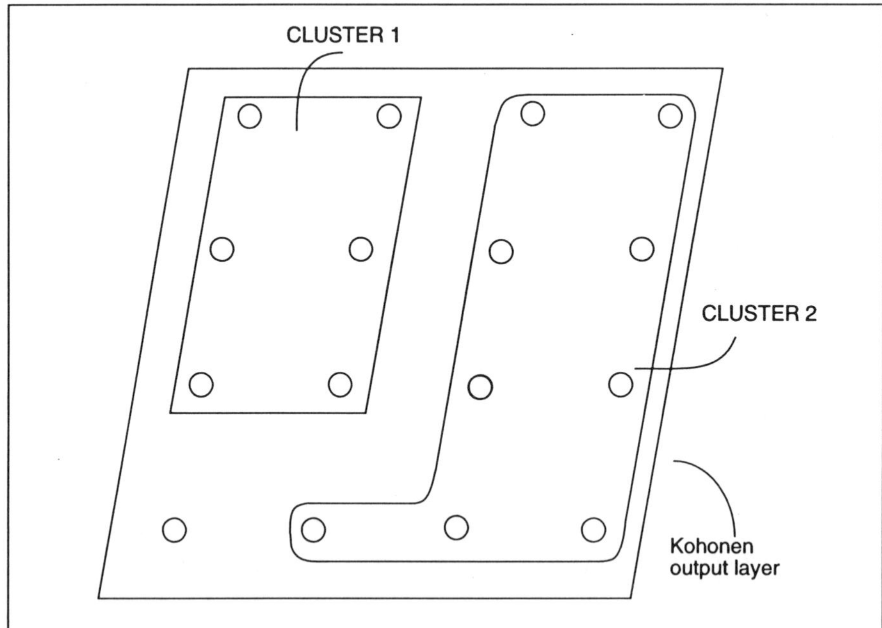

Figure 11.17 Clusters determined from common antecedents

11.5.3 Unidentified nodes and misclassification

In some situations where the clusters are defined, not all output nodes belong to a given cluster. This occurred at node (3,0) in Figure 11.17. Such nodes could represent:

1. intermediate concepts or higher-lying concepts in the concept hierarchy that have not been identified, provided they have one or more *don't care* inputs, or
2. a mixture of instances of topographically adjacent clusters and thus do not have a separate conceptual existence.

In case 1 additional clusters corresponding to these concepts are designated. In case 2 if the number of unidentified nodes is unacceptably large, a different dimensional output layer is specified, and the process is repeated until the number of unidentified nodes has been reduced to an acceptable level.

If some known concepts in the domain are not being picked up, then the net has insufficient discriminatory power. This may be solved by increasing the dimension of the output layer. However, for noisy data, a larger output layer could lead to more unidentified nodes.

11.5.4 Removal of redundant attributes

The final set of production rules might contain some negated attributes that are redundant. The final concept hierarchy is used to delete such attributes. As the notion of alternate branches in a concept hierarchy is required in this process, consider the concept hierarchy in Figure 11.18. For the concept L, the alternate branches are the sub-hierarchies rooted at M and N. Similarly, the concept M has the sub-hierarchies rooted at L and N as its alternate branches. For any concept, the alternate branches have the same parent as the concept and have roots at the same level as the concept.

When a particular concept is selected:

- All contributory attributes for the rules in the alternate branches to their leaf nodes are determined. These inputs or attributes are termed *contributory attributes for the alternative sub-hierarchies.*
- All the output nodes in the Kohonen layer that form the leaf concept clusters for the current sub-hierarchy are also identified.
- The weight components from each of the *contributory attributes for the alternative sub-hierarchies* to *all the leaf output nodes for the current sub-hierarchy* are examined.

If the weight components are zero for a particular attribute, that attribute is irrelevant for discriminating between concepts in the current sub-hierarchy.

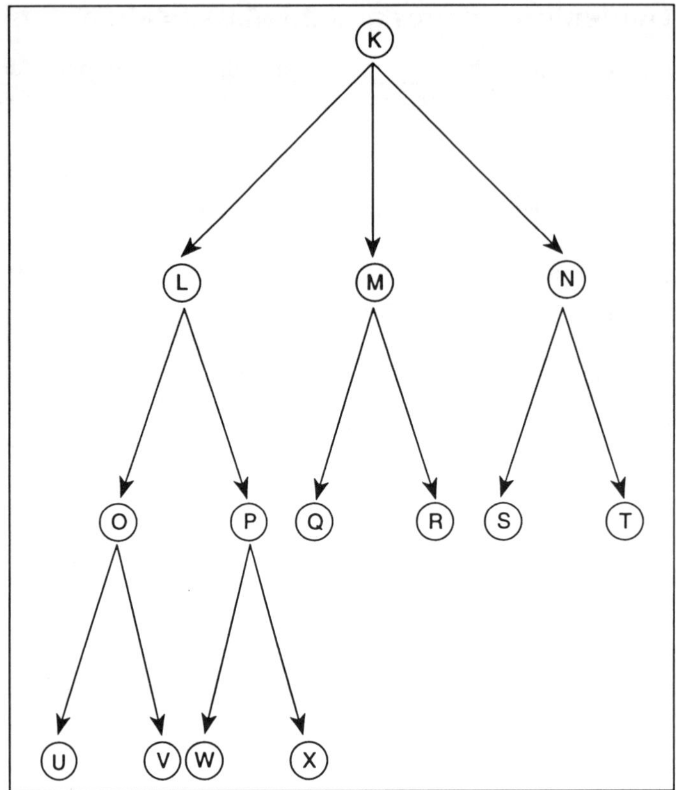

Figure 11.18 An illustrative concept hierarchy

Its negated form can be deleted from the production rules for the leaf concepts
in the current sub-hierarchy.

Consider the final concept hierarchy depicted in Figure 11.19. Assume the
production rules defining concepts B, E, and F are:

$(1) \Rightarrow (B)$
(1 AND 4 AND 5 AND NOT 2 AND NOT 3 AND NOT 6 AND NOT
7 AND NOT 8 AND NOT 9 AND NOT 10 AND NOT 11 AND NOT
12 AND NOT 13 AND NOT 14) $\Rightarrow$ (E)
(1 AND 6 AND 7 AND 8 AND NOT 2 AND NOT 3 AND NOT 4
AND NOT 5 AND NOT 9 AND NOT 10 AND NOT 11 AND NOT
12 AND NOT 13 AND NOT 14) $\Rightarrow$ (F).

On selecting concept B, the sub-hierarchy rooted at B and containing leaf
concepts E and F becomes the current sub-hierarchy. Hence, the output nodes

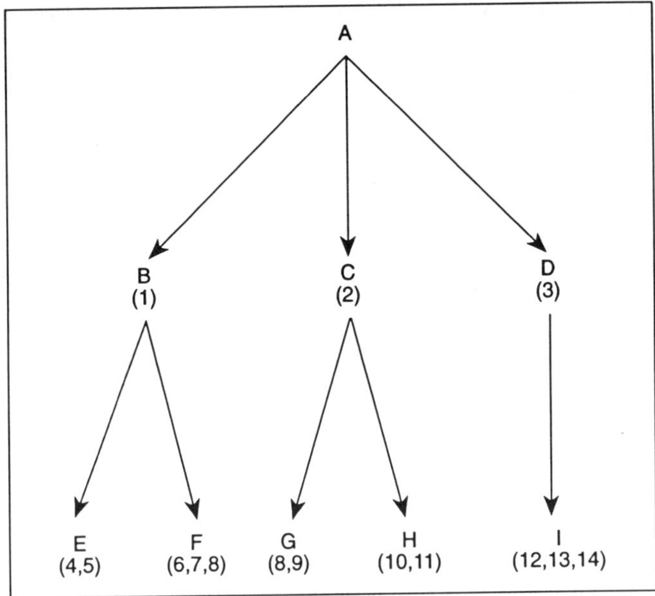

Figure 11.19 Final concept hierarchy for concepts A, B, ..., I with their associated contributory inputs listed

under consideration for this sub-net are those included in the clusters E and F. The alternative sub-hierarchies are rooted at concepts C and D and involve concepts G, H, and I. Hence, the contributory inputs for these alternative sub-hierarchies are 2, 8, 9, 10, and 11, and 3, 12, 13, and 14. The weight components from each of the *contributory attributes for the alternative sub-hierarchies* to *all the leaf output nodes for the current sub-hierarchy* must be examined. The input nodes for the attributes 2, 8, 9, 10, 11, 3, 12, 13, and 14 with a zero weight component to all the leaf output nodes in the current sub-net are determined. Assuming this is the case for inputs 2, 9, 10, 11, 3, 12, 13, and 14 the production rules defining the concepts E and F become:

(1 AND 4 AND 5 AND NOT 6 AND NOT 7 AND NOT 8) ⇒ (E)
(1 AND 6 AND 7 AND 8 AND NOT 4 AND NOT 5) ⇒ (F).

For the purpose of removing redundant attributes using the final concept hierarchy, the sub-hierarchies are examined by traversing the non-leaf concepts. This traversal is left to right for the non-leaf concepts at the same level, starting from the lowest level and moving up. For the concept hierarchy given in Figure 11.18, the sub-hierarchies are examined in the root concept sequence O, P, L, M, and N.

11.5.5   Summary of the knowledge acquisition method

The steps for knowledge acquisition can be summarized as:

1. Pre-process data to transform it into the correct format.
2. Assign a given dimension to the output layer.
3. Determine the weights of the Kohonen network using the method outlined in Section 11.4.4.
4. Delete the irrelevant attributes that are identified as having zero weight vector components to all the output nodes.
5. Use either the Threshold technique or the Breakpoint technique to determine the contributory and inhibitory inputs for the initial rules.
6. Using the antecedents for the rules, define clusters of output nodes, each cluster being associated with a given rule.
7. Assign real-world semantics to the clusters if possible, or alternatively, assign virtual labels. These define the initial set of concepts.
8. If a concept does not have any *don't care* inputs, obtain the final form of the production rule by affirming its contributory inputs and negating its inhibitory inputs in the antecedent.
9. For concepts with *don't care* inputs, form an initial rule containing the affirmation of the contributory inputs only. Explore these concepts by the method of Chapter 7 to determine if they are higher-lying concepts in the concept hierarchy.

   - If a concept is a higher-lying concept in the hierarchy, use a production rule containing only affirmation of the contributory inputs to define the concept.
   - If a concept is not a higher-lying concept, explore if it is a concept at a leaf in the hierarchy. If it is a leaf, form a production rule containing both the affirmation of the contributory inputs and the negation of the inhibitory inputs only. If the definition given in the production rule does not match a known concept, mark the corresponding nodes as unidentified, and do not process them further.

   At this stage, form a preliminary concept hierarchy.

10. Determine the number of unidentified nodes still requiring exploration. See if any of these can be assigned previously unrecognized concepts that are either intermediate or lowest level concepts. If so, using the method of Steps 8 and 9, determine their position in the hierarchy.
11. If the number of unidentified nodes is acceptable, stop. Otherwise, the number of unidentified nodes containing mixtures of instances of neighboring clusters is too high and not all known concepts have been identified. Change the dimension of the output layer and repeat from Step 3.
12. Carry out post-processing to delete negative attributes that are redundant, as described in Section 11.5.4, to obtain the final production rules.

11.6 Illustrative applications

The method for unsupervised automated knowledge acquisition has been applied to the LED digit domain and a modified version of the animal world hierarchy known here as the BIRD domain. Some of the results are reproduced from Suing (1992). These domains have been previously considered with supervised learning techniques in this book. However, here the training data set consists only of the input vectors associated with the example. The corresponding target output is not made available to the unsupervised learning technique. The advantage of using the same domain is that comparisons can be made on the rules derived. Furthermore, in applying both of the unsupervised techniques (Threshold and Breakpoint), neither the nature of the output classes that could be expected nor their number was indicated to the learning method. Hence, the situation corresponds to Figure 11.2(b) and Table 11.2(b). The network had to determine the number of clusters and the defining attributes for each cluster.

11.6.1 BIRD domain example

The BIRD domain consists of a set of data that is clean and noise-free. It is composed of 48 examples of 8 distinct types of birds, as indicated in Table 11.3, with 29 input elements or attributes for each pattern. Neither the number nor the nature of the output classes was made available to the learning process.

Name	Number of examples
BIRD	48
RUN-BIRD	5
LAND-BIRD	4
WEBBED-B	1
FLY-BIRD	43
LONG-D-FLY-B	33
PERCH-B	16
PER-B-PREY	7
PER-B-NO-PREY	9
SEA-BIRD	5
FIELD-B	12
SHORT-D-FLY-B	10
FOWL	7
LAKE-RIV-B	3

Table 11.3 Distribution of BIRD data (indents indicate hierarchical levels)

The 48 examples were repeatedly fed to the network to simulate the existence of approximately 50,000 examples. For proper learning to occur, a Kohonen network must be trained on a relatively large data set.

No target output value was associated with a particular example and thus the network carried out unsupervised learning. Furthermore, no known clusters for outputs were indicated to the net during learning. An initial assignment of a 7X7 dimension output layer was used. A small portion of the weight matrix produced after learning by the Kohonen network is given in Table 11.4. After training, the weight matrix was processed using the Threshold and Breakpoint analysis techniques.

Threshold technique

Consider the Threshold technique applied to node (3,4) from Table 11.4. The maximum weight is 0.45, corresponding to inputs 2, 3, 9, 13, and 15. These are the only contributory inputs for node (3,4) as the rest of the input weights are below the specified threshold (90% of the maximum weight 0.45). Therefore, the contributory part of the antecedent is:

Output nodes (row,col)	Input nodes 0–28									
(3,4)	0.00	0.00	0.45	0.45	0.00	0.00	0.00	0.00	0.00	0.45	0.00
	0.00	0.00	0.45	0.00	0.45	0.00	0.00	0.00	0.00	0.00	0.00
	0.00	0.00	0.00	0.00	0.00	0.00	0.00				
(3,5)	0.00	0.00	0.45	0.45	0.00	0.00	0.00	0.00	0.00	0.36	0.09
	0.00	0.00	0.45	0.09	0.36	0.00	0.00	0.00	0.00	0.00	0.00
	0.00	0.00	0.00	0.00	0.00	0.00	0.00				

Note:
* Inputs nodes (attributes in italics were determined to be irrelevant and are not considered in further analysis):

Hair	*Milk*	Feathers	Egglaying	*Pouches*
Placenta	Oceanic	Land	Tree	Field-mead
Lake-river	*Large*	*Medium*	Fly	Fly-short-d
Fly-long-d	*Five-digit*	Claws	*Hoofs*	*Odd-toed*
Even-toed	*Herbivore*	Sturdy-feet	Web-feet	*Tail*
Trunk	*Slit-eyes*	*Black-stripe*	Bird-o-prey	

* (row,col) is used to represent a particular node in the two-dimensional output layer of the (7X7) network.

Table 11.4   Portion of the weight matrix (7X7 dimension output layer)

Feathers AND Egglaying AND Field-mead AND Fly AND Fly-long-d.

All the remaining inputs are less than an inhibitory threshold of 0.05 and thus all are negated in the antecedent. Therefore, the full antecedent associated with node (3,4) is:

Feathers AND Egglaying AND Field-mead AND Fly AND Fly-long-d
AND NOT Oceanic AND NOT Land AND NOT Tree AND NOT Lake-river
AND NOT Fly-short-d AND NOT Claws AND NOT Sturdy-feet AND NOT
Web-feet AND NOT Bird-o-prey.

The listing of the contributory inputs in the antecedents with no *don't care* inputs produced by the Threshold technique for a 7X7 output layer of the network is presented in Table 11.5.

All nodes with the same antecedent are grouped into a cluster. The associated concepts or consequents of the corresponding rules can be defined from examination of the antecedents and an understanding of the domain. From knowledge of the domain, CLUSTER 8, which contains the node (3,4), matches the FIELD-B concept, giving the final production rule:

(Feathers AND Egglaying AND Field-mead AND Fly AND Fly-long-d
AND NOT Oceanic AND NOT Land AND NOT Tree AND NOT Lake-river
AND NOT Fly-short-d AND NOT Claws AND NOT Sturdy-feet AND NOT
Web-feet AND NOT Bird-o-prey) $\Rightarrow$ (FIELD-B).

Feathers AND Egglaying AND Land AND Sturdy-feet
{CLUSTER 1}

Feathers AND Egglaying AND Land AND Web-feet
{CLUSTER 2}

Feathers AND Egglaying AND Fly AND Fly-short-d AND Claws
{CLUSTER 3}

Feathers AND Egglaying AND Fly AND Fly-short-d AND Lake-river
{CLUSTER 4}

Feathers AND Egglaying AND Fly AND Fly-long-d AND Oceanic
{CLUSTER 5}

Feathers AND Egglaying AND Fly AND Fly-long-d AND Tree AND
Bird-o-prey
{CLUSTER 6}

Feathers AND Egglaying AND Fly AND Fly-long-d AND Tree AND Claws
{CLUSTER 7}

Feathers AND Egglaying AND Fly AND Fly-long-d AND Field-mead
{CLUSTER 8}

Table 11.5   The contributory inputs in the antecedents with no *don't care* inputs extracted using the Threshold technique (all unlisted inputs are negated)

As there is no *don't care* input, the rule corresponds to a concept at the lowest level of the hierarchy and is retained in full in the final set of production rules.

Now consider the Threshold technique applied to node (3,5) from Table 11.4. The maximum weight is 0.45, corresponding to inputs 2, 3, and 13. These are the only contributory inputs for node (3,5) as the rest of the input weights are below the specified threshold (90% of the maximum weight 0.45). Therefore, the contributory inputs correspond to Feathers, Egglaying, and Fly. For an inhibitory threshold of 0.05, the inhibitory inputs correspond to Oceanic, Land, Tree, Fly-long-d, Claws, Sturdy-feet, Web-feet, and Bird-o-prey. In addition, this node has three *don't care* inputs of Field-mead, Lake-river, and Fly-short-d. The antecedent extracted by the Threshold technique for the cluster containing node (3.5) is given in Table 11.6.

Feathers AND Egglaying AND Fly AND NOT Oceanic AND NOT Land
AND NOT Tree AND NOT Fly-long-d AND NOT Claws
AND NOT Sturdy-feet AND NOT Web-feet AND NOT Bird-o-prey.

{CLUSTER 9}

Table 11.6   One of the four antecedents with *don't care* inputs extracted using the Threshold technique (all unlisted inputs are *don't care*)

As the antecedent denoting CLUSTER 9 has *don't care* inputs, the possibility that it is a higher-level concept in the hierarchy is explored. Hence, using only the contributory inputs, the *re-stated rule* has the antecedent:

Feathers AND Egglaying AND Fly.

From knowledge of the domain, this can be matched with the concept of FLY-BIRD, giving:

(Feathers AND Egglaying AND Fly) $\Rightarrow$ (FLY-BIRD).

Applying the method of Chapter 7 to this rule and the rule for FIELD-B, the production rule for FIELD-B becomes:

(FLY-BIRD AND Field-mead AND Fly-long-d AND NOT Oceanic
AND NOT Land AND NOT Tree AND NOT Lake-river AND NOT
Fly-short-d AND NOT Claws AND NOT Sturdy-feet AND NOT Web-feet AND NOT Bird-o-prey) $\Rightarrow$ (FIELD-B).

This indicates that FIELD-B is a specialization of FLY-BIRD. Therefore, FLY-BIRD is a higher-lying concept. The final form if its production rule is then retained as:

(Feathers AND Egglaying AND Fly) $\Rightarrow$ (FLY-BIRD).

The resulting production rules for the BIRD domain are given in Tables 11.7 and 11.8. When the concept under consideration does not constitute a higher-lying concept, its final form must include the contributory inputs and the inhibitory inputs as negations in the production rule. The *don't care* inputs are omitted. For higher-lying concepts, the antecedents contain contributory inputs only.

When the production rule associated with each output node in the 7X7 Kohonen layer is examined, the mapping of output nodes to clusters that represent the specific concepts is obtained, as shown in Table 11.9. The concept hierarchy given in Figure 11.20 is developed by the method shown in Chapter 7.

(Feathers AND Egglaying AND Land AND Sturdy-feet) $\Rightarrow$ (LAND-BIRD)
(Feathers AND Egglaying AND Land AND Web-feet) $\Rightarrow$ (WEBBED-B)
(Feathers AND Egglaying AND Fly AND Fly-short-d AND Claws) $\Rightarrow$ (FOWL)
(Feathers AND Egglaying AND Fly AND Fly-short-d AND Lake-river)
$\Rightarrow$ (LAKE-RIV-B)
(Feathers AND Egglaying AND Fly AND Fly-long-d AND Oceanic)
$\Rightarrow$ (SEA-BIRD)
(Feathers AND Egglaying AND Fly AND Fly-long-d AND Tree AND
Bird-o-prey) $\Rightarrow$ (PER-B-PREY)
(Feathers AND Egglaying AND Fly AND Fly-long-d AND Tree AND
Claws) $\Rightarrow$ (PER-B-NO-PREY)
(Feathers AND Egglaying AND Fly AND Fly-long-d AND Field-mead)
$\Rightarrow$ (FIELD-B)

Table 11.7   Production rules derived for the lowest-level concepts in the hierarchy using the Threshold technique (all unlisted inputs are negated)

(Feathers AND Egglaying AND Fly) $\Rightarrow$ (FLY-BIRD)
(Feathers AND Egglaying AND Fly AND Fly-long-d) $\Rightarrow$ (LONG-D-FLY-B)
(Feathers AND Egglaying AND Fly AND Fly-short-d) $\Rightarrow$
(SHORT-D-FLY-B)
(Feathers AND Egglaying AND Fly AND Fly-long-d AND Tree) $\Rightarrow$
(PERCH-B)

Table 11.8   Production rules derived for the higher-level concepts in the hierarchy using the Threshold technique

SEA-BIRD	SEA-BIRD	LAND-BIRD	LAND-BIRD	LAND-BIRD	WEBBED-B	WEBBED-B
SEA-BIRD	SEA-BIRD	LAND-BIRD	LAND-BIRD	LAND-BIRD	WEBBED-B	WEBBED-B
PER-B-PREY	PER-B-PREY	FIELD-B	FIELD-B	FIELD-B	FIELD-B	LAKE-RIV-B
PER-B-PREY	PER-B-PREY	FIELD-B	FIELD-B	FIELD-B	FLY-BIRD	LAKE-RIV-B
PER-B-PREY	PER-B-PREY	LONG-D-FLY-B	FIELD-B	FIELD-B	FLY-BIRD	LAKE-RIV-B
PER-B-NO-PREY	PER-B-NO-PREY	PERCH-B	FOWL	FOWL	SHORT-D-FLY-B	SHORT-D-FLY-B
PER-B-NO-PREY	PER-B-NO-PREY	PER-B-NO-PREY	FOWL	FOWL	FOWL	FOWL

Table 11.9   Mapping produced in a 7X7 output layer using the Threshold technique

Breakpoint technique

The results obtained using the Breakpoint technique give the mapping shown in Table 11.10. From this table, some nodes in the output layer failed to produce recognizable clusters. However, the interpretation given in the Threshold technique cannot be applied here, as the contributory inputs for these unidentified nodes represent attributes that are a combination of the neighboring nodes. For example, the node marked as "**" has Feathers, Egglaying, Tree, Field-mead, Fly, Fly-long-d, and Bird-o-prey as its contributory inputs. These attributes designate the FIELD-B and PER-B-PREY clusters. Hence, this particular node has become responsive to more than one input pattern used in the learning process. This result is not new in experiments with the Kohonen network, being similar to the Phoneme Map experiment (Kohonen 1990).

Threshold versus Breakpoint

To compare the two techniques further, the learning procedure was repeated on networks with various output layer dimensions. A summary of the results is given in Table 11.11.

At some dimensions the Threshold technique can identify clusters such as BIRD, RUN-BIRD, FLY-BIRD, LONG-D-FLY-B, PERCH-B, AND SHORT-D-FLY-B. These clusters belong to the upper levels of the concept hierarchy

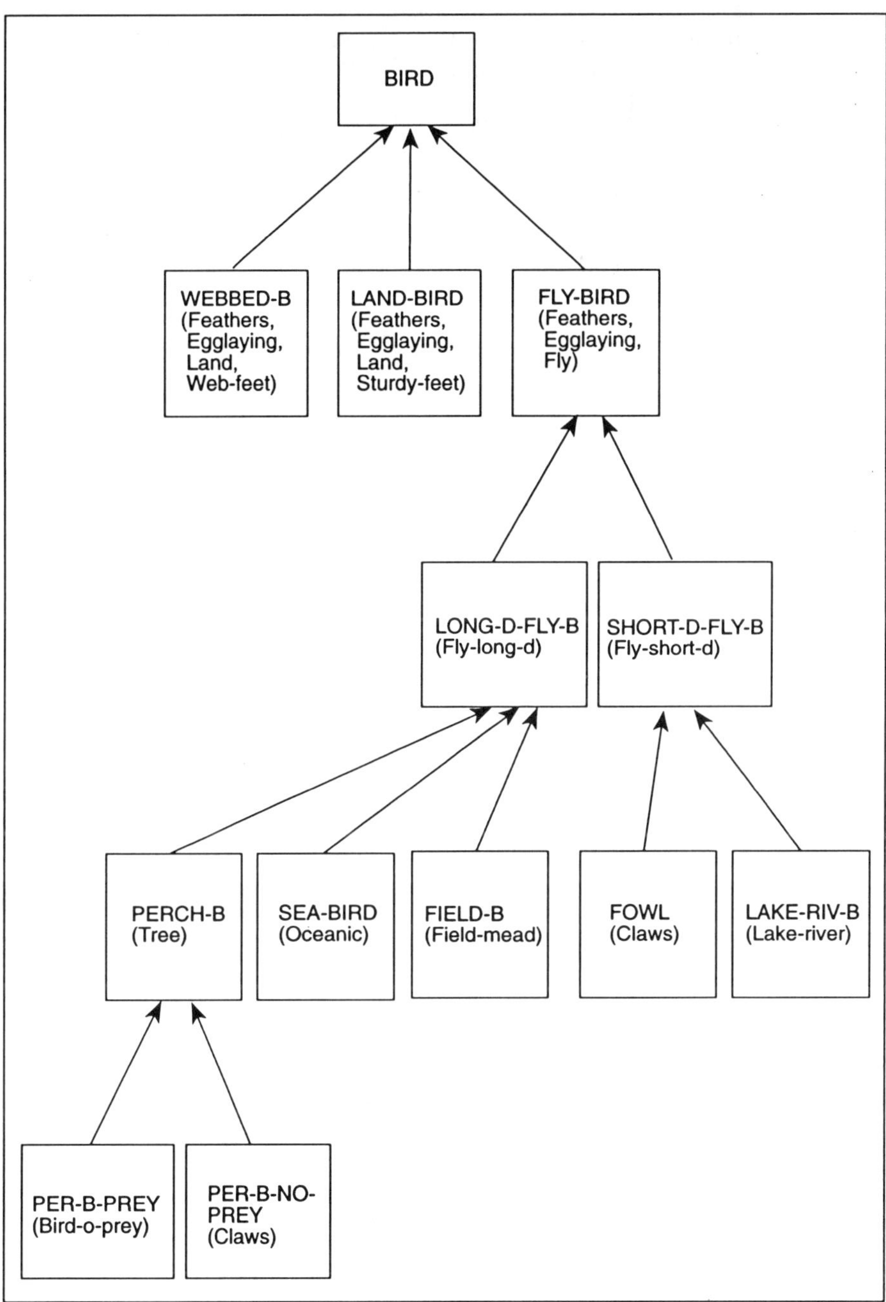

Figure 11.20 Concept hierarchy of the BIRD domain

SEA-BIRD	SEA-BIRD	LAND-BIRD	LAND-BIRD	LAND-BIRD	WEBBED-B	WEBBED-B
SEA-BIRD	SEA-BIRD	LAND-BIRD	LAND-BIRD	LAND-BIRD	WEBBED-B	WEBBED-B
PER-B-PREY	PER-B-PREY	FIELD-B	FIELD-B	FIELD-B	FIELD-B	LAKE-RIV-B
PER-B-PREY	PER-B-PREY	FIELD-B	FIELD-B	FIELD-B	*	LAKE-RIV-B
PER-B-PREY	PER-B-PREY	* *	FIELD-B	FIELD-B	*	LAKE-RIV-B
PER-B-NO-PREY	PER-B-NO-PREY	* * *	FOWL	FOWL	* * * *	* * * *
PER-B-NO-PREY	PER-B-NO-PREY	PER-B-NO-PREY	FOWL	FOWL	FOWL	FOWL

Note:
Nodes that failed to produce rules for known concepts have the following contributory and *don't care* inputs:
* Feathers, Egglaying, Field-mead, Fly, Fly-long-d, *Lake-river, Fly-short-d*
** Feathers, Egglaying, Tree, Field-mead, Fly, Fly-long-d, Bird-o-prey
*** Feathers, Egglaying, Tree, Fly, Fly-long-d, Claws, Bird-o-prey
**** Feathers, Egglaying, Fly, Fly-short-d, Claws, *Lake-river*

Table 11.10   Mapping produced in a 7X7 output layer using the Breakpoint technique

of the BIRD domain, as shown in Figure 11.21. The attributes related to these clusters are not explicitly represented by a single input pattern in the training data set, but are contained as part of several input patterns. These therefore represent abstract concepts that are generalizations of specific classes that contain instances. In object-oriented conceptual modeling, they are referred to as abstract classes (Dillon & Tan 1993).

In contrast to the Threshold technique, the Breakpoint technique failed to detect higher-lying hierarchical clusters. Instead, it extracted specific rules for concepts such as FOWL and SEABIRD. Also, the two techniques sometimes produced different rules for a given output node. For example, node (3,5) is classified as FLY-BIRD using the Threshold technique (Table 11.9), and is an unidentified node using the Breakpoint technique (Table 11.10). Thus, the Threshold technique can identify concepts at the upper level of the hierarchy, while the Breakpoint technique only deals with concepts at the lower levels in the hierarchy resulting in more specific concepts.

Rules	4X4		5X5		6X6		7X7		8X8		9X9		10X10	
	T	B	T	B	T	B	T	B	T	B	T	B	T	B
BIRD	4		2		6				4		4		1	
RUN-BIRD	2		1						2		1		3	
LAND-BIRD			2	2	5	5	6	6	3	3	13	13	6	6
WEBBED-B			1	1	4	4	4	4	7	7	3	3	2	2
FLY-BIRD	2		5				2		2				1	
LONG-D-FLY-B	2	2	2		3		1				2		2	
PERCH-B	2		1		1		1		2				3	
PER-B-PREY			1	1	1	1	6	6	7	7	15	15	21	21
PER-B-NO-PREY			1	1	3	3	5	5	2	2	12	12	22	22
SEA-BIRD			1	1	3	3	4	4	8	8	10	10	10	10
FIELD-B			2	2	1	1	9	9	16	16	7	7	13	13
SHORT-D-FLY-B	4				2		2				3			
FOWL			2	2	4	4	6	6	4	4	6	6	7	7
LAKE-RIV-B			3	3	2	2	3	3	7	7	5	5	9	9
Unidentified nodes	0	14	1	12	1	13	0	6	0	10	0	10	0	10

Table 11.11 Identified and unidentified output nodes for different sizes of the output layer (T = Threshold technique, B = Breakpoint technique)

Regardless of the technique used, the mappings in Tables 11.9 and 11.10 show the resulting self-organization of clusters. Clusters that are similar to each other are found next to each other in the map. For example, LAND-BIRD and WEBBED-B, both specializations of RUN-BIRD, are placed next to each other in all the maps produced.

Effect of the output layer dimension

This discussion refers mainly to the Breakpoint technique, since the unidentified nodes from that technique represent uninterpretable classifications and not a hidden hierarchy. From Table 11.11 an interesting pattern emerges. As the dimension of the output layer increases, fewer nodes are classified into the unidentified category up to a certain dimension. An increase from 4X4 to 7X7 in the size of the output layer results in a significant decrease in the number of unclassified nodes. Then, an increase of dimension up to 10X10 produces an increase in unidentified nodes. Therefore, the 7X7 dimension seems to be the most effective dimension for this domain.

In addition, an increase in the dimension helps in representing the statistical

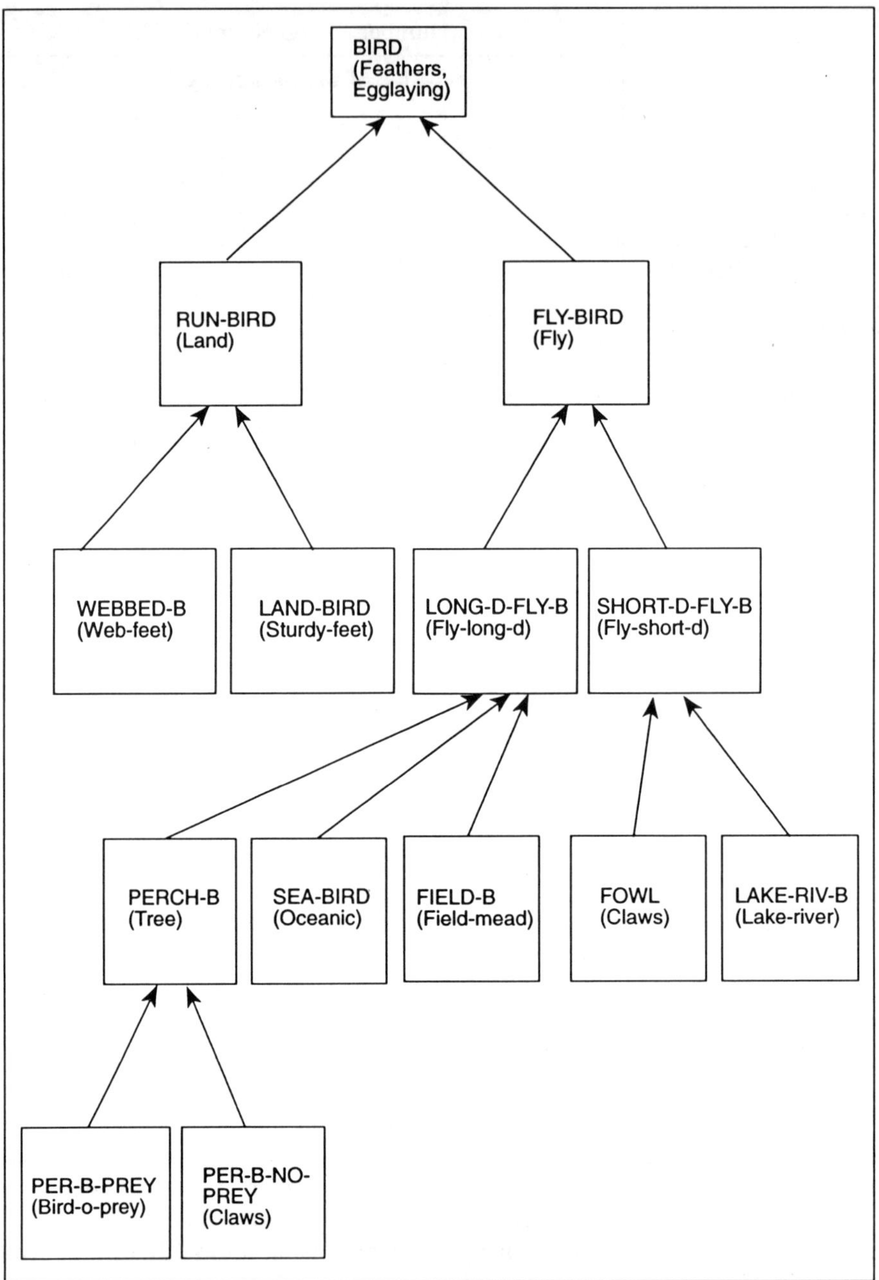

Figure 11.21 Elaborated concept hierarchy of the BIRD domain developed using the Threshold technique at some dimensions

distribution of the data set with regard to the number of nodes that respond to a given labeled cluster. A comparison of the distribution of the BIRD data in Table 11.3 and the corresponding distribution of identified nodes in the 7X7 net in Table 11.11 confirms this. The distribution of identified nodes reflects the data set distribution. This is a known feature of Kohonen nets.

11.6.2 LED digit domain example

This domain contains data defining the 10 decimal digits on LED displays. Each input pattern is composed of 7 binary attributes only. No target output vector was made available to assist the network during training. Neither the number nor nature of the output classes was indicated. Two separate training data sets were used, one comprising 1723 examples of clean data, and the other comprising 1895 examples with a noise level of 10%. As the Kohonen net requires a large data set for learning to occur, the relevant data set was repeatedly fed to the network to simulate approximately 50,000 examples. The results presented are from initial zero weight matrices.

Clean LED data

The distribution of the clean LED data used is given in Table 11.12. A portion of the weight matrix produced after learning by the 7X7 dimension output layer Kohonen network is given in Table 11.13.

Breakpoint technique

An example of rule extraction from one of the nodes in Table 11.13 is illustrated using the Breakpoint technique. For output node (6,3), the input weight components are sorted from maximum to minimum.

Name	Number of examples
ZERO	158
ONE	160
TWO	157
THREE	150
FOUR	147
FIVE	195
SIX	188
SEVEN	163
EIGHT	197
NINE	208

Table 11.12   Distribution of the clean LED data

Output nodes (row,col)	Input nodes						
	0	1	2	3	4	5	6
(5,0)	0.4472	0.4472	0.0000	0.4472	0.0000	0.4472	0.4472
(5,1)	0.4294	0.4294	0.1867	0.2427	0.1867	0.4294	0.4294
(5,2)	0.4082	0.4082	0.4082	0.0000	0.4082	0.4082	0.4082
(5,3)	0.3916	0.3916	0.3916	0.2084	0.3916	0.3916	0.3916
(5,4)	0.3780	0.3780	0.3780	0.3780	0.3780	0.3780	0.3780
(5,5)	0.3937	0.3937	0.3937	0.3937	0.1816	0.3937	0.3937
(5,6)	0.4082	0.4082	0.4082	0.4082	0.0000	0.4082	0.4082
(6,0)	0.4472	0.4472	0.0000	0.4472	0.0000	0.4472	0.4472
(6,1)	0.4472	0.4472	0.0000	0.4472	0.0000	0.4472	0.4472
(6,2)	0.4472	0.4472	0.0000	0.4472	0.0000	0.4472	0.4472
(6,3)	0.4472	0.4472	0.0000	0.4472	0.0000	0.4472	0.4472
(6,4)	0.4082	0.4082	0.4082	0.4082	0.0000	0.4082	0.4082
(6,5)	0.4082	0.4082	0.4082	0.4082	0.0000	0.4082	0.4082
(6,6)	0.4082	0.4082	0.4082	0.4082	0.0000	0.4082	0.4082

Note:
* Input nodes:
0 — Up-center   1 — Up-left   2 — Up-right   3 — Mid-center
4 — Down-left   5 — Down-right   6 — Down-center
*(row,col) is used to represent a particular node in the two-dimensional output layer of the 7X7 network.

Table 11.13   Portion of the weight matrix (7X7 dimension output layer) for clean LED data

$$W_{sortj} = [W_0, W_1, W_3, W_5, W_6, W_2, W_4]$$
$$= [0.4472, 0.4472, 0.4472, 0.4472, 0.4472, 0.0000, 0.0000].$$

A breakpoint is determined from this by finding the input weight component that is more than twice the next one, giving the inputs 0, 1, 3, 5, and 6 as contributory inputs. For $T_{inh} = 0.05$ (reflecting clean data), inputs 2 and 4 are inhibitory. Therefore, the antecedent part of the rule is constructed as:

Up-center AND Up-left AND Mid-center AND Down-right AND Down-center AND NOT Up-right AND NOT Down-left.

From an understanding of the LED digit domain, this output node can be associated with the lowest-level concept labeled FIVE, giving the rule:

(Up-center AND Up-left AND Mid-center AND Down-right AND Down-center AND NOT Up-right AND NOT Down-left) $\Rightarrow$ (FIVE).

The contributory inputs in the antecedents with no *don't care* inputs produced by this technique for a 7X7 output layer of the network are listed in Table 11.14. In this table, all the unlisted inputs are negated. They are not included for ease of reading. The associated concepts or consequents of the corresponding rules are then identified and indicated in the curly brackets. The designation of output nodes into clusters is indicated in Table 11.15.

Up-center AND Up-left AND Up-right AND Down-left AND Down-right AND Down-center   {ZERO}
Up-right AND Down-right   {ONE}
Up-center AND Up-right AND Mid-center AND Down-left AND Down-center   {TWO}
Up-center AND Up-right AND Mid-center AND Down-right AND Down-center   {THREE}
Up-left AND Up-right AND Mid-center AND Down-right   {FOUR}
Up-center AND Up-left AND Mid-center AND Down-right AND Down-center   {FIVE}
Up-center AND Up-left AND Mid-center AND Down-left AND Down-right AND Down-center   {SIX}
Up-center AND Up-right AND Down-right   {SEVEN}
Up-center AND Up-left AND Up-right AND Mid-center AND Down-left AND Down-right AND Down-center   {EIGHT}
Up-center AND Up-left AND Up-right AND Mid-center AND Down-right AND Down-center   {NINE}

Table 11.14   The contributory inputs in the antecedents with no *don't care* inputs extracted using the Breakpoint technique (all unlisted inputs are negated)

FOUR	*	SEVEN	SEVEN	ONE	ONE	ONE
EIGHT	EIGHT	*	*	HLC1/3	HLC1/3	HLC1/3
SIX	EIGHT	TWO	TWO	THREE	THREE	THREE
SIX	EIGHT	EIGHT	EIGHT	EIGHT	HLC8/9	NINE
FIVE	EIGHT	ZERO	EIGHT	EIGHT	HLC8/9	NINE
FIVE	EIGHT	ZERO	EIGHT	EIGHT	HLC8/9	NINE
FIVE	FIVE	FIVE	FIVE	NINE	NINE	NINE

Note:
Nodes that produced rules for unidentifiable lowest-level concepts are marked as "*".
Nodes marked as HLC1/3 and HLC8/9 have *don't care* inputs and are abstract higher-level concepts.

Table 11.15   Mapping produced in a 7X7 output layer using the Breakpoint technique

Using the Breakpoint technique, the clusters representing the digits 0–9 were identified and generated as rules. The remaining nodes fell into two categories:

* Nodes with *don't care* attributes that can be interpreted as higher-level concepts without a real-world significance for this domain. These can be considered as abstract concepts (Dillon & Tan 1993).
* Lowest-level concepts that are not identifiable as they represent a combination of the attributes of neighboring clusters. For example, node (0,1), which has contributory inputs of Up-center, Up-left, Up-right, Mid-center, and Down-right and negated inputs of Down-left and Down-center, is a combination of the clusters FOUR and SEVEN, as shown below:

> (Up-left AND Up-right AND Mid-center AND Down-right AND NOT Up-center AND NOT Down-left AND NOT Down-center) $\Rightarrow$ (FOUR)

> (Up-center AND Up-right AND Down-right AND NOT Up-left AND NOT Mid-center AND NOT Down-left AND NOT Down-center) $\Rightarrow$ (SEVEN).

The same situation occurred in the BIRD domain where some nodes became responsive to more than one cluster. From our knowledge of real-world domains, such nodes reflect mixtures of instances. The concept hierarchy developed from the 7X7 output layer using the Breakpoint technique is given in Figure 11.22.

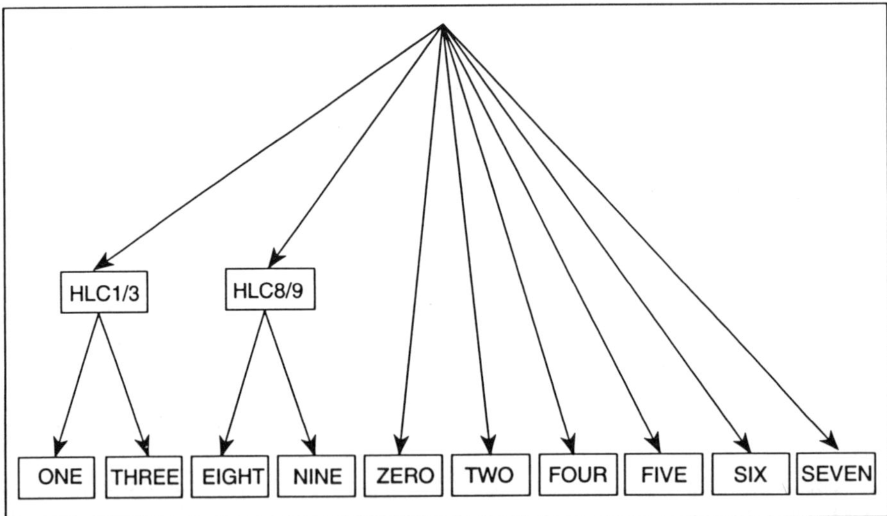

Figure 11.22   Concept hierarchy of the LED domain developed from a 7X7 output layer using the Breakpoint technique

Threshold technique

The mapping produced by the Threshold technique for a 7X7 output layer of the network learning from the same data set is given in Table 11.16. The clusters representing the digits 0—9 were identified and generated as rules. The remaining nodes all have *don't care* attributes and the majority can be interpreted as abstract higher-level concepts that do not have a real-world significance for this domain. Regardless of the technique used, the mappings produced in Tables 11.15 and 11.16 self-organize in the sense that similar clusters (such as ONE, FOUR, and SEVEN) are usually topologically adjacent.

FOUR	*	SEVEN	SEVEN	ONE	ONE	ONE
*	*	*	*	*	*	*
SIX	*	TWO	TWO	THREE	THREE	THREE
SIX	*	*	*	*	*	*
FIVE	*	ZERO	*	EIGHT	*	NINE
FIVE	*	ZERO	*	EIGHT	*	NINE
FIVE	FIVE	FIVE	FIVE	NINE	NINE	NINE

Note:
All the nodes marked as "*" have *don't care* inputs and their contributory inputs are not necessarily the same.

Table 11.16 Mapping produced in a 7X7 output layer for the lowest-level concepts (with no *don't care* inputs) using the Threshold technique

Effect of the output layer dimension

As with the BIRD domain, different sizes of the output layer were tried, and a summary of the results is given in Table 11.17. As the dimension increases, the percentage of lowest-level identified nodes generally increases. A maximum percentage of lowest-level classified nodes was reached for the 9X9 dimension. Larger dimensions also allowed for the identification of all the lowest-level clusters in the domain. Determination of the most effective dimension of the output layer is carried out by progressively testing different sizes, as explained in the algorithm. Small dimensions can lead to some sort of contraction of representation since too much knowledge or too many clusters are being mapped to a small area. Also, only a few of the known clusters may be identified with a small output layer. As in the BIRD domain, increasing the dimension of the output layer helps to illustrate the statistical distribution of the data set clearly. However, a very large dimension can be a waste of space and time during the learning process.

| Rules | Number of nodes identified — Size of the output layer | | | | | | | | | | | | | |
	4X4 T	4X4 B	5X5 T	5X5 B	6X6 T	6X6 B	7X7 T	7X7 B	8X8 T	8X8 B	9X9 T	9X9 B	10X10 T	10X10 B
ZERO							2	2	5	5	4	4	14	14
ONE			1	1	4	4	3	3	8	8	12	12	15	15
TWO			1	1	1	1	2	2	6	6	10	10	6	6
THREE			1	1	1	1	3	3	6	6	7	7	1	1
FOUR			1	1	2	2	1	1	5	5	12	12	13	13
FIVE					1	1	6	6	1	1	5	5	4	4
SIX					2	2	2	2	1	1	4	4	15	15
SEVEN			1	1	2	2	2	2	7	8	2	2	6	6
EIGHT		5		5		6	2	13	2	4	4	6	8	11
NINE		5	1	5	2	5	5	6	4	9	15	15	4	6
Unidentified nodes	16	6	19	10	21	12	21	9	19	11	6	4	14	9

Table 11.17 Identified lowest-level output nodes for different sizes of the output layer (T = Threshold technique, B = Breakpoint technique)

Effect of different amounts of noise in the data

The results of applying the Threshold and Breakpoint techniques to the LED data sets with a noise level of 10% are given in Table 11.18. Owing to the noise level, an inhibitory threshold $T_{inh} = 0.1$ was used.

For the clean data set reported in Table 11.17, a maximum percentage of classified lowest-level nodes is reached at the 9X9 dimension, and the increasing trend of classified lowest-level nodes in the network is achieved by increasing the dimension of the output layer. However, this is not the case for the noisy data set reported in Table 11.18. For small-dimension output layers, the presence of noise does not greatly affect the percentage of classified nodes. In particular, increasing the dimension from 4X4 up to 6X6 does not result in significantly different percentage of identified lowest-level nodes in the noisy data set. Therefore, a smaller-dimension output layer helps filter out noise present in the data set. For noisy data, the percentage of identified lowest-level nodes at higher dimensions decreases dramatically and both the Threshold and Breakpoint techniques show poorer performance with regard to the number of rules extracted. However, for clean data, increases in dimension up to 9X9 have the positive effect of increasing the percentage of classified lowest-level nodes.

Rules	4X4		5X5		6X6		7X7		8X8		9X9		10X10	
	T	B	T	B	T	B	T	B	T	B	T	B	T	B
ZERO							1	4	5	10	6	6	8	9
ONE			1	1	3	3	1	1	4	4	5	3	7	4
TWO			1	1	3	3	2	2	4	6	6	6	4	4
THREE					1	1	2	3	4	5	8	7	4	4
FOUR					2	2	3	3	5	6	4	4	4	4
FIVE					1	1	2	2	4	4	6	4	6	4
SIX					1	2	3	4	3	3	3	4	7	7
SEVEN			1	1	2	2	4	4	2	2	6	6	6	6
EIGHT		6		6		9	1	10	3	6	4	10	2	10
NINE		4		5	2	4	2	3	3	3	6	13	4	8
Unidentified nodes	16	6	22	11	21	9	28	13	27	15	27	18	48	40

Table 11.18 Identified lowest-level output nodes for different sizes of the output layer with 10% noise in the data set (T = Threshold technique, B = Breakpoint technique)

11.7 Recapitulation

The BIRD and LED test domains show that the developed unsupervised learning approach to automated knowledge acquisition can successfully extract knowledge in the form of production rules, concepts, and concept hierarchies. Experimentation is necessary with the dimension of the output layer to reduce the number of unclassified nodes before extracting the final rules. This study has illustrated that symbolic knowledge extraction can be successfully performed using unsupervised neural networks, where no target output vectors are available to the automated knowledge acquisition technique during training.

Acknowledgment

The authors wish to acknowledge the kind permission of M. Suing in allowing us to use some results in the two domains and material from her Honors Thesis (Suing 1992) in this chapter.

References

Beale, R. & Jackson, T. 1990, *Neural Computing: An Introduction*, Adam Hilger, Bristol

Breiman, L., Friedman, J.H., Olshen, R.A. & Stone, C.J. 1984, *Classification and Regression Trees*, Wadsworth International Group, Belmont, California

Carpenter, G.A. & Grossberg, S. 1988, "The ART of adaptive pattern recognition by self-organizing neural network", *Computer*, vol. 21, March, pp. 72–88

Caudill, M. 1987,"Neural networks primer, part I", *AI Expert*, December, pp. 46–52

Caudill, M. 1988,"Neural networks primer, part IV", *AI Expert*, August, pp. 61–7

Dillon, T.S. & Tan, P.L. 1993, *Object-Oriented Conceptual Modeling*, Prentice Hall, Sydney, Australia

Dillon, T.S., Sestito, S., Suing, M. & Witten, M. 1993, *Unsupervised Automated Knowledge Acquisition*, Technical Report, Computer Science Department, La Trobe University, Melbourne, Australia

Fukushima, K. 1980,"Neocognitron: A self-organizing neural network model for a mechanism of pattern recognition unaffected by shift in position", *Biological Cybernetics*, vol. 36, no. 4, April, pp. 193–202

Kohonen, T. 1982,"Self-organized formation of topologically correct feature maps", *Biological Cybernetics*, vol. 43, pp. 59–69

Kohonen, T. 1984, *Self-organization and Associative Memory,* Springer-Verlag, Berlin

Kohonen, T. 1988,"An introduction to neural computing", *Neural Networks*, vol. 1, pp. 3–16

Kohonen, T. 1990,"The Self-Organizing Map", *Proceedings of the IEEE*, vol. 78, no. 9, September, pp. 1464–80

Michalski, R. 1983, "Theory and methodology of inductive learning", *Artificial Intelligence*, vol. 20, pp. 111–61

Michalski, R.S., Mozetic, I., Hong, J. & Lavrac, N. 1986, *The AQ15 Inductive Learning System: An Overview and Experiments*, University of Illinois, Urbana-Champaign

Quinlan, J.R. 1986, "Induction of decision trees", *Machine Learning*, 1, pp. 81–106

Quinlan, J.R. 1987a, *Learning Decision Trees*, Technical Report 87.5, School of Computing Sciences, NSWIT, Sydney, Australia

Quinlan, J.R. 1987b, "Simplifying decision trees", *International Journal of Man-Machine Studies*, 27, pp. 221–34

Sestito, S. & Dillon, T.S. 1989, "Using neural networks for the extraction of high level knowledge representation for machine learning", *Australian Artificial Intelligence Conference (AI '89)*, Melbourne, Australia, pp. 413–28

Sestito, S. & Dillon, T.S. 1990a, "Using sub-symbolic methods for machine learning of high level knowledge representation", keynote paper, *Finnish AI Symposium (STeP-'90)*, Oulu, Finland, pp. 27–49

Sestito, S. & Dillon, T.S. 1990b, "Using multi-layered neural networks for learning symbolic knowledge", *Australian Artificial Intelligence Conference (AI '90)*, Perth, Australia, November, pp. 249–62

Sestito, S. & Dillon, T.S. 1990c, "Machine learning using single-layered and multi-layered neural networks", *IEEE Conference on Tools for AI (TAI-90)*, Washington DC, November, pp. 269–75

Sestito, S. & Dillon, T.S. 1991a, "Using single-layered neural networks for the extraction of conjunctive rules and hierarchical classifications", *Journal of Applied Intelligence*, vol. 1, pp. 157–73

Sestito, S. & Dillon, T.S. 1991b, "The use of sub-symbolic methods for the automation of knowledge acquisition for expert systems", *Eleventh International Conference on Expert Systems & Their Applications (Avignon '91)*, Avignon, France, pp. 317–28

Sestito, S. & Dillon, T.S. 1992, "Automated knowledge acquisition of rules with continuously valued attributes", *Twelfth International Conference on Expert Systems and Their Applications (Avignon '92)*, Avignon, France, pp. 645–56

Sestito, S. & Dillon, T.S. 1993, "Knowledge acquisition of conjunctive rules using multi-layered neural networks", *International Journal of Intelligent Systems*, vol. 8, no. 7, August, pp. 779–806

Stepp III, R.E. & Michalski, R.S. 1986, "Conceptual clustering: Inventing goal oriented classification of structured objects", in *Machine Learning: An Artificial Intelligence Approach, Volume II*, eds R.S. Michalski, J.G. Carbonell & T.M. Mitchell, Morgan Kaufmann, San Mateo, California, pp. 471–98

Suing, M. 1992, *Machine Learning/Automated Knowledge Acquisition using Unsupervised Neural Networks*, Honors Thesis, Computer Science Department, La Trobe University, Melbourne, Australia

Zeidenberg, M. 1990, *Neural Network Models in Artificial Intelligence*, Ellis Horwood, New York

Zhou, X. & Dillon, T.S. 1988, "A heuristic statistical feature selection criterion for inductive machine learning in the real world", *Proceedings of IEEE International Conference on Systems, Man and Cybernetics*, Beijing, China

Zhou, X. & Dillon, T.S. 1989, "Combining artificial intelligence with statistical methods for machine learning in the real world", *Proceedings of the 2nd International Workshop on AI and Statistics*, Fort Lauderdale, January

Zhou, X. & Dillon, T.S. 1991a, "A statistical-heuristic feature selection criterion for decision tree induction", *IEEE Transactions on Pattern Analysis and Machine Intelligence*, vol. 13, no. 8, August, pp. 834–41

Zhou, X. & Dillon, T.S. 1991b, "Multi-branching decision trees for induction", *Eleventh International Conference on Expert Systems & Their Applications (Avignon '91)*, Avignon, France, pp. 191–203

Zurada, J.M. 1992, *Introduction to Artificial Neural Systems*, West Publishing Company, St Paul, Minnesota

12

Manual knowledge acquisition

12.1 Introduction

In Chapter 1 we indicated that the process of manual knowledge acquisition involves a knowledge engineer eliciting the knowledge from an expert and structuring it in a form suitable for use in the knowledge base of a knowledge-based system. Figure 1.5 illustrating this process is repeated as Figure 12.1. Manual knowledge acquisition involves a considerable degree of interaction between the knowledge engineer and the expert. This interaction can take several forms, as indicated in later sections of this chapter. This approach contrasts with that used in automated knowledge acquisition, the subject of Chapters 2 to 11. As this book is primarily about automated knowledge acquisition, the present chapter presents the elements of manual knowledge acquisition without all the details and nuances.

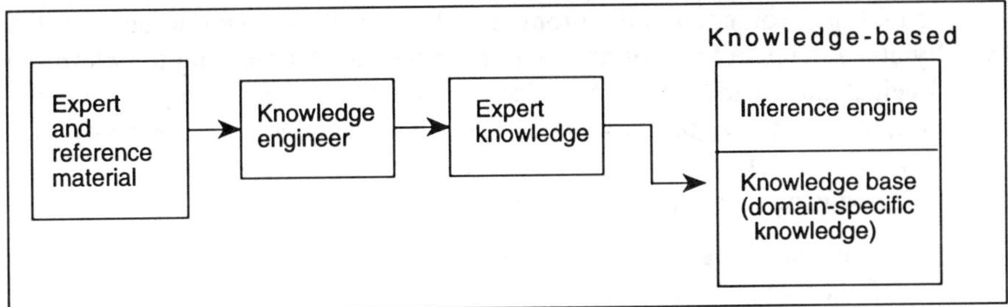

Figure 12.1   Interfacing human experts and knowledge engineers to build knowledge bases

12.2 Life cycle issues

In the early days, the process of knowledge acquisition yielded the elements of knowledge to be installed into the knowledge base at the implementation stage. Hence, knowledge acquisition resulted in a set of production rules, frames, and/or semantic nets at a level that could be coded directly in the knowledge base. There was no attempt to develop a higher-level characterization of the nature of the knowledge above the atomic units in the knowledge base. More recent studies (Chandrasekaran et al. 1992; Dillon & Tan 1993; Wielinga et al. 1992) suggest that it is important to begin the knowledge acquisition process by representing the required knowledge at a sufficient level of abstraction. This level of abstraction should allow the characterization of the problem space and the problem-solving methods. Such an abstract representation is referred to as a conceptual model.

Dillon and Tan (1993) thus argue for the use of objects, classes, rule sets, pattern-matching rules, and solution hierarchies as initial constructs for representing the knowledge. The KADS (Knowledge Analysis and Documentation System) group proposes the division of the problem into the following (Wielinga et al. 1992):

- an organizational model
- an application model
- a task model
- a model of cooperation
- a model of expertise
- a conceptual model
- a design model.

Chandrasekaran et al. (1992) argue for a task-level description of the problem. The specific representation employed is not our concern here. The important point is that the problem and the problem-solving methods have to be modeled initially at a sufficient level of abstraction, rather than attempting to determine the individual atomic units (e.g., rules, frames) used directly in the implementation.

This approach views the process of knowledge acquisition essentially as a modeling process. As illustrated in Figure 12.2, the different components of this modeling process are (Dillon & Tan 1993):

- the conceptual model
- the software structure model
- the implementation.

The conceptual model consists of a model of the real world of interest. It represents the essential characteristics of the real world that are important for the problems the software system is meant to address. When developing this model, no assumptions are made about the nature of the software structures that will be used to encode the software system. Thus no restrictions are

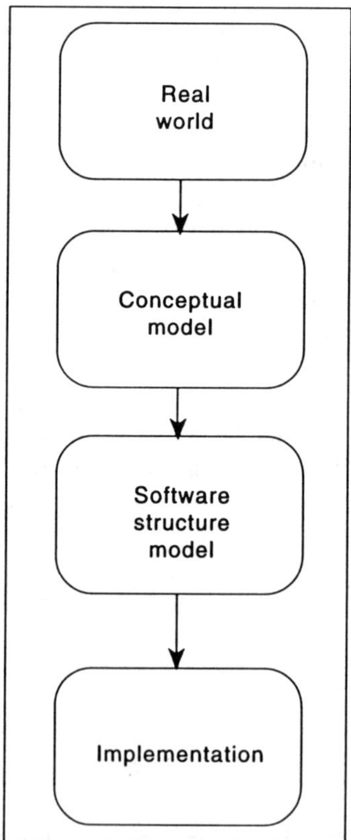

Figure 12.2 Stages in the process of software development (Dillon & Tan 1993)

placed on the knowledge constructs for knowledge representations arising from a particular software tool.

Once the conceptual model has been defined and verified, the process of its transformation into the software structure model begins. Since the software structure model defines the basis of the software implementation, sufficient attention has to be given to the kinds of structures that are available in the implementation medium. This phase yields the knowledge in the knowledge base and the basic control strategies, as well as delineating any inference mechanisms. It also introduces the modular structure of the system, if appropriate. Finally, an implementation of the process is developed using the particular software tool chosen for the task.

These three models are central to the areas of traditional applications software, database, and knowledge-based system development (Dillon & Tan 1993). The corresponding paradigms for each of these areas are illustrated in Table 12.1.

	Conceptual model	Software structure model	Implementation model
Traditional software application (e.g., structured analysis and design)	Data flow (procedural modeling)	Structure chart	Program code
Database system (e.g., relational system)	Conceptual data model [E-R diagram] (data modeling)	Logical data model [relational tables]	Physical model
Knowledge-based system	Knowledge model (knowledge modeling)	Knowledge base structure	Knowledge base code
Object-oriented system	Object-oriented conceptual model (procedural and data modeling; knowledge modeling if appropriate)	Object-oriented software structure model	Implementation model

Table 12.1   Conceptual, software structure, and implementation models

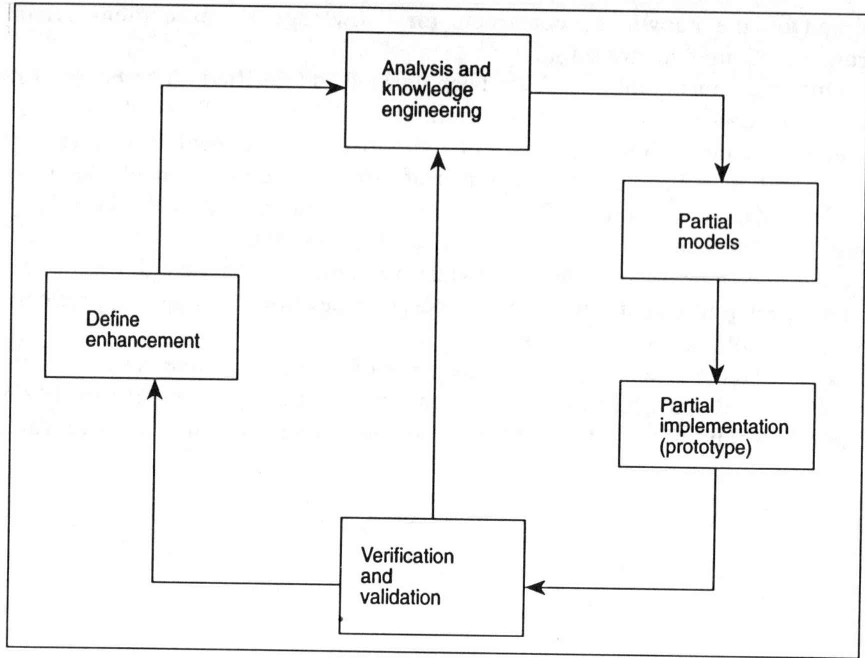

Figure 12.3 Partial modeling methodology for knowledge-based system development

It is not necessary for each stage in the process of software development to be totally completed before the next stage begins. With knowledge base development, it may be not only undesirable, but also impossible to finish each stage before starting the next. This results from having only a partial understanding of the problem and the problem space at the outset. In such a case, it is likely that only a partial conceptual model, a partial software structure model, and a partial implementation (prototype) are initially developed. Experience gained from this partial implementation should give a clearer understanding of the conceptual model and the software structure model, leading to enhanced conceptual and software structure models. This iterative approach to incremental enhanced prototyping is illustrated in Figure 12.3. Even though only partial models are developed in this life cycle methodology, this is not a justification for skipping the conceptual and software structure model stages.

12.3 Conceptual modeling

As explained, the first stage in the development of any software system is the development of a conceptual model. With traditional software, during analysis the traditional software designer has to develop a conceptual model of the problem space, as indicated in Figure 12.4. The algorithms for carrying out the required behavior are known or already exist, even though a choice may have to be made between computer algorithms during the design stage.

In contrast, in knowledge acquisition and knowledge-based systems one needs to model:

* the problem space
* the problem solver.

Thus, during manual knowledge acquisition appropriate models for both the problem solver and the problem space have to be developed, as shown in Figure 12.5.

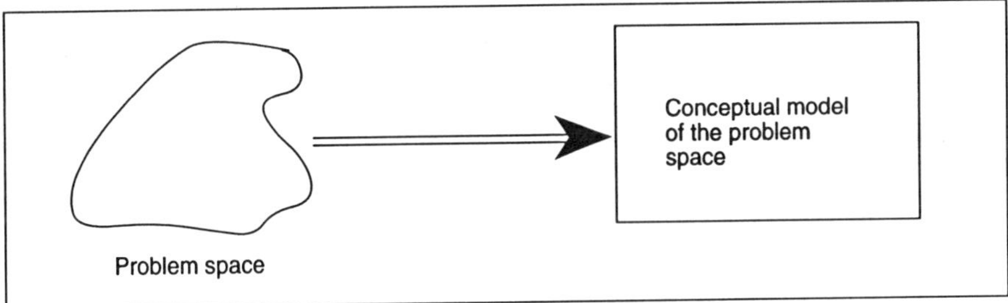

Figure 12.4 Traditional software application (Dillon & Tan 1993)

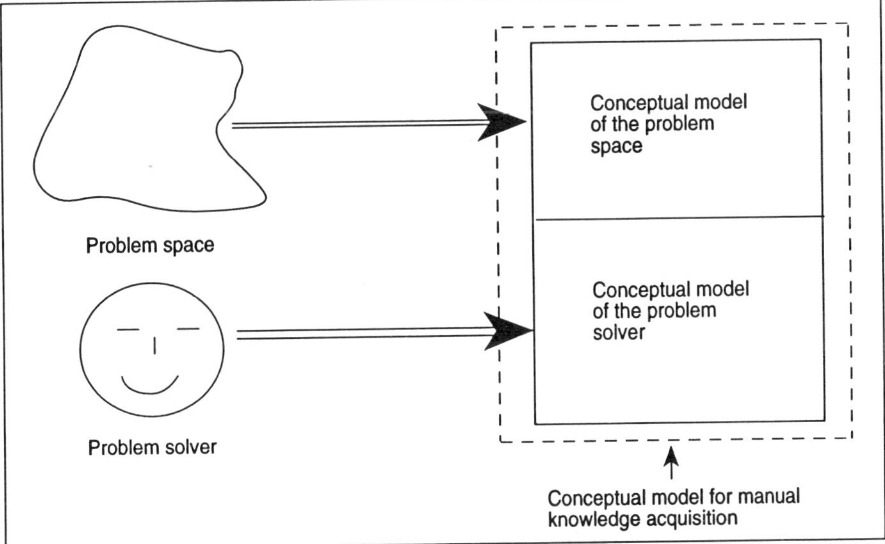

Figure 12.5 Manual knowledge acquisition – modeling the problem space and the problem solver (Dillon & Tan 1993)

The early literature on knowledge engineering and manual knowledge acquisition concentrated on attempting to develop only the knowledge used by the problem solver. Furthermore, this knowledge was represented at a very low level (the implementation level). There was little attempt to first develop a conceptual model of the problem solver. Also, very little attention was given to the notion that a conceptual model of the problem space must be developed. A detailed discussion of developing a conceptual model of both the problem space and the problem solver is given in Dillon and Tan (1993). Here we present a brief discussion of a number of the issues raised in Dillon and Tan (1993).

12.3.1 Modeling the problem space

In developing a conceptual model of the problem space one concentrates on that portion of the real world of interest. Here one needs to model:

- static properties
- dynamic properties
- constraints.

Static properties could include:

- features that describe a single entity or the component parts of a single entity;
- static interrelationships between these entities.

Dynamic properties that are important in the real world from a modeling point of view can be characterized by events and actions. Events occurring in the real world trigger an action. In contrast, an action in the real world is the carrying out of some kind of change or activity. An operation can be considered an indivisible action. The performance of an action normally results in the alteration of one or more measurable features of an entity, or simply an alteration of the state of an entity.

Representing the constraints properly is also essential to successfully model the problem space. Constraints can be implicit or explicit. Implicit constraints derive from the definitions of concepts, relationships, and attributes. Explicit constraints, on the other hand, are not contained in the definition of a concept, but are external constraints specified for the entity. These constraints can be static constraints such as an equation relating two or more attributes, limits on the range of an attribute, or an inequality that must be satisfied by two or more attributes or entities. In addition to static constraints, one needs to consider a set of dynamic constraints. These dynamic constraints can normally be expressed as a set of pre-conditions that must be met before an action is carried out or a set of post-conditions that have to be fulfilled on completion of the action (Brodie 1984).

Concepts form an important mechanism for structuring reality in conceptual modeling through the use of abstraction and generalization. This allows one to deal with a group of entities and the properties of the group together. Any conceptual modeling approach should be capable of capturing and representing these concepts. The notion of a concept used in conceptual modeling must be broad enough to capture both static and dynamic properties. A concept is thus defined by both the structure and the behaviors associated with it. The structure of the concept is represented by the set of attributes that characterizes the concept, as well as any static constraints on the concept itself or its attributes. In the case of a composite or complex concept, the definitions of component concepts that are part of the concept are also important. Dynamic properties or behaviors, on the other hand, are associated with:

- events that the concept initiates
- events to which the concept responds
- actions that the concept can perform.

An important characteristic of a concept, in addition to its structure and behavior, is that a concept and its attributes may have an existence beyond the duration of a single given execution of the system. This characteristic is referred to as the persistence of the concept. One can distinguish between the *intension* of the concept and its *extension*. The delineation of the structure, the associated behaviors, and the constraints define the concept. This definition is called the intension of the concept. It helps to identify whether something is an instance of the concept or not. In contrast, the set of all instances of the concept that exist constitutes the extension of the concept.

In traditional software or database systems one frequently relies on the intension of a concept in developing a strict definition of the concept. In knowledge-based systems such a notion of a concept could be too restrictive. For example, the definition of a dog as an animal that has four legs, barks, has hair, feeds its young with milk, and so on might be too restrictive given that a three-legged dog is also an instance of a dog. A definitional approach might be appropriate for closed precise systems of the sort found in traditional software or database systems. However, for knowledge-based systems fuzziness of a concept and imprecision might not only be tolerated, but also be necessary to capture the essential features of reality. There is experimental evidence that human beings often rely on the notion of a typical example of a concept rather than an all-encompassing definition (Smith & Medin 1981). They then rely on detecting differences between a given new example and this typical instance to help determine if the new example is an instance of the concept. This typical example is called a *prototype* of the concept (Smith & Medin 1981; Sowa 1984).

It is important to distinguish between a generic concept and an *instantiation* of a concept. A car is a generic concept and car registration number ABC123 is an instantiation of the concept car. These instantiations of a concept are called instances.

In addition to concepts, relationships play an important role in conceptual modeling. Relationships can exist between instances of concepts (instance relationships) or between generic concepts (generic relationships). There are two broad categories of relationships: hierarchical and non-hierarchical. The hierarchical relationships can themselves be divided into:

- ISA relationships
- instance-of relationships
- composition relationships
- association relationships.

Non-hierarchical relationships define relationships that link two or more concepts in an arbitrary non-hierarchical manner, such as the in-charge-of relationship illustrated in Figure 12.6.

With non-hierarchical relationships, it is important to characterize the following:

- the concepts related by the relationship;
- the degree of the relationship — binary, ternary, or n-ary;
- the connectivity of the relationship — 1–1, 1–N, or M–N;
- the name of the relationship;
- any constraints or existence conditions on the relationship or associated concepts.

Concepts can be mapped onto objects, as shown in Figure 12.7. In addition, instances of concepts can be modeled as instance objects, generic concepts can be modeled by classes represented by objects, and composite concepts

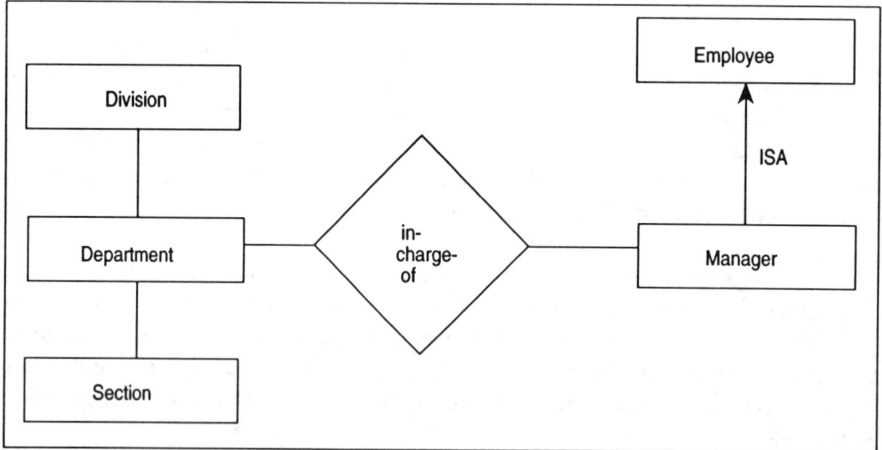

Figure 12.6 Example of a non-hierarchical relationship

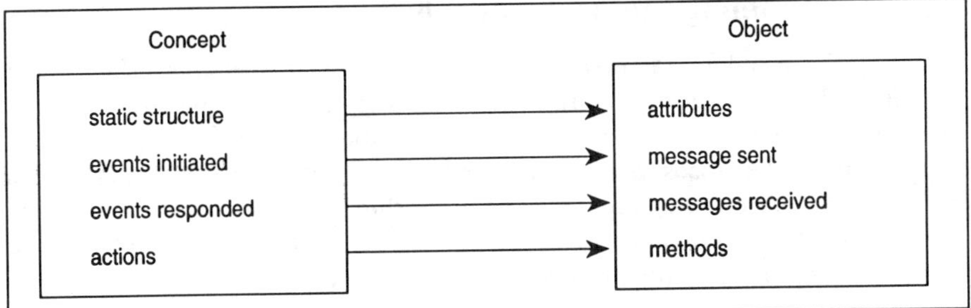

Figure 12.7 Concepts and instances as objects (Dillon & Tan 1993)

can be modeled by composite objects. The hierarchical relationships can be effectively represented through the use of ISA links, instance-of links, and composition hierarchies within an object-oriented framework. Non-hierarchical relationships have to be explicitly represented as illustrated in Figure 12.8.

In summary, the major steps in the process of developing a conceptual model involve identifying (Dillon and Tan 1993):

1. concepts, classes, and objects;
2. the structural relationships between these, and their associated constraints;
3. events and messages, and allocating these to particular objects and classes;
4. the required external behavior, and associating it with particular objects and classes;
5. the internal static structure of objects and classes; that is, the attributes and static constraints;
6. the internal dynamic structure of objects and classes; that is, actions/methods and dynamic constraints.

The first four steps in the process deal with the external aspect of objects or classes and their disposition with respect to one another. The last two steps refer to the internal structure of the objects required. The conceptual model of the problem space defined so far can be represented using Object-Property diagrams, Object-Message diagrams, and either state transition diagrams or State Controlled Petri Nets to capture the dynamic aspects (Dillon & Tan 1993).

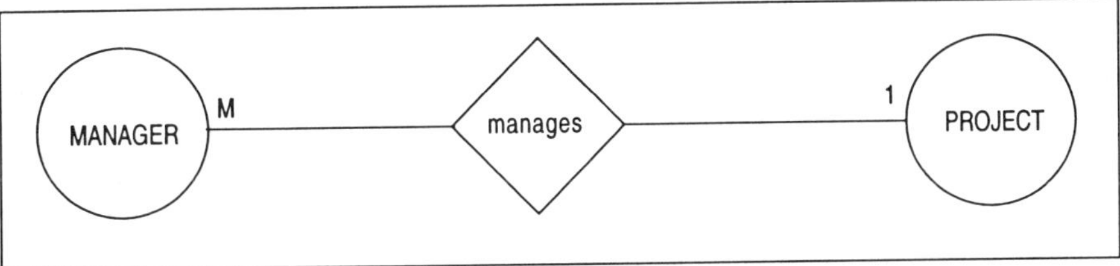

Figure 12.8 Example of an Object-Property diagram for a non-hierarchical relationship

12.3.2   Modeling the problem solver

Modeling the problem solver involves modeling the knowledge used by the problem solver to solve the problem. This knowledge is usually acquired incrementally over a long period of time by the problem solver who is a domain expert. The process is in marked contrast to traditional software algorithms or databases where the application and algorithm are known well in advance and can thus be programmed directly. The following types of knowledge are frequently employed by the problem solver (Dillon & Tan 1993).

- *Heuristics or rules of thumb. These are normally related to knowledge that the problem solver has acquired by experience and frequently are empirically determined associations.*
- *Stereotypes that are used to designate typical examples of some objects or situations.*
- *Solution hierarchies that employ different levels of looking at the problem. These are frequently associated with the level of detail the problem solver wishes to deal with at one time.*
- *Procedures that represent explicitly defined solution strategies and algorithms. The solution in this case is defined as a sequence of actions that, if carried out, leads to the required result. This type of knowledge is close to that found in traditional software applications. However, one important difference is that a procedure may only be called by the expert if it is needed or if something changes that requires it.*
- *Pattern matching a given set of conditions with a situation or the current state to see if the conditions are satisfied.*
- *Qualitative or quantitative reasoning with a model of the real-world phenomena. This frequently involves obtaining a model of the phenomena and then using it in a qualitative or quantitative simulation.*
- *Reasoning with primary case material, where it is not impossible to reduce the knowledge involved to a simple enough set of heuristics because of the highly context-dependent nature of the knowledge. Such reasoning is frequently associated with legal domains, but it also appears in other areas such as patient care (Bradburn et al. 1992).*

Heuristics can be modeled directly by production rules that are condition/action pairs of the form:

IF P THEN Q

The premise P is matched against the working memory. If it is found to be true the action Q is performed. Normally the production rule is too low a knowledge representation to be used directly for conceptual modeling. It is more appropriate for the coding stage or defining the form of the actual knowledge in the knowledge base.

When dealing with reasonably large sets of rules an additional structuring facility is necessary to group rules into related understandable chunks known as *rule sets* or *rule states*. Generally, a rule set represents a task at a higher level of abstraction than the individual rules. For instance, *Diagnose_Electrical_System* could consist of a set of rules; *Repair_Car* and *Select_Car_Seat_Cover* could be other rule sets. Once the task has been specified at this high level of abstraction then one can proceed to define the individual rules. Advantages in carrying out an initial analysis at the modeling stage using rule sets include:

- Rule sets are frequently associated with a particular purpose or area in the real world.
- Rule sets are higher-level abstractions of the rules.
- Introduction of the rule sets results in easier consistency verification and validation of the knowledge base (Liu & Dillon 1987, 1988, 1991).

Stereotypical knowledge can be very effectively captured by frames. It is useful to extend the object paradigm to have some of the properties of frames so that it can be used for modeling not only the problem space but also the problem solver. To do this, we draw on a classification of some of the differences between frames and objects given in Figure 12.9. The new notion of an *objectf* is defined as an object with some of the additional properties of frames. The characteristics of an objectf are in bold type in Figure 12.9.

<table>
<tr><td width="50%">

<u>Frame</u>
- Frame
- instance
- slots

- passive
- inheritance
- defaults
- **daemons**
- **rule attachment**
- **reasoning with a
  pattern-matching rule**

</td><td width="50%">

<u>Object</u>
- **Class**
- **instance**
- **instance attributes or
  class attributes**
- **active**
- **inheritance**
- **defaults**

- **constraints**
- **object identity**
- **encapsulation of methods**
- **polymorphism**
- **message passing**

</td></tr>
</table>

Figure 12.9   Differences between frames and objects (Dillon & Tan 1993)

Necessary extensions to the object-oriented paradigm to allow conceptual modeling of knowledge-based systems are:

- for objectfs, permitting the attachment of daemons to a slot in an object;
- for objectfs, permitting the attachment of rule states or sets to an object;
- allowing for pattern-matching rules to be added to the system;
- allowing for inheritance to be stopped at a particular class level;
- permitting the specification of reasoning hierarchies through the use of objectfs and associated rule states or procedures.

To characterize the uncertainty and imprecision often associated with knowledge-based systems, one may in addition need to use:

- fuzzy logic (Negoita 1985; Zadeh 1988)
- certainty factors (Buchanan & Shortliffe 1984)
- Bayesian reasoning (Duda et al. 1978; Pearl 1988).

When developing a model of the problem solver, the six steps referred to in Section 12.3.1 on modeling the problem space still apply. However, Step 6, relating to the identification of the internal dynamic structure, is intimately intertwined with the problem solver and is therefore postponed to a second phase. The first five steps of modeling the problem space are discussed in detail in Dillon and Tan (1993).

The process of carrying out the second phase of modeling the problem solver can be decomposed into the following stages (Dillon & Tan 1993):

1. Determine solution hierarchies and also specify any objectfs related to these.
2. Determine any pattern-matching rules.
3. Determine actions to be carried out by or performed on any objectfs.
4. Determine if the actions in 3 are performed by:

   (a) rules
   (b) methods
   (c) daemons

   and hence allocate a rule state, method, or daemon.

5. Determine the rules that go into making up any rule states.

   The solution hierarchy could correspond to one of the following:

   - an ISA hierarchy of a particular set of objectfs
   - a composition hierarchy of composite objectfs
   - a decision hierarchy that might deal with different sets of objectfs.

The ISA hierarchy is frequently used for classification problems, and the composition hierarchy for diagnosis problems. A decision hierarchy can be used with any class of problem.

Pattern-matching rules provide an important means of reasoning with objectfs from different hierarchies. As pattern-matching rules allow one to reason about structure, they are fairly high-level reasoning mechanisms. It is thus appropriate that any such rules be determined next. The following tests should be used:

- Is one trying to match objects from two different hierarchies or taxonomies?
- Is one trying to select an instance object from a hierarchy that fits a particular set of circumstances or conditions?
- Is one trying to reason about different structural relationships?

In any of these situations it could be appropriate to consider pattern-matching rules. Sometimes a pattern-matching rule can be used instead of a solution hierarchy based on a class hierarchy, a composition hierarchy, or a decision hierarchy.

The next step in determining the actions associated with the objectf involves:

- characterizing the impact of a particular external event on the objectf and its propagation through various other objectfs;
- identifying the objectf that is the final point of delivery for the required external behavior and then determining if the objectf generates this behavior alone or requires input from other objectfs.

Depending on the nature of these actions, they can be performed by:

- methods that are implemented using procedural code
- rules defined as rule states
- daemons that are implemented using procedural code.

Finally, one determines the rules that make up particular rule states.

12.4   Approaches to the process of manual knowledge acquisition

In the previous sections of this chapter, the steps and issues related to manual knowledge acquisition were covered. In this section we discuss the way in which this knowledge acquisition is carried out. Approaches to manual knowledge acquisition include interviews, case studies, protocol analysis, and ratings or judgmental methods. A structured interview combined with case studies will be detailed here, with only a brief discussion given of the other techniques.

12.4.1   Structured interviews with case studies

Interviewing has been widely used as a basic knowledge elicitation mechanism. The several different approaches to carrying out these interviews can be divided into the two broad categories of structured and unstructured interviews. Unstructured interviews are free-form interviews between knowledge engineers and domain experts. These are often recorded using audio or audiovisual equipment and then transcribed and analyzed. Unstructured interviews tend to be long and inefficient (Hoffman 1986; McGraw & Harbison-Briggs 1989).

Structured interviews have been used by a number of researchers (Prerau 1986; Senjen 1988). There are several ways in which an interview can be structured; we suggest the following approach:

Stage 1.   Initial preparation
Descriptions of the problem or problems being addressed and descriptions of the process of solution, if they exist, are examined. Any case studies are investigated. They should be divided into two groups: (i) typical or familiar cases and (ii) special or hard cases. The first group should be reviewed initially, whereas the second group should only be reviewed when the knowledge engineer understands the first group.

Stage 2.   Development of the initial question set
On the basis of the preparation in the previous stage, an initial set of questions is developed. These questions are designed as a framework rather than as a rigid requirement for the initial interview. They could be modified or augmented to allow the knowledge engineer to follow a particular line of questioning. It is important that the questions first explore typical case reasoning and knowledge before any special cases.

Stage 3.   Initial interview to develop a preliminary conceptual model
On the basis of the initial interview a first cut of the conceptual model in the form explained in Section 12.3 is made. The six steps in developing the conceptual model should be followed. This gives a preliminary model of the problem space and the problem-solving process at a sufficient level of abstraction. It identifies objects and classes, as well as the ISA, composition, association, and non-hierarchical relationships. In addition, the nature of any solution hierarchies or pattern-matching rule states is determined.

Stage 4.   Interview to finalize the conceptual model
A second set of interviews to confirm, modify, and refine the conceptual model is carried out. At these interviews it is important to obtain the necessary information to execute the second phase of the conceptual modeling process. This second phase identifies the nature of the dynamic components, allowing an appropriate choice from the following:

- rule sets
- methods implemented as procedural code
- daemons.

This allows the knowledge engineer to complete the partial conceptual model.

Stage 5.   Preliminary selection of the software tool
As a prelude to the more detailed designation of the knowledge structures, the software tool to use for implementation is selected. The knowledge engineer should now be able to do this, as the conceptual model provides a good picture, of the required knowledge structures.

Stage 6.   Interviews to determine the software structure model
There are several activities constituting the definition of a software structure model for a knowledge-based system:

(a)   identifying the components of the knowledge-based system (e.g., knowledge-based components, numerical calculation modules, databases);
(b)   identifying the flows of data between these various components;
(c)   determining the overall structure of the knowledge-based system;
(d)   determining the detail of the knowledge structures used;
(e)   determining the inference and control mechanisms used;
(f)   designing the user interface;
(g)   designing the integration of the knowledge-based components with the databases and other software components.

The knowledge engineer conducts a set of interviews with the domain experts, as well as with computer system specialists responsible for the computer environment in which the knowledge-based system will operate. The availability and format of the required data in existing databases and the design of suitable interfaces to these databases are issues to be resolved here. The computer systems specialists can clarify these issues and define any impact the new knowledge-based system might have on the existing environment.

Addressing point (c) involves determining whether the knowledge-based system will consist of:

- a conventional knowledge-based system structure with a single knowledge base and inference engine;
- a conventional knowledge-based system coupled with a numerical or qualitative simulation system, and whether the level of simulation and interaction is sufficiently deep to consider a model reference approach;
- a blackboard system with several knowledge sources;
- multiple context reasoning.

Point (d) requires determination of the specific rules in the different rule sets, the exact nature of the methods used, including any required algorithms, and the manner in which the daemons are activated. This process is iterative, as shown in Figure 12.10. After acquiring a certain amount of knowledge, it is structured into a form suitable for the knowledge base. This may involve making modifications to the hierarchical structures determined during the conceptual modeling stage. Subsequent interviews confirm the existing knowledge

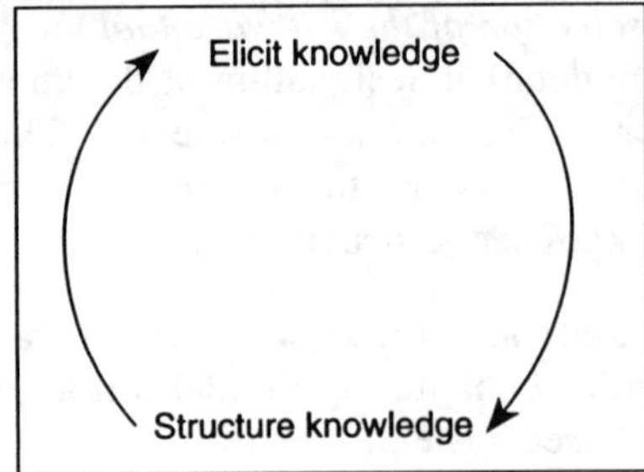

Figure 12.10 Iterative nature of the elicitation and structuring of knowledge

structures and further enhance them. At this stage it is useful to *walk through* the knowledge base with the domain expert using existing cases. This process should start with the familiar or typical cases followed by the special cases. The next point in determining the reasoning mechanisms involves issues such as whether to use forward or backward chaining, and so on.

The automated knowledge acquisition methods discussed in Chapters 2 to 11 essentially address point (d) of Stage 6. The system developer still has to resolve the whole host of remaining issues. This is achieved through a process of knowledge acquisition from interviews.

Stage 7. Specification and construction of the initial prototype
One needs to specify an initial prototype that should capture a minimal set of the core functionality, and develop a prototype implementation using the selected software tool. This is followed by an assessment of the initial prototype that forms the basis of the next stage.

Stage 8. Modifications and enhancements of the system
The modifications and enhancements are defined for the following:

- the conceptual model
- the software structure model
- the prototype implementation.

The question of the worth of audio or audiovisual recording equipment during interviews often arises. In our experience its use is counter-productive for two reasons:

- When experts are being directly recorded they frequently give publicly defensible approaches to their decision-making rather than the actual heuristics or knowledge that they used.
- Transcription of the tapes and further analysis are lengthy and tedious processes. Hoffman (1986) describes interviews with an airlift schedule planner that required 100 hours for transcription and analysis from 10 hours of interviews.

Instead of using recording equipment it is often more productive for two knowledge engineers to participate in an interview, each asking the questions in turn while the other takes notes.

12.4.2 Other techniques

Other techniques for manual knowledge acquisition include laddered grids and card sorts from problem-solving psychology and protocol analysis. Protocol analysis has been used by several researchers, including Jeffries et al. (1981) and Kuipers and Kassirer (1984). The technique consists of a domain expert thinking aloud while tackling a specific problem (Hoffman 1990; McGraw & Harbison-Briggs 1989; Newell & Simon 1972). This is recorded, and these recordings are analyzed in detail to determine the protocol used by the domain expert to solve the problem. In addition, a knowledge engineer may be present to observe any actions taken by the domain expert. Protocol analysis has to be carried out with typical or familiar problems, as well as with problems that constitute special cases.

The difficulties with this approach include:

- the assumption that domain experts can make the real basis of their reasoning explicit. As mentioned in Chapter 1, Johnson (1983) argues that a domain expert frequently advances reasons other than those actually used. The real approach could include sub-symbolic recognition of patterns that may not be easy to verbalize;
- the time-consuming nature of transcripts and analysis of recordings.

In a series of experiments comparing structured interviews, protocol analysis, card sorts, and laddered grids, Shadbolt and Burton (1990) found that, for a system classifying igneous rocks and identifying glacial landscapes, protocol analysis performed poorly and structured interviews performed best. The contrived techniques of card sorts and laddered grids came a close second. An important result from Shadbolt and Burton (1990) was that coverage of the domain was far greater when several experts were interviewed rather than just one.

12.5 Recapitulation

In this chapter we discussed manual knowledge acquisition. The technique of structured interview is the most widely used in practice by knowledge engineers, and it has been found by some researchers to be among the most effective. The method described in this chapter consisted of structured interviews supplemented by analysis of test cases.

References

Bradburn, C., Zeleznikow, J. & Adams, A. 1992, "Use of mixed knowledge representations to simulate reasoning processes in health care planning expert systems", in *Proc. of IJCAI Workshop on Representing Knowledge in Medical Decision Support Systems,* ed. C. Sarmiento, 12th International Joint Conference on Artificial Intelligence, Sydney, Australia

Brodie, M.L. 1984, "On the development of data models", in *On Conceptual Modelling*, eds M.L. Brodie, J. Mylopoulos & J.W. Schmidt, Springer-Verlag, New York, pp. 19–47

Buchanan, B.G. & Shortliffe, E.H., eds 1984, *Rule-Based Expert Systems*, Addison-Wesley, Reading, Massachusetts

Chandrasekaran, B., Johnson, T.R. & Smith, J.W. 1992, "Task-structure analysis for knowledge modeling", *Communications of the ACM*, vol. 35, no. 9, September, pp. 124–37

Dillon, T.S. & Tan, P.L. 1993, *Object-Oriented Conceptual Modeling*, Prentice Hall, Sydney, Australia

Duda, R.O., Hart, P.E., Nilsson, N.J. & Sutherland, G.L. 1978, "Semantic network representations in rule-based inference systems", in *Pattern Directed Inference Systems,* eds D.A. Waterman & F. Hayes-Roth, Academic Press, New York

Hoffman, R.R. 1986, *Procedures for Efficiently Extracting the Knowledge of Experts*, Final Report, Contract No. F49620-85-C-00013, Air Force Office of Scientific Research, Washington DC

Hoffman, R.R. 1990, "A survey of methods for eliciting the knowledge of experts", in *Readings in Knowledge Acquisition: Current Practices and Trends,* eds K.L. McGraw & C.R. Westphal, Ellis Horwood, Chichester, pp. 7–20

Jeffries, R., Turner, A., Polson, P. & Atwood, M. 1981, "The processes involved in designing software", in *Cognitive Skills and Their Acquisition*, ed. J.R. Anderson, Earlbaum, Hillsdale, New Jersey, pp. 225–84

Johnson, P.E. 1983, "What kind of expert should a system be?", *J. Med. Phil.*, vol. 8, pp. 77–97

Kuipers, B. & Kassirer, J.P. 1984, "Causal reasoning in medicine: Analysis of a protocol", *Cognitive Science*, vol. 8, pp. 363–85

Liu, N.K. & Dillon, T.S. 1987, "Detection of consistency and completeness in expert systems using Numerical Petri Nets", *Proc. Australian Artificial Intelligence Congress,* Sydney, Australia, November, pp. 170–85

Liu, N.K. & Dillon, T.S. 1988, "Artificial intelligence developments and applications", in *Australian Joint Artificial Intelligence Conference, Sydney,* eds J.S. Gero & R. Stanton, North-Holland, Amsterdam, pp. 119–34

Liu, N.K. & Dillon, T. 1991, "An approach towards the verification of expert systems using Numerical Petri Nets", *International Journal of Intelligent Systems,* vol. 6, no. 3, June, pp. 255–76

McGraw, K. & Harbison-Briggs, K. 1989, *Knowledge Acquisition: Principles and Guidelines,* Prentice Hall, Englewood Cliffs, New Jersey

Negoita, C.V. 1985, *Expert Systems and Fuzzy Systems,* Benjamin-Cummings, Menlo Park, California

Newell, A. & Simon, H.A. 1972, *Human Problem Solving,* Prentice Hall, Englewood Cliffs, New Jersey

Pearl, J. 1988, *Probabilistic Reasoning for Intelligent Systems,* Morgan Kaufmann Publishers, San Francisco, California

Prerau, D. 1986, *Knowledge Acquisition in the Development of a Large Expert System,* Report, Computer and Intelligent Systems Laboratory, GT&E Laboratories, Inc., Waltham, Massachusetts

Senjen, R. 1988, "Knowledge acquisition by experiment: Developing test cases for an expert system", *AI Applications,* vol. 2, pp. 52–5

Shadbolt, N. & Burton, A.M. 1990, "Knowledge elicitation techniques — Some experimental results", in *Readings in Knowledge Acquisition: Current Practices and Trends,* eds K.L. McGraw & C.R. Westphal, Ellis Horwood, Chichester, UK, pp. 21–33

Smith, E.E. & Medin, D.L. 1981, *Categories and Concepts,* Harvard University Press, Cambridge, Massachusetts

Sowa, J. 1984, *Conceptual Structures: Information Processing in Mind and Machine,* Addison-Wesley, Reading, Massachusetts

Wielinga, B.J., Schreiber, A.Th. & Breuker, J.A. 1992, "KADS: A modelling approach to knowledge engineering", *Knowledge Acquisition,* vol. 4, no. 1, pp. 5–54

Zadeh, L.A. 1988, "Fuzzy Logic", *IEEE Computer,* vol. 21, no. 4, April, pp. 83–93

Index